VARIETIES OF
Russian Activism

VARIETIES OF Russian Activism

STATE-SOCIETY CONTESTATION IN EVERYDAY LIFE

EDITED BY
Jeremy Morris, Andrei Semenov,
and Regina Smyth

INDIANA UNIVERSITY PRESS

This book is a publication of

Indiana University Press
Office of Scholarly Publishing
Herman B Wells Library 350
1320 East 10th Street
Bloomington, Indiana 47405 USA

iupress.org

First printing 2023

Library of Congress Cataloging-in-Publication Data
Names: Morris, Jeremy, 1974- editor. | Semenov, Andrei, editor. | Smyth, Regina, 1961- editor.
Title: Varieties of Russian activism : state-society contestation in everyday life / edited by Jeremy Morris, Andrei Semenov, and Regina Smyth.
Description: Bloomington : Indiana University Press, 2023. | Includes bibliographical references and index. |
Identifiers: LCCN 2022042998 (print) | LCCN 2022042999 (ebook) | ISBN 9780253065452 (hardback) | ISBN 9780253065469 (paperback) | ISBN 9780253065476 (ebook)
Subjects: LCSH: Social movements—Russia (Federation) | Protest movements—Russia (Federation) | Political participation—Russia (Federation) | Authoritarianism—Russia (Federation) | Russia (Federation)—Social conditions—1991-
Classification: LCC HN530.2.A8 V357 2023 (print) | LCC HN530.2.A8 (ebook) | DDC 303.48/40947—dc23/eng/20221117
LC record available at https://lccn.loc.gov/2022042998
LC ebook record available at https://lccn.loc.gov/2022042999

CONTENTS

ACKNOWLEDGMENTS

This volume emerged from the "incubator" for collaborative research established within Indiana University's Russian Studies Workshop. Supported by the Carnegie Corporation of New York, the collaborative research program was designed to foster innovative research by international teams working across disciplines, professional levels, and approaches. Our project, a look into grassroots activism in the Russian Federation between 2017 and 2021, received support from the US Russia Foundation and several Indiana University programs, including the Office of the Vice President for International Affairs (OVPIA), the Hutton Honors College, the Department of Political Science, and the Ostrom Workshop.

Our work began with an interdisciplinary workshop at the IU Gateway facility in Berlin that brought together senior scholars and students at all levels to present and discuss work on bottom-up civic activism in Russia. We are enormously grateful to the Gateway's director, Andrea Moore, and her team, who organized and ran a seamless program. We are also grateful to the participants who helped to shape the discussion and subsequent papers but did not contribute to the volume, including Karine Clément, Stephen Crowley, Tsypylma Darieva, Tatiana Golova, Ivan Gololobov, Sam Greene, Bob Orttung, Leonid Polishchuk, Katerina Tertychnaya, and Oksana Zaporozhets.

Several other scholars joined our project in the second round of chapter development as discussants at our Association for Slavic, East European, and Eurasian Studies (ASEEES) Panels, including Mark Beissinger, Valerie Bunce, Ted Gerber, Kate Grabey, Sam Greene, Olena Nikolayenko, Maria Popova, and Graeme Robertson. These panels produced lively discussion and feedback that greatly enhanced the papers. Finally, the Aleksanteri Institute and Margarita Zavadskaya gave us a chance to present the penultimate draft of the book, providing a final polish to the work.

Throughout this process, our chapter authors and coauthors provided a source of inspiration and insight to push the editorial team forward. We are especially grateful to IU Press editor Jennika Baines, who not only guided the volume through acceptance, improving it in countless ways, but also ran an exceptional professionalization and publishing session at our kickoff workshop. While we regret that Jennika could not see the volume through to publication, we are deeply grateful to Sophia Hebert for stepping in and supporting us through the final steps.

VARIETIES OF Russian Activism

1

Everyday Activism

Tracking the Evolution of Russian State and Society Relations

JEREMY MORRIS, ANDREI SEMENOV, AND REGINA SMYTH

Grassroots actions such as the 2018–2019 Moscow trash-incinerator protests that spread across Russia or the public grief in response to the tragic fire in Kemerovo in 2018 regularly grab headlines in newspapers worldwide as if they were rare or unique events. They are not. Russian citizens frequently act together to solve problems in everyday life, from the protections of local parks and schools to demands for social rights such as health care or maternal benefits. This form of active citizenship—self-organized participation in local communities and contact with local officials to secure benefits and rights—changes Russian society and increases societal capacity to make demands on government.

Because of state repression, much of the civic activism in Russia takes localized and covert forms, and this pattern is reflected in the chapters in this volume. James Scott (1990) argues that all subordinate groups employ strategies of resistance that go unnoticed by powerful economic and political leaders, which he terms *infrapolitics*. Scott (1990, 1998) challenges scholarship on dissent and protest, arguing that if we confine our conception of the political to openly declared activity, we are driven to conclude that subordinate groups lack a political life or that what political life they do have is restricted to those exceptional moments of popular explosion. This observation defines the starting point of our volume.

We address the increase in grassroots activism in Russia relying on interplay between three approaches to the study of activism: existing social identities and connections, frames, and local political opportunity structures. Russian activism did not start with the cases presented in this volume. The building blocks of social self-organization have been emerging over time—in some cases, in response to Soviet-era legacies. Our chapters demonstrate the importance of these legacies as well as the existing identities, norms, networks, and shared experiences that emerge from civic relations in communities, apartment houses, and neighborhoods to shape collective action.

Across the three parts of this volume, we show how grassroots activism increases societal capacity to solve common problems and make demands on government. This capacity is amplified as activity around one policy issue spills over into other issue areas or extends to formal politics. In the volume's conclusion, we argue that the accumulation of skills, resources, and practices; growing organizational capacity and networking among activists; and interactions with state officials increase the overall capacity of society and define a developmental model of civic society.

The Evolution of Russian Activism: Capturing the Big Picture

We define *activism* as any type of grassroots collective action aimed at redressing failures of governance, protecting rights, or demanding changes in policies enacted or imposed by political, cultural, and economic elites. These actions emerge from and redefine participants' relationships to their local communities and their perceptions of the meaning of citizenship (Fröhlich 2020). Yet, as the chapters show, activism varies widely across groups, issues, and regions. It also varies across individuals as they decide to participate or not participate, dip in and out of activism, engage in actions across issues, or move from local activism to national protest, as observed in the Navalny rallies that burst out in Russia in winter 2021.

In the Russian context, most local activists regard their actions as nonpolitical. As in other authoritarian states, the futile and aggressive nature of power politics leads citizens to distance themselves from institutionalized political arenas. For many local activists, politics is a dirty business (*politika—griaznoe delo*), and they want no part of it. In contrast, actions that address local concerns and everyday disruptions are acceptable. After 2005, many local movements limited alliances with political parties or political opposition groups to attract social support (Clément, Miryasova, and Demidov 2010). Over time, depoliticization defines a significant schism between political and civic activists (Semenov 2021).

For social scientists, any action, even localized events, taken to alter power relations, redistribute funds, or demand policy change goes to the heart of politics. Yet Nina Eliasoph (1997) argues that there is no dissonance in nonpolitical activism in a culture of political avoidance. The nonpolitical construct emerges as residents experience shared feelings and understandings based on the disruption of their everyday lives that are distinct from high politics or fights over national power or regime change (Clément 2008). In Russian society, the distinction remains crucial to the dynamics of societal participation and individuals' movement from nonpolitical to political engagement, a pattern examined in the last chapters of the volume (see also Clément 2015; Dollbaum 2020b; Zhuravlev, Savelyeva, and Erpyleva 2020).

Local activism in the post-Communist space started in cities such as Poznan in Poland to contest the European Union's imposition of an unwelcome model of economic organization and daily practices. Across central Europe and the Baltic states, the rapid spread of the neoliberal urban governance model was embodied in top-down programs focused on housing and land privatization, small business development, migration, and modernization. Citizens responded to gentrification, rising inequality, and the growth of gated communities through Right to the City movements (Domaradzka 2018; Jacobsson 2015). These local visions of everyday life stressed public transport, bike paths, and greenways over road construction and high-rise apartment buildings, and these priorities spilled over into party and electoral politics.

Russian protest actions followed a longer developmental path in the post-Soviet period. While protest was a tool of opposition throughout Soviet rule (Beissinger 2002), these events were small and limited in scope. Yet they had important legacies that shaped activism throughout the next decades (Kozlov 2020). By 1985, the Gorbachev-era reforms brought grassroots protest to the Soviet Union, focusing on human rights and economic protests (Moskoff 2016). More visibly, by the late 1980s, large-scale political actions against the Soviet system emerged in the Baltic republics as Soviet citizens organized around national identities, economic hardship, and environmental concerns to demand systemic change (Dawson 1996).

By the early 1990s, economic and political protest spread to the Russian Republic, the largest of the fifteen republics of the Soviet Union (Crowley 1997). By spring 1991, one hundred thousand protesters chanted, "Dictators will not succeed," "Save Russia from the Communist Party," and "Shame" just outside the Kremlin walls. Opposition leader Boris Yeltsin urged protesters to support striking miners and declare war on the country's leadership. When conservative forces staged a coup to stop Gorbachev's federal reforms, these protesters took to the streets to press democratic transition (Bonnell, Cooper, and Freidin 2015).

After the demise of the Soviet system, Russia's dire economic conditions created a wave of collective action to demand unpaid wages. Organized by the

Communist Party of the Russian Federation, President Yeltsin's political opposition, these events reflected discontent wrought by the social and economic collapse that followed the collapse of state capitalism (Javeline 2009). These waves of political protests aimed at undermining the incumbent leadership and bringing about systemic change.

It was less clearly understood that Russia's political and economic transformation redefined social structures—families, neighborhoods, cities, and class divisions. The effects of these changes have not been even across Russia's vast territory. With the introduction of market economics, the residents in Moscow, Saint Petersburg, and the *millionniki,* cities with populations over a million residents, have done well. In smaller cities or industrial towns in Russia's Rust Belt, citizens faced very different challenges, including rapid deindustrialization and the retreat of the paternalist state associated with communism (Morris 2016). This variation in urban life defines critical distinctions based on lifestyle, wealth, and social structures. Russian citizens continue to cope with changes wrought by economic booms and busts, as well as demographic and technological change.

These changes transformed attitudes about everyday life from "apathy to activism" (Henry and Sundstrom 2006, 3) and defined the shared grievances at the heart of collective action. Graeme Robertson's (2010) extraordinary evidence, drawn from the Interior Ministry's security reports, underscores the rise in protest events in the late 1990s across several issue areas. Anna Zhelnina's (2014) application of the Right to the City framework to Russia reinforces this picture of growing activism.

Still, scholarly work on Russian activism has focused on political initiatives. Mobilization against the nonpayment of wages (Javeline 2009) or ethnic mobilization to protect rights and demand self-governance (Lankina 2006) highlighted top-down actions facilitated by regional leaders and political parties downplaying the grassroots components of these actions.[1] Similarly, studies of civic organizations stressed the interaction between local organizations and transnational support that obscured, or at least shifted, the spotlight away from bottom-up dynamics. Yet other studies of the period illustrate the social roots of the environmental movements (Dawson 1996; Yanitsky 1999); women's rights actions (Hemment 2007; Sperling 1999); and urban movements responding to neoliberal development (Gladarev 2011).

Despite these examples, it remains a dubious and unfortunate truism that Russian society is largely passive. This impression stems from a dominant paradigm in Russian sociology in which the traumatic Soviet and post-Soviet experience engendered distrust and atomization, rendering "new social forms of interaction impossible" (Gudkov 2011, as quoted in Sharafutdinova 2019, 189). Even in critical views of this position, all kinds of observers remain trapped by the idea that sustained expression of or demand for civil liberties is all but impossible. It is a measure of the stubborn persistence of this perspective that the growth in local activism remains understudied. As Gulnaz Sharafutdinova notes, "At a minimum, intellectuals owe the public a degree of self-reflection to avoid turning their disappointment with the absence of democratic change in Russia into a suggestion that change is not possible" because of societal passivity (2019, 195). Our studies take up this point, acknowledging that Russian society has changed enormously even over the second, more repressive decade of Putin's leadership.

New Evidence: The Evolution of Grassroots Activism in Russia

The studies in our volume build on innovative data collection on grassroots actions that emerged after the 2005 grassroots mobilization in response to the end of state subsidies of social benefits. In 2004, Karine Clément founded the Center for Collective Action (IKD), which relied on activist interviews and a catalog of events to describe a new type of citizen engagement. The resulting volume (Clément, Miryasova, and Demidov 2010) showed the unlikely rise in protest even as the Putin regime revealed itself to be increasingly authoritarian, focusing on the rise in activism in response to the 2005 policy to roll back social support for vulnerable groups (see also Robertson's [2010] account of the movement). As the Putin era wore on, activism increased.

Starting in 2009, Tomila Lankina and her collaborators generated the Russian Protest Event Dataset (LaRuPed), based on crowdsourced data collected by the Russian opposition website *Na Marsh*, or To the March (Lankina and Voznaya 2015). It shows cycles of mobilization before the 2011–2012 "For Fair Elections!" campaign, followed by a decline. Figure 1.1 illustrates this wave-like pattern of collective action that resembles the dynamics of contention in democratic regimes (Tarrow 1993).

New efforts to understand grassroots activism that emerged after national protests in response to election fraud in 2011–2012 highlighted the dynamics of this pattern, linking national political protest to local actions. Work by the Public Sociology Lab in Saint Petersburg demonstrated that these protests reflected previous grassroots mobilization and contributed to further local actions (Zhuravlev, Savelyeva, and Erpyleva 2020). This dynamic is clear in the chapter on the Navalny 2017–2018 presidential campaign (see also Dollbaum, Semenov, and Sirotkina 2018; Dollbaum 2021).

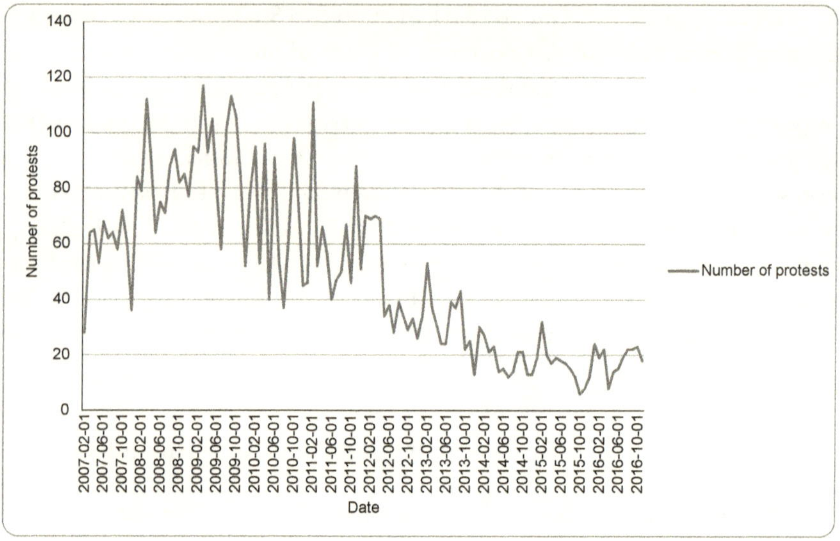

Figure 1.1. Monthly number of protest events in Russia. Source: LaRuPeD.

Sociologist Petr Bizyukov collected a data set of labor actions across Russia (Bizyukov and Dollbaum 2021). These data highlight the increase in labor protests even during the COVID-19 pandemic, including the large-scale action by medical personnel and citizens in Vladimir to contest the lack of state support (TsSTP 2020, 16). Consistent with the LaRuPed data, the new evidence incorporated new sources and methods and captured the decline in activism following the annexation of Crimea and Sevastopol after 2014 and the renewed action after 2017.

The variation in activist strategies is clear in systematic data collection efforts that began following the 2011–2012 For Free Elections protests. Andrei Semenov (2019) used press reports to compile the Contentious Politics in Russia (CPR) data set for five years, 2012–2016.[2] Table 1.1 presents three types of actions coded in the data: the total annual number of protest events, the incidents of contention focused on urban issues, and the grassroots category that captures the instances of mobilization organized by local citizens rather than institutional actors.

Consistent with Lankina's data, the CPR data show that the total number of protest events declined after the "For Fair Elections!" campaign. However, urban contention continued, encompassing issues ranging from infill construction to evictions and the protection of the architectural legacy. Between 2012 and 2016, quality of life actions constituted a steady stream (16% of the total on average) of protests and were primarily organized by local residents.

Table 1.1. Grassroots urban protest events per year. Source: CPR data.

Year	2012	2013	2014	2015	2016	Total
All protest events	2,413	2,061	1,503	1,215	1,018	8,210
Urban protests	377	406	235	134	164	1,316
Percent of total actions	15.62	19.70	15.64	11.03	16.11	16.03
Grassroots	226	222	110	56	74	688
Percent of urban actions	59.95	54.68	46.81	41.79	45.12	52.28

The data also show the spatial distribution of protest events, defying perceptions that activism is an urban phenomenon. In 2012–2015, 182 out of 543 incidents (35%) took place in the capital cities, Moscow and Saint Petersburg, and the millionniki, the ten cities with populations over one million residents. In addition, large and medium-sized cities each account for 18 percent of actions. Contention in small towns exists, but it is not very visible and therefore not well documented. This does not mean that the residents in these cities do not mobilize. Dekalchuk and Grigoriev's chapter in this book describes activism around skate-park construction in Sosnovyi Bor, a town in Leningrad oblast with 67,700 inhabitants. In other small towns, conflicts over infrastructure degradation and land allocation issues are ubiquitous and evoke collective responses. Yet it is also possible that limited resources stifle alternative resistance in these places, suggesting a need for future research.

Table 1.2 reports the nature of issues driving different actions. The evidence foreshadows our discussions throughout this work, providing insight into the types of everyday problems that provoke collective action. The data in this table also underscore how lifestyle concerns and the interactions between state and society emerge as a focus of local activism, as illustrated in the last section of this volume.

The evidence shows that mobilization against construction projects accounts for a substantial part of grassroots contention—events we focus on in the last section of our volume. Contestation over preserving recreational areas and green spaces constitutes 39 percent of the total actions. This finding resonates with the final section of this book, which provides important details about urban-planning processes and resulting contestation. Actions that tackle transportation, including road maintenance, public transport routes, and tariffs, account for 12 percent of the events. Every tenth incident concerns municipal services and evictions.

While our collective inquiry reveals a good deal more civic engagement than many observers might expect, it also shows the boundaries of activist episodes after 2013. This pattern of activism falls short of Manuel Castells's (1983)

Table 1.2. Urban grassroots mobilization by issue (aggregated numbers for 2012–2015)

Issue	Frequency	%
Construction	166	30
Transportation	63	12
Evictions	62	11
Municipal services	55	10
House investors	53	10
Recreational areas	41	9
Other	35	7
Industrial development	22	4
Heritage protection	16	3
Infrastructural projects	9	2
Waste management	9	2
Land issues	7	1
Animal rights	5	1
Total	543	

definition of urban social movements as collective action aimed at transforming social structures and urban meanings. Some protests are one-shot events; others are small, short-lived, and informal. Few actions are sustained over time or link cities, organizations, and activists across issues and geography.

Our case studies pick up at the boundaries of these data, focusing on the period after 2016, when a new wave of activism occurred. We explore this rise using case studies of local actions, or series of actions, occurring across the federation. In the next section, we draw on theories of civil society and social movements, including identities, framing, and political opportunities, to explain grassroots collective action and inaction. Many of these theoretical frameworks, developed in Western political systems, need to be adjusted to reflect the reality of the Russian context, most notably to account for patterns of state intervention and state repression.

Exploring Activism in Russia: Identities, Frames, and Opportunity Structures

To address when and how collective action emerges, our research focuses on the relations among individuals and organizations and the interactions between state and society. Each scholarly approach we rely on in this book—social capital and social identities, framing, and political opportunities—highlights interactions and contestation as the source of strategies adapted to achieve shared goals. These approaches to understanding activism are not exclusive. They provide windows into broader processes that highlight different aspects of mobilization. They are also not static. New frames, or shared understandings of common problems and potential solutions, can transform identities. Media outlets, key actors in the battle over messaging, can emerge as critical elements of the opportunity structure or suffer from repression as they did in Russia in 2021.

The interaction across these approaches to mobilization is clear in Karine Clément's pioneering work on Russian local activism. Her starting point is the Soviet legacy of top-down societal organization, which left citizens with little experience or knowledge of engaging in independent action and coordination with others. From this perspective, she argues that activism starts with the disruptions in daily life that change personal interactions with family, neighbors, and city residents (Clément, Miryasova, and Demidov 2010).

Further works (Clément 2008, 2015) highlight the crucial role that existing factors and ties within communities play with regard to collective mobilization. Urban residents share common interests embedded in microgeography, such as apartment blocks or neighborhoods, together with frequent interaction with the state over service provision or government failures. Daily interactions produce dense overlapping networks forged in common spaces that define neighborhoods, like parks, schools, and subway stations. Local landmarks, familiar walking trails, and riverside picnic grounds connect personal histories and family narratives with common interests. They are institutionalized in homeowner associations, parent associations, and days dedicated to maintaining shared spaces like courtyards and parks. Ties are reinforced through sports and music clubs and networks of families who meet on park benches. In short, activism is built on established relationships and ties that emerge from everyday life.

The Societal Building Blocks of Activism: Identities, Communities, and Social Capital

Clément (2008) underscores the first set of factors that our authors bring to the work: shared understandings, identities, networks, and experiences that influence worldviews and shared grievances. This focus on the interactions or relations among actors has much in common with the concept of social capital and the emergence of prosocial norms that enable collective action. Robert

Putnam, Robert Leonardi, and Raffaella Nanetti (1994) argue that these interactions shape the subsequent creation of norms, networks, and patterns of social trust and organizations. Research by Nobel Laureate Elinor Ostrom (2009) and other students of social capital suggests that collective action germinates from these preexisting social ties, which are marked by trust, reputation, and patterns of reciprocity.

Central to the chapters in our work, social ties also take the form of shared social, regional, and community identities forged through common heritage and history. Shared identities are constituted through interaction, held by individuals but defined by their relationships to groups. Even when identity-based actions are banned, such identities are sustained through cultural practices and traditions that are often hidden from plain sight.

In sustaining and building social identities, activism also creates new identities that can have lasting effects on future actions and political engagement (Bosi, Giugni, and Uba 2016). While these activist identities are not relevant in every context, they can be activated by new challenges or the reemergence of grievances, provoking renewed activism. Growing evidence suggests that interaction through social media fosters and sustains similar activist identities (Dollbaum 2020b; Zhuravskaya, Petrova, and Enikolopov 2020; Smyth and Oates 2015).

While Russian civil society remains underdeveloped, existing social ties and identities are the building blocks of joint action and organization. Our chapters suggest that they are at the root of activism and are strengthened and extended through activism, creating a new type of activist identity that can transcend the boundaries of local issues. They also emerge via social entrepreneurs, who shape the frames and narratives we discuss in the next section of the introduction.

Generating Grievances and Forging Solutions: Information and Framing Processes

In political contexts in which few independent social organizations or movement structures exist, social activism is coordinated through communication that emphasizes shared identities and grievance or framing. In their classic article, Benford and Snow (2000) argue that social entrepreneurs can provoke participation by providing three types of information: a diagnosis of the shared problem, a prognosis of how taking a specific action will solve that problem, and a call to arms that brings people together. Our chapters illustrate this dynamic: how individuals come to see action as a meaningful path to achieve common goals.

The approach echoes Clément's (2015) study of grassroots activism, which explores how frames generate a shared understanding of external challenges to the patterns of everyday life. She argues that by developing ways of discussing these changes, disengaged citizens, the ordinary people, come to see collective action as essential and relevant to their lives. The process of reframing the social response to change provides potential activists with a way to adjust how they feel, think, and relate to others. These small changes in action frames over time can alter individual perceptions about the need and effect of activism—building new activist identities or highlighting the importance of shared geographic, ethnic, linguistic, religious, or class identities.

Theories of autocratic systems often stress the regime's control over information and capacity to develop a shared understanding of political reality that supports regime goals. State controls over media, especially television but also major newspapers and radio, deliver pro-regime narratives that define political reality for faithful viewers. Yet state strategies also delimit acceptable speech and induce self-censorship among journalists, who are threatened with losing their jobs or subjected to physical violence.

These state-television narratives exist at a high level of political life and often cannot directly deter or counter the frames that emerge from nonpolitical grassroots actions. As a result, the regime must also limit the reach of independent media outlets, particularly regional outlets, to ensure that alternative frames are not widely available to provoke mobilization. In recent years, Russia has achieved this goal by labeling some outlets foreign agents under a vague and broad legal structure. The resulting decline in commercial sponsors forces the outlets out of business.

Our chapters, written and revised between 2018 and 2021, demonstrate that grassroots activists rely on new media and alternative tools to generate collective action frames despite these controls. These frames emerge from the daily interactions noted by Clément (2008) and articulated by activist leaders, civic organizations, and independent media. The information that facilitates frame resonance comes from daily activities such as grocery shopping, managing family budgets, or coping with outbreaks of medical problems. These personal experiences shared by family, neighbors, and colleagues counter the regime's depiction of social reality and are reinforced by personal networks, independent media, and online discussions.

Our studies show that new media platforms play important roles in developing shared knowledge and disseminating frames. By reinforcing networks and shared identities, propagating images or messages to challenge the state narratives, and providing a new online repertoire of contention, social media platforms catalyze grassroots mobilization. Activists adapt to the changing political environment by shifting across platforms from VKontakte and Facebook to YouTube, Telegram, and TikTok channels. Social influencers—a critical source of information for the next generation of activists—often shift their focus to politics in critical moments of mobilization, supporting civic action. In Russia, there is growing evidence that the market model of new media celebrities pushes influencers to forgo state incentives to promote pro-regime narratives because it undermines their followers. Throughout this volume, our case studies show that while new media does not always operate as liberation technology, these tools cannot be characterized as producing slacktivism (Diamond and Plattner 2012; Tufekci 2017).

In response to new media activism, Russian officials have deployed resources to limit counter the growing importance of new media outlets (Gunitsky 2015; Keremoğlu and Weidmann 2020). Regime intervention in the new media space includes creating regime-friendly voices, influencers, and websites, funded by the state budget. Government information portals and apps link to traditional media, reinforcing the artificial information bubble created by state media and amplifying state narratives and anti–collective action frames.

Disruptive strategies, such as using trolls to shut down discussion or alternative hashtags to swamp activists' Twitter feeds, became common tools against activist communication after the 2011–2012 protests. By 2021, new institutions such as RU.net and controls on Big Tech firms such as Google, Apple, and Telegram increased state coercion in the communication sphere. Russian-owned media platforms were forced out of business by state pressure or taken over by state-owned companies. Russian courts levied large fines when Big Tech failed to block content declared illegal under new laws. New laws criminalizing antigovernment speech as extremist threatened significant jail sentences for users and induced self-censorship.

Our focus on framing underscores how the regime's deployment of repression limits activists' capacity to generate opposition frames. It also highlights the turning point that came as this volume was going to press: an increased role of repression to limit nonpolitical mobilization. By showing the role of networks, communities, and the Russian tradition of kitchen talk, or conversations among family, friends, and colleagues, we illustrate the difficulty in stifling information in a modern autocracy. These forms of communication articulate and extend activism frames, challenging regime control of local action.

Opportunity Structures, Arenas, and Incentives for Action: State in Society

The concept of opportunity structure underscores that impulses and obstacles to mobilization vary by issue area and local context. It focuses on factors that shape the probability of collective action: the ability to engage formal state institutions, state repression, available partners within government, partners outside of government, and potential financial supporters. This list includes media allies, business support, nongovernmental organizations (NGOs) and social organizations, and other existing civic associates. As our work shows, it also includes local planning officials and priests.

An open structure offers many avenues to redress social concerns, such as legislative, executive, and bureaucratic bodies at all levels of government. In contrast, a closed system presents few opportunities within the system to influence policy formation and implementation. In nondemocratic regimes, the opportunity structure defined by the multiparty system, formal institutions, and frequent elections appears to be open. Yet the policy process—a hegemonic party, mechanisms of legislative co-optation, and bureaucratic coercion—renders the system closed. For almost two decades, the regime has increased harassment of social organizations that support local actions (Semenov and Bederson 2020) when actions previously aimed at overtly political actions have been directed at nonpolitical initiatives.

Examples of direct state action vary widely, beginning with new militarized policing forces that use artificial intelligence tools to find, identify, and arrest activists. State deterrents include the arrests of challenging cultural figures, such as stage and film director Kirill Serebrennikov; popular influencers, such as Yurii Dud'; or political figures, such as Aleksei Navalny and his team members. Similarly, as noted above, laws such as the foreign agents bill and the law on undesirable organizations limit media advertising and ties between Russian organizations and international NGOs, depriving them of resources and discrediting their motivations.

As we write, these patterns of repression continue to evolve. In winter 2021, as new parliamentary elections approached, the state doubled down on repressive actions. The level of state violence increased, and tools of politicized justice, or the use of vague laws and regulations against individual activists and NGOs, also increased. COVID-19-era laws and regulations were deployed to limit any type of opposition mobilization and to jail activist leaders but did not affect state-sponsored events or actors. The use of extremist laws against the Navalny organization discussed in the Dollbaum, Sirotkina, and Semenov chapter in this volume meant that not only officials and activists could receive long prison sentences for working with the organization but so could donors and those who spread the word on their new media platforms.

Despite increased direct state action, the chapters in this volume show that these factors vary across local contexts. Many of our chapters focus on urban action spaces, where mobilization is more likely to emerge. Population density and overlapping societal networks increase the potential for civic engagement (Anthony and Crenshaw 2014; Gould 1991). The complexity of urban life, the level of public services, and the frequency of conflict strain citizen-state relations and prompt grassroots responses (Lipset 1959; Rueschemeyer, Stephens, and Stephens 1992). These interactions inevitably shape expectations about regime responsiveness and effectiveness, generating the raw materials of social grievances (Castells 1983). Similarly, resources such as education, wealth, and leisure time predict greater individual-level participation and commitment to participation (Dalton and Welzel 2014). Internet penetration also shapes the likelihood of mobilization, especially as it extends to smaller towns and rural areas (Guriev, Melnikov, and Zhuravskaya 2021).

As our work shows, grassroots activism is most common in urban spaces, but it also occurs in small towns and rural communities or links urban and rural settings. Our studies reflect the geographic spread of contestation that is clear in high-profile events such as the Tractor March in Krasnodar Krai that contested the illegal seizure of land or the actions of the Shor, an indigenous people in the Kemerovo region, to protect ancestral lands from coal development. Social activism also takes various forms, such as the encampment protest of the Shiyes garbage dump in the Far North or the 2021 Moscow flash mobs supporting young journalists arrested for publishing *DOXA*, a student newspaper known for civic activism.

In her chapter, Anna Zhelnina relies on the concepts of players and arenas to move beyond the structural components of opportunity structure and focus on the building blocks of local movements (Duyvendak and Jasper 2015). Arenas are dynamic places where activists or players with shared identities interact. They may be physical spaces such as apartments, houses, parks, government offices, or regular protest sites. Arenas also include spaces such as online forums or, as noted above, media ecologies and even electoral campaigns. Players are also not uniform. They include leaders, activists, and potential activists, who interact within and across arenas. These interactions link arenas and bridge elements of a single movement or set of actions to other groups in the broader community.

The arenas approach does not assume that relationships imply agreement among actors or even congruent goals. It advocates scholarly attention to the tensions within alliances, coalitions, and networks, using close observation—the kind of work in this volume—to understand the nature of disaggregated networks and to look beyond broad categorizations of open and closed structures. Close study allows deeper insight into the dynamic nature of contestation and explores variation in the constraints and opportunities that shape mobilization across geography, groups, and issue areas.

James Scott (1998) reminds us that all states have the potential to intervene to reorder citizens' everyday lives to uphold basic aspects of modern life: private property, tax rolls, and social welfare benefits. Those interventions take different forms under authoritarian systems, where the lack of political accountability renders all decisions imposition from above rather than a reflection of popular input. Consistent with the actors-and-arenas approach, studies in this volume point to the usefulness of a state-in-society approach, or the idea of the mutually transformative nature of relations between state and society (Migdal 2001). In this model, the state is a multifaceted and dynamic foil for activism that demands that the autonomy and capacity of state actors be carefully disaggregated within cases.

The Russian state is not a unitary actor but a "melange of social organizations" (Migdal 2001, 49). Even in the state's seemingly least responsive periods, activism has the potential to manipulate a calculus of pressures rooted in broader state aims. For example, bureaucrats can find it useful to align themselves with, or make implicit concessions to, activists to meet these aims, especially in the arenas of social provision, education, and cultural production. This more nuanced view of state-society relations recognizes the state as both a source of grievances and a potential partner in solving the problems in everyday life.

From this perspective, it is critical to look beyond national state actions to understand the compromises inherent in authoritarian governance (Fröhlich 2012). Echoing Clément's body of work, these approaches call for a focus on how state authority operates in people's daily lives and how people come to imagine, encounter, and reimagine the state. Activism often exists in a bureaucratic ecosystem comprising what Russians call formal *volokita*—or red tape; a term formed from the verb *to drag*—and informal fixes and workarounds (Morris 2019).

From this vantage point, local systems provide a point of entry as proceduralism and microregulation render the state real to people. Still, the bureaucratic nature of interactions also means that when confronted with activism, state actors face choices, including accommodation, tacit alignment, or, in some cases, stronger coercion than the center desires. Such interactions, in turn, reveal power relationships, manipulation, and inequality. Even at its most coercive, the Russian state is vulnerable to proceduralist activism precisely because, as Galina Orlova (1999) has argued, its bureaucratic realism is subject to skillful manipulation from below as much as from above.

At local levels, Russian officials and their coalition partners do not always agree with one another; they can be divided in their response to social action. The Communist Party of the Russian Federation (KPRF) organized significant protest actions against state nonpayment of wages in the late 1990s and the monetization of benefits in 2005. However, by 2011 the co-optation of the KPRF limited its influence in local mobilization, even in response to the 2018 pension reforms designed to limit social benefits. While some regional party organizations support reforms, they do so in defiance of the national organization (Dollbaum 2020b; Semenov, Lobanova, and Zavadskaya 2016). Powerful economic actors can also support social interests to achieve vital goals. Writing about indigenous cultural contestation in Altai Krai, Gertjan Plets (2019) demonstrates the role of energy corporations in preserving cultural heritage. Douglas Rodgers (2015) makes a similar argument about a broader range of cases in which powerful energy companies side with activists against the state.

The Russian state also provides incentivizing benefits in an attempt to shape societal action. Some of these efforts co-opt or siphon off potential participants from anti-regime operations, but others offer resources to solve local problems. The Kremlin has notoriously built pro-regime youth and worker organizations that engage in all sorts of civil actions, from public education about healthy living to rallies in support of President Putin, referred to as *Putings* (Hemment 2012; Smyth, Sobolev, and Soboleva 2013). In her chapter in this volume, Anna Zhelnina identifies similar dynamics: state-sponsored organization in support of the Renovation Program. Similarly, the Russian state shapes the public space through the system of public chambers that competes with independent social forces.

Our volume recognizes the moving target of the constraints and opportunities, frames, and even identities and social structures that shape Russian grassroots activism. The studies here illustrate these changes. They show what is durable even in the face of continued repression. To underscore this capacity for adaptation to changing conditions, the last section of this introduction focuses on how groups express their grievances: the repertoire of contention.

The Repertoire of Contention: Protest, Art, and Absurdity

At its core, social activism is about communication among social actors and between society and elites, expressing preferences, interests, grievances, and demands. The range of available forms of protest actions, or repertoire, has evolved through history with changes in opportunity structures, resources, and technology (Tilly 2008). Contemporary repertoire varies in size from a protest involving tens of thousands to the action of a single citizen who engages in a picket or wears a symbolic color or piece of clothing.

A nonviolent march featuring beautifully designed and smart posters and placards expressing participants' grievances is the most recognized type of protest action. These events resemble actions familiar to our readers, such as Europe's anti-austerity protests in response to the 2008 economic crisis or American movements such as Black Lives Matter or the Women's Marches that began with President Trump's inauguration in 2017. Similar Russian actions often begin or end in rallies featuring speeches by cultural and political leaders. Music, especially anthems that symbolize the cause and inspire participants, plays a prominent role in the meetings. These meetings range in size from tens of thousands to just twenty to thirty residents joining together in a park to express shared concerns. Like their Western counterparts, Russian activists also use flash mobs, car rallies, encampments, petitions, and strikes.

The chapters in this volume demonstrate both direct and indirect state influence on activist repertoire. Government officials often refuse to authorize public rallies, forcing activists to resort to creative activities such as those described below. Single-person pickets remain legal and are common, yet frequently the line of activists waiting to take their place meet police harassment. A notable instance of picketing involved journalists who contested the false arrest of investigative reporter Ivan Golunov in early summer 2019. Moscow police planted drugs on Golunov to silence him, a tactic that could have led to a lengthy prison sentence. The public outcry led to a rare victory: authorities released Golunov and charged the officers with drug possession and evidence tampering. A similar picket occurred in 2021, against the imposition of the foreign-agent designation on media outlets and individual journalists.

Repertoire also varies with the anticipation of state response and the target of the action. In 2012, a young woman in Siberia responded to a ban on public protests by organizing a toy protest installation, inviting others to bring in toys to populate the symbolic protest. Activists in Saint Petersburg revived this tool against 2020 constitutional reform under the #MiniProtest social media campaign, leading to a criminal investigation.

Influenced by Deleuze's (1987) concept of the rhizome, Bruce Kapferer and Christopher Taylor (2012) highlight the contestation of hegemonic state processes via overlooked or less visible processes. They identify societal practices counteracting the state that are open-ended, relational, and structured by "processes that spread out laterally in all directions" (5). Clément (2015) notes that the informal mechanisms that Russians relied on to solve problems for decades can be read as infrapolitics—including the reliance on *blat,* or personal relationships, that Ledeneva (2013) notes as marking Soviet-era social relations. This rhizomatic logic is relevant to some of the more successful examples of activism in our volume.

The theme of infrapolitics reemerges throughout the volume, underscoring how everyday hidden actions shape political behavior and provide a platform for organization. Through this lens, the universal experiences of powerlessness and marginalization do not necessarily lead to anomie and atomization. Rather, hidden transcripts, which prefigure organized activism, are plentiful, from the online sharing of creative memes ridiculing the government to sophisticated forms of microresistance, such as cheat sheets on how to avoid traffic fines. These actions foreshadow our discussion in part 3 of how activism shapes state-society relations, allowing for change, in fits and starts, in both social and state structures.

The crisis also affects the actions that citizens take to pursue collective goals. During the COVID-19 pandemic, quarantine produced new types of repertoire, including online maps that report the deaths of medical personnel, platforms that report traffic alerts to protest unpopular state policies, and an online protest called For Life, livestreamed on YouTube using well-known figures to highlight state failures (Gabowitsch 2020).

The studies in this volume build on this foundation to explore the emergence and structure of more visible action. As Scott (1990) argues, social conflict grows the shoots of activism, or at least counterhegemonic practices, revealed when "imaginary overturnings of the social order" become commonplace, enabling more legible actions. It is clear in our case studies that, even when faced with threats from powerful actors, Russians organize public campaigns, file petitions, contact officials, air grievances in the media and on the internet, form coalitions with other groups, and participate in elections.

Activists communicate their grievances or advertise events much as they do in other contexts: by unfurling banners from buildings and bridges, plastering the city with stickers, handing out flyers, or expressing political ideas through graffiti. Workers strike or engage in job actions. They use social media platforms to educate and organize. NGO activities remain important, such as *Poslednii*

Adres (The Last Address), which installs plaques marking the addresses of purge victims to provide a counterweight to the state narrative about Stalin's successful wartime leadership.

Even as repression has limited some types of action, Russians developed creative and clever ways to use art, symbols, and fun to claim urban spaces and limit police intervention. The most notorious artistic actions that emerged from the Saint Petersburg–based art collective Voina, or War, gave rise to the girl band Pussy Riot. The groups in the collective filmed actions contesting corruption, posting them on YouTube to redefine the symbols and referents of state relations to history, the Russian Orthodox Church, and the West (Smyth and Soboleva 2014). In Moscow, the street-art group Monologue Art hung posters mocking national leaders around the city. The guerrilla art of the graffiti artist P1183 depicted societal concerns and garnered significant attention. Cultural activism also takes place in the organization of block parties and the designation of creative cafés or Freelabs that mix dance, music, and art with politics in cities like Moscow, Perm, and Volgograd.

The concept of *monstration*, or absurdist street actions, which was developed in the Siberian city of Novosibirsk, became a model for countering the official narrative about International Labor Day, May 1, by bridging politics, popular culture, and everyday life. In response to the nonsensical theater of politics, activists and artists transformed staid meetings into celebrations replete with costumes, street performers, jugglers, dancers, and stilt walkers. Crews of artists, activists, and ordinary citizens infiltrated the mundane communist and official May Day marches with witty and amusing slogans such as "Who has burnt off the buttons in my communal elevator?" or "Enough tolerating this! Let's tolerate something else!"

Other types of direct action resemble "insurgent citizenship" (Holston 2009) linked to inequality or injustice. Many direct actions—such as assaults on construction sites that target green zones, recreational areas, historical buildings, or infill development—are conducted anonymously to insulate activists from retribution. Spontaneous gatherings, road blockades, and seizures of construction sites usually appear uncoordinated, though closer analysis reveals that local leaders stand behind the efforts. Resource-poor groups, such as impoverished families, mount hunger strikes to claim benefits. Residents of communal apartments resist evictions through petitions, meetings, and sit-ins. Others refuse to pay utility bills to contest the poor quality and high cost of the services. These actions are less visible to outside observers and rarely get covered by the media.

By examining a range of repertoire, our authors illustrate the creativity that emerges in the face of obstacles, highlighting the role of ideas and symbols as components of collective action frames. They also show that activism can take the form of neighborly teas, improved social services, and skate parks, as well as highly publicized street protests or marches, outlining a different picture of contestation than is usual in our discussions of Russian national politics.

Our Plan

Our volume is divided into three parts that reflect the three broad patterns of mobilization observed in Russian activism. The chapters in part 1 explore how covert actions based on identities, networks, and trust can foster broader activism. Infrapolitics play an important role in these studies as activists shape collective grievances and define collective action frames. These studies underscore the scaffolding that supports coordinated but independent action, such as buying a concert ticket or learning a language. By highlighting the role of group identities, shared knowledge, and new tools, the section shows how disjointed acts of resistance become meaningful to communities and lay the groundwork for more visible collective action.

In part 2, chapter authors explore the central role that organizations play in nonpolitical mobilization. Built on the same social scaffolding that underpins infrapolitics, these actions transform resistance into new forms of visible action, the provision of public goods, or direct challenges to local political actors. This part highlights that while Russian activism is in the early stages of development, it is not entirely without structures that provide national linkages and allies for new efforts. Groups like Arkhnadzor (Architectural Sentinel) in Moscow, Zhivoi gorod (Live City) in Saint Petersburg, or Iskalechennyi Novosibirsk (Mutilated Novosibirsk) serve as a backbone for monitoring, coordination, and mobilization of neighbors. Similarly, state projects and partners such as the Russian Orthodox Church and Presidential Grants can facilitate bottom-up activism that creates new institutions and arenas for activism.

Part 3 of this book focuses on the links between activism and formal politics that force state entities to face critical challenges. These chapters illustrate governmental and economic constraints on citizens' activism, highlighting how state actions channel or repress popular discontent (Toepler et al. 2020). Yet while the state has significant resources and a monopoly of coercive power, the evidence shows ongoing contestation aimed at governance bodies, bureaucratic procedures, and elections to challenge state policy, redress everyday problems, or demand new services.

Across the chapters, authors highlight how the factors discussed above—identities and social capital, collective action frames, and local opportunity structures—can be adapted to study mobilization in an authoritarian context. Together, our work shows how these actions can evolve from infrapolitics to nonpolitical actions and, finally, to political engagement and organization building. This process increases societal capacity and mounts new challenges to the state (Clément and Zhelnina 2020). This work raises new questions about the nature of authoritarian states and emerging models of civil-society development in authoritarian contexts. We return to these questions in the volume's conclusion.

Notes

1. There are important exceptions to this generalization. See Gorenburg (2003).
2. The CPR data set is described in Semenov (2021).

Bibliography

Aidukaite, Jolanta, and Christian Fröhlich. 2015. "Struggle over Public Space: Grassroots Movements in Moscow and Vilnius." *International Journal of Sociology and Social Policy* 35 (7/8): 565–580.

Anthony, Robert M., and Edward M. Crenshaw. 2014. "City Size and Political Contention: The Role of Primate Cities in Democratization." *International Journal of Sociology* 44 (4): 7–33.

Beissinger, Mark R. 2002. *Nationalist Mobilization and the Collapse of the Soviet State*. Cambridge: Cambridge University Press.

Benford, Robert D., and David A. Snow. 2000. "Framing Processes and Social Movements: An Overview and Assessment." *Annual Review of Sociology* 26 (1): 611–639.

Bizyukov, Petr, and Jan Matti Dollbaum. 2021. "Using Protest Event Analysis to Study Labour Conflict in Authoritarian Regimes: The Monitoring of Labour Protest Dataset." *Global Social Policy* 21 (1): 148–152.

Bonnell, Victoria E., Ann Cooper, and Gregory Freidin. 2015. *Russia at the Barricades: Eyewitness Accounts of the August 1991 Coup*. London: Routledge.

Bosi, Lorenzo, Marco Giugni, and Katrin Uba, eds. 2016. *The Consequences of Social Movements*. Cambridge: Cambridge University Press.

Castells, Manuel. 1983. *The City and the Grassroots: A Cross-cultural Theory of Urban Social Movements*. Berkeley: University of California Press, 1983.

Clément, Karine. 2008. "New Social Movements in Russia: A Challenge to the Dominant Model of Power Relationships?" *Journal of Communist Studies and Transition Politics* 24 (1): 68–89.

———. 2015. "Unlikely Mobilisations: How Ordinary Russian People Become Involved in Collective Action." *European Journal of Cultural and Political Sociology* 2 (3–4): 211–240.

Clément, Karine, Olga Miryasova, and Andrey Demidov. 2010. *Ot Obyvateley k Aktivistam: Zarozhdayushiesya Socialniye Dvizheniya v Sovremennoy Rossii* [From ordinary people to activists: The emergent social movements in contemporary Russia]. Moscow: Tri Kvadrata.

Clément, Karine, and Anna Zhelnina. 2020. "Introduction to the Special Issue: Imagining a Link between Local Activism and Political Transformation; Inventions from Russia and Eastern Europe." Special issue, *International Journal of Politics, Culture, and Society* 33 (2): 117–124.

Crowley, Stephen, 1997. *Hot Coal, Cold Steel: Russian and Ukrainian Workers from the End of the Soviet Union to the Post-communist Transformations.* Ann Arbor: University of Michigan Press.

Dalton, Russell J., and Christian Welzel, eds. 2014. *The Civic Culture Transformed: From Allegiant to Assertive Citizens.* New York: Cambridge University Press.

Dawson, Jane I. 1996. *Eco-nationalism.* Durham, NC: Duke University Press.

Deleuze, Gilles, and Felix Guattari. 1987. *A Thousand Plateaus: Capitalism and Schizophrenia.* Translated by Brian Massumi. Minneapolis: University of Minnesota.

Diamond, L., and M. F. Plattner, eds. 2012. *Liberation Technology: Social Media and the Struggle for Democracy.* Baltimore: Johns Hopkins University Press.

Dollbaum, Jan Matti. 2020a. "Protest Trajectories in Electoral Authoritarianism: From Russia's 'For Fair Elections' Movement to Alexei Navalny's Presidential Campaign." *Post-Soviet Affairs* 36 (3): 192–210.

———. 2020b. "When Does Diffusing Protest Lead to Local Organization Building? Evidence from a Comparative Subnational Study of Russia's 'For Fair Elections' Movement." *Perspectives on Politics* 20 (1): 1–16.

———. 2021. "Social Policy on Social Media: How Opposition Actors Used Twitter and VKontakte to Oppose the Russian Pension Reform." *Problems of Post-Communism* 68 (6): 1–12.

Dollbaum, Jan Matti, Andrei Semenov, and Elena Sirotkina. 2018. "A Top-Down Movement with Grassroots Effects? Alexei Navalny's Electoral Campaign." *Social Movement Studies* 17 (5): 618–625.

Domaradzka, A. 2018. "Urban Social Movements and the Right to the City: An Introduction to the Special Issue on Urban Mobilization." *VOLUNTAS: International Journal of Voluntary and Nonprofit Organizations* 29 (4): 607–620.

Duyvendak, Jan Willem, and James M. Jasper. 2015. *Players and Arenas: The Interactive Dynamics of Protest.* Amsterdam: Amsterdam University Press.

Eliasoph, Nina. 1997. "Close to Home: The Work of Avoiding Politics." *Theory and Society* 26 (5): 605–647.

Flower, J., and P. Leonard. 1996. "Community Values and State Co-option: Civil Society in the Sichuan Countryside." In *Civil Society: Challenging Western Models*, edited by Chris Hann and Elizabeth Dunn, 199–221. London: Routledge.

Fröhlich, Christian. 2012. "Civil Society and the State Intertwined: The Case of Disability NGOs in Russia." *East European Politics* 28 (4): 371–389.

———. 2020. "Urban Citizenship under Post-Soviet Conditions: Grassroots Struggles of Residents in Contemporary Moscow." *Journal of Urban Affairs* 42 (2): 188–202.

Fröhlich, Christian, and Kerstin Jacobsson. 2019. "Performing Resistance: Liminality, Infrapolitics, and Spatial Contestation in Contemporary Russia." *Antipode* 51 (4): 1146–1165.

Gabowitsch, Mischa. 2020. "Regimes of Engagement and Protest in Russia: A Reply to Arnold, Sidorkina, and Shevchenko." *Nationalities Papers* 48 (2): 414–418.

Gladarev, B. 2011. "Istorikokul'turnoe nasledie Peterburga rozhdenie: Obshchestvennosti iz dukha goroda" [The historical and cultural heritage of Petersburg: The birth of the public from the spirit of the city]. In *Ot obshchestvennogo k publichnomu* [From social to public], edited by O. Kharkhordin, 71–304. Saint Petersburg: EUSP Press.

Golubchikov, O., and I. Slepukhina. 2014. "Russia—Showcasing a 'Re-emerging' State?" In *Leveraging Legacies from Sports Mega-events: Concepts and Cases*, 166–177. London: Palgrave Pivot.

Gorenburg, Dmitry P. 2003. *Minority Ethnic Mobilization in the Russian Federation*. Cambridge: Cambridge University Press.

Gould, Roger V. 1991. "Multiple Networks and Mobilization in the Paris Commune, 1871." *American Sociological Review* 56 (6): 716–729.

Greene, Samuel A. 2014. *Moscow in Movement: Power and Opposition in Putin's Russia*. Palo Alto, CA: Stanford University Press.

Gudkov, Lev. 2011. *Abortivnaia modernizatsiia*. Moscow: ROSSPEN.

Gunitsky, Seva. 2015. "Corrupting the Cyber-Commons: Social Media as a Tool of Autocratic Stability." *Perspectives on Politics* 13 (1): 42–54.

Guriev, Sergei, Nikita Melnikov, and Ekaterina Zhuravskaya. 2021. "3G Internet and Confidence in Government." *Quarterly Journal of Economics* 136, no 4 (November): 2533–2613.

Hann, C. 1996. "Introduction: Political Society and Civil Anthropology." In *Civil Society: Challenging Western Models*, edited by Chris Hann and Elizabeth Dunn, 1–26. London: Routledge.

Hemment, Julie. 2007. *Empowering Women in Russia: Activism, Aid, and NGOs*. Bloomington: Indiana University Press.

———. 2012. "Nashi, Youth Voluntarism, and Potemkin NGOs: Making Sense of Civil Society on Post-Soviet Russia." *Slavic Review* 71 (2): 234–260.

Henry, Laura, and Lisa McIntosh Sundstrom. 2006. Introduction to *Russian Civil Society: A Critical Assessment*, edited by Alfred B. Evans Jr., Laura A. Henry, and Lisa McIntosh Sundstrom, 3–8. Armonk, NY: M. E. Sharpe.

Holston, James. 2009. "Insurgent Citizenship in an Era of Global Urban Peripheries." *City & Society* 21 (2): 245–267.

Jacobsson, Kerstin, ed. 2015. *Urban Grassroots Movements in Central and Eastern Europe*. Farnham, UK: Ashgate.

Javeline, Debra Lynn. 2009. *Protest and the Politics of Blame: The Russian Response to Unpaid Wages*. Ann Arbor: University of Michigan Press.

Kapferer, Bruce, and Christopher C. Taylor. 2012. "Forces in the Production of the State." In *Contesting the State: The Dynamics of Resistance and Control*, edited by Angela Hobart and Bruce Kapferer, 1–20. Canon Pyon, UK: Sean Kingston.

Keremoğlu, Eda, and Nils B. Weidmann. 2020. "How Dictators Control the Internet: A Review Essay." *Comparative Political Studies* 53 (10–11): 1690–1703.

Kozlov, Dmitry. 2020. "'Do You Dare to Go to the Square?' The Legacy of Soviet Dissidents in Russian Public Protests of the 2000s and 2010s." *Post-Soviet Affairs* 36 (3): 211–225.

Lankina, Tomila. 2006. *Governing the Locals: Local Self-Government and Ethnic Mobilization in Russia*. Oxford: Rowman and Littlefield.

Lankina, Tomila, and Alisa Voznaya. 2015. "New Data on Protest Trends in Russia's Regions." *Europe-Asia Studies* 67 (2): 327–342.

Ledeneva, Alena. 2013. *Can Russia Modernise? Sistema, Power Networks, and Informal Governance*. Cambridge: Cambridge University Press.

Lipset, Seymour Martin. 1959. "Some Social Requisites of Democracy: Economic Development and Political Legitimacy." *American Political Science Review* 53 (1): 69–105.

Migdal, Joel. 2001. *State in Society: Studying How States and Societies Transform and Constitute One Another*. New York: Cambridge University Press.

Morris, Jeremy. 2016. *Everyday Post-Socialism: Working-Class Communities in the Russian Margins*. London: Palgrave.

———. 2019. "The Informal Economy and Post-Socialism: Imbricated Perspectives on Labor, the State, and Social Embeddedness." *Demokratizatsiya* 2 (1): 9–30.

Moskoff, William. 2016. *Hard Times: Impoverishment and Protest in the Perestroika Years-Soviet Union, 1985–91: A Guide for Fellow Adventurers*. Routledge.

Orlova, Galina. 1999. "Biurokraticheskaia Realnost" [Bureaucratic reality]. *Obshchestvennenye nauki i sovremennost'* 6:96–106.

Ostrom, Elinor. 2009. "What Is Social Capital." In *Social Capital: Reaching Out, Reaching In*, edited by Viva Ona Bartkus and James H. Davis. Cheltenham, UK: Edward Elgar, 17–38.

Plets, Gertjan. 2019. "Exceptions to Authoritarianism? Variegated Sovereignty and Ethno-Nationalism in a Siberian Resource Frontier." *Post-Soviet Affairs* 35 (4): 308–322.

Putnam, Robert D., Robert Leonardi, and Raffaella Y. Nanetti. 1994. *Making Democracy Work: Civic Traditions in Modern Italy*. Princeton, NJ: Princeton University Press.

Robertson, Graeme B. 2010. *The Politics of Protest in Hybrid Regimes: Managing Dissent in Post-Communist Russia*. New York: Cambridge University Press.

Rodgers, Douglas. 2015. *The Depths of Russia: Oil, Power, and Culture after Socialism*. Ithaca, NY: Cornell University Press.

Rueschemeyer, D., E. H. Stephens, and J. D. Stephens. 1994. *Capitalist Development and Democracy*. Vol. 22. Cambridge: Polity.

Scott, James C. 1990. *Domination and the Arts of Resistance*. New Haven, CT: Yale University Press.

———. 1998. *Seeing like a State: How Certain Schemes to Improve the Human Condition Have Failed*. New Haven, CT: Yale University Press.

Semenov, Andrei. 2019. "The Roots of the Grass: Patterns of Grassroots Urban Mobilization in Russia." *Sociological Studies* 12:29–37.

———. 2021. "The Rationale of Organizational Control: Managing the Political Opposition in Putin's Russia." *European Political Science* 20 (4): 580–591.

Semenov, Andrei, and Vsevolod Bederson. 2020. "Organizational Resilience: Russian Civil Society in the Times of COVID-19." *PONARS Eurasia*, Policy Memo 663, July 20, 2020. https://www.ponarseurasia.org/organizational-resilience-russian-civil-society-in-the-times-of-covid-19/.

Semenov, Andrei, Olesya Lobanova, and Margarita Zavadskaya. 2016. "When Do Political Parties Join Protests? A Comparative Analysis of Party Involvement in 'For Fair Elections' Movement." *East European Politics* 32 (1): 81–104.

Sharafutdinova, Gulnaz. 2019. "Was There a 'Simple Soviet' Person? Debating the Politics and Sociology of 'Homo Sovieticus.'" *Slavic Review* 78 (1): 173–195.

Shevchenko, O. 2015. "Resisting Resistance: Everyday Life, Practical Competence, and Neoliberal Rhetoric in Post-Socialist Russia." In *Everyday Life in Russia: Past and Present*, edited by Choi Chatterjee et al., 52–71. Bloomington: Indiana University Press.

Smyth, Regina, and Sarah Oates. 2015. "Mind the Gaps: Media Use and Mass Action in Russia." *Europe-Asia Studies* 67 (2): 285–305.

Smyth, Regina, Anton Sobolev, and Irina Soboleva. 2013. "A Well-Organized Play: Symbolic Politics and the Effect of the Pro-Putin Rallies." *Problems of Post-Communism* 60 (2): 24–39.

Smyth, Regina, and Irina Soboleva. 2014. "Looking beyond the Economy: Pussy Riot and the Kremlin's Voting Coalition." *Post-Soviet Affairs* 30 (4): 257–275.

Sperling, Valerie. 1999. *Organizing Women in Contemporary Russia: Engendering Transition.* Cambridge: Cambridge University Press.

Tarrow, Sidney. 1993. "Cycles of Collective Action: Between Moments of Madness and the Repertoire of Contention." *Social Science History* 17 (2): 281–307.

Tilly, Charles. 2008. *Contentious Performances.* New York: Cambridge University Press.

Toepler, Stefan, Annette Zimmer, Christian Fröhlich, and Katharina Obuch. 2020. "The Changing Space for NGOs: Civil Society in Authoritarian and Hybrid Regimes." *VOLUNTAS: International Journal of Voluntary and Nonprofit Organizations* 31 (4): 649–662.

Tsentr sotsial'no-trudovykh prav. 2020. *Kak protestuiut rossiiane: Rezul'taty monitoring protestnoi aktivnosti v chetvertom kvartale 2019 goda, podgotovlennogo Tsentrom sotsial'no-trudovykh prav* [How Russians protest: The results of monitoring of protest activity in the fourth quarter of 2019, Part 4, prepared by the Centre for Social-Labor Rights]. March 15, 2020. http://www.trudprotest.org/2020/03/15/трудовые-протесты-в-россии-в-2019-г-часть-4/.

Tufekci, Z. 2017. *Twitter and Tear Gas: The Power and Fragility of Networked Protest.* New Haven, CT: Yale University Press.

Yanitsky, Oleg. 1999. "The Environmental Movement in a Hostile Context: The Case of Russia." *International Sociology* 14 (2): 157–172.

Zhelnina, Anna. 2014. "'Hanging Out,' Creativity, and the Right to the City: Urban Public Space in Russia before and after the Protest Wave of 2011–2012." *Stasis* 2 (1).

Zhuravlev, Oleg, Natalia Savelyeva, and Svetlana Erpyleva. 2020. "The Cultural Pragmatics of an Event: The Politicization of Local Activism in Russia." *International Journal of Politics, Culture, and Society* 33 (2): 163–180.

Zhuravskaya, Ekaterina, Maria Petrova, and Ruben Enikolopov. 2020. "Political Effects of the Internet and Social Media." *Annual Review of Economics* 12 (1):415–438.

Zubarevich, Natalya. 2012. "The Four Russias: Rethinking the Post-Soviet Map." Open Democracy, March 29, 2012. https://www.opendemocracy.net/en/odr/four-russias-rethinking-post-soviet-map/.

Jeremy Morris is Professor of Global Studies at Aarhus University. His most recent monograph is *Everyday Post-Socialism: Working-Class Communities in the Russian Margins.*

Andrei Semenov is Associate Professor in the Department of Political Science and International Affairs at the Higher School of Economics, St. Petersburg.

His work appears in *Russian Politics, Social Movements Studies,* and *Post-Soviet Affairs.*

Regina Smyth is Professor of Political Science at Indiana University. She is author most recently of *Elections, Protest, and Authoritarian Regime Stability: Russia 2008–2020.*

PART 1

The Building Blocks of Everyday Activism

Identity, Networks, and Social Trust

REGINA SMYTH

Part 1 of our volume focuses on everyday political actions that take place beyond the view of repressive governments. The chapters uncover the ways in which existing social relationships, ties, and goals support collective action. Linkages, such as cultural identities, language communities, or neighborly relations, are often overlooked in studies of local activism. Yet they are the building blocks of activism and an engine of social change in response to state initiatives, new technology, and new shared understandings.

In chapter 2, Katie Stewart highlights the importance of a Soviet-era legacy, state-sponsored theaters and concert halls, to maintain shared cultural identities and values that counter the top-down imposition of national identity. Stewart shows that while many overt expressions of cultural values are prohibited, these public spaces evolved to give voice to regional identities, voiced in local languages. The chapter shows that these venues are sites of cultural contestation between the state's vision of Russian national identity and regional and local identities. This contestation is not uniform across national capitals but varies widely, shaped by history, external relations, and local communities.

Guzel Yusupova demonstrates how new technologies provide opportunities to express regional ethnic identities. Faced with restrictive language laws in 2017, the ethnic communities in Russia's republics organized to express discontent on the streets. When these actions met with a strong state response, activists turned to online tactics—connective actions—to preserve local languages. Using new media platforms from Facebook to Instagram, language activists forged an activist community and linked online and offline activism. The activists responded to legal restrictions by organizing new platforms for language learning that ranged from apps to videos and Instagram stories.

Both authors invoke James Scott's concept of *infrapolitics* to show a different type of collective action to contest state hegemony. In both chapters, actions have dual meanings: one that is symbolic of resistance and dissent and another that fits safely into everyday life experience and work to strengthen shared values.

Smyth, McCann, and Hitchcock focus on a different type of existing relationships that foster collective action. Their study showed that the social response to the Moscow Housing Renovation Program, the largest urban renewal project in the world, was built on networks of trust and reciprocity among neighbors. The complex project demanded that residents work together to secure state benefits or resist the demolition of their homes. Within apartment buildings and neighborhoods, discussions served as an important source of information to counter the governmental frames designed to limit opposition. The chapter illustrates the complex individual responses to the policy, ranging from opposition to demands for policy change and, finally, acquiescence or support of the government initiative. These shared preferences led to joint action, such as petitions, protest events, and meetings with officials.

Collectively, these chapters point to key themes discussed in the introduction and present throughout the volume. They focus on the role of infrapolitics as a form of grassroots activism, illustrating the creativity and innovation occurring out of sight in Russian society. They also show the importance of looking beyond large-scale protest actions to explore individual identities and connections as critical roots of collective action in everyday life. Finally, these chapters focus attention on the interaction between state and society across multiple arenas or sites of contestation.

2

Cultural Production as Activism

National Theaters, Philharmonics, and Cultural Organizations in Russia's Regional Capitals

KATIE L. STEWART

On July 7, 2014, famed Russian poet Yevgeny Yevtushenko recited his work and spoke to a crowd of about one hundred people in front of Kazan Federal University's main building. As part of this event, local artists performed songs and recited poetry, including some in the Tatar language, one of Russia's many minority languages. Yet in 2018 when the Tatar Public Center sought a permit to hold a public meeting to protest changes to language education law that would reduce Tatar language education, Kazan's Executive Committee denied the request. Both events supported Tatar language at a public gathering in the regional capital, but the permissible one did so by using the Tatar language as part of a larger cultural event, rather than explicitly calling on regional leaders for its defense.

In Russia, civil society is limited in its capacity to influence or challenge political leaders, but that ability is not absent. Protesting, posting political views on social media, or voting for someone other than Vladimir Putin and United Russia can result in imprisonment, job loss, or ostracization from social circles. Despite these restrictions, the cultural sphere allows citizens to articulate their own identity and values. Culture, a shared set of attitudes, beliefs, and practices "externalised by rich symbols, artefacts, social constructions, and social institutions" (Hong 2009, 4), provides a space for promoting political ideas with fewer constraints and less danger of punitive action. While some cultural activities are prohibitively expensive, street performance, festivals, and inexpensive venues provide normal citizens opportunities to strengthen shared identity and make their voices heard. Cultural activism ranges from attending music theater or performance in increasingly restricted non-Russian languages or engaging with opposition themes. It also includes more direct action, such as incorporating dance into protest or making graffiti art in public spaces.

In Russia's ethnic republics, this activism plays out in Soviet-era performance halls built to highlight non-Russian cultures and languages. For titular people such as Tatars and Bashkirs, performances bond audience members together and solidify group identity. Regional or Western productions can also signal a political or cultural identification that competes with the Kremlin's growing focus on Russian national unity. Located in regional capitals, these performers and activists also reach regional government officials who attend or take part in cultural events. This exposure to those with power enhances the influence a folk music concert or play in a regional language exerts on cultural policy, education, or regional autonomy.

To evaluate the scale and nature of cultural activism in Russia's ethnic regional capitals, I compare cultural production in three cities, Petrozavodsk, Kazan, and Ulan-Ude. Capitals of the Republics of Karelia, Tatarstan, and Buryatia respectively, they provide demographic, economic, and cultural variation that lends insight into the form and outcomes of cultural activism. My evidence is drawn from extensive fieldwork in each of the cities, along with research into online media and government and organization sites. I observed a variety of cultural activities during my fieldwork, noting audience engagement and the productions' content. These case studies elucidate the cultural structures that both pro-regime and oppositional activists use to voice and pursue political goals.

Culture, Politics, and Mobilization

Music, art, theater, and literature can both reflect and influence power relations and conflict over policy, ideology, or identity. In countries with constrained political competition, leaders employ music, national dance, and costumes at their rallies or during holidays to strengthen their citizens' emotional ties to the nation. In 2000, new to the presidency and beginning his attempts to reign in the regions, Vladimir Putin attended Sabantuy, a Tatar folk holiday, in Tatarstan, participated in dances, and wore a tubeteika, a Tatar hat (President of Russia 2000). On the other side of the equation, citizens also turn to culture to express their preferences and organize with like-minded people, especially when other avenues for political participation are blocked.

While it is relatively simple for government personnel to deny permits for protests, shutting down all autonomous cultural production would detract too much from the legitimacy that autocrats need to stay in power (Gerschewski 2013). An art show or concert brings people together with others who share their interests and facilitates discussions that could turn to the political. In addition to this organizing potential, the art or music itself can have embedded political messages, ranging from the language of lyrics to the subject of a painting. Popular and folk culture enable people to deploy "hidden transcripts" legible only to their intended audience, while not directly opposing the dominant, "public transcript" (Scott 1990, 157–158).

Those in power often attempt to constrain or guide culture to suit their own needs. Gramsci (1989) notes the importance of both dominance, coercing obedience, and cultural hegemony, obtaining consent through the distribution and reproduction of norms and worldviews in cultural life, for consolidating power. Shared culture facilitates common views of the possible, recognition of community members, and dialogue among them by providing shared points of reference, modes of expression, and collective consumption of cultural products. These possibilities make culture a contested site. Therefore, "cultural policy reflects a hegemonic struggle" as political and civic leaders support their worldviews and identities (Feder and Katz-Gerro 2012, 375).

A holdover from the Soviet Union, Russia's Ministry of Culture asserts some control in deciding which projects and performances receive federal funding or are granted distribution licenses. In contrast to the frequent and far-ranging government censorship of the Soviet era, cultural figures often engage in self-censorship, provoked by periodic arrests and harassment of high-profile figures, such as director Kirill Serebrennikov, arrested in 2018 on charges of embezzlement and fired from his position at the Gogol Center in 2021. As Yury Saprykin (2018) writes, Russian authorities today "create an environment in which cultural figures feel compelled to censor themselves." In this context, cultural activism cannot involve direct challenges to Putin and his regime without risking negative consequences, like loss of funding or one's job; however, subtle challenges and promotion of alternative identities still occur, as identified in this chapter.

This competition over power and identity is distinct in regional capital cities, where national and regional culture interact. The ethnic republics of Russia today came out of Soviet policies and institutions of ethnofederalism, regional structures defined in terms of ethnic and linguistic differences. In the Soviet Union, these regions were autonomous republics within the Russian Soviet Federative Socialist Republic whose boundaries were designed to coincide with a particular nationality. The system was intended to make socialism intelligible to people across the Soviet Union with their own languages and cultures, so they could contribute to its development and move their communities toward communism. In the 1920s and 1930s, these institutions were combined with policies of *korenizatsiia* (indigenization) that prioritized members of the titular ethnic group in leadership and promoted the development of national languages, cultures, and identities in tandem with an overarching Soviet identity.[1] These structures required Moscow to provide support to regional capitals to develop local cultures and, in turn, socialist understanding.

This legacy shapes the opportunities, frames, and interests for activists in matters of culture and identity. The republics analyzed here each have a national theater established under the Soviet Union that continues to stage productions in Karelian, Tatar, and Buryat. These productions facilitate language preservation and bring together like-minded people concerned about the status of languages under threat in other policy arenas, including education and government. With regional cultural organizations and institutions nested within all-Russian ones, artists can achieve a status of People's Artist (*narodnyy* artist) of the Republic, in addition to People's Artist of Russia, and cultural organizations request both regional and federal financial support. Soviet leaders initially formed these institutions to foster support for the central government. Today, they fulfill three functions: pro-government activism, purely leisure activities, or a locus of activism in defense of local culture, language, and identity.

Much as rock music served as a "means of cultural opposition and as a means for claiming autonomous space and identity in Russian society" (Cushman 1995, xi), attending a play in a local language or a concert espousing progressive themes can substitute for overtly political action and signal to fellow audience members and to power holders that opposition or regional identities exist. This dual use of culture, as a means of control and ideological indoctrination on the one hand and resistance on the other, left physical, behavioral, and attitudinal legacies still operative today.

Cultural production is the creation or performance of artistic, musical, theatrical, or literary works by professionals or amateurs. It can take place in the private sphere, in peoples' kitchens, in a party where a guitar is passed around, or in one's wardrobe choice, and this private production also has an impact. However, in this chapter, I focus on public cultural production in theaters, philharmonics, opera houses, and cultural organizations. Participation in or attendance at such events incorporates a collective experience where people might come in as strangers but leave recognizing the existence of a community with shared cultural, and perhaps political, values.

Russian Cultural Politics and Regional Response

By engaging in cultural politics as part of broader nation-building strategies, Russia's regime invites activism through these cultural venues and activity. To enhance regime durability, Russia's leaders have increasingly focused on constructing a version of the Russian nation that legitimates their place at the top (Stewart 2017). This construction involves a turn to greater Russification of Russian national identity, with priority given to Russian language and culture over those of minorities (Blakkisrud 2016).

Boris Yeltsin failed to construct a popular civic version of Russian nationalism in the 1990s, despite some attempts to emphasize a Russian identity based on territory and citizenship rather than ethnicity. The lack of firm commitment to a civic Russian identity and the Putin regime's increasing incorporation of ethnic components in nation-building policies and activities reflect its strategic usage as a means of gaining legitimacy in a nondemocratic regime (Goode 2019). In his speeches, Putin frequently refers to Russia as a multinational country, yet policies, official events, and language frequently elevate ethnic Russian identity. For instance, while the word *rossiiskii* (Russian in terms of state and citizenship) is still used in official communications, it has limited meaning and legitimacy for ethnic Russians who view the term as interchangeable with *russkii* (Russian in terms of ethnicity; Laruelle 2017, 95). These changes have not gone unnoticed. An activist in Karelia stated that "due to the tightening of language policy in Russia in relation to languages, regions, schools, educational programs, etc., we, of course, are losing a lot. And we should talk about this."[2]

In light of the Kremlin's nation-building attempts, culture becomes an important avenue for voicing support for and opposition to the regime. Proregime activists can show their support by gathering at houses of Russian culture, while those excluded from this central image of the Russian nation can assert rights to cultural protection by attending cultural events in their own language or showcasing minority artists. Competition over defining the national community often plays out in these cultural spaces, rather than through electoral competition.

In the following sections, I examine and compare cultural production in my three case studies: capital cities of ethnic republics with varied demographics and economic dependence on the central government. In the Republic of Karelia, only 7 percent of the population is ethnic Karel and the regional budget is dependent on federal subsidies. Situated on the shore of Lake Onega in northwest Russia, its capital, Petrozavodsk, is a city of under three hundred thousand, yet it contains many spaces and opportunities for cultural production. Within the space of four blocks, one can find the National Theater of the Republic of Karelia (RK), Musical Theater RK, Drama Theater RK, Puppet Theater RK, and the Karelian State Philharmonic. While these all receive some financial support from the regional government, they also rely on ticket sales to continue providing performances for the public. In addition to these formal spaces, Petrozavodsk is home to cultural organizations that hold events in these main theater buildings and in other areas of the city. While some of these groups' ideals mesh with Moscow's policies, others, such as promoting minority languages written in non-Cyrillic alphabets, present more of a challenge.

In Russia's Far East, Ulan-Ude provides a different cultural space for comparison. It is the capital of Buryatia, a region with an economy weaker than Karelia's and a more diverse population (30% Buryat). With around four hundred thousand inhabitants, Ulan-Ude is considered the "Buddhist Capital of Russia" and "Russia's Eastern Gateway" (Breslavsky 2012). Indicating this status, Soviet architects of Ulan-Ude's Buryat Drama Theater and Opera and Ballet Theater incorporated elements of Buryat culture and motifs into their design in accordance with the city's general plans (302). These Buryat cultural spaces, along with the Russian Drama Theater and Philharmonic, provide opportunities for supporting Buryat and Buddhist identities—identities that span beyond the borders of Buryatia and Russia.

Of the three capitals compared here, Kazan is by far the largest, regarded as Russia's third capital, after Moscow and Saint Petersburg. Tatarstan, its republic, is majority ethnic Tatar and does not rely on Moscow for its economic well-being, sending more to the center than it receives in subsidies. In Kazan, there is no shortage of spaces and opportunities for cultural production. While protesters are prohibited from gathering on the street without a permit, buskers can perform for groups on Bauman Street without police interference. Cultural production is drawn from diverse sources, including Tatar, Russian, and even Ecuadorian cultures. Therefore, there are spaces for resisting assimilation and promoting distinct identities, as well as for supporting the Kremlin's nation building.

This comparison provides a case with high levels of resources and opportunity for activism through culture (Kazan) and two cases with lower levels of resources and opportunity due to their economic vulnerability and ethnic composition (Petrozavodsk and Ulan-Ude). Kazan is an easy case for identifying culture as a means of activism, while such usage in Petrozavodsk and Ulan-Ude is likely to be less frequent and more hidden. Data from 2018 show that in a comparison of Russia's regions, Tatarstan, Karelia, and Buryatia came in fourteenth, twenty-fifth, and thirty-third, respectively, in terms of theater attendance (Rosstat 2019). While this attendance data points to more activity in Tatarstan's theaters, as expected, it alone does not indicate what popular attendance means for cultural activism.

National and Russian Theaters

Republican national theaters are subject to national oversight. While some revenue comes in through ticket sales, there is also significant support from government funds. As a result, they are subject to government oversight through regulations, annual quality control checks, and approval for hiring directors. Despite this status, theaters do have some creative control over their repertoire and staging. In addition to national theaters, each of these cities has a Russian or nonnational drama theater that focuses on Russian-language performances and is supported by the regional government.

Karelia's National Theater primarily puts on productions in Karelian and Finnish but also features some works in Vepsian and Russian. Because Karelia is the only republic in Russia without two official languages—Russian and the language of the titular nationality—opportunities to speak or hear Karelian in the public sphere are limited. One occasional attendee of performances said that she goes for language practice: "Even if you know Karelian, you will not speak Karelian in the city, because no one will understand you. Therefore, I attend events to listen to the language and understand how it is spoken, to train this skill."[3]

The performances at the National Theater combine linguistic and cultural elements, promoting both the language and the lived experience of being part of the Karelian community. *Lembi* (Love, or Sexual awakening) is performed annually with preperformance events by Nuori Karjala, a youth organization dedicated to promoting Karelian language and culture. Nuori Karjala, designated a foreign agent in 2015, faces difficulties as it attempts to restructure itself and continue organizing events with limited means. The National Theater's production of *Lembi* provides the opportunity for supporters of Nuori Karjala to come together to support linguistic preservation. Theater attendance enables supporters to both raise awareness of Karelian self-promotional efforts and bond the community together through the shared experience of viewing a play based on Karelian traditions, performed in the Karelian language, with promotional material and programs written in Karelian with the Latin alphabet. Instead of conforming to the Cyrillic standard to achieve official status, the National Theater and other Karelian-language outlets, such as the newspaper *Oma Mua*, continue to use the written form of Karelian standardized in the

1990s after attempts at standardization in the 1920s and 1930s were disrupted by shifts in Soviet language policy (Zaikov 2009).

Despite the emphasis on preserving local languages, all performances are accessible to Russian speakers with translations made available through headsets. Many take advantage of the translation and are therefore able to participate in language preservation despite not understanding it themselves. It is not uncommon for those unable to speak their national language to still promote its development. According to a survey of ethnic Karels, "only 3.7% of parents older than 50 years spoke to their kids predominantly in Karelian," though "80% of those surveyed would like their children to know the language of their nationality" (Klement'ev 2015, 69). Buying a ticket to a Karelian play and listening to it spoken onstage signals support for its preservation.

The National Theater's actors are also involved in language promotion in other ways. For example, one actor, Andrei Gorshkov, participated in and won the 2015 Mister Ethnos competition, an international competition held to preserve and develop cultures and language. The theater also hosts events organized by other civil-society organizations. In March 2016, the first day of the Eighth Congress of Karels took place at the National Theater. At this annual meeting, people concerned with language and cultural preservation and promotion discuss the effectiveness of current efforts and plan new ones. The regional government takes part in the event and its planning, but it also includes civil-society actors. Aleksandr Khudilainen, then head of Karelia, attended part of the meeting, gave a dispassionate speech in Russian, and looked bored sitting at a table on the side of the stage.[4]

After a day of presentations and discussion, the Congress ended with a performance by actors from the theater, organized by the Center of National Cultures. Organizers of such events often call on actors from the National Theater, since they can "speak in Finnish and Karelian beautifully and artistically from the stage."[5] By extending its activities outside the main building and inviting others in, the National Theater expands its usefulness as a source for activism and for demands for increased cultural support and respect.

Like Karelia's National Theater, Kazan's Kamal Tatar State Academic Theater puts on performances in non-Russian languages, particularly in Tatar, but also in other minority languages, such as Mari. With a much larger percentage of the population fluent in the titular language, translation headsets are less widely used, though available. The lack of headsets in the audience shows a large community of people maintaining and supporting the Tatar language. A Kazan resident mentioned that people will come from villages outside the city to watch performances in Tatar that are relatively inexpensive (about 200 rubles for the cheapest seats).

Next to a large concrete space with fountains, benches, plants, and a view of Lake Kaban, Kamal Theater also serves as a backdrop to outdoor cultural events, some of which are incongruent with its mission. In the summer of 2014, Kazan's Day of Slavic Writing was celebrated on the theater's outdoor steps with a Russian choir and giant Cyrillic letters.[6] In the context of calls to return Tatar to the Latin alphabet used in the 1920s and 1930s and integrate it with other Turkic languages, the celebration of the Cyrillic alphabet on the steps of a theater working to preserve Tatar can be interpreted as a political statement. While the space inside Kamal Theater is dedicated to developing the Tatar language, the space outside is more contested.

Ulan-Ude's Namsaraev State Buryat Academic Theater of Drama, founded in the first half of the twentieth century, similarly holds performances in local languages and forms bonds with other nationalities. For example, in April 2016, the theater staged *Romeo and Juliet* in Buryat as part of the annual Mongolian theater festival, Gegeen Muza (Sacred Muse). A Mongolian delegation attended to judge the performance. While independent political relations between Buryatia and Mongolia could threaten the Kremlin's central control over foreign policy, interaction within the Buryat Theater is less threatening to the Kremlin's foreign policy dominance. However, this symbolic cultural integration strengthened identification among Buryats and Mongolians, as opposed to Buryats and Russians. Karelia's National Theater also builds relations with Finland, which could present a challenge during occasional flare-ups, such as the recent call to investigate Finnish genocide of Russians in Karelia.

Russian drama theaters do not engage in similar language politics or forge international connections. In Ulan-Ude, the Bestuzhev State Russian Drama Theater is located in a different part of town than the Buryat Theater, across the Uda River and outside of the town center. A piece of art displayed inside depicts the Russian Theater, Buryat Theater, and Theater of Opera and Ballet together as a unified cultural community, though they each provide different opportunities for cultural production. As their names imply, while the Buryat Theater provides opportunities for minority-language productions, the Russian Theater focuses on productions in the Russian language.

One such production, and one that is performed multiple times annually, is *Vasili Tyorkin*, the story of an ordinary soldier fighting in the Great Patriotic War (World War II). Attending a matinee performance of this play in April 2016, I was surrounded by groups of schoolchildren on a field trip. The choice to attend this play illustrates the role of cultural production in shaping community membership and political thought from a very early age. The play contributes to the place of the Great Patriotic War in Russian identity as a source of shared victory and loss, as well as an example of how to be a good patriot and sacrifice for the country today. Attending such plays, which are performed across Russia, can demonstrate and strengthen support for the version of the Russian nation promoted by the regime, one that requires unification to ward off threats from abroad and at home.

While all these Russian theaters participate in identity building and engagement, the websites of the national theaters demonstrate that they vary in their openness to regional minorities. While the website of Kazan's Tatar theater is presented in Russian, Tatar, and English, Buryatia's theater only has a Russian option, and Karelia's is written in Russian and Finnish, rather than Karelian. By not offering translations in the titular languages, Buryatia's and Karelia's theaters make a less direct appeal for language activists to use their venues as spaces for language promotion or alternative narratives. These differences in opportunity for activism also play out in the capitals' musical culture.

Musical Theaters and Philharmonics

Musical venues enable visitors not only to hear one's national language spoken but also to hear music composed by members of the national community. These spaces often create a greater variety of cultural and political expression because of the broader expanse of performance types and styles. Despite the lack of explicit connection to a particular identity, they are still subject to official scrutiny, as evidenced by the firing of Boris Mezdrich as director of the Novosibirsk State Academic Opera and Ballet Theater for a "blasphemous" staging of Wagner's *Tannhauser* in 2015 that drew censure from Orthodox Christian officials.

Unlike Karelia's National Theater, its Musical Theater does not focus strictly on promoting regional cultures. Its opera and ballet productions draw heavily from the Russian repertoire but incorporate other European works as well. However, the Musical Theater also hosts performances by other cultural organizations and groups, some of which represent and foster a particular cultural identity. The National Ensemble of Song and Dance of Karelia, Kantele, regularly performs at the Musical Theater, exposing the audience to musical traditions of the native peoples of Karelia and enabling the musicians and dancers to engage actively in the preservation and development of this folk art, a goal the government tasked the ensemble with in 1936.

Regularly performing *Russians of Karelia* at the Musical Theater, Kantele also promotes the preservation of Russian folk culture, with an emphasis on its northern qualities. The performance begins and ends with youth aimlessly running around an airport, while the body of the work features a trip back through time, highlighting traditional Russian dance and ways of life. The narrator laments that the youth are forgetting their roots and are focused on material things and electronics. At the end of the performance I attended, and after a call for the preservation of national culture and history, the audience erupted into a very long applause, indicating support for this message.[7]

As a site open to various forms of cultural production, the Musical Theater serves as a venue for different types of activists. As at the Kamal Theater, the building and grounds are areas for celebration and protest. The Musical Theater's parking lot hosts events for important national holidays, such as New Year's Eve, Maslenitsa, and Victory Day, providing a space for the community to come together in common celebration. The Kremlin's political party, United Russia (UR), helps organize the city Maslenitsa, or early spring, celebration. Party flags hang from lampposts. A UR banner dresses the front of the stage, and a UR food stand distributes traditional blini, or pancakes.

Anti-UR events also use the steps and parking lot of the Musical Theater as a stage. On October 7, 2017, protesters gathered there for an anti-corruption rally as part of the Russia-wide action. However, this location is now off limits for use by opposition activists, as the city administration denies permits for this location or proposes other, less central sites. Like the inside of the theater, the surrounding external space provides a venue for both pro- and anti-regime activism, though the space for anti-regime activism is closing.

At Kazan's Tukay Tatar State Philharmonic, audience members can enjoy a range of compositions and performances by groups such as the State Orchestra of Folk Instruments of the Republic of Tatarstan (RT), Philharmonic Jazz Orchestra RT, and touring performers. On occasion, it hosts events that emphasize regional musicians and composers. These events provide an outlet for those who support greater protections for Tatar culture and heritage. While regional authorities constrain protest in support of Tatar identity, showing support for these aims through concert attendance is a more open avenue.

On February 3, 2016, the first Miras Festival of Tatar Music began at the Saydashev State Big Concert Hall with a performance of works by twentieth-century Tatar composer Nazib Zhiganov by the State Symphonic Orchestra. The introduction to the event began in Tatar before switching to Russian and emphasized the necessity of preserving and developing Tatar music in a modern format. President of Tatarstan Minnikhanov and the minister of culture of Tatarstan each wrote letters for the occasion, wishing luck for the festival, noting the talent of Tatar composers, and emphasizing the need for Tatar music's preservation and development. After each letter was read, the fully packed house applauded.[8] Despite the importance and media coverage of the event, regional leaders did not personally attend, signaling the politicized nature of the event.

Unlike the reserved hammer-and-sickle adornments of Petrozavodsk's Musical Theater or the monuments to Pushkin and Tukay on the outside of Kazan's Opera and Ballet, the paintings and carvings of Ulan-Ude's Tsydynzhapov Buryat State Academic Theater of Opera and Ballet overwhelm attendees with Soviet imagery interspersed with some Buryat design. A quote from Lenin, "Art belongs to the people. It should reach with its deepest roots into the very thick of the broad working masses," circles the hall, reflecting the view of art as a means of uplifting and socializing people into the dominant ideology. This setting, renovated in 2011, ensures that attendees experience all cultural events here with a sense of connection to the Soviet past, Buryatia, and the collective people. The ticket prices, however, are likely to limit attendance to the more well-off residents of Ulan-Ude or those with connections that can provide free entry.

For certain special events, Buryatia's political leaders make appearances. Unlike Tatarstan's leaders, who were absent from the Miras Festival, Buryatia's then head, Vyacheslav Nagovitsyn, and minister of culture, Timur Tsybikov, attended a performance by Saint Petersburg's Mariinsky Orchestra led by Valery Gergiev. A neighboring audience member pointed them out to me, stating, "There's our president (*prezident*)." Tsybikov, who now works at the Federal Agency for Nationalities, spoke at the event to welcome the Mariinsky Orchestra and note the connections between Buryatia's musicians and Gergiev. With their appearance, these leaders signal the importance of all-Russian culture while signifying Buryatia's integration into it.

Similar to Kazan's Big Concert Hall, the Buryat State Philharmonic is situated on the city's central square neighboring other government and arts buildings. However, it lacks its own grand entrance, sharing a building with the local United Russia headquarters on Lenin Square. The combination of United Russia and Lenin imagery both inside and outside the building lends an air of domination and official watchfulness to philharmonic events, regardless of their content. These events range from children's jazz concerts to Soviet patriotic songs commemorating Lenin's birthday and performances with traditional Buryat instruments and dress. At each of these events, the audience was large and seemed similarly enthused. The space, therefore, is open for varieties of activism ranging from support for the Soviet past to promotion of Buryat culture. As at the Opera Theater, the building's architecture and decor ensure that all performances include Soviet symbolism, incorporating the experience into a broader performance of Russian unity.

The performances, architecture, and surrounding events of these musical theaters offer opportunities for multiple types of activism and government activity. Unlike theaters focusing on drama, these spaces typically are not designated as promoting a particular national or ethnic culture. They are more flexible than national or Russian theaters and can be utilized more easily by activists with different aims, such as supporters of northern Russian culture in Petrozavodsk, the Soviet Union in Ulan-Ude, and Tatar culture in Kazan. Differences in participation or lack thereof by officials signal the extent to which the government recognizes such cultural productions and community gatherings as important, positive action in each capital.

Culture outside of State Institutions

In addition to these formal, state-administered settings for cultural production, local organizations hold smaller events in support of different ethnic identities. These avenues for identity building and cultural activism are more accessible to people with fewer means who cannot afford a theater or concert ticket.

In Petrozavodsk's Kalevala Theater, a single-screen movie theater, there is a one-room space that houses the Agriculture Club, a multifaceted group that stages cultural events, discussions, and language learning. One such event held in this space was an Ethnoball in November 2015, which Karels, Veps, Maris, and Russians attended in national costume to share their national dances (fig. 2.1). While some performed on their own, others led mini master classes, pulling audience members, including this author, into the dance.

With increasing prominence given to ethnic Russians in Russian law, funding, and discourse, smaller ethnic groups need to find other bases of support to preserve and foster their culture and traditions. Taking to the streets to challenge ethnic Russian dominance directly is risky for activists; however, engaging in cultural production at an event like the Ethnoball is a form of activism that models and corporealizes interethnic harmony, respect, and preservation in a permissible way.

This is not to say that the Agriculture Club faces no threats or challenges. One of the club's organizers acknowledged the difficulty that some have understanding an open art space that anyone can fill with theater, music, crafts, and other forms of artistic expression: they "thought up the club and developed it on the principles of democracy, and each person can come and offer something,"[9] but offering an open space for cultural production and discussion can

Figure 2.1. Dancing at Ethnoball, Agriculture Club. Photograph taken by author November 7, 2015, in Petrozavodsk.

draw detractors who do not approve of particular topics or views. For example, protesters stood outside the club as it hosted a discussion on homosexuality, smashing a cake on an organizer's head. For some issues, even cultural spaces cannot provide security for open discussion.

In Petrozavodsk, Karelian dance is also incorporated into both pro-regime and protest action around the city. For example, at the end of Petrozavodsk's 2015 National Unity Day meeting concert, a national holiday celebration supported and attended by United Russia members, the audience linked arms and did a giant Karelian circle dance as a sign of multiethnic unity.[10] In a very different context, protesters did the traditional circle dance around the Tree of Friendship, a monument to Petrozavodsk's brother-cities around the world. The city was relocating the monument to make room for a stele of military glory in a prominent location. This activism did not change the city administration's mind, but it was permitted to occur. On VKontakte, a Russian social media site, the organization To Karelian Language—Official Status in Karelia wrote, "The destruction of the symbol of friendship and its replacement with the symbol of war will be a shameful stain on the history of the city" (Pekkonen 2019). The organizer, journalist Valerii Potashov, commented, "Today we went to the old Karelian dance *'kruuga,'* to surround this monument with our love and to show that friendship is an enduring value that cannot be leveled for the sake of any historical moment" (Markelov 2019). The same dance took on very different meanings in the two contexts.

There is typically a wide range of free events to attend in Kazan as well. When I asked three twenty-to-thirty-year-olds what cultural events they had gone to recently, they chuckled and said they rarely go since money and time are tight.[11] Realizing that free events are more likely to attract attendees, and particularly young people, organizations will offer open events without a cover charge. Like events in more institutionalized settings, these can serve either a pro-regime or oppositional purpose. A leader of the Azatliq Tatar Youth Organization described the Tatar national movement as similar to the Russian opposition: some elements are systemic, "tak[ing] money from the state, cut[ting] ribbons at holidays, eat[ing] chak-chak, danc[ing] in discos," while others like Azatliq operate outside the system and make political demands in addition to their cultural outreach.[12] While a variety of Tatar organizations put on free cultural events, my interview participant differentiated between those with more or less overt and oppositional politics.

The streets of Kazan are a stage for outdoor festivals, independent musicians, and graffiti. In June 2014, the International Festival of Jewish Music in Kazan took place on Petersburg Street, a pedestrian street next to the Koltso shopping center in downtown Kazan. About two hundred people gathered to hear Jewish musicians from all over the world perform; however, news coverage of the event on Ren TV showed empty seats behind preconcert interviews, making it seem like a poorly attended event.[13] This disjuncture between attending the event in person and watching coverage of it on TV illustrates the importance and potential impact of collective viewing of cultural production. People who attended the festival could recognize the existence of a strong community and the attempts to downplay its importance in the media, despite official recognition of Judaism as of one of Russia's traditional religions.

Outdoor cultural production can also take illegal forms, such as graffiti. Writing on walls, sidewalks, and other surfaces, people claim spaces and present views potentially unvoiceable in settings that are not anonymous. In Kazan, language negotiations sometimes occur through graffiti. Those who want less Tatar in the public space demand writing in Russian and remind passersby that "Russian is also a language" (fig. 2.2). Those walking by cannot help but see these debates sprayed on the walls, giving their authors a wider audience than a letter to officials or a single meeting would obtain. This anonymous, though risky, form of cultural production contributes to language debates in Kazan that are constrained by the city's willingness to grant permits for meetings.

Regional theaters' histories, funding, and goals tie them to current regional governments and to the Soviet era when they were first developed, increasing

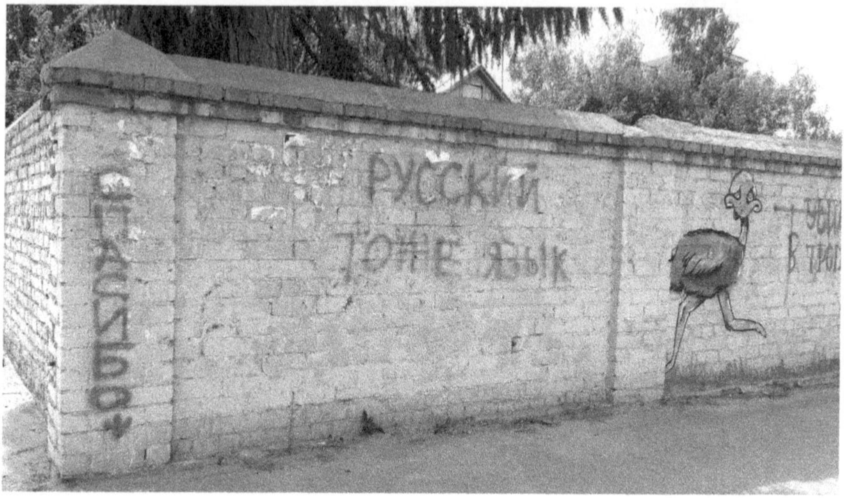

Figure 2.2. "Russian is also a language" graffiti in Kazan near Chekov Market. Photograph taken by author on July 19, 2014, in Kazan.

authorities' ability to co-opt them for their own political purposes. Cultural production outside of these formal, state-sponsored venues enables a greater variety of mobilizational forms and functions but potentially limits the reach of such action to influence policy. When cultural activities take place outside the capital centers or without official recognition, it becomes easier for authorities to limit their own and the media's attention to them.

Consequences of Cultural Activism

These cultural spaces and channels are open to activists because they are the same spaces officials use to promote their version of what it means to be a good Russian citizen. To compete with official narratives and cultural policy, activists use the same channels, but in the opposite direction. Activists do not have the same level of control over the cultural channels as the government does, and officials can attempt to block them through tactics such as funding or permit denial; however, they do have some access, because if cultural activity and venues are fully controlled or shut down, they risk losing authenticity, weakening a tool the government uses to strengthen its hegemony. Activists supporting particular cultural or linguistic development work within these channels in part because they do not view them as political. For example, a supporter of Nuori Karjala remarked:

> They tried to catch the organization in some kind of political struggle, although the organization is not engaged in any political affairs, but is engaged in the development and preservation of the language. Some tried to attribute nationalism to the organization, but these are all empty accusations, because this does not exist and cannot be. They, of course, support Karelian national culture. They are afraid of nationalism everywhere, because a very strange situation is taking place in Ukraine now. They do not want to allow this anywhere else, so they are trying to cover up all these places. But this does not apply to Nuori Karjala in any way, because people are engaged in culture.[14]

Like activism in other realms, activism in support of culture and conducted through cultural means can be construed as political activity by the government whether or not the activists themselves intend it to be.

The capitals of Karelia, Tatarstan, and Buryatia each provide many opportunities for cultural production, both inside state affiliated venues and outside of them in less formal spaces. While public protest is increasingly curtailed, cultural events serve as an alternative means of community gathering and voice. This activism is not all oppositional, however. Some cultural production and consumption complement the greater emphasis on Russian culture and language by the Kremlin, such as the Festival of Russian Choral Music in Kazan, or efforts to generate patriotism, such as a concert of patriotic songs from the USSR for Lenin's birthday in Ulan-Ude.

Other types of cultural production, such as Karelian-language theater, challenge policies unfavorable to language promotion in a permissible, less threatening manner. In Karelia, direct appeals from civil-society organizations, such as To Karelian Language—Official Status in Karelia and the Congress of Karels, to make Karelian an official language in the republic have been denied on the basis of the 2002 law requiring official languages to be written in Cyrillic. Officials have moved permitted space for anti-corruption protests from a prominent location in front of the Musical Theater to the shore of Lake Onega, away from busy streets and government buildings. Therefore, to make a stand for linguistic and cultural preservation or against those in power, Petrozavodsk citizens turn to cultural production. Attending a Karelian play, listening to a Kantele concert, and participating in a talk or meeting housed within a cultural building provide avenues for activism without directly challenging regional leaders or restrictions on public gatherings. Although in a weaker economic and demographic position than Tatarstan, Karelia still exhibits a variety of cultural spaces, both official and unofficial, for promoting minority cultures and Karelian language.

Similarly, in the context of heightened limits on permissible gatherings and topics for debate in Kazan, cultural production is a substitute for other forms of activism, such as protests and petitions. Proponents of Tatar language preservation have attempted to organize in its defense but cannot come together as a large group in public because of permit denials by the regional government. Leaders of Tatar organizations working against this policy change have faced police harassment and accusations of illegal activity. For example, Nail Nabiullin of Azatliq (Liberty) Union of Tatar Youth was detained and questioned in August 2018 on suspicion of fraud, an action Nabiullin characterizes as retaliation for his activism in support of Tatar language and culture (Radio Free Europe/Radio Liberty 2018). When avenues for demanding more official support for Tatar are closed, language promotion through cultural production in Tatar and drawing on Tatar culture can serve as a form of activism, and there are frequent opportunities for this kind of activism in Kazan's theaters and informal cultural spaces.

In Ulan-Ude, theaters and concert halls similarly provide opportunities for promoting Buryat language and culture and strengthening Buryat-Mongolian cultural connections; however, most cultural spaces in the regional capital combine Soviet and Buryat styles in a way that complements the center's vision of the greater Russian nation rather than competes with it. While activism can occur in these spaces, it is not necessarily of the oppositional sort. With fewer resources and a less widely spoken titular language, Buryatia's ability to use formal cultural spaces for mobilization is weaker. Despite the weaker mobilizing potential of Buryatia's cultural venues, activism and protest can and do occur outside of them.

As the Kremlin continues to implement new cultural policies and rely on nation building to solidify support, cultural spaces and activities will serve both as avenues to demonstrate support for the regime and as alternatives to the street or ballot box for oppositional voices.

Notes

1. For analyses of Soviet nationalities policies, see Martin (2001); Hirsch (2005); Slezkine (1994).
2. Author's interview, 2016, Petrozavodsk.
3. Author's interview, 2015, Petrozavodsk.
4. Author's observation, March 4, 2016, Petrozavodsk.
5. Author's interview, 2016, Petrozavodsk.
6. Author's observation, May 24, 2014, Kazan.
7. Author's observation, October 19, 2015, Petrozavodsk.

8. Author's observation, February 3, 2016, Petrozavodsk.
9. Author's interview, 2016, Petrozavodsk.
10. Author's observation, November 4, 2015, Petrozavodsk.
11. Author's interview, 2016, Kazan.
12. Author's interview, 2016, Kazan.
13. Author's observation, June 13, 2014, Kazan.
14. Author's interview, 2016, Petrozavodsk.

Bibliography

Blakkisrud, Helge. 2016. "Blurring the Boundary between Civic and Ethnic: The Kremlin's New Approach to National Identity under Putin's Third Term." In *The New Russian Nationalism: Imperialism, Ethnicity and Authoritarianism 2000–2015*, edited by Helge Blakkisrud and Pål Kolstø, 249–274. Edinburgh: Edinburgh University Press.

Breslavsky, Anatoliy S. 2012. "Post-Soviet Ulan-Ude: Content and Meaning of a New Urban Idea." *Inner Asia* 14, no.2 (January): 299–317.

Cushman, Thomas. 1995. *Notes from Underground: Rock Music Counterculture in Russia*. Albany, NY: State University of New York Press.

Feder, Tal, and Tally Katz-Gerro. 2012. "Who Benefits from Public Funding of the Performing Arts? Comparing the Art Provision and the Hegemony-Distinction Approaches." *Poetics* 40, no.4 (August): 359–381.

Gerschewski, Johannes. 2013. "The Three Pillars of Stability: Legitimation, Repression, and Co-optation in Autocratic Regimes." *Democratization* 20 (1): 13–38.

Goode, J. Paul. 2019. "Russia's Ministry of Ambivalence: The Failure of Civic Nation-Building in Post-Soviet Russia." *Post-Soviet Affairs* 35 (2): 140–160.

Gramsci, Antonio. 1989. *Selections from the Prison Notebooks*. Edited and translated by Quintin Hoare and Geoffrey N. Smith. New York: International.

Hirsch, Francine. 2005. *Empire of Nations: Ethnographic Knowledge and the Making of the Soviet Union*. Ithaca, NY: Cornell University Press.

Hong, Ying-yi. 2009. "A Dynamic Constructivist Approach to Culture: Moving from Describing Culture to Explaining Culture." In *Understanding Culture: Theory, Research and Application*, edited by Robert S. Wyer, Chi-yue Chiu, and Ying-yi Hong, 3–23. New York: Psychology.

Klement'ev, E. I. 2015. *Etnosotsiologiya v Karelii*. Petrozavodsk: Karel'skii nauchnyi tsentr RAN.

Laruelle, Marlene. 2017. "Is Nationalism a Force for Change in Russia?" *Daedalus* 146, no.2 (Spring): 89–100.

Markelov, Sergei. 2019. "'Mne by ne khotelos', chtoby druzhbu brosali v gornilo politicheskoy bor'by.' Zhiteli Petrozavodska proveli aktsiyu v zashchitu pamyatnika 'Derevo druzhby.'" *7x7*, June 27, 2019. https://7x7-journal.ru/articles

/2019/06/27/mne-by-ne-hotelos-chtoby-druzhbu-brosali-v-gornilo-politicheskoj-borby-zhiteli-petrozavodska-proveli-akciyu-v-zashitu-pamyatnika-derevo-druzhby.

Martin, Terry. 2001. *The Affirmative Action Empire: Nations and Nationalism in the Soviet Union, 1923–1939*. Ithaca, NY: Cornell University Press.

Pekkonen, Inna. 2019. "Petrozavodchane stantsevali v znak protesta na Alleye gorodov-pobratimov." *Karelia News*, June 27, 2019. https://www.karelia.news/news/2436227/petrozavodcane-stancevali-v-znak-protesta-na-allee-gorodov-pobratimov.

President of Russia. 2000. "President Vladimir Putin Visited the Celebration of Sabantui, a Tatar Festival." June 24, 2000. http://en.kremlin.ru/events/president/news/38707.

Radio Free Europe/Radio Liberty. 2018. "Tatar Activist Detained in Kazan, Questioned in Financial Fraud Probe." August 15, 2018. https://www.rferl.org/a/tatar-activist-detained-in-kazan-questioned-in-financial-fraud-probe/29435432.html.

Rosstat. 2019. *Regiony Rossii: Sotsial'no-Ekonomicheskie Pokazateli* [Regions of Russia: Socioeconomic indicators]. https://www.gks.ru/storage/mediabank/Region_Pokaz_2019.pdf.

Saprykin, Yury. 2018. "The Serebrennikov Case: A Theater of the Absurd." *Moscow Times*, January 16, 2018. https://themoscowtimes.com/articles/serebrennikov-case-theater-absurd-60193.

Scott, James C. 1990. *Domination and the Arts of Resistance*. New Haven, CT: Yale University Press.

Slezkine, Yuri. 1994. "The USSR as a Communal Apartment, or How a Socialist State Promoted Ethnic Particularism." *Slavic Review* 53, no.2 (Summer): 414–452.

Stewart, Katie L. 2017. "Contentious Conceptions of We the People: An Analysis of Regional Variation in Russian Nation-Building Strategies and Outcomes." PhD diss., Indiana University.

Zaikov, P.M. 2009. "Doklad predsedatelya Soyuza karel'skogo naroda P. M. Zaykova na V s"ezde 'Sovremennaya kul'turno-yazykovaya situatsiya karelov.'" In *Karel'skoe Natsional'noe Dvizhenie. Chast' 1. Ot S"ezda k s"ezdu Sbornik materialov i dokumentov*, edited by E. I. Klement'ev and A. A. Kozhanov, 175–178. Petrozavodsk: Karelian Research Center. http://resources.krc.karelia.ru/illh/doc/knigi_stati/kar_dvizh_1.pdf.

Katie L. Stewart is Assistant Professor of Political Science at Knox College. Her research, funded by the Fulbright Program and the Mellon Foundation, analyzes regional variation in Russian nation building and its effectiveness in fostering regime legitimacy.

3

The Promotion of Minority Languages in Russia's Ethnic Republics

Social Media and Grassroots Activities

GUZEL YUSUPOVA

The chapter examines Russian ethnic minorities' grassroots activities aimed at the promotion of native languages after the change in language policy at schools in 2017. Special attention is paid to the grassroots activities that have emerged from online connective action in defense of compulsory learning of local languages in schools in the national republics of the Russian Federation. Interviews with activists, participant observation, and qualitative content analysis of social networking sites reveal that the offline resistance to new language policy has been transformed into online connective action advancing grassroots activities. This has resulted in establishing horizontal social ties of support among representatives of a single ethnic group and among different ethnic groups, which evolved into interethnic solidarity based on an identification as a minority.

The Importance of Local Language Education: Policy and Scholarship

In the last two decades, Russia has charted a course toward nationalizing the state through the promotion of cultural homogenization based on a core, Russian, ethnicity (Kolstø 2015). Academic literature in Russian studies focuses predominantly on symbolic or legal aspects of this phenomenon but rarely addresses the responses of Russia's ethnic minorities to these developments from a bottom-up perspective. The most recent step in the nationalizing strategy of the Russian state—the de facto demotion of the second official local languages in ethnic republics—has provoked resistance from ethnic minorities met with overt and covert repressions from the state (Yusupova 2021). Offline mobilization failed and transformed into online connective action instead (Bennet and Segerberg 2012, 2014). This makes an interesting case for scholarly investigation and poses an important question: What were the outcomes of this online connective action?

In his speech on July 20, 2017, at the Council on Interethnic Relations in Mari El, Vladimir Putin announced the demotion of second official languages in Russia's ethnic republics and stressed that

> Russian language for us is the state language, the language of interethnic communication, and it cannot be replaced by anything else, it is the natural spiritual scaffolding of our multinational country. Everyone must know it. The languages of the peoples of Russia are also an integral part of the original culture of the people of Russia. To study these languages is the right guaranteed by the Constitution, this right is voluntary. Forcing a person to learn a language that is not native for him is just as unacceptable as reducing the level and time of teaching Russian. I would like to draw special attention of heads of regions of the Russian Federation to this.

Some might assume that this decision was caused by numerous complaints of parents of Russian-speaking children in ethnic republics who did not want to spend time learning a "useless" language (Arutyunova 2019). Others might note that this is just another step in Putin's long-term strategy of cultural homogenization across the different parts of Russia's population (Busygina 2016; Zamyatin 2016). Either way, this speech and subsequent events have raised tensions in many ethnic regions of Russia and have led to a certain degree of mobilization of ethnic minorities.

Before Putin's speech, languages of titular minorities were a compulsory subject at schools in the majority of the ethnic regions of the Russian Federation. Its presence in the school program varied across the regions from merely two hours per week in Udmurtia and Buryatia to the same number of hours as required for teaching Russian, as in Tatarstan. In September 2017, after the presidential special order, the General Prosecutor's Office began an investigation to verify whether minority-language study is voluntary in ethnic republics, with the first inspections of schools taking place in Bashkortostan and Tatarstan. The investigation revealed that minority languages in these republics were in fact still being studied on a compulsory basis. This led to the mass sacking of minority-language teachers in the ethnic republics and turned ethnic-minority-language teaching into a highly sensitive political issue. These actions then led to protest activities during the autumn of 2017 in a number of ethnic regions where the prosecutorial investigation took place. Investigations in other regions were postponed until January 2018. This tactic did not let ethnic activists from various regions mobilize at once.

This study fills the following gaps that one finds at the intersection of digital movement studies, nationalism studies, and Russian studies: First, while there is substantial research on social movements in the internet age (Castells 2012; Gunel and Baruh 2016; Howard et al. 2015), this work focuses mainly on how online activities become offline social movements and pays far less attention to hashtag activism (Yang 2016) or e-mobilizations (Earl and Kimport 2011) that never transform into offline political protests in illiberal regimes. Second, studies on social activism and social mobilization in Russia rarely focus on ethnic minority groups, particularly after the middle of the first decade of the twenty-first century, when defederalization gained strength. The few studies that do focus on local social mobilization do not focus attention on the role of digital media and do not consider long-term outcomes of such digital involvement (Greene 2012; Smyth and Oates 2015). However, such consideration sheds light on the abilities of online connective action to have real consequences for offline actions, even when offline collective mobilization has never occurred or was unsuccessful.

Finally, this chapter also contributes to the existing scholarly discussion of revitalization of substate minority languages by digital means, which rarely considers ethnic minority languages in Russia (Suleymanova 2009, Gruffydd Jones and Uribe-Jongbloed 2013; Cormack 2013; Budka 2019). Jeremy Morris's (2013) paper on ordinary internet users in Russian regions argues that social media use in fact has little or no potential for social mobilization outside of big cities, while Seva Gunitsky (2015) shows how nondemocratic regimes successfully use social media for their own purposes. This chapter proposes that this is not always the case and contributes to the field of research on local activism in Russia by considering ethnic minorities' bottom-up movement in defense of their native languages, focusing on advancing grassroots activities by means of social media.

To contribute to these debates and explore outcomes of the online connective action around local language learning, I employ several data-collection techniques that create a holistic picture. I gathered twenty-two expert interviews with activists from ten ethnic republics who were recruited and interviewed using snowball sampling, starting with activists from Tatarstan. Most of these republics are in the Volga-Ural region, although I also interviewed activists from Chechnya, Yakutia, and Buryatia. I supplement this interview data with issue-related posts on research participants' online profiles in social media networking sites (SNS). In addition to this evidence, I analyze posts related to the issue found by such digital mechanisms as hashtagging and hyperlinking on two SNS: VKontakte and Facebook. I also use my observations of WhatsApp and Telegram group discussions. Another source of information was fieldwork data gathered in Tatarstan and Chuvashia in November–December 2017 and August 2018. I also use longitudinal interviews about attitudes of ethnic minority nonactivists toward their native languages. I have used qualitative content analysis for analyzing interviews and critical discourse analysis for accessing media texts and visuals. For the sake of research participants' security, I avoid identifying them.

The Failure of Offline Mobilization and the Movement Online

As Robertson (2010) argues, the state has played a significant role in shaping the tactics and structure of opposition organizations that define the mobilization capacity in hybrid regimes; therefore, the offline mobilization tactics and consequent online resistance of ethnic minorities to new language policies were significantly shaped by the reaction of the state. The investigation in schools and the subsequent mass dismissal of minority-language teachers led to rallies held in Bashkortostan and Tatarstan in autumn 2017. Bashkortostan saw the first rallies on September 16, when more than two thousand people came to protest in the main square of the capital city of Ufa, even though local authorities had not granted them permission. Although the main reason for this rally was discontent with the regional governor, the language question played a significant role too (Krasovsky 2017). When the police tried to end the rally by arresting the leading activists, the protesters actively defended them. Nonetheless, several organizers were detained by the police at the private apartment where they gathered after the rally.

Meanwhile in Tatarstan, several Tatar activists who organized single pickets (one of the few possible ways to protest in Russia without preliminary permission from the authorities) were also intimidated or detained by police. Activists from the pro-regional-government organization Forum of Tatar Youth failed to organize a rally in Kazan too. They were not granted permission for this by the local authorities, despite repeated applications. Instead, they came up with ideas for several cultural flash mobs to raise awareness of the issue in Tatarstan. For example, one evening activists invited the most popular Tatar singers to the main street in Kazan to sing a song about their native language so that any passerby could join them.

The whole event lasted no longer than half an hour and was broadcast online on SNS. However, there was covert pressure on the participants after this event.

Leading activists received a warning from security services that "extremist" activities were not permitted and would be severely punished. Initiation of similar cultural flash mobs and following or preemptive actions by security services were mentioned by research participants from other ethnic republics of Russia:

> **Research participant:** He [security services officer] visited me about the time we intended to organize a public concert in [minority language] in response to these measures [prosecutorial investigations] in schools. He asked about my intentions, told me not to do anything stupid.
>
> **Researcher:** You talk about this as if you were acquaintances!
>
> **Research participant:** That's right. He visits me regularly since I have started to organize [some regular educational event in minority language]. You see, there is not much to do for security services here, so he visits me as a potential extremist.

Therefore, offline collective action has not become a common form of resistance. There were other ways to resist the new language policy. In the next sections, I describe several grassroots activities aimed at language revitalization and better attitudes toward the second official languages in ethnic republics that emerged from or were reinforced by the new language policy of the federal government.

The Range of Online Mobilization Actions

Limited in their ability to organize an open protest, activists from various republics started to unite online. How did they connect in the first place? There were two ways: One was by previous acquaintance offline at various meetings, conferences, or festivals organized to advance multiculturalism in Russia—on behalf of both the state's agencies in the first decade of the twenty-first century and various cross-ethnic organizations that proliferated during the 1990s. Another way was by meeting through online discussions of posts related to the new language policy. Interestingly, various platforms serve different functions and goals.

Facebook

Several special pages were created on Facebook to update all people interested in the issue and to mobilize them around particular actions, such as signing a digital petition. However, these pages were not popular for discussion. Instead, active and intense discussions of the issue and news on the topic were initiated and successfully developed as posts on activists' personal pages. One such post could gather a few dozen participants and hundreds of comments. These posts were usually open to friends and friends of friends only. Through these discussions, they befriended one another on the basis of shared ideas, political positions, and connections. During these discussions, especially when posts were reposted or had gathered many comments, activists from various republics got to know one another. Often befriending has happened after commenting on reposts from traditional media or on posts from famous scholars or journalists who specialize on ethnic issues in Russia and are followed by people interested in their unique expertise.

VKontakte

VKontakte served as a social network for gathering popular support for measures that promoted or opposed minority-language teaching in schools. There were intense discussions by ordinary people (nonactivists) on and beyond the topic. According to the research participants, activists also use this social network predominantly for communication to out-groups, both to those against the compulsory teaching of minority languages and to state officials, because they believe that all posts and groups in VKontakte will be monitored by security services and that reports to authorities will be written on this basis. This social network also serves for purposeful recruiting of new activists for newly launched initiatives, such as *Interactivismo*, a seminar on language activism.

Telegram

After prosecutions in schools began, ethnic minority activists organized several channels on Telegram dedicated to the issue of the demotion of second official languages in Russia. These channels have served to gather and disseminate news on the topic. There were channels for local audiences in each republic on minority languages and channels in Russian for a broader audience. Several activists also created a closed channel to discuss ways to resist the current language policy legally on the state level. This dual-level utilization of the social media service is a feature of Jeremy Morris's chapter in this volume. The closed channel's participants knew one another in person and avoided accepting anyone with radical views, describing themselves as "moderate" nationalists or, rather, ethnic activists to avoid the negative connotation. According to the interviews, they discussed mostly organizational and legal issues in this channel. For example, to avoid being accused of extremism while actively defending the status of second official languages in their republics, which measures must one adopt? They also consulted one another on legal means of fighting the prosecution and legislation concerning language teaching in schools, as well as international legislation concerning minority languages and other cultural rights. Moreover, they initiated and jointly wrote an open letter and a petition to the president. Then this petition was widely distributed to collect signatures. The petition and the open letter were then disseminated on various social media platforms, not least through various messengers, such as WhatsApp.

WhatsApp and Messaging Apps as "Kitchen Talk"

Aside from serving social-mobilization functions, such as sharing information on offline rallies or cultural flash mobs, WhatsApp chats on minority languages became a substitute for what in Soviet times used to be called "kitchen talk"—a crucial part of society's information landscape (Smyth and Oates 2015). WhatsApp groups comprised from one hundred to four hundred active members of each ethnic group, who actively discussed and commented on media articles, new law enforcement strategies, and popular posts on SNS. Believing that most negative comments about the compulsory learning of minority languages were being made by internet bots, group members encouraged one another to write comments on articles in local and federal media and to support positive comments and thus create the headquarters for an "informational war." They also discussed other local, regional, and global issues, like Catalonia's declaration of independence, for example. Importantly, they refrained from open discussion of this event, except for sharing the caricature made by media Azatliq (Radio "Liberty" Tatar-Bashkir service).

Meanwhile, legal investigations started in other regions of the Russian Federation, and this forced new ethnic minorities to join in the online resistance movement. After a while, media coverage and wider public interest beyond residents of ethnic republics themselves prepared the room for open discussions organized on both traditional media platforms and specially dedicated offline forums and roundtables.

In June 2018, activists created an official organization to promote minority languages and broader issues of multiculturalism and federalism in Russia—the Democratic Congress of the Peoples of Russia. This was a network of about thirty regional activists mostly but not only from Russian ethnic republics. The network aimed to foster public discussions on issues of federalism in Russia by initiating roundtables with representatives of regional activists, federal authorities, and academic experts. The new language policy was not the only reason for the creation of the organization, but the rumors of the merging of ethnic regions of Russia with nonethnic ones also inspired this initiative. In response, a special official organization emerged from horizontal networks and online activities that was solid enough to become an independent political actor and to promote ethnic minority issues at state level.

This is a rare outcome for a connective action, which is usually far more likely to be focused only on short-term "event-based" loyalties, rather than longer-term "interest-based political affiliation" (Bimber 2003). After existing for about a year, this bottom-up initiative was eventually dissolved because of the risk of participants being accused of extremism. Several attempts to register similar organizations in Ufa and in Moscow have failed. Moreover, other officially registered regional minority organizations have been later persecuted and, in some cases, accused of extremism (Interfaks Rossiia 2020).[1] This, however, stimulated discussions of overcoming the new obstacles and fostered a sense of solidarity among representatives of different ethnic minority groups.

Online Connective Action

During the first month of fierce discussion of the prosecutions, an avalanche of various memes shared in online communications enabled connective action in its classic understanding—as a wave of personal action frames when different people share their personal attitudes to the problem (Bennet and Segerberg 2014). People shared memes about their less-used languages, either with the expression of their own attitude to the problem or without any additional comments. Most of these memes expressed the risk of a particular minority language's death or despair for fired teachers. As Denisova (2015) rightly points out, memes are a coded language of dissent on the Russian internet.

One of the most influential campaigns to draw attention to the issue of the suppression of minority languages in Russia began with the online sharing of an image along with the hashtags #StopLanguageGenocide and #остановитеязыковойгеноцид on SNS addressing all minority languages of the Russian Federation. One of posts has the following framing: "Defend the languages of the peoples of Russia! If you do not say no today to these attacks, tomorrow you will speak only Russian. Share and say no to the pressure on regional languages!" This hashtag has become a popular slogan and is used for personal action frames in support of minority languages, engaging new people in the online movement. Often discussions under these personal action frames (memes with the stated personal opinion) became charged with xenophobic comments and then disappeared because the person who made the post deleted it eventually.

My findings support Sarah Oates's (2016, 403–404) argument that "by making an example through intimidation and even imprisonment of bloggers or even those who repost comments, the government can effectively create a climate of internal censorship that significantly limits the spread of political dissent online." This has worked perfectly in the case of the minority-languages movement: most people deleted posts with this and other memes after receiving accusations of extremism in comments by their "friends" on social networking sites. Extremism in this case, from many commentators' point of view, meant a claim for separatism and the disintegration of Russia, which is a criminal claim.

One of the most popular online connective action trends was to use only minority languages for communication on SNS. Many activists started to use their native languages when posting on social networking sites and when chatting with one another. Many started to share links on Russian traditional media outlets with their own comments in native language. Some Tatar activists who previously spoke in Russian with me changed our language of communication to Tatar both in speaking and writing, although most of the time I responded in Russian. "I must do everything in my ability to use my native language as much as possible and make others hear it more often, to get used to it as normality. Then maybe people like you will be less hesitant to talk in Tatar too," one research participant said to me in Tatar language, trying to explain his attempts to switch to Tatar whenever possible.

Ethnic minority activists from many republics of Russia made a call elsewhere on social networking sites to use minority languages as much as possible and bring them to the public sphere. Thus, since October 2017 the content in minority languages shared online became more visible in various SNS. This trend faded after several months, and many switched back to Russian, but many people continue to use their native languages when reasonable. This reasoning usually depends on an imagined auditorium of their messages and the information they would like to share.

There were also a few attempts by ethnic Russians to make online statements in support of minority languages. They shared stories of how important the Tatar language is for them with the hashtag #мойтатарский (my Tatar). However, these posts also often received many negative comments and disapproval from co-ethnic people. If ethnic activists or nonactivist representatives of ethnic minorities making such statements received a relatively equal share of approval and disapproval, with large support by co-ethnic people, ethnic Russians received much disapproval and less support. This surprising fact might be explained by the composition of friends and followers on SNS: the social networks of ethnic Russians are probably more ethnically homogeneous than those of ethnic minorities. However, this hypothesis needs further research.

Another example of people's online support is a campaign on Instagram in which popular and ordinary people recorded videos of themselves holding a sign reading "Stop Language Genocide" while saying another slogan, "I speak Tatar!" or singing a song about the mother tongue. Some famous Russian artists also joined the flash mob (Prokazan.ru 2017).

Other online flash mobs celebrating vernacular culture of ethnic minorities have started, like the #инстаудмурточки (#instaudmurtochki), when young girls of Udmurt origin post their pictures on Instagram with stories about why they are proud to be Udmurts. This has become a marathon with various tasks: to make videos about the Udmurt language or cuisine and answer questions, such as what Udmurt beauty is. The goal of this marathon started by one young woman is "to promote contemporary Udmurt culture, to make it prestigious to be Udmurt today, to put the end to the stigma of being a backward minority." These online connective actions and horizontal ties have resulted in the proliferation of various grassroots activities, which will be considered in the next section.

Grassroots Activities

These cases have shown how horizontal social ties among representatives of a particular ethnic group and among different ethnic groups were established in the digital domain. Have these online activities resulted in any actual offline political or social participation? What was happening in the background of intense online discussions around the topic of teaching second official languages in ethnic republics? Since the implementation of the presidential order and dismissal of minority-language teachers, the range of various grassroots initiatives aimed at the revival of minority languages in Russia has expanded.

First, preexisting initiatives, such as free courses in minority languages, have been able to recruit more volunteers. In some ethnic regions, like Mari El, for example, ethnic activists have organized free language courses because the situation revealed a demand for Mari-language lessons within the adult population. Also, minority-language courses have become available in new formats. Various thematic discussion clubs in minority languages have become popular. Of course, most of these discussions were dedicated to the question of teaching and learning minority languages. However, there was also room for other everyday topics for those who did not have a good command of their native language and for those with various levels of minority-language knowledge.

One woman who organized such a Tatar-language club in Ufa presented her project at the VIII Tatar Youth Forum in Kazan in the summer of 2018. She explained, "When I came up with this idea, the first thing I did was to consult with lawyers—would it be legal to organize such a club or might I end up in prison accused in extremist activities?" This quote shows the perception of the environment for the promotion of minority languages as repressive and hostile, particularly in the views of potential participants, who calculate the price for their participation accordingly. Nonetheless, when such clubs operate on the official level, there is significant interest in participation among ethnic minorities. For example, in Tatarstan around a thousand people signed up for official free Tatar-language courses offered by Kazan Federal University in autumn 2017. These courses were provided in the past but attracted far fewer participants. New media platforms for learning minority languages have emerged, including numerous Telegram channels, such as "Audio Books in Tatar" (Аудио-әсәрләр Исемлеге)[2] or "Tatar for Beginners," launched by the Tatarstan Muslim Religious Board. There are similar groups learning minority languages in VKontakte—several for each language. Moreover, language activists from each ethnic group have created special keyboards for computers and smartphones.

Several free applications for smartphones were created for facilitating minority-language learning. For example, Owl (tat. *Yabalak*) or Sakha [Yakut] Language (sakh. *Sakha Tyla*). At the beginning of 2019, Yakutian publishing house Bichick introduced new multimedia textbooks for learning Yakutian language, as well as smartphone games based on national folklore and the smartphone application Digital Library Bichick for reading books in Sakha language. Some ethnic groups, who did not have YouTube channels of native-language lessons before, started such channels in 2019. One of them is the Khakassian YouTube channel Khakass Speech and Some Theory (Askhyr Khakasia 2019), which was created for three different levels of language skills. Special online platforms for minority-language learning were created or updated with innovations, like the resource Ossetian Language Online[3] or the Tatar Language interactive resource (tat. *Tatar tele*).[4] Various funny and witty stickers with common phrases in minority languages were created in Telegram for personal chatting.

Artists, poets, and other representatives of ethnic minority cultural elite have also been mobilized to promote their native languages to the general public and highlight the importance of the language. For example, in their Instagram account the famous Tatar band *Gauga*, who make rock music in Tatar language, has started to publish Instagram stories under the headline "Learning Tatar" that translate some Tatar words from their songs into Russian. Not all these people identify themselves as activists. Their ethnic identification has not changed much but rather has been accentuated more often during this mobilization period.

Another example is the theatrical dance performance *Alif* by Nurbeck Batulla—a young Tatar choreographer—which won a Golden Mask award for Best Male Role in 2018. The choreography tells a story about a Tatar alphabet and is titled after the first letter of the Tatar alphabet. When awarded the prize, Nurbeck Batulla gave a speech in Tatar dedicating his show and the victory to Tatar language.[5]

Moreover, in some republics like Tatarstan and Yakutia, crowdfunding for various alternative online media in native languages is becoming more and more successful, providing resources for those media to develop and attract new followers, readers, and speakers. Editors have noticed that a greater number of ordinary citizens are donating small sums of money and that wealthier businesspeople have increased their donations. This boom in donations has helped to develop Tatar online medium Gyilem,[6] for example. Established in 2014, this online medium on the topics of science and technology in Tatar language has expanded because of increasing individual donations.

"This hype [about the] prohibition of teaching minority languages in schools has affected us surprisingly positively. Some wealthy people became interested in our media, and one has helped us with an office, another one with some facilities. Donations are significantly increased too. The only worry is what will happen when the hype fades."

After increasing interest in their activities and content, they have managed to buy the necessary equipment and recruit some staff. Before that, everyone involved worked exclusively on a voluntary basis. Interestingly, the initiator of this online media, Aidar Shaikhin, is also advancing the idea of the translation of world literature into Tatar and has already translated the first volume of the Harry Potter books. Financial support of this and similar minority-language initiatives has also come from grants from the regional governments where minority-language classes were compulsory. The Tatarstan government, for example, opened a call for several grants for the initiatives in the minority-languages domain.

Ethnic minority activists living outside Russia also started to create more online content on YouTube channels and Instagram, although in many cases they were the first to contribute to the revival of minority languages in Russia even before these events: living in the West and enabled by Information and Communication Technologies (ICT) earlier than Russian residents, they initiated Wikipedia activism, participated in online forums on minority languages, and advanced minority languages online by other means in the 1990s. Wikipedia activism has expanded since then and has received more public attention depending on the region. Currently it is most popular in Bashkortostan, where writing Wikipedia pages has become a popular activity among Bashkort elderly people. Wikipedia activist Farhad Fatkullin, who greatly contributed to the Tatar Wikipedia and to Wikipedia in other minority languages of Russia, became the first Russian citizen to be awarded an international prize from Wikipedia as the Wikipedian of the Year in 2017. He also actively promotes the use of Wikipedia in schools, with classes on how to write wiki pages and use other Wikipedia tools with a view to expand content in minority languages.

Another activity lies in the realm of ethnic commodification: the promotion of minority languages in publishing, music and fashion, and other productions and services. For example, a fashion designer from Kazan, Yaroslav Karpov, has produced T-shirts picturing the Tatar alphabet with the heading "The Trend of 2018" and highlighting in red the specific Tatar letters. In his post on Instagram, he stated:

> At the end of 2017, the question of studying the national languages of the republics within the Russian Federation in schools on an obligatory basis became acute. Arguments in favor that minority languages should be an optional form of study sound sensible: at the moment they are not required in order to build a career, they take hours from another class, the Russian language, and thus become an obstacle in the successful learning of subjects included in a Single State Exam for school students. However, there is one "but." The brand "elevenox" considers the national language to be an indispensable condition for the existence of the nation itself, its most important condition, and stands in support of the existence of a Tatar language which is native to us. When a language disappears, eventually everything connected with the people who spoke it disappears, all the huge cultural code and baggage that these people carried through the centuries disappears. We do not consider modern people culturally rich enough to put it at risk so frivolously.

Designers from other republics also promoted their native languages through commodification. For example, in Chuvashia they organized a festival with souvenirs promoting the alphabet and the language. In Buryatia and several other republics, they issued a few new books, including coloring books, and electronic games for children to learn a native language.

The sudden salience of ethnicity in public discourse and the relevance of ethnic identification to everyday routine in ethnic republics has become visible with the online mobilization, thus enabling various grassroots activities aimed at reviving the use of minority languages. This in its turn increases the prestige of minority languages in daily life, helps to build horizontal ties among activists, and boosts a feeling of solidarity by making language a symbolic political resource for a social movement.

Conclusion

The new federal language policy aimed at downgrading second official languages in ethnic republics has had many unintended consequences. First and foremost, titular ethnic minorities in all ethnic republics, including those where they dominate on the political level and are well represented among political elites, have become aware of their group vulnerability in the context of new Russian nation-building processes. Such awareness has led to their self-understanding as a political community, as a united ethnic group, and as a broader group of subordinated ethnic minorities taken together. Representatives of titular groups now have a common cause to unite to become an important actor in defining national policies toward ethnic minorities. Although their political mobilization is limited by the repressive context (Yusupova 2021), they have taken significant steps toward adopting a strong stance in public discourse on ethnic minority issues.

Unable to organize an effective social mobilization offline, ethnic activists united online instead. The resistance in cyberspace has caused the proliferation of digital platforms that address various issues and initiate public discussions. Many grassroots projects that emerged from these discussions have attracted the attention and support of cultural, political, and economic ethnic elites, thus enabling cooperation between civic society and regional economic and political powers. Although many of the digital initiatives already existed before the events discussed in this chapter, the new federal policy stimulated their spreading, expanding, and growing interest for republics' residents.

Overall, in a country as vast and culturally diverse as Russia, top-down assimilation is a poor way to shore up a spirit of national unity. Assimilation policies will always meet with resistance, even entrench it; in this case, the result is a welter of grassroots initiatives against the government's plans. It seems that the government's efforts to homogenize Russia from east to west are strengthening exactly the sort of identities they were supposed to marginalize.

However, the political goals and concerns of ethnic activists are focused predominantly on narrow problems; they do not address the core issues of democracy. Despite the experience of being restricted in the organization of open protests (a violation of the right to free assembly), misrepresented by the federal media outlets, and limited to online expression (a violation of the right to free speech), it seems that ethnic activists and the majority of ordinary people who were involved in online connective action failed to recognize the authoritarian nature of the Russian political environment. Their most overarching claim—the promotion of federalism—is seen as the basis for democratization in Russia, not vice versa. Their demands do extend past cultural rights, and they are not linked to other movements for democratization in Russia. Is this a tactic for being heard by the state and considered less dangerous? Is this a sign of a lack of political imagination? Or has the xenophobic environment forced them to be closed and focused on their own problems—in other words, to lack solidarity with other political groups? These questions require further research.

Postscript: Recent events concerning the Navalny poisoning and an acknowledgment of a new repressive turn in Russia since 2020 have shown that I should have posed the above questions from the perspective of the failures of the liberal opposition, not ethnic activists. Why have the Russian opposition and civil society long ignored the repression of ethnic and religious minorities? Didn't this repressive turn start long before the summer of 2020, and wasn't it first directed at people whose voices the majority often tries to silence?

Notes

1. For more about the repressive context and politics of fear that limits any official and informal bottom-up organizations of ethnic minorities, see Yusupova (2021).
2. https://telegra.ph/Audio-%D3%99s%D3%99rl%D3%99r-isemlege-03-17.
3. https://ironau.ru/index.html.
4. https://readymag.com/u52158107/tatar-tele/.
5. https://www.goldenmask.ru/spect_1556.html.
6. http://giylem.tatar/.

Bibliography

Arutyunova, Ekaterina. 2019. "Language Conflict in Different Dimensions: Cases of Tatarstan and Bashkortostan" [*Yazykovoi conflict v raznykh izmereniyakh: keisy Tatarstana I Bashkortostana*]. *Sociological Journal* [*Sociologicheskiy zhurnal*] 25 (1): 98–120.

Askhyr Khakasia. 2019. "Urok 1 / Khakasskaia rech' i nemnogo teorii /Shkola Khakasskogo iazyka." Video, 5:28, February 10, 2019. https://www.youtube.com/watch?v=TmBKDs_4xuo.

Bennett, W. Lance., and Alexandra Segerberg. 2012. "The Logic of Connective Action." *Information, Communication & Society* 15 (5): 739–768.

———. 2014. *The Logic of Connective Action: Digital Media and the Personalization of Contentious Politics.* New York: Cambridge University Press.

Bimber, Bruce. 2003. *Information and American Democracy.* Cambridge: Cambridge University Press.

Budka, Philipp. 2019. "Cultural Articulation, Digital Practices, and Socio-political Concepts." In *Ethnic Media in the Digital Age,* edited by S. S. Yu and M. D. Matsaganis, 162–172. London: Routledge.

Burgess, Jones. 2008. "All Your Chocolate Rain Are Belong to Us? Viral Video, YouTube and the Dynamics of Participatory Culture." In *Video Vortex Reader: Responses to YouTube,* edited by G. Lovink and S. Niederer. Amsterdam: Institute of Network Cultures.

Busygina, Iryna. 2016. "Putin's Russia: The State-Building Strategy." *Russian Politics* 1 (1): 70–94.

Castells, Manuel. 2012. *Networks of Outrage and Hope: Social Movements in the Internet Age.* Cambridge: Polity.

Clément, Karine. 2015. "From Local to Political: The Kaliningrad Mass Protest Movement of 2009—2010 in Russia." In *Urban Movements and Grassroots Activism in Central and Eastern Europe,* edited by K. Jacobsson, 163–194. Farnham, England: Ashgate.

Clément, Karine, Olga Miryasova, and Andrey Demidov. 2010. *Ot obyvatelei k aktivistam. Zarozhdaiushchiesia sotsialnye dvizheniia v sovremennoi Rossii* [From ordinary folk to activists: Emergent social movements in modern Russia]. Moscow: Tri Kvadrata.

Cormack, M. 2013. "Concluding Remarks: Towards an Understanding of Media Impact on Minority Language Use." In *Social Media and Minority Languages: Convergence and the Creative Industries,* edited by Elin Haf Gruffydd Jones and Enrique Uribe-Jongbloed, 255–265. Bristol, UK: Multilingual Matters.

Couldry, Nick. 2015. "The Myth of 'Us': Digital Networks, Political Change and the Production of Collectivity." *Information, Communication & Society* 18 (6): 608–626. https://doi.org/10.1080/1369118X.2014.979216.

Crowley, Stephen, and Iryna Olimpieva. 2018. "Labor Protests and Their Consequences in Putin's Russia." *Problems of Post-Communism* 65 (5): 344–358.

Denisova, Anastasia. 2015. "Online Memes as a Means of the Carnivalesque Resistance." Paper presented at the symposium Politics and Humour: Theory and Practice, Kent, UK. https://www.academia.edu/9865338/_2014_Online_Memes_as_Means_of_the_Carnivalesque_Resistance_in_Contemporary_Russia.

Earl, Jennifer, and Katrina Kimport. 2011. *Digitally Enabled Social Change: Activism in the Internet Age.* Cambridge, MA: MIT Press.

Enikolopov, Ruben, Alexey Makarin, and Maria Petrova. 2017. "Social Media and Protest Participation: Evidence from Russia." *SSRN*, April 7, 2017. https://ssrn.com/abstract=2696236.

Gainutdinov, D. 2017. "Surveillance in Russia." *Intersection Project*. Accessed January 12, 2020. http://intersectionproject.eu/article/politics/surveillance-russia (site discontinued).

Gelman, Vladimir. 2016. "The Politics of Fear: How Russia's Rulers Counter Their Rivals." *Russian Politics* 1 (1): 27–45.

Gladarev, Boris. 2011. "Istoriko-kulturnoe nasledie Peterburga: rozhdenie obshchestvennosti iz dukha goroda" [Petersburg's cultural heritage: The emergence of a public from the city's spirit]. In *Ot obshchestvennogo k publichnomy* [From the social to the public], edited by Oleg Kharkhodin, 69–304. Saint Petersburg: EUSP Press.

Greene, Samuel. 2012. "Twitter and the Russian Street: Memes, Networks, and Mobilization." Working paper no. 2012/1, Center for the Study of New Media and Society, New Economic School, Moscow.

Greene, Samuel A. 2014. *Moscow in Movement: Power and Opposition in Putin's Russia*. Stanford, CA: Stanford University Press.

Gruffydd Jones, Elin Haf, and Enrique Uribe-Jongbloed, eds. 2013. *Social Media and Minority Languages: Convergence and the Creative Industries*. Bristol: Multilingual Matters.

Gunel, Zeynep, and Lemi Baruh. 2016. "Social Networking Technologies and Social Movements." In *Social Networking Redefining Communication in the Digital Age*, edited by A. Kurylo and T. Dumova. Vancouver: Fairleigh Dickinson University Press.

Gunitsky, Seva. 2015. "Corrupting the Cyber-Commons: Social Media as a Tool of Autocratic Stability." *Perspectives on Politics* 13 (1): 42–54.

Howard, Phillip N., Aidan Duffy, Deen Freelon, M. M. Hussain, Will Mari, and Marwa Maziad. 2015. "Opening Closed Regimes: What Was the Role of Social Media during the Arab Spring?" *SSRN*, April 17, 2015. https://ssrn.com/abstract=2595096.

Interfaks Rossiia. 2020. "Sud v Ufe zapretil obshchestvennuiu organizatsiiu 'Bashkort' kak ekstremistskuiu." May 22, 2020. https://www.interfax-russia.ru/volga/news/sud-v-ufe-zapretil-obshchestvennuyu-organizaciyu-bashkort-kak-ekstremistskuyu.

Johnston, Hank. 2011. *States and Social Movements*. Cambridge: Polity.

Kaufmann, Eric. 2017. "Complexity and Nationalism." *Nations and Nationalism* 23 (1): 6–25.

Kolstø, Pål. 2015. "The Ethnification of Russian Nationalism." In *The New Russian Nationalism: Imperialism, Ethnicity and Authoritarianism*, edited by P. Kolstø and H. Blakkisrud, 18–45. Edinburgh: Edinburgh University Press.

Krasovsky, Alexander. 2017. "Chem na samom dele obuslovlen protest v Bashkirii." MK.ru Ufa, October 13, 2017. https://ufa.mk.ru/articles/2017/10/13/chem-na-samom-dele-obuslovlen-protest-v-bashkirii.html.

Lankina, Tomila, and Alisa Voznaya. 2015. "New Data on Protest Trends in Russia's Regions." *Europe-Asia Studies* 67 (2): 327–342.

Lewis, L. C. 2012. "The Participatory Meme Chronotope: Fixity of Space/Rapture of Time." In *New Media Literacies and Participatory Popular Culture across Borders*, edited by B. Williams and A. Zenger, 106–121. London: Routledge.

Morris, Jeremy. 2013. "Actually Existing Internet Use in the Russian Margins: Net Utopianism in the Shadow of the 'Silent Majorities.'" *Region* 2 (2): 181–200.

Oates, Sarah. 2016. "Russian Media in the Digital Age: Propaganda Rewired." *Russian Politics* 1 (4): 398–417.

Prokazan.ru. 2017. "Akter Aleksei Panin podderzhal tatarskii iazik." November 2, 2017. https://prokazan.ru/news/view/121198/.

Robertson, Graeme. 2010. *The Politics of Protest in Hybrid Regimes: Managing Dissent in Post-Communist Russia*. Cambridge: Cambridge University Press.

Semenov, Andrey. 2016. "From Economic to Political Crisis? Dynamics of Contention in Russian Regions (2008–2012)." *Austrian Journal of Political Science* 45 (4): 7–17.

Shifman, Limor. 2014. *Memes in Digital Culture*. Cambridge, MA: MIT Press.

Smyth, Regina, and Sarah Oates. 2015. "Minding the Gap: Lessons on the Relationship among the Internet, Information, and Regime Challenge from Russian Protests." *Europe-Asia Studies* 67 (2): 285–305.

Suleymanova, Dilyara. 2009. "Tatar Groups in Vkontakte: The Interplay between Ethnic and Virtual Identities on Social Networking Sites." *Digital Icons: Studies in Russian, Eurasian and Central European New Media* 1 (2): 37–55.

White, Stephen, and Ian McAllister. 2014. "Did Russia (Nearly) Have a Facebook Revolution in 2011? Social Media's Challenge to Authoritarianism." *Politics* 34 (1): 72–84.

Wiggins, Bradley. 2016. "Crimea River: Directionality in Memes from the Russia–Ukraine Conflict." *International Journal of Communication* 10 (January): 451–485.

Yang, Guobin. 2016. "Narrative Agency in Hashtag Activism: The Case of #BlackLivesMatter." *Media and Communication* 4 (4): 13–17.

Yusupova, Guzel. 2017. "Making Ethnic Boundaries in the Society of Religious Renaissance: Islam and Everyday Ethnicity in Post-Soviet Tatarstan." *National Identities* 20 (4): 345–360.

———. 2018. "Cultural Nationalism and Everyday Resistance in an Illiberal Nationalising State: Ethnic Minority Nationalism in Russia." *Nations and Nationalism* 24, no. 3 (July): 624–647.

———. 2021. "How Does the Politics of Fear in Russia Work? The Case of Social Mobilization in Support for Minority Languages." *Europe-Asia Studies* 74 (4): 620–641.

Zamyatin, Konstantin. 2016. "Russian Political Regime Change and Strategies of Diversity Management: From a Multinational Federation Towards a Nation-State." *Journal on Ethnopolitics and Minority Issues in Europe* 15 (1): 19–49.

Guzel Yusupova is a visiting scholar at Carleton University. Her research on the sociology of ethnicity and nationalism appears in *Social Science Quarterly, Nations and Nationalism, Nationalities Papers,* and *Problems of Post-Communism.*

4

From Neighbors to Activists

Shared Grievances and Collective Solutions

REGINA SMYTH, MADELINE McCANN,
AND KATHERINE HITCHCOCK

In autocratic states, top-down policy processes can embody suddenly imposed grievances or disruptions of everyday life on the citizens most affected by those policies. In the case of the Moscow Housing Renovation Program, these grievances hit very close to home. In February 2017, Moscow mayor Sergei Sobyanin faced President Vladimir Putin in a televised meeting to announce a massive citywide policy to demolish and replace the city's *khrushchevkas*, or five-story apartment buildings. This housing, constructed between the late 1950s and early 1970s, resulted from a design competition ordered by General Secretary Khrushchev to solve the postwar housing crisis that existed across the Soviet Union and its satellites. Architects came up with two prefabricated models that could be inexpensively and quickly constructed. Yet the five-story buildings were also designed as a stopgap measure, intended for replacement in twenty-five years. By 2018, many were in disrepair, with poor plumbing, leaky roofs, and tiny kitchens.

The opportunity for Muscovites to swap decaying housing for larger, modern apartments seems as if it would not spark protest. Early public opinion polls indicated that 80 percent of Muscovites supported the policy. Yet the introduction of concrete laws generated significant opposition, expressed in apartment blocks, online, and on the streets. Many residents supported the idea of modernized housing. Still, they wanted state assurance of the size, value, and location of new housing; the structure of mortgage payments; rights protections; and the preservation of green spaces.

Our chapter explores how neighborly ties shaped the social response to the Renovation Program. These interactions created common knowledge or shared understanding of residents' problems, shaping their grievances and defining their collective response. Interactions around the problem extended networks and social ties that defined residents' interests and created a foundation for the more visible public activism Anna Zhelnina writes about in chapter 6. Yet an active housing market had broken neighborly bonds for other residents and caused conflict with renters. For these residents, the policy increased cynicism about the regime and alienation from the political process. They did not join activist efforts to improve the policy provisions.

We rely on focus group interviews with residents in five-story apartments included and excluded from the program to show how neighborly ties and shared concerns about the policy outcomes shaped societal attitudes about the housing program and collective action.[1] The evidence reveals the range of responses to the program: supporters who unambiguously advocated for the Renovation Program, advocates who called for policy reform, and opponents who rejected it. We find that residents who opposed the program or wanted more legal protections relied on building- and neighborhood-level networks and reciprocal relations to overcome state control over information and articulate an alternative understanding of potential problems and grassroots solutions.

The next section of our chapter provides additional background on the program's structure, the five-story buildings, and their neighborhoods. The following two sections focus on how state information-control strategies and legislative tactics shaped popular perceptions. Relying on our focus group data, we demonstrate that shared information produced by house-level connections led to activism within the house and in the public arena. We conclude by assessing the intended and unintended consequences of the policy for future activism.

Need, Heritage, and Connections: Defining Residents' Interests

The Renovation Program was unique in that securing the benefit of a new home required residents to vote in support of the program. Scheduled for May–June 2017, the building-level votes required that two-thirds of residents confirm their support to be included in the program. This mandate fostered widespread discussion and lobbying to shape consensus. These interactions transformed residents' personal preferences and opinions into building-level collective action.

The first set of factors defining interests and shaping responses were practical, tied to measurable considerations such as apartment quality, condition, and location. The second set of factors were more symbolic, rooted in place attachment and tied to individuals' historical and emotional connections. These considerations shaped a complex landscape of individual interests that served as the raw material for grassroots activism.

Figure 4.1. Construction of five-story panel buildings, Moscow 1959–1960.

The quality, location, and condition of individual apartment buildings and apartments played a key role in shaping incentives for supporting or opposing the Renovation Program early on. From the start, the government defined the Renovation Program's scope narrowly, in terms of khrushchevkas, or five-story buildings, because the abundant material problems with these buildings were well known. Despite uniform design objectives, the condition of these buildings varied significantly. Two models were constructed: the first made of bricks and the second of concrete panels. The brick buildings proved superior in terms of noise containment and heating. The inferior concrete-panel construction complicated repairs because the plumbing was embedded in the concrete. Our respondents reported problems with batteries, also embedded in the concrete, exploding in their buildings. Figure 1 shows the construction process of a panel building, the more vulnerable construction pattern.

Figure 4.2. A collage of brick and panel five-story building facades with balconies. Photograph by Karina Gorbacheva.

Satirizing the widely recognized dilapidation of these khrushchevkas, Russians sometimes refer to them as *khrushchoba*, invoking the word for slum, *truschoba*. Yet many five-story buildings are very nice and are located in the most desirable neighborhoods in central Moscow. In recent years, many residents of these buildings have undertaken costly personal investments in renovation and repair, shaping the apartments into comfortable spaces despite poor structural conditions and the quality of construction at their outset. Figure 2 is a collage of five-story building facades that show both the variation in deterioration in the exteriors of different types of buildings and the key indicator of internal renovation—new modern windows that are weatherproof.

Residents' responses to the Renovation Program also reflected emotional place attachment, defined as "the bonding of people to places" (Altman and Low 2012). Attachment symbolically connects individuals to their ancestors or cultures (Billig 2006; Mazumdar and Mazumdar 1993) and reinforces social ties and community membership (Hidalgo and Hernandez 2001). In conjunction with physical factors such as quality and location, strong symbolic, historical, and communal ties played an important role in shaping housing preferences.

Khrushchevkas typically carry personal and historical significance for their residents—a sentiment reflected by some of our focus group respondents who grew up in their apartments. In the 1950s and 1960s, the five-story buildings marked a new stage of Soviet life. A departure from the previous norm of cramped, communal living spaces, these single-family apartments marked the first time since the 1917 revolution that privacy at home became possible. Many of these apartments have been passed down through generations, creating strong local identities linked to family history (Mikhaylyuk 2017).

These buildings also provided a structure that allowed communities to emerge. Each building had several shared entrances, with a handful of apartments on each floor of the entrance, creating natural connections (or conflicts) around the upkeep of shared spaces. Complexes of four or more buildings encompassed tree-filled courtyards, with playgrounds and green spaces that came to serve as residents' gathering places. In the crowded urban center, these courtyards also provided parking—a valuable perk in Moscow's crowded city center. Collections of these buildings, called micro-raions or microdistricts, provided services such as schools, nurseries, medical offices, and movie theaters or clubs, further ensuring interaction among residents. They resembled Western planned communities or estates that combine housing and services to sustain modern lifestyles.

The potential that new residents would overload these services triggered a fear that new construction would lead to a stressful disruption of everyday life. Research has shown that when a place becomes threatened, people living there often report stronger attachment and increased awareness of that place's benefits in terms of social ties and neighborhood infrastructure (Anton and Lawrence 2014). In the focus group discussions, we find that emotional and symbolic attachment to place echoes this argument, shaping perceptions of the Renovation Program and defining the benefits of the program.

Variation in the location, condition, and attachment to place and community across individual residents plays a significant role in shaping their policy preferences. The policy process, including the state's attempt to shape beliefs and the interactions among neighbors, also defined expectations. These interactions had the greatest influence on policy opponents who rejected the intrusion into their lives and the advocates who supported the program but wanted significant legal assurances that policy implementation would succeed. Residents of buildings included in the renovation program were skeptical about the size and location of new housing, the loss of private parking, and their ability to secure new mortgages. Neighborhoods were concerned with dust, traffic, noise, the strain on local infrastructure and parks, and the imposition of high-rise buildings that would transform the cityscape. As we show in the next section, the regime framed the program in a way that would allay these fears but was unable to eliminate opposition.

Moscow's Playbook: Disrupting Common Knowledge and Shaping Political Opportunities

The Renovation Program illustrates how authoritarian officials influence political opinions using powerful information-based tools, including framing, disinformation, and state media control. Contemporary autocrats use these tools to maintain elite support and secure political stability. This informational approach to understanding autocratic stability also demonstrates how information politics can limit contentious politics by shaping state-society relations. Government frames diagnose problems, define solutions, and propose actions to maintain regime support or preclude opposition mobilization. Broadcast on state-controlled television, hegemonic frames delimit appropriate speech and acceptable political action. They are important tools for incumbents to deflect blame or shift responsibility, mask unpopular policies, or obscure endemic corruption.

In contemporary autocracies, the state also constructs frames and disinformation narratives to disrupt the accumulation of common knowledge about opposition attitudes and the articulation of alternative viewpoints. Increasingly in Russia, information politics are also regulated through vague legal frameworks that impose significant penalties on citizens who engage in critical speech, damage others' religious beliefs or patriotic zeal, or repost anti-regime sentiment. These laws foster self-censorship and profoundly constrain citizens' articulation of their true beliefs, their knowledge of one another, and, ultimately, their willingness to act together to make demands on the government. Without this shared knowledge, grassroots action is unlikely.

Renovation as a Demonstration of Governmental Responsiveness

Russian analysts advance many explanations for why the state embarked on this risky and extraordinarily resource-intensive Renovation Program in 2017. While many of the buildings were in disrepair, creating a need for reconstruction, these were not the only buildings included in the program. In our view, the decision to embark on this project also represents a highly publicized demonstration of regime responsiveness, designed to address citizens' apolitical demands to bolster incumbent electoral support. There were also economic reasons to embark on the Renovation Program. The program will protect Moscow's budget surplus, infuse cash into the lagging construction industry, and win elite support by distributing rents—or informal streams of income through graft and bribery.

Past studies of public opinion show that many Russians would welcome the regime's intervention to improve housing. Studies conducted after 1991 have consistently reported that housing is a highly salient concern for Russian citizens (Levada Center 2022). Borisova, Polishchuk, and Peresetsky (2014) argue that most Russians believe that the government should be responsible for costly capital improvements to substandard Soviet-era housing. These sentiments are reflected in our focus group discussions. As one young woman who opposed the program pointed out, "I know very many people who are sitting and waiting for the state to give them an apartment. Among my acquaintances or work colleagues, somehow, they all sit and wait. And when they are given an apartment, they still sit and wait." Echoing these sentiments, when Moscow mayor Sergei Sobyanin and President Vladimir Putin introduced their plan in February 2017, the mayor told Putin, "We have mass appeals [for demolition from] the residents, municipal deputies, associations of deputies, and the Public Chamber of Moscow. We have reason to say that this is a people's project." In city-level debates, Moscow Duma deputy Stepan Orlov echoed this sentiment, arguing, "The bill was born of countless citizens' complaints. Hundreds of thousands of Moscow households are waiting for reform. This [Renovation Program] is a chance to move to comfortable modern apartments and make Moscow even more beautiful" (Filonov 2017).

This argument defined the program in terms of residents' demands and urban modernization, publicizing the regime's ability to consider everyday citizens' wishes without compromising power relationships or needing to engage in systemic reform. Given this framing, it is not surprising that in early fall 2020, the government announced a program expansion to cover five-story buildings across Russia. Although there have been some successful housing renovation programs in Russia's regions, this move to expand the program is risky because it is unlikely to come to fruition due to the COVID-19 economic slowdown and the lack of available funding beyond Moscow and Saint Petersburg. This program expansion remains at the center of political discussion although not all regions are engaged in significant policy planning.

Shaping the Flow of Information

The second element of regime's strategy is to disrupt the accumulation of common knowledge among citizens. Shared information, or common knowledge, is at the heart of civic activism. To make demands on the state, citizens must realize that others share similar grievances or policy positions. This shared knowledge that others will join you if you decide to act is a critical first step in sparking collective action (Chwe 2013). The second step is for citizens to agree on tactics: actions that communicate those grievances to officials and demand response (Smyth 2020a).

After the announcement of the program, the regime worked to shape the informational environment through several channels. The city government distributed special issues of the free, state-run newspaper, *Vechernaya Moskva*, and launched an article series in the economic newspaper *Kommersant*, whose editor sat on the program's financial board. Mayor Sobyanin frequently appeared on television, engaging in project-related activity. The city government also extended the scope of its web portal, Active Citizen, to educate Muscovites. These outlets deliver the regime's narrative: rosy pictures of benefits, falsified polling data, and reports of parallel vote counts in buildings excluded from the program to show broad social support (Litvinova 2017). As is now common in Russia, state agencies also created pro-demolition online advocacy groups (Kovalev 2017).

The regime also built a significant public education project about the process and outcomes of the policy. Moscow city architects constructed scale models of imagined apartments and invited Muscovites to visit them, despite the lack of concrete architectural plans. Mayor Sobyanin used his social media accounts to update Muscovites about program details and even posted pictures of himself touring the hypothetical apartment models. The cities' web portal, Active Citizen, provided up-to-the-minute news about the provisions in revised laws, online forums to discuss the program, and graphics to explain the process of relocation to potential participants.

Our respondents were aware of this public education project. One older woman who opposed the program colorfully cited Boris Yeltsin's prime minister Viktor Chernomyrdin when she spoke about the state's position: "He had a brilliant phrase: We wanted the best, but it turned out as always. It seems to me the phrase characterizes the Renovation Program because, in their words [the government's], everything is so wonderful, so good. Look at how they advertise it: Mom, Dad, and I are happy, a close-knit family, happy children walking along."

Yet despite highly publicized public education projects, a male respondent who was a dubious supporter went on to highlight the complex and contradictory information that made it difficult to discern the true nature of the program: "Over time, it [the program's legislation] has become so overwhelmed with details, with all sorts of amendments, that you have to go online or go somewhere and pick up the latest edition of documents to get all these details. At first, everything was simple; now, it is no longer simple. If you want to be generally aware of all changes and details, you won't know anything if you don't put time and effort into this." As the respondent notes, the iterative policy process constituted another state effort toward disinformation and obfuscation.

Another focus group participant who supported the program was also very cynical about this mode of online communication. He argued, "You cannot resolve anything if the authorities do not hear, and the authorities are not particularly interested in this. They create all sorts of portals, such as *Dobrodely*, so that you write there. Sometimes they give you some kind of a formal reply, and all for nothing."

As these sentiments foreshadow, our focus groups illustrate that despite state efforts to instill a positive and uniform view of the program, residents formed very different views. These views were rooted in their everyday experiences, discussions with neighbors, online forums run by NGOs and activists, gossip, and conspiracies. As we will show in the next section, communication between residents generated common knowledge of shared attitudes toward the project—often in defiance of the state's framing and information campaign—allowing individuals to begin defining their actions to pursue common goals.

The New Autocracy: Merging Opportunity Structure and Information Politics

Beyond working to quell discontent through optimistic messaging, the state also worked to shape the political opportunity structure available for citizens to engage with the program, creating spaces for engagement and developing various feedback mechanisms. These tools included online and face-to-face meetings with officials from across the political system: from the national-level State Duma to deputies on neighborhood councils. Yet the demand for interaction also prompted counternarratives among those affected by the program. Opportunities to engage in deliberation within legislative bodies or Dumas took place at every government level, from neighborhood councils to the national legislature, the State Duma. As Kolesnikov and Volkov (2017) point out, organizers were careful to use these events to send a message of responsiveness. Proceedings were packed with program supporters to create an atmosphere of overwhelming support.

As has become common in political contestation in Moscow, officials also used protest events and counterprotest rallies to shape public opinion. In a report based on a leaked transcript of a Moscow city government meeting on April 24, Deputy Mayor Anastasia Rakova, who is reported to be the program's architect, argued that rather than fight protesters, the regime must organize actions including policy supporters (Vinokurova 2017). These actions, organized by pro-Renovation groups supported by the city government, remained very small, reflecting the general disengagement of the Renovation supporters that is also evident in focus group evidence. However, they carried new information and a counterweight to grassroots mobilization.

This type of structured policy input through formal and informal channels is not limited to this housing project. A growing literature on complaint explores how contemporary autocratic regimes design political mechanisms that channel discontent into individual expressions or demands rather than reveal shared grievances (Cook and Dimitrov 2017; Henry 2012; Libman and Kozlov 2017). As noted above, participation included a wide variety of online spaces for policy engagement through offline forums, hearings, and meetings with officials.

The state also developed a complex policy process—a new twist on the political opportunity structure—which proliferated essential points of popular engagement. Early in the policy process, the mayoralty indicated that citizens living in houses included in the program would vote to affirm their acceptance of the benefits.

The vote emerged as a crucial point of engagement that made building-level organization a critical component of the policy process. Existing ties within houses and house governance structures became the focus of agitation. The house elder, an informal official who deals with building management issues, emerged in some houses as a figure to interpret state intent and educate fellow residents. These interactions became the first major site of activism in response to the project as individuals began to seek out information and, in many cases, attempt to influence their neighbors' opinions regarding relocation.

Citizen Responses: Everyday Life as the Locus of Popular Challenges

Despite the state's significant investments into shaping public opinion regarding the program, social networks and everyday life experiences played a key role in defining our identified categories of program opponents, supporters, and advocates. An examination into how each of these groups developed illustrates the limit of the state's disproportionate power to control informational narratives and patterns of civic participation.

Initial apprehensions regarding the program were rooted in various individual-level factors, including apartment quality, construction materials, relationships with neighbors, and the need for state assistance to rectify housing problems. Despite the state's efforts to maximize program support through framing and disinformation, these apprehensions led to the emergence of a significant number of program opponents who disliked all aspects of the program and referred to it as demolition (*snos*) rather than renovation. Their opposition was rooted in the program's inherent uncertainty, the potential for property rights violations, and fears about the transformation of the urban landscape. Many were simply attached to their place through family history. Several older residents lamented that they were being removed from the apartments and neighbors that had defined their life histories.

This group also contested the core narrative about the poor quality of five-story buildings. Many, such as the activist Lyubov Zolatova (2017), took pride in purchasing and renovating their apartments to suit their tastes and lifestyles. This personally financed work constituted a significant investment that would not be compensated. One young man who opposed the program described his apartment: "It is comfortable and warm. I did the renovation myself. Everything is as I wanted. We have a standard three-bedroom in a nine-story building, on the sixth story, with parking places. It is cool, comfortable, and warm." Note the stress on comfort and heating and cooling in this response, a set of commonly held complaints about such buildings and a core element of the regime's claim that they could not be repaired. One of our respondents even pointed out that similar buildings had been reconstructed in other post-Communist states and emerged as a part of the vibrant urban landscape.

Recognizing the shared reality of these sudden concerns emerging from the state's policy initiative, many communities began to articulate salient, collective objections to state action. As Zhelnina describes in chapter 6, nonstate organizations, such as existing city-level NGOs, new grassroots organizations, and house-level and neighborhood associations, also generated opportunities for Muscovites to weigh in on the policy provisions. As other chapters in this volume illustrate, similar policy impositions have generated rapid mobilization across Russia.

The second interest group to emerge, supporters, largely echoed the idea that the state is the best housing manager and frequently repeated the government's call to modernize homes and their districts. Wholeheartedly embracing the state's framing of the project, this pro-Renovation movement was initiated with significant state support. As Zhelnina points out, this effort included state-sponsored online groups that developed a counter-presence to spontaneous anti-Renovation groups. This interest group encapsulated popular enthusiasm for the program, which promised to relieve occupants of the burden of undertaking extensive repairs to their apartments and the communal spaces in their buildings. Our respondents who supported the program articulated physical complaints about their apartments, including the lack of soundproofing, insulation, and space. As one young woman argued, somewhat tongue in cheek, addressing the poor-quality housing was daunting given the number of problems. When asked about what she likes about her apartment, she responded, "I only like my husband, nothing else. I got the apartment from my parents, and renovations need to be done. I do not like doing renovations. I've never done it myself, naturally. I'm not going to do it, because there is no time. For the time being, we will rent. I want to choose everything for a new apartment." Similar sentiments were also clear on social media, where the vision of a better future life was prevalent.

A quote from a program proponent in Andrei Kovalev's long report on the For SNOS organization aptly illustrates why many Khrushchev-era apartment dwellers welcomed assistance to secure new housing: "We live in a dilapidated house without an elevator and a garbage chute. We walk along broken-down staircases, and the windows in the entrance haven't closed since the time of perestroika. The water from the roof flows from the basement, and it stinks. Plaster falls in our faces."

In addition to concerns with their apartments' physical state, some of the program supporters cited social issues as a reason to move. They highlighted conflict with neighbors, complaints about smoking and noise, and discomfort with non-Russian residents, immigrants to Moscow, who crowded into neighborhood rental apartments.

Among program *supporters*, the effect of privatization and marketization of apartments loomed large in their support for state intervention. Many respondents spoke of the difficulty in maintaining neighborly relations, given the rental market and frequent turnover. Even social media connections, through WhatsApp or Telegram, could not sustain the links among neighbors. As one middle-aged supporter of the program argued, "Take our house, previously we knew all the neighbors, talked with them. And then [their apartment] is all for sale. Then these apartments are sold again. Now, it is impossible to communicate with the neighbors. Either people do not live in their apartment, or they rent it. It is very difficult to find an owner."

Residents who espoused this view linked it to the decline of building self-governance and the desire for state management. They also cited the complexity of regulations and interaction with the states. One man argued, "The tenants simply can't do it all. First of all, it is necessary to have a graduate school of buildings of some kind to understand all these SniPs and GOSTs rules.[2] It is then necessary to have a law degree, too, something higher, to defend it later in the courts. Which tenants can deal with this? They all have families and children." For these residents, the complexity of urban life, the proliferation of regulations and the legal structures encouraged reversion to state-centric solutions for building management and renovation.

Politically, supporters were divided on the role of the state. Some supported the program because they trusted local officials to ensure that the program would be fair. Others simply believed that resisting the state's imperatives was futile and that the state would act regardless of citizen response. Identifying the hidden and selective preferential treatment common in Russia's system, some respondents came to believe that they would be punished for opposing the program or rewarded for agitating on its behalf.

Advocates represent a more complex form of program support. These residents separated the policy's intentions from the dangers of its implementation—core concerns that led to opposition. These citizens were willing to engage in nonpolitical action to represent those whose rights were violated, advocating changes to key provisions and legal structures included in the legislation. The advocates began in small group meetings and house-level discussions, as well as online discussion groups. Andrey Pertsev (2017) outlined their concerns, many of which were confirmed in our focus groups: the delegation of concrete policymaking to local officials, the value of new apartments and size of replacement buildings, the potential for developers to petition to include buildings in existing construction sites, and the violation of property rights. When the focus group moderator asked a young man who fell into the advocate category what he wanted from the program, he argued for a responsive policy: "I don't know. The same kind of renovation is organized to protect residents' rights: they are relocated to the same area. They have the same square meters, and some wishes are accounted for to preserve their living conditions." For many residents like him, the introduction of the project transformed citizens' aspirations into concrete demands for fair and adequate housing.

While most residents whose apartments were slated for demolition wanted new homes, they felt cautious about the policy's risk and spoke of the potential for being scammed. Included residents also spoke about the potential to be moved to the city's outer regions with little recourse to protect their interests. As one advocate in our focus groups argued, "You know, if you look at the Renovation from the point of view of an owner, for example, of one of the *Khrushchevka*, I think that they would see it as simply a gift from God—how lucky we are to move into a new apartment. Still, I need some guarantees from the state about where my home will be, what kind of quality it will be, what apartment I will receive."

Advocates demanded regime responsiveness and state protection from apartment management companies and real estate developers, even as they agitated in support of the program. For example, according to one advocate, "In principle, the state must fulfill everything. They have all the mechanisms, some kind of control, specially trained people. But they must listen to people. They must be open to people." This general concern about the government acting to enrich itself and contractors at the people's expense was a strong theme across the focus group discussions. Yet, consistent with a conception of nonpolitical protest, very few respondents directly criticized Mayor Sobyanin or President Putin instead of focusing on economic elites and bureaucrats and specific policy demands.

Neighborly Ties: Informing Opinions, Generating Common Knowledge

Our focus group interviews indicate that neighborly connections shaped the information flows at the heart of grievance formation. These effects were particularly clear in the views of opponents and advocates who were linked by existing neighborly connections that ranged from strong, multigenerational relationships to simple, polite ties. These connections provided conduits to spread ideas that challenged state narratives. Ultimately, these ties allowed individuals to overcome the first obstacle to grassroots mobilization: recognizing and articulating shared goals and potential strategies.

The Nature of Neighborly Ties

The historic nature of the five-story buildings frequently created communities rooted in shared experiences of growing up and being educated together. As one young man said, "There everyone knows each other. Everyone studied together at some point, went to discotheques. Some fights, some girls, some parties. We grew up like that." These historical roots of the Khrushchev buildings provided a foundation for social interactions.

These ties stand in contrast with conventional wisdom and even survey-based findings of low levels of social capital in Russian society. In our focus groups, many respondents noted that they turn to their neighbors when faced with emergencies. They documented efforts to solve maintenance issues and spoke admiringly about neighbors who initiated these projects, collected money and materials, and led the efforts.

Outside of the Renovation context, participants shared stories of neighbors helping one another by lending household items, watching over one another's apartments, and even caring for the sick when needed. One respondent, a program opponent, emphasized the importance of these kinds of relationships to daily life: "The people in my neighborhood are good. I can't speak for everyone, but in general, I've had problems. I was in the hospital once, and almost twelve people from the house came to visit me. I believe that it is necessary to live with people humanely."

These ties are rooted in everyday life and transcend social divisions such as generational divides. Some participants specifically cited young people as a source of help in their buildings, contributing to a foundation of reciprocity and mutual aid. For example, one interviewee explained, "For help, I can go, of course, to my younger neighbors. Once it was necessary: grandfather died directly in the apartment, and it was necessary to get help to lift him. I had nobody to turn to. I ran out; a boy came and helped. As for salt or onions and things, there's always someone." This juxtaposition of the mundane and extraordinary challenges of life demonstrates that proximity brings interaction. Despite the common perception that Russians are aloof, disengaged neighbors, this discussion demonstrates that this is not the case in all buildings. The elements of social capital described in the introduction of the volume exist in these communities. These established connections provided pathways through which neighbors share ideas and information and understand one another and their ideas about politics in the local context.

We find that neighborly ties in Moscow's buildings and neighborhoods varied widely, influencing neighborly interactions, information gathering, and actions. Some focus group members confirmed Zhelnina's evidence of unexpectedly high levels of social capital. Yet most of our evidence suggests that weak ties are more common. Granovetter (1973) defines weak ties as networks of individuals who share a common culture or set of experiences. Even if individuals are not acquainted with everyone in the network, ties to others and shared experiences extend connections and recognition of other residents as people who are like oneself. Given this, individuals are more likely to trust one another and the information that is provided.

Informing Opinions, Generating Common Knowledge

In the context of the state imposition of a vague policy, engagement in basic norms of trust and reciprocity enabled many neighbors to discuss the Renovation Program with one another despite the short timeline before the vote. For example, when asked whether he was acquainted with his neighbors, one respondent explained, "Yes, of course. Over twenty years, everybody has become acquainted. Can I say that it is a close relationship? No. But let's say we have normal, neighborly relationships. We greet each other. We were able to discuss some questions when this Renovation Program was announced. There was a heated discussion on this theme, including among neighbors."

Neighborly relationships, therefore, created informal spaces that exposed individuals to information beyond tightly controlled state narratives surrounding the project. Furthermore, our focus groups also demonstrate efforts to persuade neighbors through courtyard conversations and house meetings. According to one focus group participant:

> My uncle Jora, who lives under us, came to my home and asked about the Renovation Program. He asked not as an agitator but from the point of view of a person who did not understand what was happening. I showed him the short video about which you spoke, FBK [an educational video released by Navalny's team]. There were a few short videos on the subject. We watched it together, and then it happened. We realized that almost all the apartments in our entrance would vote against the program. We did not yet go to other entrances, but we thought that if we had such movement, then probably, it was so everywhere.

This response hints at the development of a kind of bandwagon effect. Through conversation and interaction with neighbors, apartment officials, and governmental representatives, residents formed a sense of the balance of support and opposition within their buildings. As a result, they either disengaged from the process or felt coerced into adapting the majority viewpoint. In some cases, the result was the animosity and difficult relations among neighbors detailed in Zhelnina's study in the next section.

In these ways, neighborhood ties created formal and informal spaces for discussion and recruitment through education. Discussions revealed new information about the program and its specific provisions, increased the visibility of various opinions, and shaped consensus around strategies. Critically, the common knowledge regarding the balance of opinions—societal frames—played a key role in mobilizing individuals and fostering collective action in response to the Renovation Program.

From Common Knowledge to Collective Action

As illustrated in the previous section, after the project's announcement, even weak ties facilitated neighborly discussion of the program. As individuals began to develop a sense of the balance of opinions for and against the project among their neighbors, they gained critically important common knowledge. This information was essential as a catalyst for collective activity.

Grassroots action calling for reform or elimination of the program consisted of actions to influence the formal political process and actions that applied pressure outside the system. Within-system actions included sending petitions to local deputies, attending meetings with city officials, contacting representatives through letter-writing campaigns, using web portals to communicate with officials, voting for inclusion within the apartment building, and voting in regional and local elections. The pressure from outside the system came from protests and pickets described in the previous chapter. External pressure also manifested from efforts to contest the regime's narratives through blogs, Twitter, and Telegram debates, as well as flyers hung in building vestibules and reports on alternative television and radio.

While, in some cases, split opinions generated significant pressure and conflict within buildings (see chap. 6), we found that communication with neighbors frequently influenced opinions, created critical common knowledge, and sparked mobilization. This was common as supporters became advocates. As one focus group participant noted, "At first, I was not very strongly involved. I only attended one discussion. Everyone thought—oh, OK, now they [the state] will give us apartments—and I also expressed support. When people began signing petitions against the program, and it became clear that this was nonsense, I also came and signed against the program." Once individuals were recruited into new networks, they became more likely to act. This momentum reinforced ties. The focus group discussions show that participating with their peers strengthened both the quantity and quality of neighborly relationships—a finding confirmed in statistical analysis (Borisova, Smyth, and Zakharov 2021).

One illustrative quote from the focus group interviews effectively highlights the socializing effect of neighborhood-level political engagement: "[I am acquainted with about] 60 percent [of my neighbors]. Moreover, this 60 percent was stretched in connection with the Renovation. I've seen so many new faces. Such activated people, before I didn't see them. Here you look, one came to discuss the vote, the second came concerning this vote, then we all gathered in the yard." In these ways, neighborhood ties created new formal and informal spaces for interaction and information sharing. Yards, entrances, and teas became sites of agitation that engaged residents and raised the salience of their concerns and complaints.

As Anna Zhelnina demonstrates in chapter 6, once individuals and neighborhood groups became active, NGOs and existing civic structures played a key role in amplifying concerns, providing access to reliable information regarding the project, and channeling modes and methods of political engagement in response to the project. Three years later, this activism remains significant as the regime continues to hammer out the project's details. The proposal to build new structures within the Two Bears park in June 2020 provoked a significant petition drive and an additional appeal to the General Prosecutor's Office to limit construction because face-to-face meetings with citizens could not be held during COVID-19 quarantine. Additional actions broke out when developers agitated to include new apartment blocks because they were located in prestigious economic growth corridors. Because mortgage subsidies fueled unprecedented housing construction in 2019, conflict is likely to grow.

The Outcomes: Ongoing Engagement, New Social Capital, and Perceptions of Regime Responsiveness

The complex policy process around the Renovation constituted a new twist on the idea of the opportunity structure as citizens' engagement in hearings, meetings with officials, and voting channeled their activity toward state-run actions as a mechanism to build social support. As this chapter and Zhelnina's chapter in this volume illustrate, this tactic applies to the housing policy and other programs designed in Moscow and then passed on to local officials to hammer out the details.

Our findings show a society increasingly frustrated by the lack of state responsiveness to social demands and the regime's unwillingness to listen to its citizens. Interestingly, respondents who were most supportive of the program were also the most cynical. They pointed out that only lucky people would receive good apartments and that the probability of coming out ahead was about 50 percent. As one woman argued about the likelihood of corruption in the policy implementation, "You have to get used to it. We live in Russia." This sense of alienation or disengagement extended to individuals' engagement with formal politics, such as the Moscow mayoral election in September 2018.

Activism was more pronounced among program opponents and advocates, but the advocates were unique in their expectations of state response. Their expressed conviction that activist engagement yields results has been critical in maintaining nonpolitical protest and resisting spillover into political action. As one advocate argued: "I always thought [the leadership of Moscow doesn't listen to the opinions of Muscovites], but in reality, they do." This sense of collective efficacy among those who have advocated for specific policy implementation measures is an important component of ongoing activism as well as a source of regime support.

The program also highlighted growing social support for NGOs and their role as citizen advocates. As another advocate, a newcomer to action, argued, "If it were not for these [civic] associations, for example, the law on Renovation would have been adopted in the first reading and would have been very tough. If people hadn't come to the rally, had not raised a fight, then those influenced by the Renovation . . . their rights would be even less than now. Therefore, any resistance is a plus." Many of our respondents agreed that the alliance between residents, NGOs, and some local officials improved the policy by demanding—and getting—regime responsiveness to popular demands.

The policy changes made during the early stages of the program helped to influence these attitudes. Soon after the program's announcement in 2017, legislators added new provisions amid great fanfare to respond to these concerns (Voronov and Chernykh 2017). Newspapers reported the legislative response to citizens' concerns, including issues with the lack of legal protection or recourse in the process, the disposition of land under the houses to be demolished, access to parking in new apartments before and after the permanent move, guarantees of the terms of relocation, and the size and value of subsequent apartments. Provisions of the laws governing the buildings, the range of eligible buildings, and collective decision-making processes continued to be adjudicated even after the residents' voting period. President Putin also responded to protest demands, promising that he would not sign any bill that violated property rights (Voronov 2017).

Today, the Moscow city government maintains an active online information portal and hosts regular monthly meetings and receptions designed to gather and address citizen concerns regarding the ongoing program. Online portals, including the Moscow Residential Development Fund website, emphasize examples of state responsiveness and the desire for constructive dialogue between the state and those affected by the program (the Moscow Residential Development Fund).

Not only has the regime's strategy been successful in winning support for the policy (evident in the fact that nearly 90% of included buildings voted for the proposal) but it has also managed to build a significant amount of support for state actors. Yet, in winning this support, the city government altered expectations about citizens' ability to hold their government responsible and demand policy change. Since the demolitions began, the government refused all new protest permits and made it more difficult for residents to participate. In summer 2020, friction between government officials and residents arose because of the overreliance on online meetings and portals rather than face-to-face interactions with citizens. Officials argued that this change was due to the COVID-19 pandemic. However, residents who signed petitions argued that the government disregarded negative votes and comments through online systems and reported positive outcomes (Voronov 2020). Many online groups, such as Snoska, continue to monitor program developments and organize affected residents through VKontakte and Facebook.

This activism reflects an unexpected consequence of the Renovation Program's structure. Although activism was built on existing ties that allowed the citizens to transcend alienation and cynicism and coordinate with their neighbors to lobby for stronger legal protections, it also strengthened these ties. The interactions contributed to the emergence of new relationships and networks among neighbors, increasing societal capacity to respond to suddenly imposed grievances. The program forged new links among neighbors and Muscovites living in khrushchevkas and affected microdistricts, a finding confirmed by statistical analysis of a survey of Muscovites conducted by the authors (Borisova, Smyth, and Zakharov 2021; McCann 2019).

The program also linked house-level social capital to existing NGOs and activist communities that were already engaged in the everyday issues of urban life. Finally, the program created new ties between society and local and city officials, making the municipal council deputies and institutions more relevant. Our analysis reinforces Zhelnina's finding that nonpolitical activism led to more-engaged citizens and provided a bridge between activism and elections. The multilevel policy process raised the visibility of opposition municipal deputies who provided activists with allies within the government, altering the opportunity structure largely closed to opposition groups. As Vice Mayor Rakova acknowledged, "Moscow is a big village. As soon as two or three opposition deputies appear in any district, a cry is heard all over Moscow about problems. It immediately takes on an urban scale. And then, we will have the gubernatorial election, and the problem of the municipal filter may arise" (Vinokurova 2017).

Citizens also recognized this link between their interests in political action. The Renovation policy process politicized neighborhood councils and led to significant support for opposition candidates in fall 2017 and even greater protest in summer 2019, when opposition candidates were banned from running (Smyth 2018, 2019). Aside from its effect on Moscow's cityscape, this outcome may be the longest-lasting effect of the housing policy. The program is an example of how Russian society's capacity to challenge the government at all levels through urban activism constitutes a visible manifestation of development.

Our chapter foreshadows Anna Zhelnina's exploration of the grassroots response to suddenly imposed grievances in chapter 6. We focus exclusively on ties among neighbors that produced shared understandings of the Renovation Program. These ties defined the common interests in improving the policy and the coalitions around potential social responses. In contrast, Zhelnina's study explores the linkages within and across neighborhoods, nascent organizational ties, and emerging and established civic activists' role in shaping engagement. These chapters uncover elements that shape activism: existing social structures that give rise to new narratives, shared problems, and potential solutions. Read together, this work highlights how state policy can strengthen ties among individuals and increase societal capacity to demand government responsiveness.

Notes

1. We conducted focus groups in early winter 2018 at the start of the demolition process. The Moscow-based public opinion research firm the Levada Center facilitated eight groups that included sixty-one respondents. The groups were organized on the basis of two social and political divisions: supporters and opponents of the program and the age of the participant. The goal of the design was to allow for deep discussion of common concerns rather than confrontation.
2. GOST is the State Union Standard, a legacy of the Soviet period, that oversees the certification system for construction and housing. SniP is the subset of regulations imposed by Russia and Kazakhstan.

Bibliography

Altman, Irwin, and Setha M. Low, eds. 2012. *Place Attachment*. Vol. 12. New York: Springer Science and Business Media.

Anton, Charis E., and Carmen Lawrence. 2014. "Home Is Where the Heart Is: The Effect of Place of Residence on Place Attachment and Community Participation." *Journal of Environmental Psychology* 40 (December): 451–461.

Billig, Miriam. 2006. "Is My Home My Castle? Place Attachment, Risk Perception, and Religious Faith." *Environment and Behavior* 38, no. 2 (March): 248–265.

Bolotov, I. 2017. "Khrushchevkas—a Nightmare and Horror. Their Destruction Is Necessary." [Khrushchevkas—to kashmar and uzhac. Ikh nuzhno snocit. Ili Nyet?]. *Meduza*, February 23, 2017. https://meduza.io/feature/2017/02/23/hruschevki-eto-koshmar-i-uzhas-ih-nuzhno-snosit-ili-net.

Borisova, Ekaterina I., Leonid Polishchuk, and Anatoly Peresetsky. 2014. "Collective Management of Residential Housing in Russia: The Importance of Being Social." *Journal of Comparative Economics* 42 (3): 609–629.

Borisova, Ekaterina, Regina Smyth, and Alexey Zakharov. 2021. "The Policy-Based Accumulation of Social Capital in Autocratic Systems." BOFIT Working Paper Series, Helsinki, Fall 2021.

Cheskin, Ammon, and Luke March. 2015. "State–Society Relations in Contemporary Russia: New Forms of Political and Social Contention." *East European Politics* 31 (3): 261–273.

Chwe, Michael Suk-Young. 2013. *Rational Ritual: Culture, Coordination, and Common Knowledge*. Princeton, NJ: Princeton University Press.

Cook, Linda J., and Martin K. Dimitrov. 2017. "The Social Contract Revisited: Evidence from Communist and State Capitalist Economies." *Europe-Asia Studies* 69 (1): 8–26.

Filonov, Dmitry. 2017. "Who Will Carry Whom? Map of the Opposition of Moscow Districts." *Republic*, May 12, 2017.

Golunov, Ivan. 2015. "Whose 'My Street.'" *RBK*, October 20, 2015. https://www.rbc.ru/newspaper/2015/10/20/56bc92e99a7947299f72b9f9.

Granovetter, Mark S. 1973. "The Strength of Weak Ties." *American Journal of Sociology* 78, no. 6 (May): 1360–1380.

Henry, Laura A. 2012. "Complaint-Making as Political Participation in Contemporary Russia." *Communist and Post-Communist Studies* 45 (3–4): 243–254.

Hidalgo, M. Carmen, and Bernardo Hernandez. 2001. "Place Attachment: Conceptual and Empirical Questions." *Journal of Environmental Psychology* 21 (3): 273–281.

Kolesnikov, Andrei, and Denis Volkov. 2017. "Defending One's Backyard: Local Civic Activism in Moscow." Carnegie Moscow Center, May 2, 2017. https://carnegie.ru/2017/05/02/defending-one-s-backyard-local-civic-activism-in-moscow-pub-69822.

Kovalev, Andrei. 2017. "How Mayor Sobyanin Deceives Muscovites Out of Their Own Money." *Limp Noodle Blog*, May 15, 2017. https://noodleremover.news/sobyanin-lies-48ea41d458f5.

Levada Center. 2022. "Societal Opinion—2021, Annual Yearbook." Moscow, Levada Center, April 20, 2022. https://www.levada.ru/2022/04/20/novyj-vypusk-ezhegodnika-obshhestvennoe-mnenie-2/.

Libman, Alexander, and Vladimir Kozlov. 2017. "The Legacy of Compliant Activism in Autocracies: Post-Communist Experience." *Contemporary Politics* 23 (2): 195–213.

Litvinova, Daria. 2017. "Campaigning to Destroy: How Moscow Authorities Promoted Mass Housing Democracy." *.coda*, July 13, 2017. https://www.codastory.com/disinformation/campaigning-to-destroy/.

Mazumdar, Shampa, and Sanjoy Mazumdar. 1993. "Sacred Space and Place Attachment." *Journal of Environmental Psychology* 13, no. 3 (September): 231–242.

McCann, Madeline. 2019. "The Neighborhood as a Site of Political Mobilization: Challenging Housing Renovation and Pension Reform in Moscow." Master's thesis, Russian and East European Center, Indiana University.

Mikhaylyuk, Vitaly. 2017. "The Condemned: Living in a Khrushchyovka." *Russia behind the Headlines*, May 5, 2017. https://rbth.com/longreads/khrushchyovki/.

Pertsev, Andrey. 2017. "Moscow Housing Demolition Program Creates a New Wave of Angry Urbanites." Carnegie Moscow Center, May 2, 2017. https://carnegie.ru/commentary/?fa=69821.

Smyth, Regina. 2018. "How the Kremlin Is Using the Moscow Renovation Project to Reward and Punish Voters." *PONARS Eurasia Policy Memo* 513, March

2018. https://www.ponarseurasia.org/memo/kremlin-using-moscow-renovation-project-reward-punish-voters.

———. 2019. "Moscow's Municipal Elections Illustrate the Growing Political Crisis in Russia." *Conversation*, September 19, 2019. https://theconversation.com/moscows-municipal-elections-illustrate-the-growing-political-crisis-in-russia-123262.

———. 2020a. *Elections, Protest, and Authoritarian Regime Stability, Russia 2008–2020*. New York: Cambridge University Press.

———. 2020b. "Explaining Urban Protest in Illiberal Regimes: An Emphasis on Russia." *APSA | Comparative Politics Newsletter* 1, no. 1 (Spring): 75–84.

Vinokurova, Ekaterina. 2017. "Moscow Is a Big Village." *Znak*, April 24, 2017. https://www.znak.com/2017-04-24/meriya_moskvy_provela_s_rukovoditelyami_prefektur_zakrytoe_sovechanie_po_snosu_domov.

Voronov, Alexander. 2017. "Residents from Demolished Five-Story Buildings Will Be Relocated in the Same District." *Kommersant*, April 26, 2017. https://www.kommersant.ru/doc/3282637.

———. 2020. "The Prosecutor's Office Is Connected to the Renovation Program." *Kommersant*, June 6, 2020. https://www.kommersant.ru/doc/4371914.

Voronov, Alexander, and Alexander Chernykh. 2017. "There Will Be No Carpet Demolition." *Kommersant*, April 4, 2017. https://www.kommersant.ru/doc/3261724.

Zolatova, Lyubov. 2017. "How I Fell Prey to the Moscow Renovation Programme." *Russiaknowledge.com*, July 12, 2017. http://www.russiaknowledge.com/2017/07/12/how-i-fell-prey-to-the-moscow-renovation-program/.

Regina Smyth is Professor of Political Science at Indiana University. She is author most recently of *Elections, Protest, and Authoritarian Regime Stability: Russia 2008–2020*.

Madeline McCann is former Program Coordinator at the Program on New Approaches to Research and Security in Eurasia at the George Washington University. She holds an MA from Indiana University, and her research focuses on environmental activism and natural resource development in the post-Soviet space.

Katherine Hitchcock is a legislative correspondent for the US Senate. She holds a BA from Indiana University, where she studied political science, history, and Russian and East European studies.

PART 2

Organizational Roles in Mobilization for Activism

Communication, Cooperation, and Conjunction

JEREMY MORRIS

A key observation among the contributors to part 2 of our volume is that cooperative activism helps build organizational capacity in response to some shortcoming in relation to the state. Building on the invocation of infrapolitics in the first part, chapters explore the emergence and structure of more visible, situated, and confrontational contestation: protests, petitions, and organization—demonstrating actions in which actors consciously work together, often in conjunction with organizational actors, to bring individuals together to pursue common goals. This part covers different types of activism in which organizations play a role in mobilization but the claims and outcomes are largely apolitical. These actions transform resistance into new forms of visible protest actions, the provision of public goods, or direct challenges to local political actors.

One noteworthy finding is how often instances of urban activism in Russia are similar to those in polities around the globe. Even when faced with threats from powerful actors, Russians organize public campaigns, file petitions, contact officials, air grievances in the media and on the internet, form coalitions with other groups, and participate in elections. Activists make themselves visible and communicate clear and memorable messages of dissent and, more importantly, demands. Workers strike or engage in direct and coordinated actions.

John Burgess explores the partially hidden activism of grassroots church figures operating within the constraints of the conservative and state–co-opted Orthodox Church. His case presents something of a transition between the previous part of the volume; it shows how locally shared grievances and social needs that are invisible or ignored by the state can still build activism—under the radar—within a structure that is based on hierarchy and distance (church leaders) and is subordinate to state interests. Burgess also indicates that divisions between city and country are less and less relevant. Instead of boundaries, entrepreneurial church activists see countryside and neglected locales as the terrain of opportunity in doing good works that the broader church neglects in its pursuit of politically supplicant power and self-aggrandizement.

Anna Zhelnina studies housing activism through the prism of gradual networking over the long term within and between closely connected apartment buildings—networking that, with the inevitability of water flowing downstream (a key metaphor) joins up with other currents: other neighborhoods, NGOs, and finally election activism. "Mundane" and highly situational "civic" activism around housing serves as a school for potentially wider and more substantive action. Zhelnina also takes up an important theme first developed by Karine Clément and continued in Morris's chapter: that shared activist activity has an affective element that serves to break the cycle of feelings of powerlessness. This chapter also demonstrates the importance of social media as supporting mobilization effects and communicative coordination as well as countering bureaucratic and other constraints that emanate from the antipolitical blocking of the state.

Jeremy Morris's chapter complements the insights of Zhelnina to highlight how important the process of trust building and shared experience—but not necessarily shared identity—is in producing the necessary solidarity for activism to emerge from common grievances and political dissent. A further insight in this chapter is how seemingly local actions exhibit signs of diffusion—union activists in Saint Petersburg "teach" locals in Kaluga how to build an independent union, socialist groups "lend" politically dedicated supporters to labor unions willing to engage in more confrontational and agitational work, and a new YouTube generation of leftists nomadically gravitate to ripe locations for mobilization of exploited workers. Tactics, frames, and organizational tools travel between political and nonpolitical contexts. It is a particularly twenty-first-century form of activism that combines mobility and responsiveness to produce an experiential density and commitment to activism.

Similar to Zhelnina, Anna Dekalchuk and Ivan Grigoriev show how initial activism in support of a public skate park met all kinds of structural, political, and bureaucratic barriers that were overcome only by a new partnership between local officials, and in particular corporate managers, and the activists. The skate park in Sosnovyi Bor resulted from long-standing ties among residents who grew up together and found shared meaning and pride in their city. This essay also links local networks to new NGOs designed to support subsequent organizational efforts and a wider range of activism.

Overall, the chapters in this part illustrate how close observation allows our authors to identify the linkages between hidden action and more open contention to explore the mechanisms that underpin the emergence, development, and decline of activism in contemporary authoritarian settings. Citizens in authoritarian states often combine less visible practices with distinctly political forms, petitions, protests, rallies, and strikes, transforming the institutional structure of new or existing civic organizations. A number of our essays use process-tracing techniques to identify changes in existing organizations. Both Jeremy Morris and John Burgess, writing about different institutions, invoke the legacy of the Soviet experience on church- and union-based activism to explain current patterns of engagement, showing that path dependency, while important, does not preclude vibrant and politically meaningful activism.

5

Social Activism in the Russian Orthodox Church

JOHN P. BURGESS*

Western observers frequently regard the Russian Orthodox Church as closely allied with the nation's ruling elites and therefore as unresponsive, and even opposed, to grassroots citizen initiatives. In contrast to Ukraine, where Orthodox and other religious leaders were prominent in the 2013–2014 Maidan Revolution, Orthodox clergy in Russia rarely speak out against government injustices.[1] Instead, the church regularly benefits from state interventions that pit it against local citizen interests. In particular, government plans in recent years to allow construction of churches on corners of public parks in Moscow and Yekaterinburg have catalyzed citizen protest. The church hardly seems a reliable partner for those Russians who seek political or social change.

However, just as other chapters in this book demonstrate that the Russian state is not monolithic and that government officials and grassroots activists interact in complex ways, this chapter demonstrates that the Russian Orthodox Church too is multifaceted. Even if church officials rarely oppose the state publicly, they nevertheless regard the church as an independent social actor with its own institutional and ideological interests. This chapter describes how Orthodox believers have stepped into the breach when the state has been unable to respond quickly or efficiently to social problems, such as drug abuse and physical and mental disability. Those who participate in these initiatives develop political agency. They see themselves not as passive subjects of the state but rather as activist citizens who have a voice in shaping their society.

In examining these initiatives, this chapter expands our understanding of social activism in three significant respects. First, it demonstrates that religious social work is a form of social activism with implicit if not always explicit political significance. Second, the chapter establishes the significance of a national organization (the church) for linking urban and rural social action. Third, the chapter shows how religiously based social movements depend both on hierarchical organization (spiritual authorities) and on established local communities (church parishes), whose members share key social values and forge partnerships among themselves and with other social actors to realize these values.

Undoubtedly, the current head of the church, Patriarch Kirill, will continue to affirm the church's loyalty to the Russian nation and state as currently constituted politically. In present circumstances, it is inconceivable that he would endorse a political rival to President Putin, such as Aleksei Navalny. But, as this volume demonstrates, citizen engagement can take "under the radar" forms (Scott 1990). Politics is not only about participating in state decision-making but also about forging grassroots partnerships and alliances, which contribute to the formation of civil society. Indeed, as political scientists have argued, civil society may be the soil from which political activism (in the narrower sense) sprouts (Smith and Freedman 1972).

The Russian Orthodox Church

Russian Orthodoxy traces its roots to the founding of Christianity in the first century. At that time, the unity of the Roman Empire guaranteed the unity of the "one holy catholic and apostolic church."[2] By the eleventh century, however, West and East had diverged politically and religiously. In Western Europe, the Roman Catholic Church emerged, while Orthodoxy (sometimes called Eastern Orthodoxy) predominated in Byzantium. A pope headed the Catholic Church, whereas Orthodoxy was constituted by different national-ethnic churches, each of which had its own patriarch. Theology and worship also developed differently. In Orthodoxy, icons (paintings of saints) became especially important as aids to prayer and communion with the spiritual world.[3]

Orthodoxy became the religion of the Eastern Slavic peoples with the conversion of Prince Vladimir (or Volodymyr, Ukrainian spelling) in 988 CE. When Constantinople, the capital of Byzantium, fell to Muslim invaders in 1453, Muscovy and its rulers assumed the mantle of divinely appointed protectors of Orthodoxy, which they regarded as the only true religion. At the same time, however, the Russian state increasingly controlled the church. Even as Orthodox ritual and practice continued to shape Russian culture and everyday life, Peter the Great abolished the patriarchate in 1721, and, later in that century,

Catherine the Great closed many of the monasteries and nationalized their lands.[4]

State control of the church became almost complete with the rise of communism in 1917. The Bolsheviks viewed religion as the "opiate of the people" and equated the church with the old political order. By 1941, Stalin had nearly eradicated public, institutional Orthodoxy. Nearly all religious edifices had been closed or destroyed, and most church leaders had been exiled or executed. However, the Nazi invasion of the Soviet Union brought about a new relationship between church and state. The state allowed the church to exist, while co-opting it politically (beginning with the war effort). Only with the dissolution of communism in 1991 did the church receive the constitutional right to manage its own affairs.[5]

Today, as many as 70–80 percent of ethnic Russians identify as Orthodox. Moreover, with its nineteen thousand parishes and several hundred men's and women's monasteries, the Orthodox Church is Russia's largest nongovernmental organization.[6] However, church and state have worked closely together to expand the church's institutional presence and social prominence. Putin and many government authorities identify themselves as Orthodox, direct money to the church, and promise to defend traditional moral values, including social respect for the church and its leaders.[7] In cooperation with the Office of the Mayor, the church is currently building two hundred new churches in Moscow, where available land is at a premium. Public schools provide instruction on how Orthodoxy has shaped Russian culture.[8]

Orthodoxy traditionally has a hierarchical structure, and Patriarch Kirill has further centralized power. Bishops exercise close oversight of priests, and the patriarch expects the loyalty of bishops. While parishes on paper have church councils in which lay believers participate, bishops and priests make all key decisions. Church authorities may consult those beneath them, but democratic participation, as it has developed in many Protestant churches in the West, is still foreign to Russian Orthodoxy. Nevertheless, the church's most dynamic social projects depend on what we may call "lay activism" (cf. Knox 2004, 76). Ordinary church members devote their personal time and resources to addressing urgent social needs, both on their own initiative and in response to church priorities (Bacon 2016; Luehrmann 2019; Mitrokhin 2004; Khodzhaeva 2014; Zabaev et al. 2013).

Spiritual Authority and Social Partnerships

Social activism is especially apparent in urban contexts, where intellectual and financial resources are concentrated. In cities, too, high rates of social change threaten citizen interests and motivate protest and response. A similar dynamic characterizes church-related activism. The church's largest and wealthiest parishes, most gifted priests, and most active lay believers are urban. A religious motivation to reach out to people in need impels them to respond to urban problems of poverty, unemployment, addiction, and inadequate social services.

Social activism in the Russian Orthodox Church is often catalyzed by a visionary priest who commands people's allegiance and harnesses their energies and resources. This kind of priest has not only institutional but also charismatic authority. He wins a popular reputation as a "spiritual father," a godly man of extraordinary spiritual wisdom and power. The spiritual father helps people resolve personal dilemmas, such as whether to marry, undergo a surgery, buy an apartment, or look for a new job. His followers ask him to pray for their well-being when they are physically ill, emotionally distraught, or struggling with an addiction. A "spiritual family" gathers around the priest, and he may ask one member to reach out to another who needs, for example, medical or legal assistance.[9]

From a Western perspective, the spiritual father hardly looks like an "activist." However, a closer look reveals that he does not focus his followers on otherworldly concerns at the expense of life here and now. On the contrary, he engages them in "politics," if by politics we understand how people shape the structures and dynamics of their common life. The spiritual father calls on his spiritual children to think about family, society, and nation. He asks them to take responsibility for their lives and the lives of those around them. He wants them to act with compassion and honesty and to work for the common good.

In post-Communist Russia, some of Moscow's most prominent priests have exercised this kind of spiritual authority. Especially well known are Father Vladimir Vorob'ev (b. 1941), Father Dmitrii Smirnov (1951–2020), Father Vladimir Volgin (b. 1949), and Bishop Panteleimon (Shatov; b. 1950). Each has several hundred spiritual children, including cultural, political, and economic elites. Although many of these spiritual children are not active in parish life (indeed, less than 2–3% of Muscovites regularly attend church), they nevertheless seek out a charismatic spiritual authority who relates to them compassionately and helps them with personal issues that lie hidden behind their professional successes.

In turn, a spiritual father may recruit these elites, because of their professional expertise, to address particular social needs that he has identified. Father Vorob'ev is the founder and rector of St. Tikhon's Orthodox University, one of the country's most prestigious nonstate institutions of higher education. Its mission is to train a new generation of Orthodox believers for leadership not only in the church but also in economic, cultural, and political arenas. Father Vorob'ev's spiritual authority has enabled him to raise money from leading businessmen, including Arkadii Rotenberg, a close associate of President Putin. Although Rotenberg is of Jewish heritage, Father Vorob'ev and other leading church figures have interested him in Orthodox spirituality, and he has traveled to Mount Athos and its famous monasteries.

Father Smirnov, who for a time headed the church's Synodal Department for Interaction with the Armed Forces and Law Enforcement Agencies, successfully recruited elite support of social projects "in defense of family life" and traditional moral values. Father Volgin is close to Svetlana Medvedev (wife of Dmitrii Medvedev, the former prime minister), among other elites. Although he has not played a prominent role in church-related social causes, Father Volgin has helped organize several major parishes in Moscow, as in Arkhangelsk, an exclusive, gated community outside Moscow, and in the nation's television-broadcasting headquarters in Ostankino, a Moscow suburb.

Bishop Panteleimon directs the church's Synodal Department for Church Charity and Social Ministry. He depends on urban elites not only for financial support but also for volunteer services. Several of his major social projects are located at Moscow's Martha and Mary Monastery, where he serves as spiritual confessor to the sisters. After being closed by the Bolsheviks in 1926, the monastery has again taken up the socially activist vision of its early twentieth-century founder, Elisabeth Feodorovna Romanova (sister-in-law to Czar Nicholas II). Its programs for autistic children and for people caring for elderly relatives are groundbreaking for Russian society.

Similar patterns appear in provincial areas, such as in the Belgorod region, four hundred miles south of Moscow. At the time of the disintegration of the Soviet Union, Father Sergii Kliuiko (b. 1960) left his job as a sports trainer to go into the priesthood. After serving as a chaplain in a prison and in a psychiatric hospital, he became the spiritual head of a newly constituted women's monastery in Belgorod, the provincial capital (pop. 400,000), and organized an Orthodox sisterhood (inspired by the example of Elisabeth Feodorovna Romanova) to serve people in financial and spiritual need. Since 1999, his responsibilities have expanded to include a parish in the village of Nikol'skoe, on the outskirts of Belgorod. His spiritual children now include members of the monastery and sisterhood, his parishioners, and local civic and political leaders. His abilities as an organizer and as a spiritual guide complement each other.

Another activist priest, Father Nikolai Germanskii (b. 1953), serves a parish in Rakitnoe, a town of five thousand inhabitants, forty miles west of Belgorod. During the late Soviet era, a renowned Orthodox holy man, Father Seraphim

Tiapochkin (1894–1982), lived here. Father Germanskii lectures and writes about the elder, receives visitors in the elder's cell (where his icons and priestly garments are preserved), prays with people at the elder's gravesite, and promotes the elder's canonization. Father Germanskii's spiritual authority undergirds his social activism. He organizes an annual Orthodox Day of Youth in Rakitnoe that draws several hundred participants. Like Father Kliuiko, he has forged close relationships with local elites and offers them spiritual guidance. Especially important is a religious-cultural journal that he edits and distributes to local civic and political leaders (and which the regional governor has supported financially).[10]

The dynamics of church social activism that we find in large cities such as Moscow have an added dimension here. Father Kliuiko and Father Germanskii bring urban resources to their rural settings, and their rural settings attract urban elites. The two men travel almost daily between their parishes and Belgorod, and their spiritual children and supporters in the city regularly travel to them. Father Kliuiko conducts their weddings or baptizes their children in Nikol'skoe. Those who know Father Germanskii make pilgrimage to Rakitnoe to experience the special spiritual atmosphere that he has cultivated there.

Two other parishes offer further insight into these urban-rural dynamics: the parish of Saint George in the village of Georgievskoe in the Ivanovo region and the parish of the Vladimir Icon of the Mother of God in the village of Davydovo in the Iaroslavl' region. In both cases, a priest with recognized spiritual authority has organized a social project to address a specifically urban problem. In both cases, well-educated urban professionals offer essential support. While neither parish is typical of the Russian Orthodox Church, both exemplify the creative possibilities that exist for religiously based social activism.

Saint George's Parish

Saint George's parish lies directly on the banks of the Volga River in a rural area that has suffered severe economic decline since the collapse of the Soviet Union. The fields that once belonged to large communal farms now lie fallow. Young people have abandoned the countryside to look for work in urban areas, leaving the elderly and the poor behind. The church of Saint George is at the end of a long, ill-maintained dirt road. The car ride to the closest city, Kineshma, can take several hours, depending on road and weather conditions, and the train trip between Kineshma and Moscow (only once a day, each direction) takes another eight. Nevertheless, the natural setting is stunning: the Volga here is nearly two miles wide, and brilliant stars light up the sky on a clear night.

In 1988, the local bishop appointed a priest-monk, Father Mefodii (Kondrat'ev), to renew religious life in the parish (see fig. 5.1). Father Mefodii (b. 1957) was from Ufa, a large city in Siberia. In 1975, he came to Moscow to study physics. Classmates remember his extraordinary intellect. He had a good sense of humor but was also serious, always asking questions about the meaning of life and reading philosophical literature. Knowing nothing about Christian faith, he stepped one day into an Orthodox church. Its beauty transfixed him. He returned to Ufa and taught at the city's medical institute but was discontent. In 1984, he moved to the Ivanovo region to be close to his spiritual father, the local bishop. The bishop soon tonsured him and ordained him to the priesthood.

In the early nineteenth century, Saint George's parish had united several prosperous villages. The large brick church had three altars and a bell tower. By the time Father Mefodii arrived, no one lived any longer in the village of Georgievskoe, and several neighboring villages had been abandoned. Father Mefodii dreamed of founding a small monastic community on the site. For guidance, he relied not only on his spiritual father, the bishop, but also on a renowned spiritual elder, Naum Baiborodin (1927–2017) in the historic Holy Trinity-St. Sergius Lavra, north of Moscow.

On one of Father Mefodii's visits to the elder, in 1994, a young man from Belarus, Oleg Reubo, approached Naum to ask his blessing to take monastic vows. Naum replied, "You want to be a monk? Go help this man, Father Mefodii." Father Mefodii gave the young man instructions on how to travel to Saint George's parish. Two weeks later the man arrived. In 1997, the bishop tonsured him and gave him the name Siluan, in honor of a great holy elder on Mount Athos. Father Mefodii and Father Siluan kept a monastic regime; began restoring the village church, which during the Soviet era had been sorely neglected; conducted religious services; and ministered to the parishioners who remained in nearby villages.

In 1991, Father Mefodii met Elena Rydalevskaia, who worked for a drug rehabilitation center in Saint Petersburg. In the late 1980s, when she was still in her twenties, Rydalevskaia, like other young intellectuals in the waning years of the Soviet Union, had begun searching for a deeper meaning to life than Marxist-Leninist ideology could provide. As happened to Father Mefodii, a new world opened to her in Orthodoxy. She began making regular visits to Father Vasilii Borin (1916–1994), a Russian Orthodox priest and spiritual father in Estonia. The love and acceptance that she experienced in his parish inspired her to become religiously and socially active. She soon heard about Father Mefodii and his spiritual wisdom, visited Saint George's parish, and became one of his spiritual children.

Figure 5.1. Father Mefodii (Kondrat'ev), Saint George's Parish (Ivanovo region). Photo with permission of Father Siluan Reubo.

Other people from Moscow and Saint Petersburg began to make regular pilgrimages to the parish, such as Evgenii Livadnii, the director of a large technology corporation in Moscow. He and Father Mefodii had been classmates in the technical university in Moscow. Livadnii, like many of Father Mefodii's urban spiritual children, travels to the parish only intermittently. Others, however, with assistance from the brothers, have bought abandoned houses, turned them into dachas, and now live in the village much of the summer.

Rydalevskaia and Father Mefodii discussed her drug rehabilitation work, and in 1992 she brought several of her clients to visit the parish. In 1993, Father Mefodii agreed to allow one of the young men, who had no other place to live, to remain at Saint George's for several months. The monks had no idea how to relate to a recovering addict. At first, they mostly left him alone. Gradually, however, they saw his humanity, even as he told them of the terrible crimes to which drug addiction had once driven him. Father Mefodii came to believe that God was calling the brothers to develop a drug rehabilitation program. The program would be unique in attending not only to the therapeutic needs but also to the spiritual condition of the young men. In 1998, the parish began regularly accepting patients (see fig. 5.2).

Today, five monks live in the parish, as do, at any one time, ten to fifteen young men. The young men have completed a first stage of recovery, often at Rydalevskaia's center in Saint Petersburg, and spend up to a year at Saint George's. They work in the community garden, construct and maintain buildings, participate in group and individual therapy, receive religious education, and join in the monks' rhythms of prayer and worship. Some learn Church Slavonic and sing in the church choir. For many, Saint George's is their first experience of the healing beauty of the natural world, far from the hyperstimulation and destructive temptations of the city. In addition, Saint George's is their first encounter with the kind of loving, trusting community that Rydalevskaia and others of Father Mefodii's spiritual children have found there. For those young men who return to Saint Petersburg, Rydalevskaia's center links them with parishes and offers follow-up counseling. Saint George's claims a success rate of 60 percent or higher (in comparison to 25% for Russian rehabilitation programs in general).

Since 2010, Father Mefodii has coordinated the drug rehabilitation work of the entire Russian Orthodox Church. He regularly leads seminars for priests who wish to begin programs in their parishes. In 2013, in further recognition of Father Mefodii's talent and experience, the patriarch appointed him bishop of a diocese in the Urals. Because Father Mefodii is rarely present anymore at Saint George's, Father Siluan now heads the parish and the rehabilitation center. But Bishop Mefodii continues to serve as the community's spiritual father. He still has his cell, and Father Siluan asks his counsel and blessing for all important decisions.

By ordinary definitions, Saint George's does not count as an example of political activism. It did not organize itself in opposition to a government action, it does not seek to influence state policy, and it has a hierarchical, not a democratic, structure of governance (externally, it is subject to the local bishop; internally, Father Siluan determines how the parish and its rehabilitation program will operate). Nevertheless, Saint George's is a striking example of infrapolitical activism in contemporary Russia. Its rehabilitation program arose in response to the drug crisis in Saint Petersburg, and it developed a model program of drug rehabilitation when government efforts were still lagging. Bishop Mefodii's spiritual children, themselves mostly from Moscow and Saint

Figure 5.2. Rehabilitants, St. George's Parish (Ivanovo region). Photo with permission of Father Siluan Reubo.

Petersburg, actively participate in the parish's life and surround the young men with their love. As one woman says, "The young men watch us and see what healthy relationships look like." The urban pilgrims and the young men share work, meals, and prayer. Especially on holidays, the parish becomes one large extended spiritual family composed of local parishioners, the *dachniki* (dacha owners), urban pilgrims, the monks, and the young men. A hierarchical power structure does not prevent people from actively shaping a way of life and cultivating solidarity with one another.

The flow of resources between city and countryside is also evident in the parish's financial structure. Like other parishes of the Russian Orthodox Church, Saint George's receives no subsidies from either the diocese or the patriarchate; on the contrary, the diocese and the patriarchate require parishes to contribute money to them. The young men pay nothing for the rehabilitation program. Saint George's parishioners are poor and few in number; they donate small amounts of money in exchange for candles and prayer requests. In contrast, some of Bishop Mefodii's urban supporters are able to contribute generously, as when at Christmas or Easter they bring expensive food items from the city or make monetary gifts.

In addition, church people from outside of Russia have supported the parish's building and renovation projects. For a number of years, a well-to-do German Lutheran was a major donor; an American Presbyterian church worker also promoted the monks' work and raised money for the parish. Recently, the parish received a Russian Presidential Grant for the Development of Civil Society, which enables the monks to take the young men on excursions to provincial museums and theaters. As Dekalchuk and Grigoriev illustrate in another chapter in this volume, this same program has enabled young people in Sosnovyi Bor to build a skate park when the local government failed to act.

Even at "the end of the road," life at Saint George's does not remain static. What began as a daring experiment in communal Christian living in Russia's boonies is becoming, perhaps predictably, more regularized, more institutionalized. Indoor toilets are replacing outhouses. The new guesthouse will have a hot shower. Gradually, city people who are attracted to the remote beauty of the area and know nothing of the parish are buying or building dachas, while Elena Rydalevskaia has sold hers. Local government officials are even talking about improving the road. The parish's supporters deeply respect Father Siluan, but they miss Bishop Mefodii and still regard him as their spiritual father, even if their contact with him now is sporadic and mostly by phone. For now, however, Saint George's has succeeded in carving out a free space for an alternative politics.

The Parish of the Vladimir Icon of the Mother of God

The possibilities for social activism in the Russian Orthodox Church are also evident in the parish of the Vladimir Icon of the Mother of God, in the village of Davydovo in the Iaroslavl' region. While Davydovo's natural setting is neither as remote nor as beautiful as Saint George's, it does have a magic of its own. The surrounding countryside belonged to the heart of medieval Russia. Velikii Rostov, one of the cities on Russia's Golden Ring, is only an hour's drive away. Its medieval kremlin and churches have earned it the status of a World Heritage Site. The fourteenth-century Boris and Gleb Monastery, a favorite of Russia's first czars, lies halfway between Rostov and Davydovo.

According to archival records, Davydovo had a church by the early seventeenth century. The current structure dates from 1834. At that time, the village was a prosperous trade and agricultural center for smaller villages nearby. In the early twentieth century, the area had perhaps a thousand inhabitants. But

Figure 5.3. Father Vladimir Klimzo, parish of the Vladimir Icon of the Mother of God (Davydovo). Photo with permission of Father Vladimir Klimzo.

the Soviet years proved devastating. The agricultural economy of the area declined as young people were recruited to work in factories in Moscow. In 1972, the village school closed. By the end of the Communist era, the surrounding villages had been abandoned, and fewer than a hundred people remained in Davydovo.

Father Vladimir Klimzo (b. 1956) grew up in Moscow (see fig. 5.3). After briefly studying medicine, he married and made a living building and selling guitars. Although neither he nor his wife knew much about church life, they had a growing if vague sense that God was calling them to make a difference for good. In 1991, wanting to get closer to the natural world, they moved to the Karelia region, near the Finnish border, where Father Klimzo learned construction and farming. But he and his wife soon found the area too remote, especially for the schooling of their three daughters, and in 1994 the family moved to Davydovo. When they settled in and confronted the dire circumstances—demoralized villagers whose principal activity was drinking—Father Klimzo and his wife suddenly understood that they had discovered their life calling: to renew the village, beginning with the church.

Whereas Saint George's had escaped government confiscation after the October Revolution, state authorities closed the Davydovo church in 1935 and used it successively as a club, a movie theater, and a granary. By the time the Klimzo family arrived, the church building was in ruins. The dome had been removed, the roof had collapsed, the walls were buckling, and the interior was wet and moldy. In 1998, Father Klimzo began organizing the villagers to restore the building. As they rebuilt the church, they discovered, says Father Klimzo, that the church was also "rebuilding" them. They began praying and reading scripture together and restoring parish life.

In contrast to Father Mefodii or Father Siluan, Father Klimzo never had a spiritual father. People nevertheless regard him as a spiritual authority. Several Orthodox believers in Moscow, wanting a deeper sense of spiritual community than they could find in their city parishes, heard about Davydovo. Father Klimzo helped them move there, buy property, renovate houses, and learn how to farm. They too poured their energies and resources into restoring the church. One of the new residents, a trained iconographer, began preparing new icons for the church. Other supporters of the parish, while continuing to live in Moscow, regularly drove out to Davydovo on weekends and holidays. In 2005, the local bishop ordained Father Klimzo to the priesthood, thereby allowing him to celebrate the liturgy and the sacraments.

Renovation of the church has continued; as of 2022, the dome had been replaced, the walls had been secured, and the central nave had been painted and was being used for worship. An annual religious procession from the Boris and Gleb Monastery to a holy well in the countryside now includes a stop at the Davydovo church. The parish's restoration work so inspired one member of the procession, a well-to-do woman from Moscow, that she commissioned a beautiful icon of the Vladimir Mother of God for the church.

The parish has organized a nursery school and an elementary school. An important component of the educational program is Orthodox religious instruction, including training in singing Orthodox liturgical music, and some of the children now participate in the church choir. In addition, the children are introduced to Russian folklore and folk songs, which, according to Father Klimzo, help communicate Orthodox values of loyalty to one's people and country. During Maslenitsa, the week of feasting and revelry that precedes Lent, the village organizes a great festival. The children wear traditional folk costumes and perform skits. At such moments, it is clear that Davydovo, like Saint George's parish, is an extended spiritual family whose members seek to care for one another.

One day an itinerant monk appeared in the village. He stayed only briefly, hardly said a word, and disappeared without a trace. A few months later, Father Klimzo received a call from a woman in Moscow who heads a social program for children with physical and psychological disabilities. The monk had told her that Davydovo would be a wonderful place for an excursion for the children. Father Klimzo invited them. The only accommodations that he could offer were in an unused house, with the beds pushed up against each other so tightly that there was hardly room to move. But the children were able safely to roam the village and enjoy the outdoors. Over the years, other people had come to the church in search of help—alcoholics, drug addicts, and homeless people—but after this encounter, ministry to disabled children became Father Klimzo's priority.

During the Soviet period, disabled people were institutionalized out of sight of the general public. One of the church's most famous monasteries, northeast of Saint Petersburg on the island of Valaam, was converted into a home for so-called *invalidy*, including severely disabled soldiers from World War II. Similarly, children with disabilities were often removed from their homes. Since the fall of the Soviet Union, attitudes have not changed quickly, and state resources for families with disabled children are limited.

Davydovo has stepped into the breach, just like Saint George's with drug rehabilitation. Since that first meeting in 2006, the parish of the Vladimir Icon of the Mother of God has organized camps each summer for physically and mentally disabled children and their parents. The program has become so popular that the one camp (two weeks) has now expanded to three or four, with up to twenty children and their parents attending each (see fig. 5.4). People from the parish assist, as do volunteers from Moscow and elsewhere, including physicians and psychologists.

Families with disabled children often feel isolated socially, especially in the city. In Davydovo, however, they connect with other families and develop networks of support. At the end of each day, everyone gathers in the church for vespers, led by Father Klimzo. In the city, the children would be regarded as a nuisance and disturbance. Some rock back and forth, pace the floor, or grunt or cry out inarticulately. In Davydovo, in contrast, they feel welcome and safe. This special atmosphere of love and acceptance is so powerful that families return year after year. Indeed, several families are now planning to move from Moscow to Davydovo to raise their disabled children.

Davydovo also changes the volunteers. Father Klimzo tells of a woman in Moscow who, after receiving a degree in psychology, wanted to work with children with disabilities. Searching the internet for possibilities, she stumbled across Davydovo and began volunteering in the summer camp. She had never participated in church life before, but now she was suddenly praying every day, receiving Father Klimzo's spiritual direction, and experiencing such loving

Figure 5.4. Vespers with children from the camp for disabled people, parish of the Vladimir Icon of the Mother of God (Davydovo). Photo with permission of Father Vladimir Klimzo.

Christian community that she asked to be baptized. Another volunteer, a police officer from Germany, has helped out in the camp for several years. He has fallen in love with one of the Russian volunteers and is now converting to Orthodoxy.

In 2020, construction began on an assisted living facility for adults with disabilities. Each resident will have his or her own three-room apartment. Nearby, a second building will serve as a health center. Emergency medical treatment, physical therapy, arts and crafts supplies, sensory-quiet rooms, and a small gymnasium will be available. Residents will be integrated into the life of the village, including parish worship services. As at Saint George's, major funding has come both from Father Klimzo's spiritual children and from international church organizations.

The parish of the Vladimir Icon of the Mother of God has organized its efforts without direct support or oversight of either state or church authorities, although they are happy to advertise the social good that it does. Like Saint George's parish, it does not threaten their power. Neither parish engages in "politics," in the sense of political activism that seeks to change church or state policies. Father Klimzo's theology, fully in accord with traditional Russian Orthodoxy, gives him cover. He publicly expresses loyalty to his nation and church. Because he makes no demands on them and says that he simply wants to serve them, he is able to carve out a free space "under the radar."

Father Klimzo maintains a relatively low public profile in comparison to those priests in Moscow or the Belgorod region who have organized large-scale social projects with the help of high-powered elites. His spiritual children are mostly middle-class, Orthodox, urban professionals who are seeking a safe place to raise their families away from the trials and temptations of the big city. They support Davydovo because it, like Saint George's parish, offers them a loving community.

It is nevertheless unclear how long Davydovo will be able to sustain itself as a quiet spiritual community. State authorities eventually insist on licensing social service programs and agencies. Church authorities typically rein in priests who operate too independently. An additional challenge is transition in leadership, as Father Klimzo grows older. While he does not see himself as indispensable, his spiritual authority currently holds the parish and its programs together. It is not yet clear what will become of Davydovo when he retires.

Father Klimzo says that he would like to develop an organizational structure that can function independently of his leadership. In this regard, a key "political" question arises: Will a hierarchical organizational structure evolve into a more democratic one? And if it does, what will be the consequences, to use the terminology of German sociologist Max Weber (1965), of replacing *charisma* with *bureaucracy*? Places such as Davydovo offer rich material for understanding Russian society as a whole and the future of social activism in a country in which religious and civil authorities regulate most civic organizations tightly.

A key institutional factor has helped both Saint George's parish and Davydovo protect their free space: they enjoy the support of the patriarchate's Department of External Church Relations and its Commission on Spiritual Formation and Religious Education. The secretary of the commission, Margarita Neliubova (b. 1962), has extensive international connections. She wants the Russian Orthodox Church to learn from the social ministries of churches in the West. She is concerned about such issues as AIDS/HIV and domestic violence. Father Mefodii and Father Klimzo share their experience at seminars that she organizes. This connection to the patriarchate has elevated the stature of each program, attracted international sponsors, and ensured that local state and church authorities do not undermine the parishes' work.

Social Capital and Political Protest

Russia's state and church leadership are highly controlling, even authoritarian, but, on the ground, free spaces do exist in which creative social activism flourishes. Orthodox priests who win spiritual authority exercise considerable social influence. They communicate Orthodox social values to elites and activate their participation in social projects. Their spiritual children help one another negotiate personal crises. In gratitude, these lay activists reach out beyond themselves to urban populations that have specific social needs: at Saint George's, drug addicts; at Davydovo, people with disabilities. From an Orthodox (and, indeed, Christian) religious perspective, religious worship and social service are inseparable.

As other chapters in this volume have demonstrated, social engagement in Russia rarely translates into organized efforts to oppose the state's exercise of power. Indeed, given present political realities, cooperation with the state may be the best strategy for advancing church interests. Being a dissident seems not to go anywhere in contemporary Russia. None of the priests or lay believers featured in this chapter are active in political parties or opposition political movements. Indeed, church regulations prohibit priests from holding political office and discourage them from taking political stands. Moreover, in its official statements, the church claims to be "above politics."[11]

Nevertheless, Saint George's and Davydovo, as we have seen, are best understood not as "above" but rather "under" politics. They have a "hidden" political transcript (Scott 1990). Without claiming to be political (in the sense of influencing state policy), they nevertheless live politically by shaping a way of social life that implicitly challenges the logic of state power. Significantly, they are able to use the church's organizational structures to their advantage. In these communities, hierarchical spiritual authority impels rather than represses lay participation. An institutional framework (parishes as parts of dioceses within a patriarchate) does not so much regulate as protect creative local initiatives. Remote rural locations paradoxically provide possibilities for addressing urban problems.

Moreover, rather than opposing religious and nonreligious actors, Saint George's and Davydovo build bridges. Because "Orthodoxy" in Russia does not imply active church participation, these communities are able to present religious affiliation not first as adherence to church doctrine or ritual but rather as commitment to social well-being. Just as people in some Western European countries perceive "Christian" hospitals or nursing homes as more humane and compassionate (and less driven by profit), Russians who rarely or never attend church may nevertheless see "Orthodox" social projects as contributing positively to social and national life. For their part, the leaders of Saint George's and Davydovo do not require religious conversion before one can volunteer or receive services, although they do see participation in their programs as a step into church life. Recall again Father Klimzo's maxim: as we rebuild the church, it rebuilds us.

Another way to think about the political implications of religiously based social activism is suggested by Smyth, McCann, and Hitchcock and by Zhelnina in their chapters in this volume. They argue that social service projects develop what sociologists call social capital (Putnam 2000). Participants grow in their ability to identify problems in their society, to negotiate solutions, and to organize responsive action. While the hierarchical structure of the Orthodox Church means that priests and bishops always have veto power, the authority of a spiritual father depends on his ability to build trust with his spiritual children. His relationship to them is dialogical, not simply dictatorial. He draws out his followers' talents, rather than squelching them. They, in turn, forge partnerships with one another and with other social actors that share their values.

The nascent civil society that emerges in such places as Saint George's and Davydovo may be "managed" (to borrow from President Putin's term *managed democracy*), but that does not make it politically insignificant. They open up a space in which people seek to make their society more just and compassionate. Their social activism in the form of charitable activity gives them confidence that they can shape their corner of the world, however small, for good. Whether they vote for Putin or not, they do not expect the state to solve every social ill. Indeed, they doubt that it can. They believe that they themselves must take responsibility. They claim a voice for determining the future of their nation.

To be sure, Saint George's and Davydovo are exceptional parishes with exceptional priests. Many Russian Orthodox priests, like religious leaders anywhere in the world, are content to be mere "religious services providers." They make their living by performing rituals for those who request them. However, there will also always be activist leaders who are energized by connecting people and motivating them to realize particular social goods. Saint George's and Davydovo may be unique, but it does not take long to discover priests in Russia who are organizing other kinds of local social initiatives: community folk music ensembles, local history programs, or parish libraries and museums. None of these initiatives can be managed merely in a top-down manner. Their success depends not only on the vision and energy of a charismatic priest but also on lay volunteers who invest themselves personally and financially.

As we have seen, church social activism is by no means limited to urban parishes. As Yusupova also demonstrates in her chapter, urban activism can link urban and rural communities. Indeed, urban Orthodox activists sometimes find that they have a greater ability to respond to urban problems by addressing them in a rural rather than an urban setting. The flow of resources between city and countryside demonstrates that "urban" activism extends beyond city limits. Grassroots activists have reshaped the character of the villages of Georgievskoe and Davydovo, even as village life has helped these activists cultivate a deeper sense of spiritual community than they find in the big city.

Because we do not yet have comprehensive sociological analyses of the nature and extent of church social initiatives in Russia and the reasons elites and professionals do or do not support them, we cannot draw firm conclusions about the larger significance of parishes such as those that we have investigated in this chapter. However, we do have evidence that some priests and parishes, especially in Moscow and Saint Petersburg, are taking on a more explicit political agenda. The "hidden transcripts" of loving, compassionate community that certain spiritual fathers and spiritual children have long rehearsed, as at Saint George's and Davydovo, are breaking out into the open. Some Orthodox believers have built enough social capital to be able to say aloud to the state, enough is enough.

In the summer of 2019, peaceful but unauthorized street demonstrations took place in central Moscow in protest of state manipulation of city elections. Many of the demonstrators were in their teens and twenties. The police responded aggressively, especially on June 27, chasing demonstrators from the streets and making more than one thousand arrests. Several Orthodox churches in Moscow opened their doors when protesters sought refuge.

One of these parishes, the Church of Cosmas and Damian, is known for its social activism in the tradition of Aleksandr Men' (1935–1990), a great spiritual father of the late Soviet period (Daniel 2016). The head priest, Father Aleksandr Borisov, was one of his spiritual children and, like Men', has organized creative educational and social programs. The parish offers free psychological counseling, a shelter and jobs training program for homeless people, and outreach to prisoners. Members of the parish volunteer professional services.

This spirit of social activism, cultivated over many years, shaped the parish's response to the demonstrators. Father Ioann Guaita, an assistant priest, met with the young people, expressed his admiration for their courage, and prayed with them. He did not directly criticize state authorities. But several months later, he and Father Borisov joined more than a hundred other Orthodox priests and lay leaders in signing an open letter to the government. They criticized the harsh sentences that the courts were handing down. Significantly, the signatories included not only urban but also rural priests, and not only Muscovites but also people in other Russian cities (*Pravmir* 2019).

Some conservative priests and bishops objected to this letter, arguing that the church should not get involved in politics. However, divergent factions of the church did unite around a different political event. In the spring of 2020, the Ministry of Defense completed construction of a massive cathedral outside of Moscow. Its architecture and art celebrate Russian military victories from the Middle Ages to the present. Prior to Patriarch Kirill's consecration of the church on June 14, controversy arose. Journalists viewed an interior mosaic that celebrates the "peaceful" annexation of Crimea in 2014 and includes portraits of President Putin, Minister of Defense Sergei Shoigu, director of the Federal Security Service (FSB) Aleksandr Bortnikov, and other government officials. In a panel that celebrates the Soviet victory in the Great Patriotic War, Joseph Stalin appears on a banner.

Father Leonid Kalinin, head of the church's Commission for Church Art, Architecture, and Restoration, and a prominent Moscow parish priest, argued that the mosaics were in accord with church tradition and canons. In the past, he noted, the church has often built cathedrals to celebrate Russian war victories. Portraits of emperors and warriors, such as the thirteenth-century grand prince Aleksandr Nevskii, regularly appear in Russian churches.

In response, a group of conservative academics and intellectuals, many of whom have prominent posts in Moscow and participate in the church hierarchy's decision-making bodies, published an open letter to the patriarch. They objected to the inclusion of Stalin, who had relentlessly persecuted believers and destroyed churches and monasteries in the 1930s (*Radonezh* 2020). Church representatives on the more liberal side of the church were even sharper. One priest publicly called the mosaics "a sacrilegious outrage against the very essence of a church. They turn it into a neo-pagan symbol that gives a sacred status to the government and its armies and leaders" (*Grad Petrov* 2020).

Others noted that the cathedral seemed more intended to celebrate the nation's armed forces than to offer a place for worship and communion with Christ, "the Prince of Peace." In the end, President Putin asked that his own portrait be removed, and church and state authorities eventually decided to move both mosaics from the church to a museum at the site.

These examples demonstrate that the Russian Orthodox Church, despite its close relations to the state, can also speak and act in accordance with its own interests. The church is not consistently supportive of state policies. It does not always submit to the state or support its ideology. Moreover, these examples show that the official pronouncements of the patriarch and his representatives do not reflect the church's actual theological and political diversity. Even categories such as liberal, traditionalist, and fundamentalist (Papkova 2011, 45–69) fail to capture the full range of Russian Orthodox belief and practice. Russian Orthodoxy involves a constant renegotiation of different Orthodoxies—official and unofficial, institutional and popular, hierarchical and local, traditionalist and reforming.

Samuel Kincheloe, a well-known Chicago sociologist of the urban church in the mid-twentieth century, would tell his students, "If it ain't local, it ain't real" (Gustafson 2004, 111n6). If we are to understand the Russian Orthodox Church today, we must look not only at the relationship between President Putin and Patriarch Kirill but also at particular parishes and priests. What happens locally in the Russian Orthodox Church has real political significance. Even when believers do not directly challenge political power structures, they develop a voice that is able to speak to society. They become political agents. To be sure, religiously motivated social activism in Russia is not of one political stripe. Only some of it moves in the direction of democracy. But all of it contributes to a civil society that offers a counterweight to state political authority and domination.

Notes

* The research for this chapter, which included visits to parishes and extensive interviews with church representatives, was supported by the Fulbright Scholar Program (2018–2019) and the American Councils for International Education (2019). The chapter builds on my work in Burgess (2017).

1. A chapter about the church in a recent book about life under the Putin regime highlights "the last free priest," who is punished by his bishop for speaking out against the church's authoritarian, centralized power structures, which resemble the Kremlin's. See Yaffa (2020, 122–163).
2. A phrase from the Nicene Creed, one of Christianity's most ancient statements of belief (fourth century).
3. For good introductions to Orthodox history, worship, and spiritual practice, see Ware (2015); and McGuckin (2020).
4. See the essays on Russia in Meyendorff (1996).
5. For the history of the church under Soviet communism, see Davis (2003).
6. The canonical territory of the Russian Orthodox Church extends to other countries of the former Soviet Union. In Ukraine, the church has twelve thousand parishes and hundreds of monasteries.
7. In 2020, amendments to the Russian Constitution included "the preservation of traditional family values" as one of the goals of the Russian Federation.
8. For a good overview of Russian Orthodoxy, including contemporary developments, see Agadjanian and Kenworthy (2020).
9. For a history of "spiritual eldership" in Russian Orthodoxy, see Paert (2010).
10. Its title is *Vozvrashchenie* [Return].
11. See the chapter on "Church and State" in "The Basis of the Social Concept," Russian Orthodox Church, August 2000, https://mospat.ru/en/documents/87559-tserkov-i-gosudarstvo/. For one analysis, see Papkova (2011, 26–32).

Bibliography

Agadjanian, Alexander, and Scott Kenworthy. 2020. *Understanding World Christianity: Russia*. Minneapolis: Fortress.

Bacon, Edwin. 2016. "The Church and Civil Society in Russia." In *Russian Civil Society: A Critical Assessment*, edited by Alfred B. Evans Jr., Laura A. Henry, and Lisa MacIntosh Sundstrom, 110–125. Abingdon: Routledge.

Burgess, John P. 2017. *Holy Rus': The Rebirth of Orthodoxy in the New Russia*. New Haven, CT: Yale University Press.

Daniel, Wallace. 2016. *Russia's Uncommon Prophet: The Life and Times of Father Aleksandr Men*. DeKalb: Northern Illinois University Press.

Davis, Nathaniel. 2003. *A Long Walk to Church: A Contemporary History of Russian Orthodoxy*. 2nd ed. Boulder, CO: Westview.

Grad Petrov. 2020. "Krest, serp i molot" [Cross, sickle, and hammer]. April 28, 2020. https://www.grad-petrov.ru/broadcast/krest-serp-i-molot/.

Gustafson, James M. 2004. *An Examined Faith: The Grace of Self-Doubt*. Minneapolis: Fortress.

Khodzhaeva, Ekaterina. 2014. "Participating in the Global Community: The 'Syndesmos' Experience of the Kazan Orthodox Youth." In *Orthodox Paradoxes: Heterogeneities and Complexities in Contemporary Russian Orthodoxy*, edited by Katya Tolstaya, 184–192. Leiden: Brill.

Knox, Zoe. 2004. *Russian Society and the Orthodox Church: Religion in Russia after Communism*. London: Routledge.

Luehrmann, Sonja. 2019. "'Everything New That Life Gives Birth To': Family Values and Kinship Practices in Russian Orthodox Antiabortion Activism." *Signs: Journal of Women in Culture and Society* 44, no. 3 (Spring): 771–795.

McGuckin, John Anthony. 2020. *The Eastern Orthodox Church: A New History*. New York: Oxford University Press.

Meyendorff, John. 1996. *Rome, Constantinople, Moscow: Historical and Theological Studies*. Crestwood, NY: St. Vladimir's Seminary Press.

Mitrokhin, Nikolai. 2004. *Russkaia pravoslavnaia tserkov′: Sovremennoe sostoianie i aktual′nye problemy* [The Russian Orthodox Church: Contemporary Condition and Current Problems]. Moscow: Novoe literaturnoe obozrenie.

Paert, Irina. 2010. *Spiritual Elders: Charisma and Tradition in Russian Orthodoxy*. DeKalb: Northern Illinois Press.

Papkova, Irina. 2011. *The Orthodox Church and Russian Politics*. New York: Oxford University Press.

Pravmir. 2019. "Otkrytoe pis'mo sviashhennikov v zashchitu zakliuchennykh po 'Moskovskomu delu'" [Open letter from priests in defense of those imprisoned

in the "Moscow Case"]. September 18, 2019. https://www.pravmir.ru/otkrytoe-pismo-svyashhennikov-v-zashhitu-zaklyuchennyh-po-moskovskomu-delu/.
Putnam, Robert D. 2000. *Bowling Alone: The Collapse and Revival of American Community*. New York: Simon and Schuster.
Radonezh. 2020. "Orkrytoe obrashchenie k Patriarchu moskovskomu i vsia Rusi Kirillu v sviazi s izobrazheniem I.V. Stalina v Glavnom khrame Vooruzhennikh sil Rossii" [Open appeal to Kirill, patriarch of Moscow and all Rus', in relation to the image of Stalin in the Main Church of the Armed Forces of Russia]. May 3, 2020. https://radonezh.ru/2020/05/03/otkrytoe-obrashchenie-k-patriarhu-moskovskomu-i-vsya-rusi-kirillu-v-svyazi-s/.
Scott, James C. 1990. *Domination and the Arts of Resistance: Hidden Transcripts*. New Haven, CT: Yale University Press.
Smith, Constance, and Anne Freedman. 1972. *Voluntary Associations: Perspectives on the Literature*. Cambridge, MA: Harvard University Press.
Ware, Timothy (Metropolitan Kallistos of Diokleia). 2015. *The Orthodox Church: An Introduction to Eastern Christianity*. 3rd ed. New York: Penguin.
Weber, Max. 1965. *Politics as a Vocation*. Philadelphia: Fortress.
Yaffa, Joshua. 2020. *Between Two Fires: Truth, Ambition, and Compromise in Putin's Russia*. New York: Tim Duggan Books.
Zabaev, Ivan V., Daria A. Oreshina, and Elena V. Prutskova. 2013. "Spetsifika sotsial'noi raboty na prikhodakh russkoi pravoslavnoi tserkvi: problema kontseptualizatsii" [Peculiarities of Social Work in Russian Orthodox Church Parishes: An Issue of Conceptualization]. *Zhurnal Issledovanii Sotsialnoi Politiki* [Journal of Social Policy Studies] 11 (3): 355–368.

John P. Burgess is Professor of Systematic Theology at Pittsburgh Theological Seminary. He is author of *Holy Rus': The Rebirth of Orthodoxy in the New Russia*.

6

The River of Urban Resistance

Renovation and New Civic Infrastructures in Moscow

ANNA ZHELNINA

Moscow's urban renewal, the so-called Renovation Program announced in early 2017, promised to demolish about five thousand Soviet-era residential buildings and relocate their residents to new high-rises. The announcement produced emotional turmoil among residents of the condemned buildings and triggered the biggest housing-related mobilization in Moscow history. The city was split: some Muscovites saw Renovation as a chance to move from outdated and dilapidated homes into shiny new buildings; others were appalled by the city administration's shameless attempt to grab their property. The months after the announcement of the project saw emotional and exhausting interactions among pro-Renovation residents, anti-Renovation residents, and the authorities. During the spring and summer of 2017, people fought for their buildings to be included or excluded from the final list of buildings to be demolished (see Smyth, McCann, and Hitchcock in this volume).

I explore the continuity of activism by demonstrating the role of the previous housing- and neighborhood-related mobilizations in the neighborhoods affected by the Renovation, as well as the outcomes of the Renovation-related interactions and mobilization. This chapter is inspired by the discussions about the continuity of social movements, and in particular Crossley's notion of "waveless" feminism and the "river" metaphor for social movements that helps interpret them as a continuous flow instead of series of disconnected "waves" (Crossley 2017, 20).[1] Taking the river metaphor even further, I suggest looking at Moscow's urban social movements as flows that have a potential to build a river by creating their own path, avoiding or carving out obstacles, and merging multiple smaller flows into one large river body. Social movements, like rivers, create their own infrastructures, choose alternative tactics when encountering obstacles, build alliances, and grow—or get lost: not all flows end up in the sea; some disappear under the ground. In contrast to the notion of social movements as waves, the river understanding of mobilization foregrounds the continuous development and the gradual accumulation—and losses—of civic infrastructure along the way.

Although it is too early to evaluate the long-term effects of the Renovation, which is ongoing and is scheduled to run until 2032, several years have passed since the announcement of the program, allowing me to trace changes in the buildings and neighborhoods I studied over this time. In what follows, I demonstrate how the civic infrastructures that had emerged in Moscow before Renovation helped Muscovites during the Renovation-related struggles; I also show that the mobilization during the summer of 2017 had lasting effects on the later activist efforts. In doing so, I address the questions raised in the introduction: What are the social and political implications of activism, and what kinds of learning and reimagining of civil society occur as people mobilize to protect their living environment?

The responses to Renovation were not necessarily collective or visible. Some residents of the condemned buildings, unhappy with the prospect of forced relocation, took matters into their own hands and moved out of the buildings included in the Renovation before the official relocations began. Some sold their flats to move into five-story buildings that successfully fought off Renovation; others were deeply traumatized by the project and moved out of Moscow altogether. The real estate market responded to Renovation immediately, too: shabby apartments in the included buildings were advertised as investments in future, better housing. There is also some evidence of exchange deals between opponents and supporters of Renovation who lost in their buildings: opponents would move into buildings that fought off the Renovation, allowing the frustrated supporters to move into would-be demolished five-stories. In this chapter, however, I focus on the more organized and collective forms of activism.

This chapter is based on a qualitative study in four neighborhoods of Moscow affected by Renovation, combining interviews and observation with digital ethnography of neighborhood-based online communities dedicated to the Renovation.[2]

What Are Rivers Made Of: Civic Infrastructures

Social capital and its derivatives—civic capacity and collective efficacy (Sampson et al. 2005)—have been celebrated by many scholars as foundations for civil society and the productive participation of citizens in social affairs. There is an organizational dimension to this foundation (voluntary associations, nonprofits) and a related feeling of collective efficacy that characterizes the members of a community. Sampson, Raudenbush, and Earls (1997, 918) define collective efficacy "as social cohesion among neighbors combined with their willingness to intervene on behalf of the common good." At the neighborhood level, people need some mutual trust and solidarity to be able to act for the common good (See Smyth et al. this volume), this connectedness emerges from collective events celebrating community—"whether pancake breakfasts at the local fire hall, fundraisers for cultural causes, ethnic festivals, or neighborhood block parties" (Sampson et al. 2005, 676). However, the same researchers observe that the best predictor for collective action at the neighborhood level is the density of nonprofit organizations, not the density of social ties and neighborly exchange. Communities need infrastructure to be able to formulate and pursue collective goals.

Putnam (1993) emphasizes the importance of the normative, ideological dimension of civic infrastructures and calls for the development of "norms of trust, reciprocity, and civic engagement." The organizational side, "a dense network of civic associations," and the "ideological" side, "an active culture of civic engagement," are both important in shaping a healthy democracy (103). If people share this culture, their communities are more likely to be built on "horizontal collaboration among equals" instead of "vertical patron-client relations of exploitation and dependence" (103). Variability in civic infrastructures can explain why some communities are better off than others: if they have the necessary infrastructures, their citizens engage more actively and take control over their neighborhoods.

Civic infrastructures can include a spectrum of arenas, networks, and repertoires to assist civic participation. These may be formal, legally established tools of participation available to citizens, such as voting, membership in voluntary associations, municipal self-governance, homeowners' associations and cooperation, and participatory budgeting. These tools regulate the relations of citizens and governmental bodies. Civic infrastructures can also include informal associations and networks of family and friends that focus on the creation and maintenance of a common good (Zhelnina and Tykanova 2019). Arenas—spaces where participants of the political process interact and compete (such as courts, public hearings, and street rallies)—are elements of these civic infrastructures (Jasper and Duyvendak 2015).

Civic infrastructures help maintain the continuity of activist efforts but are also created as they develop and encounter new obstacles and dilemmas. The recent research on gains and losses of social movements reveals the complicated nonunidirectional dynamic of a movement's impact: the choices the protesters make transform their environment as they create new arenas and players, build or break up alliances, and choose tactics (Jasper et al. 2022). This chapter focuses on the gradual process of the development of civic infrastructures triggered by a shock imposed on Muscovites by the Renovation Program.[3] The processes activated by the announcement of Renovation go beyond the mobilization of the residents of the affected buildings to opt in or out of the program. Even if some Muscovites eventually "won" or "lost" the fight (and their buildings were excluded or included), there were additional outcomes of the mobilization: new networks, skills, and organizations.

Origins of the Flows: Housing and Activism before Renovation

Moscow, Russia's capital and largest city, experienced massive population growth and urbanization in the twentieth century, especially after the 1960s, when the construction of large-scale housing estates, including khrushchevka areas, expanded the housing opportunities for Muscovites (Rudolph and Brade 2005).[4] After the collapse of the Soviet Union, former socialist cities saw immense transformations and spatial changes and the reconfiguration of state-business relations, in recent decades guided by neoliberal urban policies (Büdenbender and Zupan 2017; Golubchikov, Badyina, and Makhrova 2014; Vendina 1997). Ordinary Muscovites were the first to experience these changes.

The current housing situation in Russian cities is a result of privatization that allowed tenants to own, for a symbolic fee, the quarters they occupied. Every pre-1991 apartment building is a mix of tenure types: homeowners (both those who privatized or inherited and those who bought apartments on the market), social renters, and commercial renters (renting apartments from the homeowners) live next door to one another. Unique configurations of tenure types in each building may be a challenge for building maintenance and residents' cooperation, but few Muscovite residents paid attention to their neighbors' ownership status before it became an issue in Renovation-related discussions.

One of the causes of the uneven character of privatization and the resulting mix of tenure types is that housing privatization meant not only the transfer of property from the state to individuals but the transfer of responsibility for the property's maintenance; Verdery (2004) notes that not only "goods" but also "bads" were distributed during privatization in post-Socialist countries. The quality of the distributed housing varied, and some people received liabilities along with their property rights; some privatized spacious apartments in solid buildings, while others were left with small flats in crumbling and nonprestigious khrushchevkas. Regardless of condition, building maintenance became the residents' responsibility: homeowners were expected to organize and create associations to hire maintenance companies. In many cases, however, this self-organizing never took place, and the same municipal companies continued to take care of the buildings and often fail to do so adequately.

Gradually, the situation started to change; the flow of housing activism was fueled from different sources, some explicitly political, others more pragmatic and apolitical. One source was the grassroots housing activism boosted by the passing of the Housing Code in 2005, as Clément (2008) vividly portrays. Another source was the national protest mobilization of 2011–2012, which emerged to address political issues of national significance but eventually redirected some attention to local politics (Zhuravlev, Savelyeva, and Yerpyleva 2014).

Homeowners were central to activism in the seemingly apolitical post-Socialist contexts (Szczepańska 2015; Vihavainen 2009). As Aidukaite and Fröhlich (2015, 5) note, the transfer of responsibility "profoundly changed the relationship between individuals and the state. Most notably, this concerned the notion of citizenship in the new post-Soviet societies." Some homeowners, even those avoiding politics, wanted to have a say in managing their homes, and this pragmatic interest sometimes worked as a gateway into larger politics. Still, these active homeowners were a minority.

For example, Vihavainen (2009) talks about the difficulties of establishing self-governing bodies after the housing reform of 2005, which transferred all maintenance duties to residents and encouraged self-governance in the apartment buildings. Not everyone noticed these changes, and most buildings retained a pleasant lethargy. Even if people have routinely complained about poor maintenance of common areas in their buildings, few have taken a proactive position in caring for their living environment, placing responsibility for it on authorities and maintenance companies, over which people have not exercised any real control.

But everything is different when home is threatened: researchers have documented the emergence of urban social movements, including those addressing issues of housing and the quality of the living environment, in Moscow and elsewhere (Aidukaite and Fröhlich 2015; Clément, Miryasova, and Demidov 2010; Fröhlich 2019; Ivanou 2016; Shomina, Kolossov, and Shukhat 2002). Semenov (2018) calculated that different "urban" problems, including the issues of undesired construction, quality of the environment, and loss of home due to construction fraud, were the most popular causes for protests in 2012–2013. Threats to home shake even politically apathetic Russians out of their lethargy (Zhelnina 2020).

An alternative source of increased attention to local issues has been the protest politics at the national level: the large mobilization against electoral fraud in 2011–2012 caused an influx of fresh forces into local politics and activism, including municipal-level elections. Zhuravlev, Savelyeva, and Yerpyleva (2014) identified new activist groups that developed from the national-level political protests into local activist initiatives in several Moscow neighborhoods. Activists began to monitor municipal councils, produce leaflets and newspapers with important local information, and engage directly with local projects (protesting the destruction of parks, road extensions, etc.). Municipal elections also became an arena for oppositional activists in 2012: in several municipal districts, activists participated as candidates, and sometimes won, and in three districts the opposition and independent candidates received the majority of the votes (*Gazeta.ru* 2012).

The shock of Renovation forced private individuals, many of whom had no interest in collective action or political participation, into interactive arenas: to succeed (save their building or ensure it was demolished) people had to face their opponents, who often lived right next door. Preexisting networks and organizations were crucial in helping the new activists to navigate the complexities of the urban political structures in Moscow.

Building the Riverbanks: Infrastructures for Resistance and Support

Although it was in preparation for a couple of years before it was publicly announced (Golunov 2017), Renovation officially began after Mayor Sergei Sobyanin's meeting with President Vladimir Putin on February 21, 2017. At this highly publicized meeting, the mayor complained about the difficulties with capital repairs and the poor quality of socialist-era housing in Moscow, and the president suggested that the relocation and demolition process begin.

Muscovites began to organize right after the prospect of the program became real. Two days later, Facebook users Kari Guggenberger and Natalia de Kirsche created a group that soon became an important arena for anti-Renovation resistance, sharing information, experiences, and emotions. While only one of the many anti-Renovation groups online, it became the largest (with almost twenty-eight thousand members in the summer of 2019). The two admins had no reputation as local activists.

Eventually, Guggenberger became a symbolic leader and public figure, integrated in the Moscow-wide urban activist networks, showing the role technology can play in supporting connective action (see Yusupova's chapter in this volume). In this Facebook group, people posted Renovation-related news and updates on the legislation and voting process and looked for neighbors to start organizing together. This platform also became the main arena for the mobilization of participants of the large offline events: the anti-Renovation rallies that took place in May 2017.

The evolution of local activism in Moscow between the 2012 and 2017 mobilizations created important foundations for the anti-Renovation activities and attracted new attention and new participants. For example, in 2014, Yuliia Galiamina, a professor from the Higher School of Economics, and municipal deputy Natalya Shavshukova founded an independent School of Local Self-Governance. The project held lectures and workshops to help activists organize to contest local issues, but the primary goal was to prepare them as candidates for upcoming municipal elections. Galiamina was elected as a municipal deputy in Timiriazevskii municipal district and worked on the promotion of local self-governance across Moscow. She is founder and editor in chief of the independent newspaper *Nash Sever* (Our North), which focuses on the Northern Administrative District of Moscow.

Independent municipal deputies were central to Moscow-wide resistance to Renovation: as Gorokhovskaia (2018) notes, they used their official status to apply for rally permits and demand amendments to the Renovation bill. Galiamina became an important activist on this issue: she formed the Headquarters of the Defense of Muscovites (Shtab Zashity Moskvichei) and announced the School of Defense of Muscovites to specifically address the problems created by Renovation. The Headquarters became a hub of information, legal support, and guidance for Muscovites who wanted to get their houses off the demolition lists.

These preexisting efforts resulted in the creation of new arenas for people to exchange information, learn about the capital's governance structures, and provide emotional and technical support for new activists. Emotionally, this could mean breaking the feeling of isolation and powerlessness, a strong barrier preventing mobilization and activism in politically apathetic societies. Learning to navigate the city's bureaucracy using real-life examples and even acquiring document templates were important new skills.

The "schools" for activists, seminars, and workshops organized by Moscow-wide activist networks and politicians provided critical tools and education for some of my interviewees. Such efforts emerged in many neighborhoods: local activists organized to educate their neighbors about housing maintenance, their rights, Moscow's governance structures, and relevant legislation. These schools and clubs of local, building-level activism appeared long before Renovation happened, but the accumulated knowledge and contacts proved very valuable when the threat of relocation hit.

Diana, who praised her neighborhood for being actively against Renovation, explained the importance of such networks when I asked why her neighborhood was much better than many others in fighting off the inclusion in demolition lists: "I can't say that we have a close-knit neighborhood (*druzhnyi raion*), but there are, indeed, many structures. Historically, in our *okrug*, activists live here—N in the neighboring district, and NN in ours. Well, it's formally not our neighborhood, but she founded a school of housing management, and people have been going there a few years now. They make notes of everything; in general, some kind of education is happening. People see something, they listen." Activist learning, or education, as Diana calls it, prepared the residents of the neighborhood for the Renovation crisis. They knew one another; they knew where to seek help and generally were more alert and aware of what their rights were.

Activists could also build on another element of civic infrastructure: neighborhood social media groups. Online communities existed for every Moscow neighborhood, with the number varying from six to thirty-two per neighborhood (Davydov and Logunova 2018). Some of these groups acted as arenas for the formation and maintenance of local activist networks; others were dedicated to more mundane local news, events, and discussions. My research shows that many of these groups became arenas where Muscovites connected with their neighbors to organize against or for the inclusion of their building in Renovation.

The neighborhood groups also became arenas of debate about the program: some users posted shocked or appreciative messages, and long discussions of the details of the Renovation Program took place in the comments section. Renovation-related posts and emotions sometimes exhausted and annoyed the unaffected users of the groups, prompting activists to create neighborhood-specific groups, such as Neighborhood N against Renovation, where all the mobilizing proceeded. Muscovites against Renovation kept a list of neighborhood-based local groups to help neighbors who were not part of their local social media platforms to find one another.

Online actions complemented the offline activist groups, which also proved an important resource for the anti-Renovation efforts. For example, Alisa, a neighborhood activist whose *stalinka* was initially included in the program but was excluded after the neighbors mobilized against it, told me how existing activist networks and skills benefited her case:[5]

Anna: Did you know each other before?

Alisa: Yes. But we became much closer now, of course. I live there [in her neighborhood—AZ] for a long time, and we had some activity in our district before; I knew active people in the neighboring buildings. We discussed things.

Anna: What kind of activity? Was it the road extension or something else?

Alisa: The road, too, and the construction. . . .

Anna: You had some experience with the authorities by then, so you were prepared and knew what to do?

Alisa: Yes, sure. And who to consult with, this is the most important: we had this team (*kollektiv slozhivshiisia*), who could help and give advice. We have enough lawyers, knowledgeable people, who know how to compose documents.

Our conversation illustrates that experienced activists were happy to share their knowledge and connections with the first-time activists.

Activism was not only about preserving personal homes. Many activists wanted to limit demolition lists to stop the construction of high-rise buildings that would dramatically alter neighborhood life and landscapes. As Smyth, McCann, and Hitchcock show in their chapter in this volume, attachment to place was an important motivation for the anti-Renovation activists. Saving the atmosphere of the area instead of that of individual apartments became a preferred strategy. Elizaveta, a new activist in her building, was surprised that her remote neighbors were willingly dedicating their time to help her:

Elizaveta: They knew all about the documents related to apartments, land, and they had prepared it.

Anna: And they were ready to share it with you?

Elizaveta: Yes! And what surprised me most, with strangers! Without a profit, in their own time, and they spent a lot of time!

Elizaveta's surprise in the quote above is an indication of her implicit social mistrust, something she revised after her experience of mobilization. She learned a few things not only about the city's governance structures but also about people and civic networks in her neighborhood. These people's altruism challenged some of her assumptions about society and made her trust civic networks more.

Sometimes new activists found individual mentors and advisers among experienced and renowned activists; this proved very helpful in most cases but could also backfire. Nadezhda told me about her mentor and adviser, an experienced and "absolutely saintly" activist, as she called her. Her advice, guidance, and emotional support provided Nadezhda with confidence but posed a risk: the reputation and personal idiosyncrasies of the mentor affected the choices and the alliances new activists could build. It also muted their radicalism: in Nadezhda's case, when the activists had an opportunity to get help from an official with whom the mentor had issues, "she persuaded us [not to push further]. It even sounded like a threat, that she might even use her own leverage. And it was so emotional, as I see now, but at that point, because of our lack of experience, it stopped us." The advantage of having an experienced ally had a trade-off. Gaining access to knowledge and other resources that her mentor could provide came at a cost of limiting her networks and freedom to engage with new allies in new arenas. Experienced activists carried their preexisting relationships into the Renovation-related arenas, and sometimes new activists had to share the burdens and not only the advantages of their experience.

Rocks in the River: Fighting and Learning

The announcement of Renovation created a lot of uncertainty and anxiety, and both experienced and new activists had to make decisions and take action when the details of the program were still unknown. Under such uncertain circumstances, the residents wishing to stay put had to get acquainted with the local- and city-level governance institutions and their processes.

The first learning point was the identification of the urban governance structures of Moscow. The activists soon learned that "the *upravas* are as powerless as we are," as Irina, a supporter of Renovation, told me. Muscovites realized that local administrations make no decisions and only execute the decisions made at the level of the Moscow Mayor's Office. Therefore, the most active ones made sure that copies of their documents (collected signatures, open letters, protocols of the homeowners' assemblies) reached all levels of government, starting with *upravas* and maintenance companies (*Zhilishnik*) and going as far as the Mayor's Office, State Duma, or the President's Administration.

Activists also explored other arenas where they could influence the consequential decisions. Some of the anti-Renovation Muscovites began their fight against demolition before the lists of the buildings were published. After the meeting of the mayor and the president, both online and offline groups emerged: some of my interview partners "ran to their neighbors" right away. They started preemptively collecting signatures against the demolition of their buildings, which they then submitted to local (*uprava*) and district administrations (*prefektura*). Diana, whose building was not included in the lists, believes her preventive action was key:

> There were lists with signatures. I don't remember exactly, but there was some sort of a deadline. I think the *upravas* got an instruction to collect opinions first. And there [in *uprava*] was a Renovation office [*kabinet Renovatsii*], there was a responsible clerk. Every resident could come and ask questions; usually this employee was useless, nevertheless. We, I ran [through her building's apartments—AZ] with these signature lists, and in the process, I realized that many of those who opened the door—signed it. And we took a stack of pages [saying] that we, the residents of such and such building, are against, and this is our property, so go to hell. And then we realized that if we want to be safe, we need to hold a homeowners' assembly. I knew who we were dealing with already—you can't be sure of anything, they might open the door and say: we're waiting to be relocated to Biriulevo since 1958.[6] So, we held the assembly, and it was the same: the majority was against.

Diana and her neighbors quickly realized that the tools provided by the government were false arenas:[7] homeowners could not control the outcomes of the "collection" of public opinion by Renovation offices; hearings in local administrations were only supposed to inform the citizenry about the vague program. They took the situation in their building into their own hands and organized a homeowners' assembly. Homeowners' assemblies are a common tool of self-governance at the building level, but during Renovation, they were repurposed as an arena for Renovation-related decision-making. As a collateral effect, people also learned that this tool existed and could be used for other housing-maintenance tasks.

Organizing a homeowners' assembly requires sophisticated preparation: if some of the formalities are not observed, the decisions of the assembly risk being dismissed. Among such formalities are the timing and ways of announcing the assembly's date and place, the process of electing the counting committee, and the time frame for absentee voting. Observing these formalities became a challenge for activists who had no experience in organizing: this is where the networks and legal skills of the experienced activists became an asset. Some organizers hired professional lawyers to help them organize a legally impeccable assembly, which required money.

Apart from these challenges, local administrations in some districts added more difficulty to the anti-Renovation organizers: to properly inform all the homeowners about an assembly and to hold a vote, the organizers needed official rosters of homeowners, which the local administrations refused to provide, citing privacy concerns. Zhanna, who failed to hold an assembly in her building, points out the importance of timing and prior experience:

> **Zhanna:** We had a month, and there is this huge pile of [required] documents. If you've never done it before . . . we've spent a month trying to get the [list of homeowners], you see.
>
> **Anna:** In the uprava?
>
> **Zhanna:** Yes. They wouldn't give it to us. Only gave it to us after a scandal. But we lost time! And they already launched their wave of propaganda.

Zhanna had no direct access to activists who could have helped her with alternative ways of getting the roster: some of the activists in her neighborhood had paid commercial companies to get rosters, and the "scandal" in the uprava after which they started providing the rosters was also the result of local activists' efforts.

Timing, as both Zhanna's and Diana's cases show, was crucial: those activists who mobilized well in advance, collected preventive signatures, and worked with their neighbors before the state machine launched its massive pro-Renovation propaganda had a better chance to secure their neighbors' support and get their buildings out of the program. Zhanna, however, lost crucial time and did not succeed in organizing the assembly. The local administration successfully used the lack of experience among the residents and did not provide them with the tools they needed.

Regardless of when they took place, homeowners' assemblies were rarely peaceful: neighbors with different positions confronted one another face-to-face. It got especially heated after the official deadline for holding Renovation-related homeowners' assemblies had passed, but some pro-Renovation organizers still attempted to hold them. Preventing these "illegal" assemblies became a collective task for the Moscow-wide anti-Renovation community, which had already grown strong by that moment. The anti-Renovation activists in buildings where an assembly was scheduled posted announcements on social media to invite like-minded supporters; Moscow-wide activist groups and organizations would also send representatives, bring legal help, obtain video equipment, and record the violations at the assemblies. Sometimes such interventions created a lot of confusion and even aggression from the pro-Renovation organizers. Live broadcasts of this hostility on anti-Renovation social media provided an important emotional boost for organizers at the building level.

Liudmila, who felt powerless and fearful in the face of her majority pro-Renovation neighbors, described the importance of these expressions of solidarity: "I was so scared [at the assembly]—because these people, some were drunk, some with their [walking] stick. What to do? But I posted about this assembly in our [neighborhood] group, and people came. . . . They came, a few people from our group, they already had conducted their assemblies. They made pictures. It was just good to have some external observers. They came and told me quietly: stay cool. There are not many of you, your main strategy now should be to prove that they organized this assembly with violations." The support group not only provided emotional help for Lyudmila but also advised her on the best course of action at the meeting.

Supporters of Renovation could also get similar help from state officials and proxies: pro-Renovation deputies or representatives of upravas could show up and give speeches to convince people to vote for the program. Even when local administrations did not provide direct help, they were interested in what was going on in individual buildings and, allegedly, were involved in persuading residents to vote for Renovation. Upravas could even exert some influence through the public councillors (*obshestvennye sovetniki*; sometimes interviewees also called them "building elders," *starshye po domu*): representatives of the residents of the building, appointed by the uprava, who were selected as intermediaries between the local administration, maintenance companies, and the residents. These positions are often dormant: even if neighbors know that there should be such a contact person among them, the person is often inactive or their activities are invisible. During Renovation, this player was activated in some buildings: some of them mobilized their potential authority and contacts with upravas to promote their own interests (mostly they were blamed for being pro-Renovation and suspected of looking for extra benefits by convincing others to vote for Renovation).

Alisa, who was previously a public councillor but was removed for her lack of loyalty, explained:

> **Alisa:** In some buildings these people are pro-uprava. They received instructions to walk around and convince people.
>
> **Anna:** But what's their motivation?
>
> **Alisa:** Their motivation was, and many people know it: they were promised that their building would be among the first to relocate, they were promised a better location, something else better. . . . We have one scandalous building; they organized an assembly. . . . It was one big violation of the assembly

protocol. And it was clear who initiated it, it was all those paid-for (*zakaznye*) people.

Anna: Those public councillors?

Alisa: Yes.

Before Renovation, many residents were not aware of the institution of public councillors, and some of the new activists tried to volunteer for these positions. As it is not an elected or transparent position, their odds were low. But some considered this an opportunity: Inna, whose whole block of several buildings opted out of the program after a strong mobilizing effort, described her active neighbor's plans to become a public councillor:

> [One activist from the group] went even further. She dug out this information, that our buildings have some kind of public observers in the uprava, there are even their portraits with names on their website. And no more data. No phone, not how to find them, not what they do: nothing. So, she got interested, found out who these people are and how they are selected. It is the uprava that selects them. But for that, there must be some nomination from the buildings. She now tries to understand their functions and says she's ready. At least it is a good way to establish some connection. It's like an intermediary between the building and uprava. We would have some information about what's going on there. What are the plans, what's coming?

Inna formulated the main motivation for interacting with the local governance structures: to know "what's coming," to get access to the decisions about the living environment that are made behind the closed doors of the administration.

One of the main issues with Renovation was its sudden imposition without information about the actual plans or the time frame of the program's implementation, an uncertainty that resulted from the absence of real public discussion of the project before its launch. Residents were forced to make a decision within a couple of months. Before the bill describing the conditions of the program was signed into law, citizens were not allowed to voice their concerns in a meaningful way: the numerous meetings with heads of upravas, *prefecturas,* and other officials were designed as "informational" sessions rather than discussions. The officials themselves did not have complete information during these sessions. Most public meetings featured emotional outbursts and were a difficult enterprise for everybody: the officials had to deal with more people in a more open environment than they were used to, and the residents often did not get the desired information or were frustrated to see that not everybody was on the same side.

One result of the mobilization was a learning process for many new activists: they discovered Moscow's political and governance institutions, and their responsibilities and potential, for the first time. People learned about upravas, maintenance companies, and city parliament deputies and drew conclusions about the most and least efficient ways of promoting their housing-related interests in this system. Mostly, people learned that the political system was unresponsive to citizens' requests and was even destructive. For some, it was a bitter disappointment.

Lidiia, a resident of a five-story building included in the program, formulated this feeling of disillusionment and powerlessness as one of her discoveries from her Renovation-related experience: "I believed [before] that if there are some laws and they get violated, it is enough just to point it out. Take a letter to a deputy—and they would say: what are you talking about! We will now investigate and fix it all! I thought that the head of uprava is a person who is responsible for protecting citizens' rights, and not to saw off billions [*pilit' den'gi*]. During these three months that I'm [immersed] in this topic, so much negative has revealed itself!"

Some Muscovites, like Lidiia, were diverted from political engagement because of such frustrating experiences. For others, however, the workings of the local governance institutions were exposed to scrutiny. These institutions were overwhelmed by the increased citizen participation and strove to discourage collective action and maintain the sense of futility that interactions with them caused in many people. Uprava heads were suddenly exposed to angry people who acted collectively and could exercise more pressure than before.

Residents who had been active in the neighborhood before and knew the uprava bureaucrats had some advantages in pressing demands on the government. They knew where to go and whom to contact. But the bureaucrats resisted. They tried to avoid collective action and to stick to their preferred one-on-one interactions, as in this example Tania, a local activist, told me about:

> N called me and said: we want to go; can you go with us [to the head of uprava office hours—AZ]? I said, yes, of course! And I wrote an application, that I need to get the homeowners' roster, and we signed up all together. ... He was so outraged that we came all together! And I remember that it was even like their common tactic, to divide everybody. Divide and conquer, maybe that's it, because they really don't like when a group comes in. We

> said that we have one issue, and he says—no, you can't! You come in first, and then you. But we insisted and entered all together.

New activists had to learn about local political and governance structures and their ways. Those who had had some experience with maintenance companies or upravas before, or had participated in local activist efforts, had an advantage: they required less time to figure out how to navigate the system. But those residents who had never had activist experience could get help from the more experienced ones: the accumulated skills and knowledge helped the newly mobilized people as well. Even if the fight for one's building was lost, these networks, knowledge, and experience were important gains that may be used in future activist efforts in the neighborhoods.

Flows That Disappeared: Frustrating Consequences of Mobilization

The positive and empowering effects of Renovation-related mobilization are not present in every building and neighborhood; there are also disruptive and frustrating cases. To pick up the river metaphor again, it's possible to say that not all smaller flows with the potential to join the river and eventually meet the sea achieve that: some disappear under the ground or get diverted and form isolated lakes instead.

For example, when Viktor organized neighbors to vote against Renovation, he didn't realize that his action might lead him into very unfavorable lands. He had been active in his building and neighborhood before: a responsible homeowner, he took care of the condition of the building and the territory around it and regularly contacted the local administration to make sure they provided the appropriate services. He used his knowledge and authority during the Renovation but later became an object of blame: some pro-Renovation neighbors accused him of depriving them of the chance for a better life and sabotaged his further efforts in building maintenance and improvement. Viktor now has a problem: his neighbors no longer cooperate. When he tried to set up a driveway access gate in his building's courtyard, he ran into opposition: "Even if I manage to get them to a meeting, they would be against me, just out of principle. If I come and say, let's have the gate, Moscow is ready to pay for it, no way. Just because it's me." The frustration caused some neighbors to avoid any collective action, even the kind that could benefit them.

This experience was not unique. Viktoria, a new activist who organized neighbors in the building to vote against demolition, became actively engaged in housing issues, but her efforts were blocked by her adversaries. She explained, "We need to address the project of capital repairs in our building now, and I should, theoretically, hold an assembly before March 1, to define what we want and how we want it. . . . And it is impossible. They don't talk to me. Or they say 'hi' like that [through clenched teeth]. It's terrible, they see me—and they go—yikes! Or start like: 'Why do you come here, what do you want, you've come again!' Like I did something bad in the building!"

New obstacles in the activist terrain are not the only reason that mobilized "flows" disappear. Some "flows" do not have enough power to reach the main channel of the activist river: many mobilized residents were only interested in keeping their building in or out of the demolition lists, and their experience of engagement was not enough to convince them that activism was worth their time and effort.

After reaching their minimum goal, these people returned to their previous apathetic state and refused to participate in any collective efforts, even with the people with whom they had just shared an emotional and empowering experience. For example, Marianna told me about her fellow activist who organized an assembly in her building and performed most of the legwork to ensure that neighboring buildings would do the same but refused to do anything to help opposition candidates during municipal elections because of her basic mistrust of politicians. However, some new networks and connections proved useful during the municipal campaign in 2017: "But she stepped back, she said: when they get into power, they will become shit. . . . But another woman, who was more emotional, she agreed to let them come to her building. I can't say I helped a lot, but I told them which doors to knock on, where they could find support, because I knew the building's composition and knew who could theoretically be supportive of them, because people, who were once united by a common undertaking, they will as a rule support one another in another undertaking, too."

Social networks and familiarity with neighbors thus were significant outcomes of mobilization, with potential to create some trust or at least less fear of strangers in the building, which may be important for future endeavors. However, they did not automatically lead to the establishment of working civic infrastructures. On the one hand, some neighbors got to know one another and other activists from their neighborhood, felt an emotional boost of solidarity and empowerment, and developed new social ties (see also Smyth, McCann, and Hitchcock in this volume). On the other hand, sometimes peaceful relations and cooperation suffered from the divisiveness of the program, and the potential for any collective action diminished. The specific outcome depended on a set of factors, such as the familiarity of neighbors before the controversy, and especially the perception of activists as either newcomers or old-timers; tactics selected by the activists; the emotional dynamic they created; and the level of divisiveness they allowed. The exploration of these factors is a subject for a different study.

During the anti-Renovation resistance in Moscow, new players (both individual and collective) emerged and existing players transformed: there were new activists, organizations (such as active house councils), and activist networks on the neighborhood and city levels. These players explored and rediscovered the existing but abandoned or underused arenas of city politics: they gave homeowners' assemblies a new life and meaning, explored the possibilities of the "public councillors" with the upravas, and most notably made municipal elections an active arena in many of Moscow's neighborhoods in September 2017.

Boosted by anti-Renovation sentiment, the municipal elections brought more victories to the independent municipal candidates: the opposition received the majority in ten municipal councils (out of 125), and about 200 candidates supported by the democratic opposition were elected in total (Golunov 2017). Municipal elections became one of the arenas where Muscovites, mobilized in response to Renovation, could continue their political efforts. Increased attention to the municipal elections is one example of how Renovation transformed Moscow's politics.

The solidarity built during the anti-Renovation struggles brought new players to the municipal election arenas: as voters, as electoral observers, and as candidates. Ekaterina formulated such a connection; while she lost the fight for her own building, the unity and solidarity she felt with other neighborhood activists and her new interest in neighborhood-level politics kept her in the political domain: "The most interesting part is that our group became so consolidated and active, that when we heard the call for people to become municipal deputies, we had a large core group (*kostiak*), about 8 people, who were ready to fight till the end (*do pobednogo*)."

Not all of these campaigns succeeded, of course; even when they did, the newly elected candidates faced serious difficulties: they often had to deal with a majority United Russia municipal council that sabotaged all efforts by independent deputies or encountered factions between different subgroups of activists. The analysis of these issues is a subject for a separate study, but the emergence of these newly elected players created an important effect, as Larisa formulated:

> We have talked about it before, that people don't believe that they can do anything. And when they meet these people who are ready to spend their personal time and work on public issues—it inspires. And people are

> attracted to it, even if they can donate very little of their time, when they see that—oh! There is someone! . . . I think it is a huge advantage, that it motivates people, even if they are just observing it—there's no disillusionment in everything, or this feeling that you're ready to throw in the towel (*opushennye ruki*), that we can't influence anything. This is a result.

The political institutions and tools formally existed previously, but the influx of new active players transformed them into arenas, where the fate of buildings and neighborhoods were at stake. New players—indignant Muscovites outraged by the violation of their rights during the Renovation campaign—emerged in these arenas, enforced the formal rules (by acting as observers at the municipal elections, for example), and with such actions managed to flip the balance in some municipal councils in favor of independent candidates.

Conclusion: Where Is the Sea?

In this chapter, I have used the river metaphor to outline the ways in which Renovation-related activist efforts developed, using the infrastructures and force of the preexisting urban activist efforts but also adding new power and new "riverbanks" to this flow. First, existing personal connections between activists, knowledge of whom to consult in a situation of shock and crisis, provided anti-Renovation activists with important resources and helped them react to the crisis relatively quickly and efficiently. These connections were further reinforced by the mobilization, and people "became even closer" and developed new relationships that involved others who were not previously active. Not all such efforts had positive outcomes: in some buildings, people's relations and ability to act collectively were hindered by the heated fights and divisions triggered by the announcement of the program. I compared this to the flows that get lost in dry lands—meeting obstacles around which they could not find a way or lacking the energy to continue.

The flow of a social movement does not require all the minor streams to join the main channel to make an impact on the landscape and reach the sea: it is enough if a critical number of the most creative and forceful join together. However, at this moment in the Renovation's progress, it is not yet clear what the "sea" looks like or where it is.

Notes

1. For an example of a creative use of the river metaphor in the study of social-movement identities, see McKee Hurwitz and Felsher (2019).

2. The interview data were collected in summer 2017, spring 2018, and summer 2019. The sample includes people from different sides of the conflict (sometimes direct opponents from the same building), as well as people with different levels of involvement (varying from indifference to activism). Digital ethnography of online communities concerned with renovation, both supporting and opposing the program, spans the two-year period (February 2017–summer 2019). In contrast to the retrospective analysis of online posts, digital ethnography suggests the copresence of the researcher in the online communities and real-time observation of the discussions and their evolution over time, along with the offline events.
3. In this chapter, I focus only on the anti-renovation efforts, but it is worth noting that the pro-renovation activists and the Moscow government often mirrored what their opponents created. For example, when social media platforms became an important tool of mobilization and communication among the anti-renovation Muscovites, the Mayor's Office tried to arrange a similar "online equipment" for the pro-renovation people. They were maintained and populated by young members of United Russia and the Youth Parliament (their so-called Dvizhok project; Kovalev 2017).
4. *Khrushchevka*: a prefabricated building with "cost-optimized" size and layout of flats constructed in the 1950s–1960s.
5. *Stalinka* is a term used for five-story buildings constructed during the rule of Joseph Stalin (1928–1953). Usually these are more solid buildings than the khrushchevkas, five-stories constructed in the late 1950s–1970s as part of Nikita Khrushchev's housing plan.
6. Biriulevo is a district on the outskirts of Moscow that became eponymous for remote and nonprestigious residential areas.
7. Jasper (2006, 168) notes that false arenas don't allow players to influence the decisions but can provide a feeling of participation. Still, false arenas can be transformed into real ones.

Bibliography

Aidukaite, Jolanta, and Christian Fröhlich. 2015. "Struggle over Public Space: Grassroots Movements in Moscow and Vilnius." *International Journal of Sociology and Social Policy* 35 (7/8): 565–580.

Büdenbender, Mirjam, and Daniela Zupan. 2017. "The Evolution of Neoliberal Urbanism in Moscow, 1992–2015." *Antipode* 49, no. 2 (March): 294–313.

Clément, Karine. 2008. "New Social Movements in Russia: A Challenge to the Dominant Model of Power Relationships?" *Journal of Communist Studies and Transition Politics* 24 (1): 68–89. https://doi.org/10.1080/13523270701840472.

Clément, Karine, Olga Miryasova, and Andrey Demidov. 2010. *From Ordinary People to Activists: The Emergent Social Movements in Contemporary Russia* [*Ot Obyvatelei k Aktivistam: Zarozhdayushiesya Socialniye Dvizheniya v Sovremennoi Rossii*]. Moscow: Tri Kvadrata.

Crossley, Alison Dahl. 2017. *Finding Feminism: Millennial Activists and the Unfinished Gender Revolution*. New York: NYU Press.

Davydov, Sergey, and Olga Logunova. 2018. "Communities of Moscow's Districts on Social Media: Content and Moderation" [Soobshestva Moskovskikh Raionov v Sotsial'nykh Media: Kontent i Ego Moderatsiia]. *Monitoring of Public Opinion: Economic and Social Changes* [Monitoring Obshestvennogo Mneniia: Ekonomicheskie i Sotsial'niye Peremeny] 1 (March): 204–221. https://doi.org/10.14515/monitoring.2018.1.10.

Fröhlich, Christian. 2019. "Urban Citizenship under Post-Soviet Conditions: Grassroots Struggles of Residents in Contemporary Moscow." *Journal of Urban Affairs* 42 (2): 1–15.

Gazeta.ru. 2012. "Results of the Municipal Elections in Moscow" [Rezul'taty Munitsipal'nykh Vyborov v Moskve]. Accessed November 15, 2020. https://www.gazeta.ru/infographics/politics/rezultaty_cik_municipalnyh_vyborov_po_moskve.shtml.

Golubchikov, Oleg, Anna Badyina, and Alla Makhrova. 2014. "The Hybrid Spatialities of Transition: Capitalism, Legacy and Uneven Urban Economic Restructuring." *Urban Studies* 51 (4): 617–633.

Golunov, Ivan. 2017. "Who Invented Renovation: Moscow's Authorities Have Been Planning the Mass Demolition Program for Three Years, and Then Decided to Turn It into a Political Project" [Kto Pridumal Renovatsiyu: Moskovskie Vlast Planirovali Massovuiu Programmy Snosa Tri Goda, a Potom Reshili Sdelat' Ee Politcheskim Proektom]. *Meduza*, August 15, 2017. https://meduza.io/feature/2017/08/15/kto-pridumal-renovatsiyu.

Gorokhovskaia, Yana. 2018. "From Local Activism to Local Politics: The Case of Moscow." *Russian Politics* 3 (4): 577–604.

Ivanou, Aleh. 2016. "Social Problem Ownership at Taganka, Moscow: Explaining Urban Protests against Infill Development Projects." *Rationality and Society* 28 (2): 172–201.

Jasper, James M. 2006. *Getting Your Way*. Chicago: University of Chicago Press.

Jasper, James M., and Jan Willem Duyvendak, eds. 2015. *Players and Arenas*. Amsterdam: Amsterdam University Press.

Jasper, James M., Luke Elliott-Negri, Isaac Jabola-Carolus, Marc Kagan, Jessica Mahlbacher, Manès Weisskircher, and Anna Zhelnina. 2022. *Gains and Losses: How Protestors Win and Lose*. Oxford: Oxford University Press.

Kovalev, Alexey. 2017. "And in Pursuit of the Sobyanin Bots—Hello, Is This the Noodleremover?" [I Vdogonku k Cobianinskim Botam—Allo, Eto

Lapshesnimalochnaia?]. *Limp Noodle Blog*, May 2, 2017. https://noodleremover.news
/mayorbots-5d294abc7383.
McKee Hurwitz, Heather, and Brianne Felsher. 2019. "What Happened to Occupy? Collective Identity Transformations across a Protest Wave." Paper presented at the ASA 114th Annual Meeting, August 10, 2019. New York City.
Meduza. 2017. "Moscow Election Results in Five Maps. Where Did United Russia Take 100% of the Seats in the Councils of Municipal Deputies? Where Is 0%?" [Rezul'taty vyborov v Moskve v piati kartakh. Gde "Edinaia Rossiia" vziala 100% mest v sovetakh munitsipal'nykh deputato? A gde 0%?]. September 11, 2017. https://meduza.io/feature/2017/09/11/rezultaty-vyborov-v-moskve-v-pyati-kartah.
Putnam, Robert D. 1993. "What Makes Democracy Work?" *National Civic Review* 82 (2): 101–107.
Rudolph, Robert, and Isolde Brade. 2005. "Moscow: Processes of Restructuring in the Post-Soviet Metropolitan Periphery." *Cities* 22 (2): 135–150.
Sampson, Robert J., Doug McAdam, Heather MacIndoe, and Simon Weffer-Elizondo. 2005. "Civil Society Reconsidered: The Durable Nature and Community Structure of Collective Civic Action 1." *American Journal of Sociology* 111 (3): 673–714.
Sampson, Robert J., Stephen W. Raudenbush, and Felton Earls. 1997. "Neighborhoods and Violent Crime: A Multilevel Study of Collective Efficacy." *Science* 277 (5328): 918–924.
Semenov, Andrey. 2018. "Protest Activity of Russians in 2012–2013" [Protestnaia Aktivnost' Rossiian v 2012–2013]. *Sotsiologicheskie Issledovaniia*, no. 11, 53–63.
Shomina, Yelena, Vladimir Kolossov, and Viktoria Shukhat. 2002. "Local Activism and the Prospects for Civil Society in Moscow." *Eurasian Geography and Economics* 43 (3): 244–270.
Szczepańska, Magdalena. 2015. "Social Aspects of Managing Homeowner Associations." *Real Estate Management and Valuation* 23 (1): 55–62.
Vendina, Olga I. 1997. "Transformation Processes in Moscow and Intra-urban Stratification of Population." *GeoJournal* 42 (4): 349–363.
Verdery, Katherine. 2004. "The Obligations of Ownership: Restoring Rights to Land in Postsocialist Transylvania." In *Property in Question: Value Transformation in the Global Economy*, 139–159. Oxford: Berg.
Vihavainen, Rosa. 2009. *Homeowners' Associations in Russia after the 2005 Housing Reform*. Helsinki: Kikimora.
Zhelnina, Anna. 2020. "The Apathy Syndrome: How We Are Trained Not to Care about Politics." *Social Problems* 67 (2): 358–378. https://doi.org/10.1093/socpro/spz019.

Zhelnina, Anna, and Elena Tykanova. 2019. "Formal and Non-formal Civil Infrastructures: Contemporary Research on Urban Local Activism in Russia" [Formal'nye i Neformal'nye Grazhdanskie Infrastrucktury: Sovremennye Issledovaniia Gorodskogo Lokal'nogo Aktivizma v Rossii]. *Zhurnal Sotsiologii i Sotsial'noi Antropologii* 22 (1): 162–192.

Zhuravlev, Oleg, Natalia Savelyeva, and Svetlana Yerpyleva. 2014. "Individualism and Solidarity in the New Russian Civil Movements." *Zhurnal Issledovanii Sotsialnoi Politiki, Journal of Social Policy Studies* 12 (2): 185–120.

Anna Zhelnina is Postdoctoral Researcher at the Institute of Urban and Regional Studies (Urbaria) at the University of Helsinki. Her research focuses on urban politics, citizenship, and urban redevelopment.

7

Activists and Experiential Entanglement in Russian Labor Organizing

JEREMY MORRIS

Research on labor activism in Russia asks whether organized workers can overcome the quiescent legacy of trade unionism in the USSR and after its collapse (Ashwin 1999; Crowley and Ost 2001; Crowley 2002; Gorbach 2019; Mandel 2000; Vinogradova, Kozina, and Cook 2012). Despite major strikes in 1989–1990 and at the end of the 1990s—particularly by coal miners—in the long term, trade unionism has failed to articulate key worker grievances effectively. A paradox emerged: workers proved they could mobilize and had structural power, but this did not translate into associational leverage to ameliorate the 1990s "Shock Therapy" economic reforms.[1]

The disparity between structural and associational working-class power remains notable in Russia (Hinz and Morris 2017). Federative and trilateral bodies linking state and society have been unable to force any kind of class compromise from state or private capital since 2000. One reason has been the effective co-option of existing unions by the state along with the draconian 2001 Labor Code. Nonetheless, what I call "plural" forms of labor protest remain widespread—including many forms of action short of a strike that take place in waves, not only during periods of economic distress and not only in unprofitable enterprises (Greene and Robertson 2009; Vinogradova, Kozina, and Cook; 2012).

As illustrated by Irina Olimpieva's chapter in this volume, unions officially affiliated with Russia's main trade union umbrella organization, the Federation of Independent Russian Trade Unions (FNPR), are cowed, unsure of their role, and sensitive to further erosion of their chimerical institutional power. They are unwilling to advocate for workers. While still Europe's largest federative union, with approximately twenty million members in 2018, FNPR rarely initiates strikes or protests, despite the increase in labor protests elsewhere in Russia. These bureaucratic organizations reject class conflict, and their track record in voicing worker demands is poor (Olimpieva 2012). Since their founding in 1990, they have defended their institutional "partnership" position, rather than deal with the deterioration in conditions, pay, and security (Ashwin and Clarke 2002; Mandel 2004; Vinogradova, Kozina, and Cook 2012).

At the same time, an atmosphere hostile to labor organizations in Russia cannot completely extinguish labor strife. Labor protests elude the repressive code or use "hidden transcripts" of resistance, individualized tactics, or online campaigns. Key sectors like auto and service industries, with intense exploitation and fewer traditional unions, represent niches for new activist organizers. This chapter focuses on two examples of grassroots labor activism: the establishment and organization of a new independent union, MPRA (Interregional Trade Union Workers' Association), at the Kaluga Volkswagen plant after 2007 and the recent attempts to organize food couriers in Moscow, many of them migrants.

These examples contribute to our understanding of activism by drawing attention to long-term effects of activist learning and experience; the propagation of activism across domains of contention (from electoral politics to labor relations); and the significance of horizontal category networking ("netness") as a characteristic of Russian activism.

The rest of this chapter is organized as follows: The next section develops my concept of entanglements to explore the emergence of labor activism. Second, I trace labor mobilization in Russia after 1991 to contextualize the appearance of new activist unions and their members. Using this framework, I sketch the successes and failures of this new union approach using the case study of Volkswagen (VW) in Kaluga, where I previously carried out research. I reinterpret the Kaluga materials to trace the flows of activist experience as well as their dispersed networks and mobility. I then compare the Kaluga case to the ongoing food-courier activism in Moscow, highlighting similarities and differences. The final section discusses the themes of activist "experiential entanglement." My empirical materials are mainly from two sources: the VW case rests on numerous interviews with activists, as well as participant observation of auto-plant workers, largely from the years 2009–2010 and 2013. The second case—of the Moscow couriers—comprises mainly virtual ethnography from summer 2020.[2] These materials are interviews, Telegram channel announcements, and other online discussions by different self-proclaimed unions purporting to represent couriers. I also make use of media reports and social media account posts—particularly from VKontakte and YouTube.

Conceptualizing Entanglements

Netness (and the accompanying term *catness*) derives from Charles Tilly's (1978) proposed association between relations and identities in contentious politics.[3] *Netness* refers to the knitting together of embedded and reciprocal social relations. Anthropologists also propose *netness* to describe the entangled connectivity of loose, easily collaborating, value-generating nodal points in any network (not just human ones)—often facilitated by technology (Case 2011).

Catness (*category-ness*) refers to the effects of shared identities. A network might have high netness, such as with a group of close friends, but lack catness because of quite different personal, social, professional, or political characteristics. For Tilly, organization in the cause of contention occurs when both catness and netness intersect—his example is a local printers' union. Tilly's conceptualizations have been considered in relation to Chinese (labor) activism—on how the density of informal interpersonal networks engenders trust, solidarity, and reliability in protest mobilization (Liu 2016) yet fails to translate into coordination and solidarity between different workers (Yongshun 2006, 6). In a recent study of the long-haul-trucker dispute in Russia, Crowley and Olimpieva (2016) consider the inherently limited catness of these types of Russian labor protests.

The callback to Tilly underlines my main argument—that experiential density and shared commitment in activist networks are worthy of greater attention. However, I argue that both *identity* and *network* are too container-like and ultimately static as categories. My proposal is to look at experience and practices as intersubjective phenomena—"*within* relationships and *between* persons" (Jackson 1996, 26)—to chart a course between overly subjectivist (agency-based) and objectivist (structural) accounts of activism. Essentially, this is a main task of phenomenologically inspired scholarship. As McAdam (2003, 283) notes, a network approach comes with its own blinders. Beyond structuring variables, one needs to search for mechanisms of "[cultural] *content*" (McAdam 2003, 287, original emphasis) that shape contentious politics. In other words, the dynamics of the social setting matter a lot; McAdam reflects on the limits of structuralist approaches to social movements and proposes more of a role for "agency." Geography and anthropology have recently both made important contributions to how emotion, (copresent forms of) solidarity, and creativity affect the understanding of new and hybrid forms of resistance that are written into everyday life and that are not reducible to intentionality (e.g., Hughes 2016; Pottinger 2017).

However, emotional and affective perspectives are not enough on their own to do justice to the phenomenological approach I favor. "New" unions and labor activists are typically more loosely institutionalized and less hierarchical. They lack the permanent copresence and density of netness that institutions and traditional workplaces provide and instead are entangled in a wider web of looser affinities and contingent alliances.

The classical unity of the union may be lacking, yet activists, despite their dispersal, draw on the shared experience of political collaboration in concrete actions and overlapping and uninterrupted lines of (particularly online) communication to intensify their sense of solidarity and cause. I call this process *experiential entanglement.* Shared causes are actualized by the lived experience of activists as workers *and* activists, as well as their encounters with others and with union organizing. Entanglement in common experience (in working as a food courier, participating in a protest picket, or just hanging out in a YouTube livestream) shortens the time horizons for possible actions. By the same token, our perspective on activism moves beyond the static and sometimes contentless containers of identity and network.

Entanglement is a solution to two conceptual problems. It overcomes a subject-object division, where purposive action is delegated to the individual or the movement according to rules of hierarchy. Experience is a way for participants to share transformation via contention. As Mattingly argues (2019, 419), the "phenomenological point is not that social categories and conditions should be disregarded but that experience cannot be reduced to what they encompass or call attention to." Ways of thinking and acting in common emerge as a consequence of entangled experience. This is the phenomenological challenge to agentic intentionality or structural accounts of networks (Jackson 1996, 22; Mattingly 2019, 423).

New Unions Occupy Activist Niches in the Years 2000–2009

As mentioned above, Russia's trade union umbrella organization is the largest in Europe. Affiliates are the inheritors of former official unions, which were directly subordinated to the Communist Party. With few exceptions, they occupy a position akin to managing labor discontent by administering benefits in kind from employers. This Soviet legacy makes unions into something distant from their image of sometimes militant counterparts in liberal democracies. Instead, in the USSR, and in a much more truncated way since its dissolution, unions bridged the gap in the incomplete welfare state under communism. Important elements of what was called the "social wage" were at least partly under the purview of unions—including things like vouchers for holiday trips. Other aspects of the social wage were subsidized food, a fast track to housing, access to kindergartens, and so on. Whether the union had a real role in provision of these or not, their image was indelibly linked to discretionary (yet important, expected, high-value) job perks.

Even before 1991, this hybrid welfare state started to break down, and in the 1990s, with social wages increasingly eroded and wage arrears becoming the major generator of labor unrest, these paternalist unions lost much of their rationale for existence and proved unable to reform themselves. While unions still promote the illusion of institutional power via intensive cooperation with the state, FNPR affiliates' associational power is inexorably eroding, with massive loss of members since 1990 and a lack of serious organizational restructuring. However, this lack of adaptation presented a major opportunity for more activist organizers.

From 1990 onward, there were serious attempts to build alternative unions, suggesting that transformation of the established and inflexible industrial relations system might be possible (Biziukov 2003; Greene and Robertson 2009). However, these attempts failed, partly because of internal conflicts and partly because of continued state support for FNPR unions. While alternative unions were able to demonstrate structural power, especially in manufacturing and transport, they failed to gain stable associational power or meaningful institutional power. Their most significant achievement was the emergence of an alternative federation in 1995, the Confederation of Russian Labor (KTR), which was able to carve out its own space legally as a more activist-focused organization and gain about two million members. Nonetheless, employment relations in Russia are still dominated by the traditional FNPR unions.

The growing significance of foreign firms in Russia in the period from 2000 to 2009 created an opportunity for alternative trade unionism (Chetvernina 2009). Like the alternative unions of the 1990s, small unions at company level grew out of conflicts not because wages were in arrears—which was still a problem in Soviet-style factories dominated by the old unions—but precisely because these multinationals sold jobs as "high-tech" and "modern" yet made deals with regional politicians to keep wages low. Unions made use of workers' strong marketplace and workplace bargaining power in the automotive industry, mobilizing large groups of workers in the production process to achieve demands relating to wages but also to working time and health and safety. Most small local unions are affiliated with the Interregional Trade Union of

Autoworkers (Mezhregional'nyi Profsoiuz Rabochaia Assotsiiatsiia [MPRA]; Olimpieva 2012).

Not surprisingly, the VW plant in Kaluga, which Sarah Hinz and I studied from 2009 to 2013, was rapidly and successfully unionized by the MPRA, shortly after the factory opened (Hinz and Morris 2017). By 2012, with twelve hundred workers organized, the union gained legal recognition from management, though membership was only around 20 percent of production operatives. Relations between management and the MPRA were tense and difficult. The German management underestimated MPRA's ability to gain access to the plant and salt the workers with at least one highly competent and experienced activist.[4] In 2012, the union entered collective bargaining (significant because of the high threshold required for recognition), and in 2013, it successfully called for strikes (ruled unlawful by a court) and protests. The novelty of this kind of labor activism lies in unconventional tactics—such as protest, political pickets of non-VW car dealerships, sabotage of production, and work-to-rule, known in Russian as the "Italian strike." The union won concessions on pay and reductions in agency labor contracts. Spurred on, their second campaign sought to reduce shift and working-week lengths. Today the union remains the key player at the plant but is less able to mobilize than before.

Before moving to discuss micro-level activism, it is worth noting a different form of entanglement: that of old and new forms of labor organization. "Old" and "new" unions should not be understood as in rigid opposition. It would be a mistake to oppose new to old in terms of active-passive, confrontational-collaborative, or institutional-devolved. MPRA mixes traditional institutionalized markers with a much looser and more flexible orientation and opportunistic approach. This translates into a corresponding model of interactions and relationships among its activists. Indeed, a notable and unanticipated aspect of new activism in MPRA is how it becomes entangled in some of the welfare activities associated with FNPR unions.

MPRA as a Case Study in Diffusion and Brokerage between Sites of Activism

Even at the time of my original fieldwork, it was apparent that local MPRA success at Kaluga was primarily due to professionalized activism with significant outside support, not only from MPRA nationally but also from anti-capitalist groups then affiliated with the Russian Socialist Movement (RSD).[5] While the main organizer in Kaluga had not previously been a professionalized activist, the involvement of others presents a classic example of what Tilly calls diffusion of a relatively small number of frustrated leftist political activists looking for causes.[6] *Diffusion* refers not only to the migration from one cause to another but also the transfer of information along lines of interaction (McAdam, Tarrow, and Tilly 2001, 333).

The relatively unconventional forms of contention that took place were indications of transference, sometimes approaching a hybrid of traditional methods of labor protest and the politics of the street (including criminal damage to private property). At the same time, the MPRA case seemed to illustrate McAdam, Tarrow, and Tilly's (2001) concept of brokerage—linking previously unconnected social sites. Anti-capitalist activists migrated between disparate causes—from the well-known environmental campaign to save a Moscow forest from roadbuilding, to labor activism with MPRA.[7] As Laura Henry (2006, 109) notes, changes in information technology mean that the term *organization* is increasingly plastic and that small groups or even individuals can be effective in seeding activism once transplanted from one site to another, perhaps especially so in the febrile environment of niche activism in a wider social field where action is politically constrained (102).

In the MPRA case, two visible activists were clearly supported morally, informationally, and tactically by a virtual network of others—some of whom were peripheral to the union movement. While stressing their independent journey into activism, they emphasized the intellectual influence of RSD and anti-fascism as a common cause among activists. MPRA nationally was materially supported by IG Metall (the powerful German autoworkers' union) and was also in touch with other international labor activists. While this environment socialized the greenhorn activists to the importance of the union as an institution, much of their personal philosophy was "workerist" or autonomist—they repeatedly conceptualized activism as "revolution from below"—and related to horizontal teaching and learning.

Despite RSD influence, they continually stressed the experiential—that witnessing and experiencing injustice in the course of working life had politicized them. When asked about initial involvement, they emphasized that consciousness developed through concrete events and experiences and that this insight required focus on day-to-day life in the plant. Here, there was an admission that even new unions had to balance conflict with a sensitivity to the concerns of traditional unions—the little things workers moan about in various places, including online. Despite years of experience in MPRA, when interviewed in 2013 they still emphasized learning from experience and then transmitting that learning—particularly through the local union's active VKontakte pages. A remarkable aspect of union work was the thriving and very open discussion online. Many thousands of posts were made in response to member and non-member questions in this small space of activism.

The union also regularly published printed materials with wide-ranging commentary on issues at the plant but also on national and international topics such as tripartite unionism, precarious work, and political economy. These were a crucial form of subversion of official transcripts. For example, writers attacked the notion of partnership between plant and workers. The large-format double-sided newsletters were eagerly consumed by nonunion members, who felt that reading and discussing sheets of paper in private was safer than participating online. Thus, the newsletters and their consumption serve as an example of infrapolitics in action, where political socialization takes place in ways almost invisible to the wider society.

Can we translate this into an assessment of netness and catness? It both falls short and exceeds them. On the one hand, some of the nodes that we could ascribe to the dense network that facilitates MPRA's success are transitory. At best, brokerage is intermittent, and the pathways of diffusion, well, a little diffuse. There was evidence of moral encouragement, some training through mobility of activists, the use of IG Metall as an interface internationally, and sporadic local interaction with RSD. On the other hand, this slack netness creates different kinds of potentially useful contingencies and mutual obligations. In turn, over time the local nonprofessional activists developed their own hybrid set of strategies (including responding to mundane and nonpolitical demands of workers and even nonunion members).

When the Interior Ministry's anti-extremism unit arrested an activist, it was workers at the plant in his immediate vicinity who provided help—the loose catnet tightened. While catness operates both locally (among workers) and nationally (among RSD activists), it is based on shared indigenous experience. This experience is as transformative to participants' relations—entangling them in cause and loyalty to each other—as cultural (Tarrow's [1993] term), emotional, or, indeed, cognitive models of contentious mechanisms.[8] Borrowing, adaptation, and spontaneous local growth of novel organizational forms (the idiosyncratically transparent and responsive VKontakte pages) characterize this activism.

Gig Worker Organization and Activism: Reproducing Divisions between Passive and Active Unions?

The second case presented is the Moscow food-courier dispute that began in late 2019. Food couriers are a recent global manifestation of precarious labor on city streets. They use public, private, or hired transport—from scooters to cars—to collect meals from producers and deliver to private clients. What distinguishes them from traditional delivery drivers is that they lack a formal or informal labor contract with the food producers. Sometimes this shift in how production and labor intertwine is described as part of the "sharing economy," the idea being that different food preparers make use of the same dispersed labor delivery force, which is then more productively utilized using supply and demand allocating algorithms and geolocated mobile phones.

Critical views question the term *sharing* as misleading, since many examples, including food delivery, are not really peer-to-peer economic transactions. Instead, most models like Uber result in greater rates of (often micro) capital exploitation (cars as taxis, private accommodation as mini hotels, etc.). Low wages are typical, and precarious self-employed workers are forced to sweat their assets. In the food-delivery business, the "uberization" of services has led to cutthroat competition between aggregator third parties who develop the software and own mobile application architecture, as well as to falling wages and negative socioeconomic externalities such as pollution and congestion. Former Soviet states are no exception to this trend, although sharing platforms continue to coexist with lo-fi semi-informal modes where risk is individualized, as in the infamous informal taxis (Kovács et al. 2017).

The Moscow food-delivery market is commensurate with the city's wealth, size, and large number of fast-food chains (see fig. 7.1). Demand for couriers expanded massively during the COVID-19 pandemic, and notably couriers were exempted by the Moscow government from lockdown in 2020 (Orlova and Morris 2020). There are three major players in the Moscow market: Delivery Club (the target of labor activism), Yandex Eda, and Sbermarket. Delivery Club was fulfilling one million orders a week in the middle of April 2020.

Delivery workers are highly visible because they are required to dress in the brightly colored livery of the particular platform/aggregator they are currently working for, carry branded color-coordinated cube-shaped insulated backpacks, and have to wait publicly in eateries, travel by public transport, or move about on foot, bike, or scooter. Many are visible ethnic minorities from Central Asia, underlining the work's low status, precariousness, and caste-like character. This visibility partly facilitated self-organization and communication with activists migrating from other causes. However, as becomes clear, this is not a case of activists colonizing this new space of activism (and reproducing ethnic hierarchies). While demands are articulated mainly through white activists (to the media, via Telegram channels), the genealogy of the dispute and the success of rapid mobilization—which could not come without

Figure 7.1. Food-delivery couriers on bicycle in central Moscow. Photograph taken by author in July 2021.

trust building and negotiation among couriers—shows more synergy than opportunism.[9]

Before the pandemic, labor activists in different parts of the world had tried to organize couriers because of the dangerous and unhealthy conditions they work in. Low piece-rate pay and aggregator companies' delegation of all risk to the courier by contracting out each individual job on a demand basis, denying workers employee status, make them a visible group of precarious workers. Notable cases of attempted labor organization of these so-called gig workers occurred in Canada and California among Uber drivers and in New Mexico among baristas. In some European jurisdictions, Uber has been denied a license to operate.

The 2020 Canadian Food and Commercial Workers union dispute with Uber had three aims: to force payment for all hours worked, to allow recourse to a legally binding grievance procedure, and to have contracts legally recognized, making workers employees rather than contractors. In 2018, Uber drivers won the right to be recognized as workers rather than self-employed contractors in the UK, with the case reaching the Supreme Court in 2020 on appeal. This campaign had more of the character of a legal action than of organized unionism. California's Supreme Court in August 2020 ruled that Uber and Lyft should treat drivers as employees and pay sick pay, unemployment insurance, and holiday pay. However, this was overturned in November 2020 by a statewide vote (Proposition 22) heavily funded by gig companies.

In Russia, independent unions had previously been involved in some solidarity activism with service workers in the food sector and with striking Ozon e-commerce delivery workers in October 2019 (KTR 2019). Because of the legal restrictions of the 2001 Labor Code, it is vital that legally recognized unions do not allow the authorities to accuse them of actively participating in the organization or the unionization of other professions. However, in the Ozon case, it is almost certain that activists from a KTR union did provide administrative and legal aid—KTR cloaked their involvement in the euphemistic phrase "giving support." Since 2018, taxi drivers, increasingly exasperated by the dominance of a single Uber-type app platform called Yandex-taxi, have attempted to self-organize online (via the Russian-developed, cloud-based Telegram instant messaging service) using coordinated boycotts of the Yandex app.

This effort proved a salutary reminder of the limits of slacktivism, with a significant social media presence and clearly identified and articulated grievances failing to translate into any coordinated action. In some respects, the taxi drivers' case echoes that of the Blue Buckets Society of car owners (Evans 2018). Car owners made use of a limited repertoire of complaint culture actions and a too-narrow framing of disputes. Those involved eschewed wider framing of disputes and more activist mindsets and sought apolitical or technical solutions, which often made the emerging taxi union look more like a self-help group than an association for bargaining.

By contrast, food couriers' militancy and potential for self-organization are shown by spontaneous actions in 2019. The death from a heart attack of a young Saint Petersburg courier from Kyrgyzstan drew press coverage and interest among left-leaning groups online (Petlianova 2019).[10] In Kazan, a significant unofficial strike occurred in September of that year. Coordination efforts made use of Telegram chat. In November 2019, a new Telegram channel called "SKR Russian Union of Couriers" appeared with a Moscow-based coordinator, but its activism resembled that of the taxi drivers, emphasizing self-help, information, and dialogue. It garnered around one thousand subscribers with a small sub-chat group.

Then Moscow-based group Courier Union appeared on Telegram. Its aggressive approach and politicized language had obvious links to a broad network of activists with leftist credentials. This channel clearly focused on two grievances: delays in pay for couriers working for Delivery Club and financial penalties for small infractions of rules. In June and July 2020, Courier Union threatened strikes and picketed the Delivery Club's parent company. The main organizer, Kirill Ukraintsev, successfully created a popular online space for the communication of more radical activism. He also generated enough short-term traction among couriers that the threat of strike was taken seriously by the company and the mainstream media.

Relatively detailed, if not completely sympathetic, accounts of the dispute were covered by business sites RBC and Forbes. By taking on the role as spokesperson for the "union," Ukraintsev was able to leverage and combine online and offline resources. As of the time of writing in late August 2020, Delivery Club's parent company was promising to make good the debt to the couriers, with the activist claiming that millions of rubles of arrears and worker penalties had already been paid.

New Labor Activists Entangled in Public-Personal Networks of Shared Experience

As in the case of MPRA in Kaluga, the Courier Union example allows us to look up close at activist entanglement. Kirill Ukraintsev, the face of the Courier Union campaign, was previously visible as an emerging leftist YouTuber. It is worth noting the degree of candor and fearlessness of this new generation of activists and a new degree of social leveling,[11] at the same time as highlighting their links with the "older" generation while avoiding the trap of romanticizing technopolitics and its potential for strengthening reaction (Sierra Caballero and Gravante 2018; Weidmann and Rød 2019).

Nonetheless, the Ukraintsev case underlines that internet activism and real-world activism are difficult to separate; they reinforce each other, present a particular form of entanglement of the public and the personal, and increase connections without necessarily implying the density or intensity of netness or catness. Both are important in maintaining momentum for activists in a political environment where opportunities for real contention come and go and where the severity of authoritarian repression also varies. Ukraintsev has a history of informal association with activists from RSD, the Left Front, KTR, and MPRA. In taking up the cause of couriers, he also had some contact with an activist formerly of StopXam and Nashi, organizations associated with regime-inspired youth activism.

However, before the courier dispute, he was known exclusively as a leftist YouTuber. Notable was Ukraintsev's ability to rapidly mobilize from his wide yet loose network of comrades from different anti-capitalist shades of opinion and translate some of his online ideas into offline action. Mobility takes on another facet of significance, though: in the courier actions, meetings took place between Saint Petersburg and Moscow union activists; Saint Petersburg MPRA lent resources of various tangible and intangible kinds to the Moscow campaign; and leafleting (typical of groups such as Socialist Tendency) took place in far-flung Nizhnii Novgorod. Ukraintsev himself is an interesting example of several hands-on new left activists who are not from Moscow and are less wedded to a strong embeddedness in one particular group.

In a number of long public online discussions and interviews, Ukraintsev talks about his politicization and activist genealogy. He is comfortable discussing the minutia of leftist ideas, but like the MPRA activists, he emphasizes practical action and experiential embeddedness as a motor of contention and a means for further political enlightenment. When asked by a fellow leftist YouTuber about how he became involved in the courier dispute, he talks about the importance of self-organization of the base, of linking this to the wider issue of gig workers, and of the tactical decision not to frame disputes as class struggle "because we know we can get a sympathetic audience among pension protestors and those against in-fill building developers" (*Sovetskoe Televidenie* 2019).

Ukraintsev is associated with other YouTube channels, one of which (*Vestnik Buri* [Stormbringer]) is probably the most popular left politics channel in Russian, with two hundred thousand subscribers and many videos on a variety of subjects. All have a consistently anti-capitalist or Marxist flavor, and a few of them garner over a million views. In the same interview, Ukraintsev talks about developing this YouTube "revolutionary propaganda channel" and discusses the vlogger team's political positioning as "the only socialist/communist players of the general oppositional field." The point of the videos is to retain a left identity without falling into liberal narratives. Left group collaboration with figures like Aleksei Navalny is not to be avoided but to be embraced to show that the Left has broad concerns and that they constitute a non-factional assembly.

Ukraintsev is currently an activist of the Left Bloc [*Levyi Blok*]—a loose affiliation of socialist groups that emphasize the right to independent action, created at the end of 2015. He has been vlogging since 2017 but has been an activist since the politicizing Bolotnaia election protests in 2011. Acknowledging that this politicization was gradual, he talks about the educating and enlightening power of exposure to various currents—including libertarian communist organizations such as Autonomous Action, Siberian anarchists, RSD, and MPRA. As a libertarian left socialist activist,[12] he talks about the reflexive need in the nonsystem left to be flexible and collaborative and for different activists to figuratively meet one another. Indeed, a livestream on YouTube about the dispute included a Q&A from the virtual public.

This new type of connectedness moves beyond the limits of union or party activism. This is entanglement in activism appearing as novel forms of transfer and interfacing that use technology. Indeed, in one talk, Ukraintsev mentions what in his view is novel about this activism: that Telegram allowed the campaign to activate a groundswell of solidarity among *consumers* of couriers' services for the first time—a further entangling. Talking about post-2012 left activism, Ukraintsev says, "We're dealing with the shards of movements that were strong in the aftermath of Bolotnaia and which got a second wind due to labor disputes like the trucker protests."

He sees the dynamic of protest as reinvigorated by the potential of social media and vlogging. This dynamic also is linked to moving away from party affiliation and narrower electoral activism that tends to lead to rapid demobilization between elections.[13] Ukraintsev and his associates clearly tend to be less invested in a single organization, network, or cause, and this strategy appears to be partly mediated by generational positioning and the disappointment after 2011–2012. The distributed logic of digital communication is projected onto political activism, bringing with it questions about the relative strength of open "reciprocal action" (as Ukraintsev says) and of bounded networks.

The Paradox of Experiential Entanglement

In this summarizing discussion, I reflect on points of connection between the MPRA and Courier Union cases. I also develop the concept of entanglement and the role of technology that are important to the field of activism in Russia today and their relationship to some of the classic ideas about contention outlined earlier in relation to Tilly and Tarrow.

The horizontal networking between relatively diverse yet committed individuals, groups, and loose affiliations is important. Moreover, mobilization, if not fully successful in both MPRA and Courier Union cases, depends on reciprocity among activists, their long-standing yet loose social relations, which allow easy diffusion (transfer of information and personnel) and collaboration, facilitated by technology that allows them to be geographically or physically dispersed but still closely connected.

Anthropologists inspired by Actor-Network Theory have called netness a form of entanglement (Case 2011). Tilly's use of *netness* is a separate coining that emphasizes membership and density of connecting points and only indirectly indicates the importance of social embeddedness. Entanglement emphasizes that shared or lived experiences contribute to network relations and that technopolitics entails a tighter knitting together of quasi-public political identity and the personal than was possible before the internet.

Let us step back for a moment and compare the concerns of this chapter with those of others in this volume. Matti Dollbaum, Andrei Semenov, and Elena Sirotkina's chapter on the success of the Navalny 2017–2018 mobilization campaigns stressed activist experience and genealogy as factors. Seasoning in prior experiences of campaigning and the generation of informal networks sustained online in fallow periods were important. Activists gravitated toward the Navalny campaign not just because of a strong commitment to this one cause but because of diverse and cumulative grievances.

Zhelnina in this volume emphasizes processes of trust building, collaboration, and horizontal networking as a kind of experiential learning about how not to be powerless. Like Dollbaum, Semenov, and Sirotkina's chapter, these are long-term processes with origins in other grievances or moments of contention. I also wish to emphasize the focus in these chapters on the "processual" development of activist potential through both cognitive and "unconscious" experiential learning. The focus on processual insights aligns with Clément and Zhelnina's recent (2020) development of more phenomenologically inflected perspectives on how activism, pragmatic politics, and networks are mutually constituted and "grounded" in everyday experience, practices, and routines. These are not cognitive, affective, or structuralizing arguments.

While the present study is composed of a self-selecting sample of dedicated activists, their meta-reflection on the success or failure of different campaigns and approaches and on the genealogy of the Left in Russia is worthy of note. After all, it also frames activism as sensitive to the meaning of the "experiential" side. The cases give us an unusual insight into the long-term problem of a lack of coalescence among antisystem groups, long seen as a barrier to a more unified opposition (Smyth 2006; Kolstø 2016; Semenov 2017). However, despite the pragmatic rhetoric of triangulation between causes and groups, their story is really one of a post-coalescence perspective—another example of activist learning.

The 2011–2012 Bolotnaia protests are a watershed event after which these activists, more or less disillusioned with electoral politics, turn to the base, grassroots causes and to propaganda (a term they use repeatedly). This is a tendency shared by very different activists in the studies of this book. Ironically, while conditioned partly by the failure of Bolotnaia, this dynamic recalls the very origins of syndicalism in the late nineteenth century and the eternal dilemma of labor politics—what the relationship should be between socialists and, as Lenin famously put it, parliamentary cretinism.

It is not surprising that there is an elective affinity between this branch of left politics generally and a sympathy for the experiential and grounded struggle-as-life at the core of these activists' performative identity. For them, recurring narratives act as mobilizing resources: the direct action of workers and the role of the strike—elements that Georges Sorel identified as important "myths" in producing revolutionary energy for syndicalists (Schecter 1990). What is new is the reframing of struggle from the national labor movement to the global Left's struggle. This young generation is well versed in the need for the Left to address identity politics and postcolonialism. Thus, they are keen to link traditional labor politics to novel and—for activists—sometimes esoteric theoretical ideas such as the multitude, the global precariat, and left accelerationism.

This outward-looking stance is still resolutely based on the primacy of lived experience and even self-transformation through action. Indeed, this focus on action was clearly so important to some activists that as an internalized disposition it actually threatened my ability as researcher to win their trust and connect with them. The suspicion and "vetting" that I was subject to only underlines this; a professor lacks the capacity to adequately speak with, or for, left groups because he has not entangled himself in struggle or lived injustice.[14] Here again we encounter a paradox of this mode of activism: while globally aware, activists present themselves as not embedded in a particular ideology (not even syndicalism) and *not* shaped by a common history of struggle (against Putin, for example). Their netness is loose and their catness opportunistic or even pluralistic and intersectional.

In their choice of action, connection, and articulation of grievances, they attempt to escape easy incorporation into any of the well-known or visible vehicles of opposition in Russia today—be it nationalism, the co-opted Left (systemic parties), the so-called liberal intelligentsia opposition. They would likely think of Tilly's brokerage as too static a conceptualization because it presupposes a fixity of positions, rather than their experience of a more contingent, uncertain politics. This is a version of nomadic activism that evokes the theorizing of late capitalism and the resistance to its engine, the state, by Deleuze and Guattari (1987) and others. For Paolo Virno, movement and mobility—characterized as the potential for "defection"—become more important as tactics of resistance than are traditional modes of activism bundled as openly oppositional protest (2004, 76).

* * *

Combining objective and subjective accounts of actors with phenomenological perspectives strikes me as important. In the 1980s, new social movement theories began grappling with the problem of the individual and collective action, cognition, and emotion. This resulted in a different kind of political science pioneered by Alberto Melucci (1989) that would not reduce movements to coherent groups with a structural integrity or imperative. Instead, Melucci highlighted intermediate processes between the levels of individual and of movement. In a sense, this was a parallel approach to that undertaken by Tilly in political sociology's turn toward relational and network modes of inquiry.

Both Melucci's and Tilly's approaches offer points of departure into what I have called the experiential approach to activism. Melucci (1989) writes of the importance of attending to the "submerged" reality of movements, to avoid the abstraction of "networks." Tilly (2001) writes about the "integration of cognitive, relational and environmental." Nonetheless, both Melucci and Tilly are accused of remaining culturally reductionist (Bartholomew and Mayer 1992; Brubaker 2010). In this chapter, I have argued that while shared cognitive motivation is important to networks, the experiential entanglement of activism is also worthy of consideration. This has cognitive, reflective, and also non- or precognitive significance as "lived experience." I describe the experiential side of activism as phenomenological because this emphasizes the importance of intersubjective lifeworlds inhabited by activists.[15] These lifeworlds might have reflexive surfaces in "talk," but they also have prediscursive, prerational foundations (Charlesworth 2000, 4) in the unarticulated embodiment of injustice (the experience of the weight of the courier's backpack, the long-term injuries of class from the auto assembly line), as well as in the shared experience of being in a march, picket, or contentious action.

Activism is considered the beginning of building institutionalization and scaling up movements. But what is missing is a close inquiry into the mechanisms of struggle—the "being in the world" that produces potentiality. This isn't a restatement of agency versus structure in phenomenological clothing.[16] Instead, in showing how entangled activists meet, organize, and further share experiential struggle, I wish to challenge the deterministic interpretation that favors consciousness and intentionality over transformations through social activity. This is also in contrast to encountering the world of contention only at the discursive level—the rebuke of the activist to the professor. The chasm between saying and doing is where most people falter.[17]

Notes

1. *Structural power* refers to one of Erik Olin Wright's (2000) three typologizations of working-class power.

2. Ideally, I would have liked to do "connective ethnography" (Dirksen, Huizing, and Smit 2010), in which researchers connect online with informants as well as doing research physically at a site that includes interviews, participant observation, and other qualitative methods. However, the courier strikes are better described as examples of "virtual ethnography" as my interactions with participants took place online and my tracing of networks and actions by participants relied entirely on online sources.
3. Tilly in turn based *catness* and *netness* on his interpretation of Harrison White's work on group taxonomies to identify where group identities and networks coincide, which the latter called "catnet" (1978, 63).
4. "Salting" as a tactic introducing an activist to a plant to agitate and organize is discussed widely in professional union literature but less in academic work.
5. Interview with KTR employee Dmitrii Kozhnev from April 13, 2013, on RSD's website (Ovsiannikov and Kagarlitskii 2013). This interview details Kozhnev's activist work in Kaluga and gives an idea of the relatively compressed social networking of RSD, KTR, and anti-capitalist activists as well as their literal and political mobility.
6. I use the term *leftist* as a compromise between the common use of *ultraleftist* by the liberal Russian press to describe these activists and the terms they use to describe themselves, which vary from *anti-capitalist* to *socialist* and *communist*.
7. Cf. Tarrow's (1993) discussion of modular transferability during a cycle of contention, where he examines the process of diffusion. For another discussion, see Wada (2012).
8. McAdam, Tarrow, and Tilly make the point that local relations can be contingently strong without being categorical (i.e., knitted through shared identity).
9. Ukraintsev discusses at length the processes of communication, negotiation, and mobilization in a long online stream from August 22, 2020, later published on the small *Luch* YouTube channel run by Marxist-Leninists. He mentions that the couriers couldn't wait and were a driving force of self-organization before his involvement. He also talks about the support received from a spectrum of leftist groups. The previous actions by couriers lend weight to his account. "Общение с председателем профсоюза 'Курьер,'" , August 22, 2020, video, 1:40:55, https://www.youtube.com/watch?v=XpMnSPIUVco&feature=youtu.be.
10. The portal vc.ru featured a call for unionization by a prolific blogger on the problems of "freelance" labor, the new digital precariat, and collective action. ("Курьерам 'Яндекс.Еды' и Delivery Club нужен профсоюз," December 19, 2019, https://vc.ru/legal/98134-kureram-yandeks-edy-i-delivery-club-nuzhen-profsoyuz.)

11. Although it is beyond the scope of the chapter, it is worth highlighting the relevance to labor activism of the effect of social leveling. What I mean by this is that young people increasingly gain a higher education but experience the same precarious experience of work as those without the opportunity of extended schooling. Similarly, the emergence of YouTubers with political agendas indicates complementary leveling-up the other way, with organic intellectuals emerging from their engagement with social media and online resources for self-education.
12. In Russian it is possible to distinguish between *libertarianskii* and *libertarnyi.* In correspondence with me, Ukraintsev requested to clearly distinguish between the former, a non-socialist form of liberalism, and the latter, which can collocate with *socialist.* Online correspondence, December 1, 2020.
13. For a discussion of the view that the failed attempt to create a visible party sufficiently to the left of the Russian Communist Party has "debilitated" leftist politics despite the Left's "potentiality," see Luke March (2017).
14. A draft of this chapter was shared with Ukraintsev, who made some corrections to biographical and ideological details.
15. The term *lifeworld* (after Schütz and the phenomenological tradition more generally) emphasizes the domain of the everyday, immediate social experience and practical activity. See Jackson (1996).
16. James Jasper's work has emphasized the cultural context of social movements and individual agency, as well as emotion (see Jasper 2004, 2007, 2018, respectively). My approach is grounded in phenomenological anthropology, which has points of contact with such cultural turns in social movement research but remains highly suspicious of unqualified terms such as *culture, subjectivity,* and *identity* as points of entry into explaining social phenomena.
17. I owe this insight to an informal discussion in spring 2020 started by Gregory Afinogenov on Trump-era activism in the United States.

Bibliography

Aronoff, Myron J., and Jan Kubik. 2013. *Anthropology and Political Science: A Convergent Approach.* Oxford: Berghahn Books.

Ashwin, Sarah. 1999. *Russian Workers: The Anatomy of Patience.* Manchester: Manchester University Press.

Ashwin, Sarah, and Simon Clarke. 2002. *Russian Trade Unions and Industrial Relations in Transition.* Basingstoke: Palgrave Macmillan.

Bartholomew, Amy, and Margit Mayer. 1992. "Nomads of the Present: Melucci's Contribution to 'New Social Movement' Theory." *Theory, Culture and Society* 9 (4): 141–159.

Biziukov, P. V. 2003. "Al'ternativnye profsoiuzy: tri epokhi." In *Profsojuznoe prostranstvo sovremennoi Rossii*, edited by V. Borisov and S. Klark, 98–125. Moscow: ISITO.

Brubaker, Rogers. 2010. "Charles Tilly as a Theorist of Nationalism." *American Sociology* 41:375–381.

Case, Amber. 2011. "Netness." Wiki entry for the project *Cyborg Anthropology*. Last modified August 17, 2011. http://cyborganthropology.com/Netness.

Charlesworth, S. J. 2000. *A Phenomenology of Working Class Experience*. New York: Cambridge University Press.

Chetvernina, T. 2009. "Trade Unions in Transitional Russia: Peculiarities, Current Status and New Challenges." RRC Working Paper Series 16, Russian Research Center, Institute of Economic Research, Hitotsubashi University, Kunitachi, Japan, June 2009.

Clément, Karine, and Anna Zhelnina. 2020. "Beyond Loyalty and Dissent: Pragmatic Everyday Politics in Contemporary Russia." *International Journal of Politics, Culture, and Society* 33 (7/8): 143–162.

Crowley, Stephen. 2002. "Explaining Labor Quiescence in Postcommunist Europe." Paper presented at the Biannual Conference of Europeanists, Chicago, March 15–17, 2002.

Crowley, Stephen, and Irina Olimpieva. 2016. "Russian Labor Protest in Challenging Economic Times." *Russian Analytical Digest* 182:2–6.

Crowley, Stephen, and David Ost. 2001. *Workers after Workers' States: Labor and Politics in Postcommunist Eastern Europe*. Lanham, MD: Rowman and Littlefield.

Deleuze, Gilles, and Félix Guattari. 1987. *A Thousand Plateaus: Capitalism and Schizophrenia*. Translated by Brian Massumi. Minneapolis: University of Minnesota Press.

Dirksen, V., A. Huizing, and B. J. Smit. 2010. "Piling on Layers of Understanding: The Use of Multiple Methods for the Study of (Online) Work Practices." *New Media & Society* 12 (7): 1045–1063.

Evans, A. B., Jr. 2018. "Protests in Russia: The Example of the Blue Buckets Society." *Demokratizatsiya: The Journal of Post-Soviet Democratization* 26 (1): 3–24.

Gorbach, Denys. 2019. "Underground Waterlines: Explaining Political Quiescence of Ukrainian Labor Unions." *Focaal—Journal of Global and Historical Anthropology* 2019 (84): 33–46.

Greene, Samuel A., and Graeme B. Robertson. 2009. "Politics, Justice and the New Russian Strike." *Journal of Communist and Post-Communist Studies* 43 (1): 33–54.

Henry, Laura. 2006. "Shaping Social Activism in Post-Soviet Russia: Leadership, Organizational Diversity, and Innovation." *Post-Soviet Affairs* 22 (2): 99–124.

Hinz, Sarah, and Jeremy Morris. 2017. "Trade Unions in Transnational Automotive Companies in Russia and Slovakia: Prospects for Working Class Power." *European Journal of Industrial Relations* 23 (1): 97–112.

Hughes, Sarah M. 2016. "Beyond Intentionality: Exploring Creativity and Resistance within a UK Immigration Removal Centre." *Citizenship Studies* 20 (3–4): 427–443.

Jackson, Michael. 1996. "Introduction: Phenomenology, Radical Empiricism, and Anthropological Critique." In *Things as They Are: New Directions in Phenomenological Anthropology*, edited by Michael Jackson, 1–50. Bloomington: Indiana University Press.

Jasper, J. M. 2004. "A Strategic Approach to Collective Action: Looking for Agency in Social Movement Choices." *Mobilization* 9 (1): 1–16.

———. 2007. "Cultural Approaches in the Sociology of Social Movements." In *Handbook of Social Movements across Disciplines*, edited by B. Klandermans and C. Roggeband, 59–109. New York: Springer.

———. 2018. *The Emotions of Protest*. Chicago: University of Chicago Press.

Kolstø, Pål. 2016. "Marriage of Convenience? Collaboration between Nationalists and Liberals in the Russian Opposition, 2011–12." *Russian Review* 75 (4): 645–663.

Kovács, Borbála, Jeremy Morris, Abel Polese, and Drini Imami. 2017. "Looking at the 'Sharing' Economies Concept through the Prism of Informality." *Cambridge Journal of Regions, Economy and Society* 10 (2): 365–378.

Krinsky, John, and Ann Mische. 2019. "Formations and Formalisms: Charles Tilly and the Paradox of the Actor." *Annual Review of Sociology* 39:1–26.

KTR (Konfederatsiia Truda Rossii). 2019. "Kur'ery internet-magazina OZON ob'iavili zabastovku." October 6, 2019. http://ktr.su/content/news/detail.php?ID=6462&fbclid=IwARonIL3f53chGttDdaR3pjgFTTqwy7MNYcsSqAIoY4f-3Fe4ENqdlqhyqik.

Liu, Jin. 2016. "Credibility, Reliability, and Reciprocity: Mobile Communication, Guanxi, and Protest Mobilization in Contemporary China." In *Asian Perspectives on Digital Culture: Emerging Phenomena, Enduring Concepts*, edited by Sun Sun Lim and Cheryll Soriano, 69–84. New York: Routledge.

Mandel, David. 2001. "Why Is There No Revolt? The Russian Working Class and Labor Movement." *Socialist Register* 37 (March): 171–195.

———. 2004. *Labor after Communism: Auto Workers and Their Unions in Russia, Belarus and Ukraine*. Montreal: Black Rose Books.

March, Luke. 2017. "The 'Post-Soviet' Russian Left: Escaping the Shadow of Stalinism?" In *Systemic and Non-systemic Opposition in the Russian Federation*, edited by Cameron Ross, 97–120. Farnham: Ashgate.

Mattingly, C. 2019. "Defrosting Concepts, Destabilizing Doxa: Critical Phenomenology and the Perplexing Particular." *Anthropological Theory* 19 (4): 415–439.

McAdam, D. 2003. "Beyond Structural Analysis: Toward a More Dynamic Understanding of Social Movements." In *Social Movements and Networks: Relational Approaches to Collective Action*, edited by D. McAdam and M. Diani, 281–298. Oxford: Oxford University Press.

McAdam, Doug, Sidney Tarrow, and Charles Tilly. 2001. *Dynamics of Contention*. Cambridge: Cambridge University Press.
Melucci, Alberto. 1989. *Nomads of the Present: Social Movements and Individual Needs in Contemporary Society*. Edited by John Keane and Paul Mier. Philadelphia, PA: Temple University Press.
Olimpieva, Irina. 2012. "Labor Unions in Contemporary Russia: An Assessment of Contrasting Forms of Organization and Representation." *Journal of Labor and Society* 15 (2): 267–283.
Orlova, Galina, and Jeremy Morris. 2020. "City Archipelago: Mapping (Post) Lockdown Moscow through its Heterogeneities." *City & Society* 33 (1). https://anthrosource.onlinelibrary.wiley.com/doi/pdf/10.1111/ciso.12331
Ovsiannikov, Ivan, and Boris Kagarlitskii. 2013. "Vazhno sviazat' teoriiu s neposredstvennym opytom liudei." *Rossiiskoe sotsialisticheskoe dvizhenie*, April 10, 2013. http://anticapitalist.ru/archive/analiz/tovarishhi/dmitrij_kozhnev_%C2%ABvazhno_svyazat_teoriyu_s_neposredstvennyim_opyitom_lyudej%C2%BB.html.
Petlianova, Nina. 2019. "Smert' kur'era." *Novaia gazeta*, April 23, 2019. https://novayagazeta.ru/articles/2019/04/23/80325-smert-kuriera.
Pottinger, Laura. 2017. "Planting the Seeds of a Quiet Activism." *Area* 49 (2): 215–222.
Schecter, Darrow. 1990. "Two Views of the Revolution: Gramsci and Sorel, 1916–1920." *History of European Ideas* 12 (5): 637–653.
Semenov, Andrei. 2017. "Against the Stream: Political Opposition in Russian Regions in the 2012–2016 Electoral Cycle." *Demokratizatsiya: The Journal of Post-Soviet Democratization* 25 (4): 481–502.
Sierra Caballero, Francisco, and Tommaso Gravante. 2018. *Networks, Movements and Technopolitics in Latin America: Critical Analysis and Current Challenges*. Cham: Springer Nature.
Smyth, Regina. 2006. "Strong Partisans, Weak Parties? Assessing the Assumptions of Cohesiveness within Russian Party Organisations." *Comparative Politics* 38 (2): 202–228.
Sovetskoe Televidenie. 2019. "Ia tak liubliu svoiu stranu. . . ." *YouTube*. Interview with Kirill Ukrainstev, recording of livestream, January 18, 2019. https://www.youtube.com/watch?v=LuWm2EZk3WI.
Tarrow, Sidney. 1993. "Modular Collective Action and the Rise of the Social Movement: Why the French Revolution Was Not Enough." *Politics and Society* 21 (1): 647–670.
Tilly, Charles. 1978. *From Mobilization to Revolution*. New York: Random House.
Vinogradova, Elena, Irina Kozina, and Linda Cook. 2012. "Russian Labor. Quiescence and Conflict." *Communist and Post-Communist Studies* 45 (3–4): 219–231.

Virno, Paolo. 2004. *A Grammar of the Multitude: For an Analysis of Contemporary Forms of Life*. Translation by Isabella Bertoletti, James Cascaito, and Andrea Casson. Los Angeles: Semiotext(e).

Wada, Takeshi. 2012. "Modularity and Transferability of Repertoires of Contention." *Social Problems* 59 (4): 544–571.

Weidmann, N. B., and E. G. Rød. 2019. *The Internet and Political Protest in Autocracies*. London: Oxford University Press.

Wright, E. O. 2000. "Working-Class Power: Capitalist Class-Interests, and Class Compromise." *American Journal of Sociology* 105 (4): 957–1002.

Yongshun, Cai. 2006. *State and Laid-Off Workers in Reform China: The Silence and Collective Action of the Retrenched*. London: Routledge.

Jeremy Morris is Professor of Global Studies at Aarhus University. He is author most recently of *Everyday Post-Socialism: Working-Class Communities in the Russian Margins*.

8

Skateboarding Together

Generational Civic Activism and Nontransition to Politics in Sosnovyi Bor

ANNA A. DEKALCHUK AND IVAN S. GRIGORIEV

One of the important effects of the stabilization and economic growth of the years 2000–2009 in Russia was the diversification in consumption patterns of the Russian population and the rise in the subculture-oriented activities among Russian youth. Over time, these processes contributed to the restructuring of urban spaces in response to new visions of everyday life (Zhelnina 2011). In this chapter, we explore patterns of civic activism that emerged among young people who came of age in the 1990s and seek to express their vision of life in surrounding city structures such as skate parks.

Indeed, skateboarding experienced a renaissance in Russia in the 2010s. As of 2019, at least 180 dedicated skate parks existed in Russia, most of them constructed after 2010.[1] Furthermore, whereas initially they mostly featured the more lightweight and movable plywood and steel constructions, later a trend toward building concrete skate parks emerged: twenty-eight such parks were built after 2013, and sixteen of those were constructed in 2018–2019 alone. Skate parks thus become an important element of the modern Russian cityscape.

Building skate parks is complex and expensive.[2] Most concrete parks are proactively provided by local authorities to fulfill state mandates to support youth-related activity and are embedded into existing municipal sports facilities by specialized companies. Of the twenty-eight concrete skate parks in our sample, only ten were financed and owned by private firms. Most of these are located within newly built residential apartment complexes to attract families with children.

This chapter explores an unlikely case of skate-park construction promoted, lobbied for, and built by a local youth community in Sosnovyi Bor, a town eighty kilometers from Saint Petersburg. It took the local skaters ten years to self-organize, lobby for the park, negotiate with the authorities and the city community, secure financing, oversee and take part in the actual construction, and finally go through the tedious and nonobvious process of legalizing the newly built park.

The first section puts our case into the broader theoretical perspective of local civic activism. The second introduces Sosnovyi Bor, the setting for our case study. We use the third and fourth sections to describe the activists behind the effort to build the skate park and then focus on the actual campaign in the fifth and sixth. Our analysis is based on thirteen semi-structured interviews with local skaters, representatives of the broader youth community, and the local deputies and the town administration officials involved in the process. We supplement these interviews with local media reports and extensive insider knowledge.

Skate Park as a Sandbox for Civic and Political Activism

Before the 2010s, skateboarding in Russia was largely a street culture activity. As such, it created significant damage and disruption to city infrastructure. As Howell (2008, 476), in his description of the US experience, puts it, "Without sanctioned places to practice, skateboarders had been occupying parking lots, empty swimming pools, drainage ditches, plazas, sidewalks, streets, schoolyards, building foundations, and just about any other paved space they could get their wheels on. Municipalities have tended to perceive this occupation as an impediment to traffic flows and as a potential danger to pedestrians and the skateboarders themselves."

Using street furniture, stairs, and handrails also causes structural damage. As a result, urban managers came to see skate parks as a solution to a range of skateboarder-related problems. The urge to control and contain the damage created by the skaters motivates and explains the local communities' involvement and, in fact, leading role in constructing skate parks—a development we also observe in Russia.

Unlike an uncontrollable force that should be contained, skaters themselves are also interested in promoting skate parks they can use. Yet it is rare that we observe the skater community lobbying for and getting their skate parks built where the local authorities are not proactively promoting one. This pattern makes the case of Sosnovyi Bor a remarkable success story for local activism and an important example of the activist provision of collective goods.[3]

What makes such successful collective action by the skater community hard to achieve is the peculiar nature of the skate park as a *public good* that can be used simultaneously by many skaters and that no one can be denied access to. Furthermore, skateboarders also face the problem of self-organization to achieve their interests. While they may share an interest in building the park, mobilizing to secure support is difficult. It takes effort for the group to define common interests and pursue political support. The process is especially hard since most skaters are young people without political representation or voice in community matters (Farthing 2010; Weller 2006). It takes time to earn political standing in the community, and throughout this process, the skaters must preserve group cohesion while learning how to engage in political decision-making.

Meanwhile, for city residents, the cost of building parks is dispersed, but the negative effects produced by a noisy skate park in the neighborhood are not.[4] As costs shift from urban streets to specific neighborhoods, they often produce NIMBY (not in my backyard) activism. When that happens, neighborhood leaders can serve as entrepreneurs who personify the public opposition to a skate park, informing both residents and city officials and creating new hurdles to hinder the skater community.

Finally, as the whole process becomes public, skaters must convince the policymakers that building a skate park would counterbalance the negative externalities they produce. Simultaneously, they must convince the rest of the community that they are working toward a public benefit and are a constructive and useful group that *deserves* support. Launching a public campaign is hard, and citizens often perceive skateboarders as undeserving, unproductive, and antisocial. The community's natural reaction is to suppress their activities and limit their perceived deviant behavior instead of encouraging it (Schneider and Ingram 1993).

As we show, Sosnovyi Bor was a success story in all of these respects: the skater community managed to stay united as the skaters were growing up, to frame a positive plan and present it to the community, to learn to work with the Mayor's Office and City Council, and ultimately to have their park built and go fully operational in 2019. Building the skate park proved a successful political action and possibly a springboard for the youth groups' future political engagement. Yet in our interviews the activists, despite having accumulated the resources and know-how to convert their social standing into political influence, revealed a consistent aversion to politics throughout the construction process and even after success. They wished to continue their social activities and participate in community decision-making—without engaging in politics.

This result contributes to the discussion exploring the linkages between social movements and political engagement and is consistent with the argument that civic activism may preempt political participation and political activism (Eliasoph 1998). We add to the discussion on how civic activism preempts political participation by showing its cultural embeddedness: the activists show aversion to politics, which is culturally rooted and is a matter of their core nonconformist values and beliefs rather than of any practicality. Not going into politics for them is conditioned by their values, rather than by insurmountable structural obstacles. In the conclusion, we relate this observation to broader themes of civic activism in Russia developed in this volume.

Conditions for Activist Success: Emergence of Local Identity and Sosnovyi Bor's Opportunity Structure

To explore the structural and institutional factors that led to this success, we focus our research on Sosnovyi Bor, a small nuclear town some eighty kilometers west of Saint Petersburg.[5] For much of its history, Sosnovyi Bor was a closed city. To enter the town, one would have to be a registered resident or have a special pass.[6] During the Soviet period, closed status implied better supplies and generally a more comfortable living. The city also adopted a Scandinavian-like approach to city planning, integrating infrastructure into the natural landscape dominated by pine trees growing on the Baltic dunes. As a result, Sosnovyi Bor was a desirable place to stay and start a family.

Typical of many closed cities, Sosnovyi Bor grew from a small settlement in 1970 to a medium-sized city of around fifty thousand by 1990. Those who relocated were mostly young specialists: recent technical school and university graduates placed at the nuclear power plant for their first jobs, or scholars and engineers placed at the newly established research facilities. These early settlers, now in their sixties and seventies, came from all over the Soviet Union.

The closed city and relatively small population produced a close-knit community with a compressed social geography typical of cities in the former Soviet Union (Morris 2016). The people are aware of the town's situation, informed enough to control the local authorities, and integrated enough to exercise influence. The political and economic elite that rose to prominence in the 1990s comes from among the first settlers. They keep close informal relations with the rest of the town's population with whom they share the experience of settling in. They buy groceries in the same shops, used to live in the same late-Soviet apartment buildings, and remain connected to the rest of the community through the multitude of connections typical of small towns. These dense networks define the political context of Sosnovyi Bor and the civic identities of its residents.

City life is also significantly informed by the economic structure of the city. The state is the largest employer, offering jobs at eight research facilities, the nuclear power plant belonging to the state corporation Rosatom, and LSK Radon, which is part of the federal agency for construction, among other places. At the same time, a few enterprises are privately owned, including ZAO ECOMET-S, a nuclear waste processing facility, and, most importantly, Titan-2, a construction company that builds new generating units.[7] In contrast to the state-owned enterprises, Titan-2 is active in politics. The firm has consistently followed a strategy of active local entrenchment and strong community embeddedness to secure ongoing contracts to service the power plant and build its new units.[8] As a result, much of the political leadership in town originates from Titan's top management. Some functionaries even spilled over into regional politics.[9]

This public-private ownership structure created a precarious balance in Sosnovyi Bor's local politics and defined a relatively open political process. Without this economic competition, Sosnovyi Bor would probably be just another company town entirely dominated by the power plant's leadership and thus responsive to Rosatom rather than to its population. However, by participating in the open democratic process controlled by the local forces, Titan managed to establish its control over the town in the first place while also keeping national players out. Therefore, Titan is strongly interested in sustaining the relative openness of the political process, which secures its stronger standing even as it makes politics more transparent and responsive to citizens than it would have been otherwise—an effect strongly reinforced by the local community's peculiar cohesion.

The town's unique generational dynamics enhances this relative openness. The early settlers who arrived at approximately the same time found themselves in a political void. They built the town and established networks and stable social connections in the 1970s–1980s. After the collapse of the Soviet Union, this generation defined the new political and economic reality of Sosnovyi Bor. The transition reinforced the influence of the 1970s' generation throughout the 1990s and the years 2000–2009 (Gel'man and Travin 2016), and the first settlers still effectively retain control over the town's political life. As a result, community governance emerged as a dialogue between a strong state, embodied in the power plant, and a strong society. Titan-2, a company created by the early settlers, can be seen as an instrument for the society to protect its control over local politics.

By the 2010s, the early settlers faced the challenge of generational change as their children came of age. This second cohort, born in the 1980s, grew up in

Sosnovyi Bor and therefore had a stronger shared identity than their parents. Their group identity was defined by shared cultural experiences: their exposure to punk, grunge, heavy metal music, and urban sports activities such as roller-skating, skateboarding, and BMX biking. It would later also be supplemented by values typical of nonconformist youth, including claims over public spaces and freedom from external control (Krutskikh 2019). This identity formed initially as belonging to the same age cohort. It was articulated collectively through local punk and heavy metal bands rehearsing in the late-Soviet concert halls built by their parents in the 1980s. By the years 2000–2009, this second generation produced a constellation of local activists whose development we document in this chapter, beginning with the story of their early experiences in the next section.

The Formative Years

The activists lobbying for a skate park in Sosnovyi Bor were not teenagers. In fact, they were in their late twenties to early thirties, born in the 1980s and raised together in the 1990s—the generation influenced by the MTV channel, which began broadcasting in Russia in 1998 (Garza 2008, 221–222; Omel'chenko 2012, 248). Many still believe the channel to have "sowed the seeds of new knowledge and good taste in people," "inspired and explained," and "talked to you as if you were its old buddy" (Dud' 2018).[10] The channel exposed Russian teens to the world of Western music, pop culture, and extreme sports.

This cultural exposure felt like a revolution across Russia, including in Sosnovyi Bor. As one of our respondents recalls: "Do not forget that we were at the turning point, [living] in the transformative period when it was all becoming popular. We were influenced by these fashion and culture when this was being conceived [in Russia]. Why was it so popular to wear Adidas T-Mac VI? Because they were Yankee, because B-boys [wore them]. It had even to do with clothing. We were buying [stuff] in the Pionerskaia secondhand fare and then wearing it for ages. And I got the confiscated Doc Martens' shoes somewhat [semi-legally]" (activist interview, August 7, 2019).

This revolution had a substantial impact on the town. In the early years of the first decade of the twenty-first century, Sosnovyi Bor becomes a center of gravity for the young people from Saint Petersburg and the broader Leningradskaya region but also from the rest of the country. The town was well known for its *Korobka*[11] skate park, with its diverse metal elements and a metal half-pipe and its active community (or *tusovka*) of roller-skaters, skaters, graffiti artists, B-boys, DJs, and music bands. An annual festival, Street Adrenaline Zona LAES, launched in 1999, reinforced the town's reputation and status.[12] The festival was believed to be the first event of its kind in the country to bring together youngsters from the neighboring regions who were crazy about the new street culture and extreme sports (Dolgikh 2015; for more details, see *Roller.Ru* 2005).

Even though this may sound too ambitious for a small town, it is still how those who were eleven to nineteen at that time remember the turn of the century. In a TV interview, one skate-park activist noted: "We are now the 9th concrete skate park in Russia. Yet, we have every chance to become what we once were: 15 years ago, we were the capital of extreme sports in Russia because our metal skate park was the first to open in Russia" (stv24news 2016c).

This heyday of street culture would prove short-lived. By the years 2007–2009, the skate park was in decay. It would later be relocated from the open hockey rink to the city sports center's backyard, where it attracted fewer and fewer newcomers. The last Street Adrenaline festival took place in 2004. According to one of the organizers, the city administration stopped providing any assistance around 2005 (activist interview, August 3, 2018; activist interview, August 14, 2019)—a tectonic shift compared to the active administrative support and $3,000–$4,000 in financial assistance that funded the first two festivals in 1999 and 2000 (*Delovoi Peterburg* 2000).

One plausible explanation for this change of heart is rooted in the network-based governance described above. The primary organizers of the first two festivals were the early settlers. They occupied positions at LAES and relied on the personal support of Mayor Valeriy Nekrasov to launch the festival (*Delovoi Peterburg* 2000; *Roller.Ru* 2005). As this older generation stepped aside in 2001–2002, the younger organizers lacked the close connections with both LAES and the local authorities to keep the festival afloat. High personnel turnover in the city hall among the civil servants who were charged with running youth and sports programs also complicated interactions with the administration (activist interview, August 14, 2019).

Despite fewer events and their declining visibility, the tusovka did not disintegrate completely (activist interview, September 11, 2018). After graduating from high school, many of these teenagers decided to stay in the town and enrolled in one of the two technical schools (*PTUs*) or the local branches of the Saint Petersburg universities. Moreover, many of those who had left to study in Saint Petersburg returned after graduation. Those who did not leave for good considered themselves to be a part of a distinct tusovka with a shared identity. The group spent a lot of time skating and coaching the younger generation, making music, drawing graffiti, and gathering at the Batareinaia Bukhta, a beautiful bay fifteen minutes away from Sosnovyi Bor. They also engaged in the midsummer Youth Day events organized by the city administration and LAES (activist interview, August 6, 2018). On a symbolic level, these activities showed their engagement and aspiration for a stronger ownership over the town.

The New Generation of Activists

One early manifestation of these ownership claims was a 2007 street art event. On a summer night, a group of graffiti artists painted the huge ugly concrete letter blocks forming the town's name at the entry to Sosnovyi Bor with colorful stripes. This action embraced their claim to the city and showed their strong emotional attachment to it. The act also symbolized their desire to create something good for the town. They called the event an act of "kind vandalism." Despite knowing that their action was illegal (activist interview, August 14, 2019), they also did not try to hide; they uploaded a series of photos from the event on VKontakte, the Russian analogue of Facebook.[13]

By 2020, these "vandals" headed one of the most successful socially oriented NGOs in Sosnovyi Bor, Studio Gorgona.[14] Ironically, the NGO's most well-known project today is STOPVANDAL, which aims at changing the attitudes of the city residents toward their common spaces, such as the entrances of their apartment blocks, bus stops (see fig. 8.1), and the city beach.[15] The regional authorities commissioned the NGO to paint and decorate the town bus stops, reclaiming them from ads, leaflets, and graffiti. Now each bus stop has a unique look and a small plaque detailing the history of the surrounding area (activist interview, July 31, 2018). Working with municipal cultural organizations, Studio Gorgona also fights tagging by providing young artists with legal spots to draw. The name they chose for the central spot, Art Dvor Adrenaline (Art Yard Adrenaline) refers to the activists' shared experience of participating in the Street Adrenaline festivals.[16]

Those involved in the NGO activities believe that all of this became possible in 2013 after the amendments to the Nonprofit Organizations Act. The amendments were widely criticized by the Russian NGO sector and Russian and Western scholars because they limit international collaboration (Bogdanova, Cook, and Kulmala 2018). But local activists report that this law has had significant positive implications, providing legal standing and recognition from the authorities. Newly registered NGOs became eligible for funding from state-sponsored programs like the Presidential Grants for developing civil society and local grant programs run by Rosatom and LAES. With this new status, they are now able "to launch a dialogue with the city administration or the president, if you would like, on a legal level" (activist interview, August 3, 2018).

Figure 8.1. Bus stop with a plaque in Kandikjulja, a village a five-minute drive from Sosnovyi Bor, painted by the Studio Gorgona NGO. Image credit: Gorgona Studio Nikodim Antoninov.

The idea that voice, funding, and success are only possible if the organization is registered is now so salient for the leadership of Studio Gorgona that they have launched a second nonprofit. The organization is called Sosnovyi Bronx, the tusovka's nickname for the town during their high school years (activist interview, July 31, 2018). Sosnovyi Bronx provides legal assistance to young city dwellers seeking to register and promote their social initiatives. In his interview for the local newspaper, Nikodim Antoninov, the major driver behind the activities of the NGO, notes, "Today we are focusing not solely on the drawing. We are trying to spark the civic initiatives and organizations in the town which could exist legally and receive funding. We are trying to wake them up because many people in our town sit at home and do nothing while they could have pushed through their ideas and projects" (Doronina 2018). This ethic and shared identity are clear in the NGO's motto: "Discover your town's culture. You are a part of it."

The city administration has been keenly supporting the activities of these two NGOs for two major reasons. The first one has to do with their zeal, self-reliance, and ability to raise money through diverse regional and federal state-sponsored programs, a focus promoted among town-based NGOs since late

2014 (local official interview, August 13, 2019). Almost all our respondents argue that the administration's role is usually reduced to approving projects that target the town's property (like bus stops) or writing letters of support and recommendations when these NGOs apply for grants. To illustrate this point, in his interview, a representative of the local authorities notes that he "cannot recall them asking for money to buy spray paint even once" (local official interview, February 21, 2019). Second and no less important for the administration is that both NGOs aim to provide pure public goods and care for the local commons (local official interview, March 3, 2019).

Studio Gorgona and Sosnovyi Bronx create positive services for the town and also a positive image for the tusovka, which is still sometimes referred to as the *neformalnaya* youth (or *neformaly*) by the broader public. In the late 1990s, this label was popular among the Russian youth and helped to distinguish skaters, roller-skaters, graffiti artists, B-boys, and the like from Russian skinheads or *gopniks* and to point out their choice for an alternative lifestyle. But when the media or the local officials use the term today to label the activists, it seems to bear a negative connotation of something shadowy, covert, or even illegal. This connotation is rooted in the late Soviet period, when the young Komsomol bureaucrats coined the notion to label "self-organized youth groups which positioned themselves as 'the Other' in relation to the formal structures, those of the Pioneers, the Komsomol and the Communists" (Omel'chenko 2006, 162; Pilkington 1994, 113–161).

As one respondent argues, the term defines the attitudes they act against: "The word *neformaly* is a dumb word. These people [from the administration] know little [about the street culture] and for them we are neformaly. Why is it so?" (activist interview, August 6, 2018). Entering their thirties, these activists now strive to show that while they are different, they still deserve to be a part of the town, that they are not something shadowy or out of place, something that must be hidden.

Let the Park Be—or Not?

The lobbying activities surrounding the skate-park construction and led by the town's skaters from the tusovka also aimed at changing the authorities' and population's attitudes toward the skaters—to use the 1990s catchphrase popular in the United States, they wanted to show that "skateboarding is not a crime." Yet these activists also needed to secure extensive administrative support and substantial financial contributions. The skate park would also be much less visible for city residents than were the colorful bus stops or other initiatives by Studio Gorgona. This civic initiative required a change in interaction between the activists and the administration—from a peaceful and mutually beneficial coexistence to a complicated transactional relationship.

While the turn of the century saw the Korobka skate park attracting many teenage roller-skaters and skaters spurred on by the Street Adrenaline festivals,[17] the years 2005–2010 was a period of stagnation for the extreme-sports movement in Sosnovyi Bor (stv24news 2019a). Tellingly, hardly anyone interviewed for this study recalls the year when the metal elements from the open hockey rink found their new home in the backyard of the SKK city sports center (Sportivno-Kulturnyi Kompleks, the Sports and Culture Facility—an abbreviation used in Russia for most such structures). It happened in 2011 (activist interview, August 6, 2018), but by that time, the Korobka park had already been in disrepair for several years, and the skaters had taken to the town's streets anyway.

Relocating the park to the SKK's backyard had proved difficult and involved negotiations between the local authorities and the LAES administration (local official interview, August 13, 2019). Yet even after getting a place to perform their tricks, the skaters were still not fully satisfied, and they insisted that they needed a big concrete base for their movable metal and plywood elements, built specifically for the skate park (activist interview, August 6, 2018; local official interview, August 13, 2019). This idea of building a specialized skate park in the town was first articulated as early as in 2010 by Leonid Zaitsev, one of the town's most experienced skaters and a major engine behind the park's construction (stv24news 2015b). Since then, he and his fellow skaters have lobbied the city administration to provide a new skate park. How would they do it?

Through active engagement in organizing the city-sponsored Youth Days, they have become personally acquainted with the administration and the civil servants in charge of dealing with the youth, sports, and culture. However, the first half of the 2010s showed that having those connections was not enough (activist interview, August 6, 2018), so activists pursued all possible strategies to make their campaign visible. One of them joined the Sosnovyi Bor TV station STV to cover skateboarding. And indeed, although the number of TV spots about city skaters and the metal skate park did not increase per se, their substance and tone changed. Having a fellow skater on the STV team provided activists with a platform to broadcast their message to the administration and the community.[18] The message was straightforward: demand for a new park came not from the older skaters (who should have had better things to do with their adult lives) but rather from a socially much more deserving group (Schneider and Ingram 1993)—a younger generation who did not want to damage curbs, monument bases, and other pieces of infrastructure while performing their tricks (stv24news 2014b).

The actual window of opportunity for a full-scale campaign opened in spring 2014 when the concrete fencing around SKK began to disintegrate, posing a safety hazard. Activists used this event to frame the situation as a pressing demand by young residents: "Since there are a lot of kids skating here, there is a direct threat to their lives" (stv24news 2014b). The administration reacted quickly and promised relocation to a brand-new skate park. The authorities' rapid reaction was also shaped by LAES (legally, the owner of the SKK sports center), which made it clear to both the skaters and city hall that they no longer wanted this land used as a skating spot (stv24news 2014b; local official interview, August 13, 2019).

The relocation of the park elements was planned to take a month since the new location, an asphalt skating ground in the residential area, was not ready. However, once it became clear what the new location would be, the neighborhoods close to the proposed park launched a large-scale NIMBY campaign against the construction, pointing to the noise pollution that skating produces (activist interview, August 6, 2018). Throughout the spring and summer of 2014, the tenant leaders brought piles of identically worded signed petitions to the city hall. By summer 2015, it became clear that the NIMBY campaign made it impossible for the administration to proceed as planned (local official interview, August 13, 2019): the skaters' concentrated benefits collided with the NIMBYs' concentrated costs.

To maintain momentum, the skaters made another move: despite the unsafe conditions of their old skating spot, in summer 2014, they opened an extreme-sports school, eXcourse, for the kids who wanted to master the art of skateboarding (stv24news 2014c), demonstrating the pressing demand for a skate park (local official interview, August 13, 2019). The school was a follow-up to the TV show *eXcourse*, which aired on STV in 2012–2013.[19] By early 2015, one of the school's students won third place in a regional skate contest. In the TV spot reporting the victory, contest participants and the reporter argued that the skate park in Vsevolozhsk, the town where the contest took place, was what Sosnovyi Bor needed for the kids to get proper coaching (stv24news 2015b).

Effectively, the skaters' campaign proved there was a demand for a new park from the community. At the same time, the NIMBY campaign demonstrated that moving the park into one of the city's existing sports facilities would not be an option. In this context, it was very timely that the former minister Aleksei Kudrin's Committee for Civic Initiatives and the European University at Saint Petersburg launched a program of experimental participatory budgeting in

Sosnovyi Bor. The program provided activists with a final piece of leverage to gain support for a new park (stv24news 2014a; Dimke, Shilov, and Grebenshchikova 2016). The activists applied for funding twice. First, in early 2015, they failed, but they showed their resolve to attract some financial support of their own. Then in early 2016, they succeeded to secure four million rubles of support for a project to build an open shed for the park. Importantly, by that time the construction of the park itself had started, and the idea of a shed made much more sense (stv24news 2016b, 2016c).[20]

Winning Over the Authorities

In October 2015, the contractor began construction preparations in a remote area close to the city beach (stv24news 2015a). Some of those involved in the lobbying process attribute this sudden breakthrough to the advent of the new city mayor, Vladimir Sadovskii, previously the CEO of a company related to Titan (activist interview, August 5, 2018; activist interview, September 11, 2018). To get the new mayor on board, the activists approached him directly and invited him to look at the training conditions at SKK. They admitted that the park was noisy but argued that it was wrong that they had been "pushed out from the town." At this moment, the authorities made the decision to build a solid concrete skate park (local official interview, March 3, 2019). Our respondents agree that Sadovskii considered the skate park his signature project (activist interview, August 6, 2019; activist interview, September 11, 2018; local official interview, August 13, 2019).

Mayoral support was also critical to secure funding. Since the town's coffers could not support the project, the mayor secured charitable donations from its biggest enterprises.[21] The main parts of the park, built by the professionals from the two companies affiliated with Titan and the skaters themselves, were completed by mid-August 2016.[22] On August 13, 2016, the skate park was inspected and unofficially opened by the mayor, the Speaker of the City Council, the deputy governor of the Leningradskaya region, and the heads of LAES and Titan (stv24news 2016a). The skate park was nearly complete: it had to be fenced, put into operation, and transferred in operative management to an activist-established NGO legally charged with running it. Registering the NGO would also allow the activists to unfreeze the funding obtained through the participatory budgeting instrument in 2016 and to start building a shed over the park (activist interview, September 11, 2018; local official interview, February 21, 2019; local official interview, March 3, 2019; local official interview, August 13, 2019).

It would take two and a half years to complete these steps, as 2017 brought technical and legal complications. The DIY construction method meant that some of the necessary technological solutions had not been used, and in 2017 the concrete surface started to generate dust, making it almost impossible to use the park. And since the skate park was not fit for skating, it was legally impossible to put it into operation. The situation was complicated by the administration's reluctance to provide additional budgetary funds to repair the surface (Selin 2016). Finally, the activists themselves contributed to the alienation of the authorities by launching a widespread complaining campaign that city hall civil servants perceived as uncooperative and unfair (local official interview, February 21, 2019).

As a result, by early 2018 the city administration was considering transferring the skate park onto the balance sheet of the municipal youth center, Dialogue (stv24news 2018), run by much older people with no interest in sustaining skateboard culture (activist interview, August 6, 2018). By relying on a deputy in the City Council whom they had known since their university studies, the activists managed to avoid this scenario. As early as in April 2018, this deputy put the skate park's transfer on the agenda of the permanent deputy committee for social issues. After hearing the administration representatives, she explicitly requested "the City Hall to finally decide which organization would be charged with running the skate park" (TERA-Studiia Teleradiokompaniia 2018). At that moment, though, because the activists had not yet registered their own NGO, the Dialogue youth center was the only organization available to accept responsibility for the park's management. This was the moment when fellow activists and friends from Studio Gorgona and Sosnovyi Bronx provided crucial support.

In summer 2018, the latter actively helped settle legal issues and register a nonprofit organization charged with running the concrete skate park. And then by autumn 2018 the skaters and the leadership of Studio Gorgona decided that there was no need to establish another NGO and that the Sosnovyi Bronx center would be happy to have the skate park in operative management (activist interview, September 11, 2018). Meanwhile, in July 2018 the skaters were finally able to secure additional funding to repair the concrete surface and fencing (the total sum amounted to 1.7 million rubles from the town's coffers), and in early 2019 the concrete skate park was finally transferred to the balance sheet of the city's Committee for Managing Municipal Property and put into operation. Sosnovyi Bronx was awarded operative management (stv24news 2019b).

The skaters and the Sosnovyi Bronx center immediately submitted several applications for regional and federal grants to introduce skate-park

Figure 8.2. The concrete skate park next to the city beach in Sosnovyi Bor, painted by the Studio Gorgona NGO. Image credit: Gorgona Studio Nikodim Antoninov.

improvements, including sealing the surface with special paint, building a small office for the park administration, and installing benches, lighting, and surveillance cameras (see fig. 8.2). These efforts secured an award of a million rubles from the Presidential Grants fund. The work was done before a big festival to celebrate the fact that skateboarding had become an Olympic sport and, of course, the new skate park (activist interview, August 6, 2019; activist interview, August 14, 2019).

The two-day Street Olympic festival took place on August 17–18, 2019. It incorporated everything from the 2000–2005 Street Adrenaline festivals: extreme-sports contests, performances by B-boys and graffiti artists, DJs, and local bands.[23] Even the organizers were the same, albeit fifteen years older (activist interview, August 6, 2019; activist interview, August 14, 2019). One of the participants of the festival described his feelings about the event: "In my childhood, we had such events. These were the 2000s and the Street Adrenaline fest at Korobka. And I am so happy that this is happening for us again. We have become grown-ups already, and now it is the third generation of kids growing up and learning new sports and tricks here" (stv24news 2019a). This shared identity was key to the construction of the concrete skate park—a major success for activists united not only by the common cause but also by a common past and common values.

Conclusion

Development of activism in Russia seems to follow an evolutionary trajectory from no activism or activism only for existential reasons (such as striking and blocking roads to fight wage arrears in the 1990s) to nonpolitical activism seeking narrow community goals, political protest, and political activism (Robertson 2013; Gorokhovskaia 2018; Smyth 2020). Our chapter shows how infrapolitical practices such as graffiti and music festivals can forge networks, resources, and identities that sparked activism to provide particularistic goods and, finally, formal organization.[24]

In the case of Sosnovyi Bor, we observe all of the necessary conditions for that development to occur: the group-level factors facilitating the skaters' collective action, as well as an open opportunity structure that included a network-based governance structure, balance between the major economic entities, and partnership with the mayor. We also observe all the necessary process-related conditions: the skaters managed to self-organize, strike strategic alliances with potential partners and the authorities, and fence off the opponents' attempts to thwart their campaign (Tarrow 1989). As a result, the case we describe falls squarely into the second-generation nonpolitical local activism. Still, the progression seems to stop there, as the activists expressly seek no institutionalized direct political engagement.

This finding is consistent with the argument that civic activism does not always translate directly into political participation and political activism (Eliasoph 1998). Yet, in the context that we study, it is surprising. First, if anything, managing to have the skate park built should have proved that politics, however imperfect, works. The activists seem to understand the benefits of political engagement: a telling episode is one of the leaders of Studio Gorgona publicly reproaching the new mayor Mikhail Voronkov for not inviting the NGO's representatives to the local anti-vandalism commission.

Second, the hurdles and setbacks the project faced over the years have proved that politics matters. Having a stronger and more self-reliant political standing (which could be earned by becoming a local deputy, for instance) could help overcome the hurdles that still lie ahead. As we show above, the political process remains relatively open, and our interviews (not reported in this chapter) show that youths do get elected to the City Council in Sosnovyi Bor. Even if the skate-park activists do not consider running themselves, they could still promote candidates from the tusovka and help them get elected. However, the young local politicians who run and even get elected are not part of the local nonconformist youth community.

Finally, the resources, know-how, and reputation the activists have accumulated over the years could be converted into stronger self-reliant political standing. Instead of taking that path, the activists reject such possibility point-blank simply as a matter of their self-declared aversion to politics (even despite their obvious involvement in some community-level political activities). The most neutral terms the activists use to explain their attitude toward politics are that it is a "dirty business" they would never go into and that politicians are "hypocritical comrades" they could never become. As one of the activists exclaimed: "Why would I waste resources [becoming a politician] when I can create something unique? I am not sure I would be excited to be behind curbs' maintenance, for instance. And what for? How would I motivate myself? [Politics] is simply a waste of one's life energy, lucid mind, and a positive attitude. There are good people there who could have spent their time on something good but must spend it on the paperwork instead."

Importantly, in our case, the activists were not driven away from politics by any prior negative experiences, and they seem to have a broader political agenda extending beyond building the skate park. Their generation simply happens to adhere to antipolitical values and despise formal politics. This depoliticization is the main reason this generation stays out of politics. Their culture and values (Willis 1978) prevent them from the power they could have if they refocused their energy.

Notes

The Basic Research Program at the National Research University Higher School of Economics funded this research.

1. The authors collected these data from open sources. FK-Ramps, Russia's biggest skate-park design firm (in business since 2005), claims to have built 450 objects overall (which include indoor and outdoor skateboarding and BMX cycling facilities).
2. The price tag can vary by a factor of ten: from the equivalent of tens of thousands of dollars to many hundreds of thousands.
3. A similar process unfolded in the skate-park construction in Rostov-na-Donu, where two sisters, Alina and Maria Vyskrebentsevy (both students at the Rostov University), launched a campaign to build a skate park, raised sufficient funds, and connected city authorities to a construction company.
4. These include noise, vandalism, deviant behavior related to nonconformism, and insubordination (Woolley and Johns 2001; Németh 2006; Chiu 2009), as well as an increased burden on public health care (Macdonald et al. 2006).
5. Comparable cases include other nuclear towns and the so-called *Naukograds*: Soviet-era closed towns hosting secret research facilities.

6. This restriction ended very recently. Now to enter the town, one must produce a passport at border control.
7. On December 29, 2017, *Vedomosti* reported that half of Titan's voting shares were sold to *Rosenergoatom*, *Rosatom*'s subsidiary.
8. In all other nuclear monotowns in Russia, contractors who rebuild power plants are all directly owned by *Rosatom*.
9. For example, one of the Titan's executive officers, who is also the former longtime mayor, served as vice chairman of Leningradskaya region's Legislative Council.
10. Yury Dud', one of the most influential YouTube bloggers in Russia and a member of this generation, titled his documentary *MTV—The Main Channel of our Childhood*.
11. *Khokeynaya korobka* (literally, a hockey box) is Russian for open hockey rinks. The skate park initially was stationed in the rink.
12. See the piece written for the roller.ru website by one of the participants of the Second Street Adrenaline festival in August 2000 (2 Международный Фестиваль Экстремальной Культуры 2000).
13. Commenting on the uploaded photos, one of the participants noted, "It is still there. We worried it would not last even a week, and yet. The authorities liked it. In the local newspaper, this was presented almost as a gift to the town" (Vladimirov 2007).
14. The name comes from the tag originally used by the two cofounders when they were graffiti artists who met and worked together in the late 1990s.
15. See the project's public page on VKontakte (Dvizhenie STOPWANDAL n.d.).
16. See the project's public page on VKontakte (Art Dwor n.d.).
17. The 2002 amateur video profile is still available on YouTube (Sosnovy Bor Video 2012).
18. One of the activists says it provided an opportunity "to draw even more attention to skateboarding" and "to say it out loud that there is skateboarding in the town" (activist interview, September 11, 2018), thus reiterating the narrative of the youths' wish to have their ownership of the town recognized by the rest of the community.
19. Hosted by Leonid Zaitsev and Sergey Krainov, another experienced skater, the show presented a series of master classes that taught the audience how to perform tricks. (See, e.g., the first episode of the show, Bazara NET 2012.)
20. Skate parks typically have no sheds. However, because it has just about seventy-eight sunny days a year, with temperatures about or below zero between November and early April, if it did not have a shed over it, the park would be inaccessible for skaters for most of the year.
21. We assume that building the skate park as a DIY project assisted by the big businesses located in the town (*metodom narodnoi stroiki*) was the only way

forward since it was much cheaper for the local budget and allowed the authorities to avoid engaging in public procurement procedures. This solution also insulated the city hall from accusations of frivolous spending while overlooking more urgent projects demanded by the general public, such as the refurbishment of a nursery school.

22. The video about the construction process is available online (Bazara NET 2018).
23. Video of the festival is available at https://www.youtube.com/watch?v=4PQ-vZ_1Hlg.
24. These networks and resources would include not only the enduring ties of friendship within the tusovka but also informal ties to the town's decision-makers used by the activists to gain access to policymaking. As Morris, Semenov, and Smyth mention in the introductory chapter, resorting to these informal personal mechanisms can be in itself seen as an infrapolitical practice adopted to navigate through the political environment and to solve problems that cannot be effectively solved through formal procedures.

Bibliography

Art Dwor. n.d. VK. Accessed September 1, 2022. https://vk.com/artdwor.

Bazara NET, dir. 2012. "EXkurs #1." To chatter, video, 6:03, December 18, 2012. https://www.youtube.com/watch?v=CzoIpDj77yQ.

———. 2018. "Gluhovka Skatepark." To chatter, video, 2:38, May 7, 2018. https://www.youtube.com/watch?v=iO3bTHyIBz4.

Bogdanova, Elena, Linda J. Cook, and Meri Kulmala. 2018. "The Carrot or the Stick? Constraints and Opportunities of Russia's CSO Policy." *Europe-Asia Studies* 70 (4): 501–513. https://doi.org/10.1080/09668136.2018.1471803.

Chiu, Chihsin. 2009. "Contestation and Conformity: Street and Park Skateboarding in New York City Public Space." *Space and Culture* 12, no. 1 (February): 25–42. https://doi.org/10.1177/1206331208325598.

Delovoi Peterburg. 2000. "LAES Vedet Zdorovyi Obraz Zhizni." August 18, 2000. https://www.dp.ru/a/2000/08/18/LAJES_vedet_zdorovij_obraz.

Dimke, Dar'ia, Lev Shilov, and Tat'iana Grebenshchikova. 2016. *Partitsipatornoe biudzhetirovanie: Kak privlech' grazhdan k upravleniiu gorodom?* Saint Petersburg: Evropeyskii universitet v Sankt-Peterburge. https://eu.spb.ru/images/RESPUBLICA/PB/PB_booklet_e.pdf.

Dolgikh, Ekaterina. 2015. "Tsvetnaia skazka." *Gazeta "Maiak,"* September 29, 2015. http://mayaksbor.ru/news/dosug/tsvetnaya_skazka_/.

Doronina, Irina. 2018. "Nikodim Antoninov: Nechego sidet' doma, nuzhno rabotat'!" *Gazeta "Maiak,"* April 25, 2018. http://mayaksbor.ru/news/society/nikodim_antoninov_nechego_sidet_doma_nuzhno_rabotat/.

Dud', Yuriy. 2018. *MTV—Glavnyi Kanal Nashego Detstva / VDud'*. https://www.youtube.com/watch?v=YQRmaQ14-LA.

"Dvizhenie STOPVANDAL." n.d. VK. Accessed September 1, 2022. https://vk.com/stopwandal.

Eliasoph, Nina. 1998. *Avoiding Politics: How Americans Produce Apathy in Everyday Life*. Cambridge: Cambridge University Press.

Farthing, Rys. 2010. "The Politics of Youthful Antipolitics: Representing the 'Issue' of Youth Participation in Politics." *Journal of Youth Studies* 13, no. 2 (April): 181–195. https://doi.org/10.1080/13676260903233696.

Garza, Thomas J. 2008. "«Не Трожь Молодежь!»: A Portrait of Urban Youthspeak and the Russian Language in the 21st Century." *Russian Language Journal/Русский Язык* 58:213–230.

Gel'man, Vladimir, and Dmitry Travin. 2016. "Fathers versus Sons: Generation Changes and the Ideational Agenda of Reforms in Late-Twentieth-Century Russia." In *Authoritarian Modernization in Russia*, 34–50. Abingdon, UK: Routledge.

Gorokhovskaia, Yana. 2018. "From Local Activism to Local Politics: The Case of Moscow." *Russian Politics* 3, no. 4 (November): 577–604. https://doi.org/10.1163/2451-8921-00304006.

Howell, Ocean. 2008. "Skatepark as Neoliberal Playground: Urban Governance, Recreation Space, and the Cultivation of Personal Responsibility." *Space and Culture* 11, no. 4 (November): 475–496. https://doi.org/10.1177/1206331208320488.

Krutskikh, Polina. 2019. "Skeitbording Kak Instrument Prochteniia Goroda." *Monitoring Obshchestvennogo Mneniia: Ekonomicheskie i Sotsial'nye Peremeny*, no. 1, 292–310. https://doi.org/10.14515/monitoring.2019.1.14.

Macdonald, Duncan J. M., Sile McGlone, Alan Exton, and Sam Perry. 2006. "A New Skatepark: The Impact on the Local Hospital." *Injury* 37, no. 3 (March): 238–242. https://doi.org/10.1016/j.injury.2005.10.015.

Morris, Jeremy. 2016. *Everyday Post-Socialism: Working-Class Communities in the Russian Margins*. London: Palgrave Macmillan.

Németh, Jeremy. 2006. "Conflict, Exclusion, Relocation: Skateboarding and Public Space." *Journal of Urban Design* 11, no. 3 (October): 297–318. https://doi.org/10.1080/13574800600888343.

Omel'chenko, E. L. 2006. "Nachalo Molodezhnoi Ery Ili Smert' Molodezhnoi Kul'tury? «Molodost'» v Publichnom Prostranstve Sovremennosti." *Zhurnal Issledovanii Sotsial'noi Politiki* 4 (2): 151–182.

———. 2012. "Subkul'tury, Pokoleniia, Solidarnosti? K Voprosu Kontseptualizatsii Novykh Form Kommunikatsii v Molodezhnoi Srede." In *XII Mezhdunarodnaia Nauchnaia Konferentsiia Po Problemam Razvitiia Ekonomiki i Obshchestva*, edited by E. G. Yasin, 3:243–263. Moscow: Izdatel'skii dom NIU VShE.

Pilkington, Hilary. 1994. *Russia's Youth and Its Culture: A Nation's Constructors and Constructed*. Abingdon, UK: Routledge.

Robertson, Graeme. 2013. "Protesting Putinism." *Problems of Post-Communism* 60, no. 2 (March): 11–23. https://doi.org/10.2753/PPC1075-8216600202.

Roller.Ru. 2005. "Interv'iu s Sergeem Sheianovym." Accessed November 7, 2020. https://www.roller.ru/content/cat-181/article-1731.html.

Schneider, Anne, and Helen Ingram. 1993. "Social Construction of Target Populations: Implications for Politics and Policy." *American Political Science Review* 87, no. 2 (June): 334–347. https://doi.org/10.2307/2939044.

Selin, Stanislav. 2016. "Skeit-park na Glukhovke pochti gotov." *Gazeta "Maiak,"* August 17, 2016. http://mayaksbor.ru/news/society/skeyt_park_na_glukhovke_pochti_gotov_/.

Smyth, Regina. 2020. *Elections, Protest, and Authoritarian Regime Stability: Russia, 2008–2020*. Cambridge: Cambridge University Press.

Sosnovy Bor Video. 2012 [2002]. "777 zastavka." To chatter, video, 2:00, filmed in 2002, posted July 27, 2012. https://www.youtube.com/watch?v=bOn7Bmmzd3A.

stv24news. 2014a. "Ia Planiruiu Biudzhet." Sosnovoborskoe televidenie-CTV, video, 2:42, March 13, 2014. https://www.youtube.com/watch?v=X6nGhtWZefo.

———. 2014b. "Skeitbord." Sosnovoborskoe televidenie-CTV, video, 3:01, April 3, 2014. https://www.youtube.com/watch?v=CWp1VBBot_E.

———. 2014c. "Vybor Za Skeitom." Sosnovoborskoe televidenie-CTV, video, 3:14, August 28, 2014. https://www.youtube.com/watch?v=yYNM2cq9U5M.

———. 2015a. "Da Budet Park!" Sosnovoborskoe televidenie-CTV, video, 2:30, October 8, 2015. https://www.youtube.com/watch?v=PBS6Bm_bBb4.

———. 2015b. "Ot Trenirovok k Uspekhu." Sosnovoborskoe televidenie-CTV, video, 3:05, June 11, 2015. https://www.youtube.com/watch?v=5C2Nd3nbifM.

———. 2016a. "Predstaviteli Pravitel'stva Posetili Skeitpark." Sosnovoborskoe televidenie-CTV, video, 1:22, August 17, 2016. https://www.youtube.com/watch?v=PICvWrBW81o.

———. 2016b. "Proekty Pobediteli." Sosnovoborskoe televidenie-CTV, video, 2:19, June 17, 2016. https://www.youtube.com/watch?v=w7iXADYRZdE.

———. 2016c. "Triuki Vysshego Pilotazha." Sosnovoborskoe televidenie-CTV, video, 2:41, October 17, 2016. https://www.youtube.com/watch?v=ooHd6X1lrfo.

———. 2016d. "Vziali v Rabotu." Sosnovoborskoe televidenie-CTV, video, 3:47, August 4, 2016. https://www.youtube.com/watch?v=5H2CJqmzA3A.

———. 2018. "Kak Obespechit' Bezopasnost' Na Zaniatiiakh v Budushchem Skeit-Parke?" Sosnovoborskoe televidenie-CTV, video, 1:14, January 23, 2018. https://www.youtube.com/watch?v=OOA4bbkck9w.

———. 2019a. "Festival' Ekstremal'nykh Vidov Sporta 'Olimpik Strit.'" Sosnovoborskoe televidenie-CTV, video, 5:41, August 20, 2019. https://www.youtube.com/watch?v=W_A1Fft2cfY&fbclid=IwARoSp74pro8cMpwwGs8cTnclsAbw48Wpn46J68N4OSI81vC7aM1UTYAXohk.

———. 2019b. "Komissiia Po Sotsial'nym Voprosam." Sosnovoborskoe televidenie-CTV, video, 2:09, February 27, 2019. https://www.youtube.com/watch?v=ALyKbG6yaSw.

Tarrow, Sidney G. 1989. *Democracy and Disorder: Protest and Politics in Italy, 1965–1975*. Oxford: Clarendon Press.
TERA-Studiia Teleradiokompaniia. 2018. *Deputaty Obsudili Sud'bu Skeit-Parka v Sosnovom Boru*. Accessed November 7, 2020. https://www.youtube.com/watch?v=OKunRPaospY.
Vladimirov, Artemy. 2007. "Dobryi Vandalizm Ili Kak Eto Bylo . . ." VK, August 14, 2007. https://vk.com/album876605_2045744.
Weller, Susie. 2006. "Skateboarding Alone? Making Social Capital Discourse Relevant to Teenagers' Lives." *Journal of Youth Studies* 9, no. 5 (November): 557–574. https://doi.org/10.1080/13676260600805705.
Willis, Paul. 1978. *Learning to Labour: How Working Class Kids Get Working Class Jobs*. Abingdon, UK: Routledge.
Woolley, Helen, and Ralph Johns. 2001. "Skateboarding: The City as a Playground." *Journal of Urban Design* 6, no. 2 (June): 211–230. https://doi.org/10.1080/13574800120057845.
Zhelnina, Anna. 2011. "«Zdes' kak muzei»: torgovyi tsentr kak obshchestvennoe prostranstvo." *Laboratorium* 3, no. 2 (January): 48–69.

Anna A. Dekalchuk is Associate Professor in the Department of Political Science and International Affairs and Senior Research Fellow at the Centre for Comparative Governance Studies at HSE University. Her research on EU studies, reforms in democracies and autocracies, and social reforms in Russia appears in *Journal of Contemporary European Studies* and *Democratization*.

Ivan S. Grigoriev is Associate Professor in the Department of Political Science and International Affairs and Research Fellow at the Centre for Comparative Governance Studies at HSE University. His research on judicial politics and business-state relations in Russia and reforms in Russia and the post-Soviet space appears in *Post-Soviet Affairs, Research and Politics, Russian Politics,* and *Democratization.*

PART 3

Institutional Environment and Opportunity Structures for Urban Activism

ANDREI SEMENOV

The chapters in the previous section explored the relations between the activists and the organizations, highlighting that organizational support plays a key role in transforming the disparate grievances and identities into sustained mobilization. Organizations accumulate resources and knowledge necessary for the collective action and facilitate their transfer across time and space. Both activists and organizations, however, operate in an environment filled with rules and institutions. The compliance with existing regulations established by the regime circumscribes the strategic goals, available repertoire, and payoffs, shaping the scale and direction of the mobilization. The studies in this section focus on institutional constraints and political opportunities that serve as a context for urban mobilization.

The two chapters by Eleonora Minaeva and by Carola Neugebauer, Andrei Semenov, Irina Shevtsova, and Daniela Zupan highlight the important and often neglected aspect of urban mobilization—the urban-planning process. Minaeva's contribution makes a strong case for the relevance of the urban-planning instruments, such as strategic master plans for understanding the political developments across Russian cities. She shows how the policy transfer initiated by the powerful actors in the city of Perm failed to achieve its initial goal but at the same time sparked a broad public discussion on the future of urban development. Given the spread of novel planning instruments regarding urban commons' governance, her study is particularly valuable as it highlights the limitations of the policy transfers in authoritarian settings.

In their chapter, Neugebauer and colleagues take a step further and compare the entire set of institutions and urban-planning practices in Perm and

Bonn—cities with contrasting political conditions. Apart from describing planning regulations and institutions, they highlight the key similarities and differences between the two cases. They conclude that while the planning process is inherently complex, preventing the citizens from engaging with urban affairs, the institutions might help facilitate civic participation by either easing access to the policymaking process or incentivizing powerful allies to act on behalf of the activists.

Zooming out of the particularities of the planning institutions, chapters by Irina Meyer-Olimpieva and by Jan Matti Dollbaum, Andrei Semenov, and Elena Sirotkina show how existing or newly built organizations fit into the electoral autocracy conditions. Using the mobilization against pension reform led by trade unions during the summer of 2018, Meyer-Olimpieva demonstrates how the preexisting ties with the regime circumscribed the unions' range of available repertoire, rendering the protests toothless. The regime's ability to co-opt and control both official and independent unions helped forestall the transformation of the mass discontent with the reform into street actions. However, the widening gap between the leadership and the rank-and-file activists reveals the limits of the co-optation.

Dollbaum, Semenov, and Sirotkina further explore the relationship between the centralized structures and the regime. The authors demonstrate how Aleksei Navalny's 2017–2018 presidential campaign exploited the limited opportunities for mobilization presented by the regime. By studying the local offices' performance, they also reveal the tensions within the organizational structure and the local context's impact on the key campaign's characteristics.

Overall, the chapters in this section showcase the enormous variation in the contextual features that the activists face in the course of mobilization, confirming that institutions and opportunity structures remain useful analytical tools for studying the interactions between the citizens and the state.

9

Policy Activism in Urban Governance

The Case of Master Plan Development in Perm

ELEONORA MINAEVA

The world of urban policymaking is an area where specific local policies often serve as an international model or the current fashion of urban governance. González observes: "Some cities acquire a 'paradigmatic' or 'celebrity status' like Bilbao and Barcelona, which have become 'meccas for urban regeneration, from industrial cities of a post-authoritarian regime to culturally vibrant magnets of visitors'" (González 2011, 1397). Urban policies, such as participatory budgeting, planning, sustainable cities, and community programs, also extend to the global level and are routinely promoted by transnational institutions such as the World Bank.

Scholars describe the rise in urban policy transfers in terms of the emergence and entrenchment of entrepreneurial modes of urban governance (Harvey 1989). Diffusion of best practices is also often associated with the idea that "policy should be based on what works best, rather than on a particular ideological position" (Campbell 2002, 89). In this context, city assets can be mobilized as a resource to develop competitive development strategies (Scott et al. 2018). Actors or organizations who participate in policymaking hope for a future return of time, energy, and money invested in policy innovation (Mintrom and Norman 2009).

Scholars have made great strides in developing theories explaining political innovation, including urban policy transfer. However, most theoretical research still refers to decentralized democratic regimes and not autocratic states (Zhu 2017). This focus is limited to systems where political accountability and policy infighting are combined with economic competition. As a result, the current theory applies to a distinct set of political institutions and actors.

This gap raises an important question: How do these new policies emerge, spread, and become entrenched in electoral authoritarian regimes? To address this broad question, I focus on two critical aspects of these regimes. First, I explore the role of the institutional environment through which policy innovations flow. Second, I highlight the influence of uneven power relationships among actors engaged in policy diffusion.

This chapter explores the creation of new urban planning instruments in Russia. The study focuses on the diffusion of a strategic urban planning system usually dubbed "master planning." The master plan is regarded as one of the documents that guides the planning, development, reconstruction, and other types of urban development. The plan considers the wide spatial, sectoral, institutional, and environmental context of the city's development for several years ahead.

The empirical focus is on Perm, Russia's fourteenth-largest city, located on the Volga River in Perm Krai. Through close observation and evidence from semi-structured interviews, I demonstrate how Perm's master plan was designed as a new urban planning instrument and how the local stakeholders responded. My study relies on a policy transfer approach to uncover the mechanisms through which Perm's political leaders borrowed this urban governance instrument. By tracing the policy diffusion process, the chapter reveals many types of urban activism. It can be launched by politicians who desire to significantly change current ways of doing things or seek possible returns in the form of reputation or other dividends. I support my argument with evidence drawn from media reports and interviews with urban planners, architects, government officials, and developers.

The Historical Roots of the Master Plan Strategy

As spatial development documents, master plans emerged in response to the rapid postwar growth of Western European cities. They embodied the ideas of decentralization, openness, and participation of various reference groups in the decision-making process aimed at urban transformation (Zupan 2015). In the Western context, these documents emerged from the programs of competing political parties and assumed the use of public-private partnership mechanisms, consultative institutions, and public discussions. These policymaking tools created opportunities for various interests, from economic developers to users of recreational areas, to influence the process (Gerrits, Rauws, and de Roo 2012).

In contrast to Western European urban practices, the Russian planning system inherited from the USSR was centralized, and it prioritized state and business interests (Golubchikov 2004). This existing urban planning system could not meet the challenges most important to social interests, such as shrinking recreational areas, infill development, demolition of historical and cultural heritage, and expansion of roads. As a result, there has been an increase in grassroots mobilization to contest these concerns since 1991.

Similarly, the Soviet-era document of urban planning, the general plan, did not address the urban environment's strategic prospects, such as creating a compact city or preserving urban communities. Instead, the general plan presents a technical scheme of the objects' location on the city map for specialists such as planners and architects. The demand for negotiation over strategic prospects and emerging social interests required a shift to new urban planning practices. This new approach would account for different relationships among elites and between the public and private sectors and would legitimize the possibility of public participation in the political and administrative process.

Unlike the Soviet-era general plan, a master plan is not a legally binding document. In a sense, the master plan reflects an agreement among key players, including local authorities, citizens, and developers, on the prospects for the city's development. In contrast, the general plan and other documents are a direct guide to implementing these prospects. Thus, the distinction between a general plan and a master plan is a specific feature of post-Soviet urban planning, highlighting its accessibility for civil society and other reference groups. The demand for negotiation over strategic prospects and emerging social interests required a shift to new urban planning practices. This new approach would reflect different relationships among elites and between the public and private sectors. It would also legitimize public participation in the political and administrative process.

In the years 2000–2009, the idea of importing European urban planning practices, and in particular master plans, has spread as one of the options for preventing or mitigating urban conflicts. The idea of developing a master plan first appeared in Perm in 2008–2010, defining the transformation of the regional capital into a compact European city as a development goal several decades ahead.[1] Yet the plan provided a strategic framework for the general plan, without the status of law.

Initiated by individual policymakers, the Perm master plan is considered an example of top-down urban activism. As political entrepreneurs, regional policymakers sought to reimage local urban governance by "selling" the city in terms of new strategic planning practices based on the best European practices. As a result, top-down activism produced a new arena for interaction among the public authorities, developers, and citizens. Despite the best intentions behind the project, the local community first opposed it. The imposition of the master plan on the urban community was combined with the lack of institutional platforms for hearing the voices of various interest groups. At the same time, the new practice of strategic urban planning has been taken up by the federal center and several other regional and local governments.

The Policy Transfer Approach

Policy transfer analysis is an approach to policy development that theorizes a process or set of processes in which knowledge about institutions, policies, or delivery systems at one sector or level of governance is used in the development of institutions, policies, or delivery systems at another sector or level of governance (Evans 2009, 243–244). The theoretical models of policy transfer differ across conceptual foundations, particularly in terms of the mechanisms that shape how policies travel across geopolitical and issue boundaries. Scholars in these debates describe these processes in terms of convergence, emulation, diffusion, social learning, policy learning, bandwagoning, and lesson drawing.

The literature focuses on mechanisms involved in diffusion and transfer, the interactions between them, and the ways they evolve. One approach suggests highlighting four such mechanisms: learning, coercion, competition, and mimicry (Marsh and Sharman 2009). Dolowitz and Marsh (2000, 13) propose conceptualizing transfer as "lying along a continuum that runs from lesson-drawing to the direct imposition of a program, policy or institutional arrangement on one political system by another." Competition (global or local), in turn, implies that the policy transfer pathway is associated with the need to fight for markets and human and financial resources (Simmons and Elkins 2004). Finally, in some cases, the purpose of the transfer is to emulate the best practices and standards to acquire legitimacy without significant change. Researchers label these actions as mimicry (Marsh and Sharman 2009, 272) or symbolic imitation (Braun and Gilardi 2006; Shipan and Volden 2008).

Policy transfers become even more complex when they move across international boundaries and are applied to the local level. Classic studies of policy transfer in the American context by Crain (1966) on the adoption of water fluoridation and Knoke (1982) on municipal reform fixed transfers to local polities as early as the 1960s and 1970s. They distinguish among and find evidence for four mechanisms of policy diffusion. More recent studies of municipal antismoking policy in US cities find that imitation is a more short-lived diffusion process than learning, competition, or coercion. Besides, larger cities are better able to learn from others, are less fearful of economic spillovers, and are less likely to rely on imitation (Shipan and Volden 2008). Others focus on the pursuit and dissemination of policy information, instead of the transfer of specific policies. Relying on a survey of US mayors, scholars have found that the local heads select models according to comparative aspects, such as the distance and similarity of the initial locale, and policy attributes, such as the expected effects of the implemented policies (Einstein, Glick, and Palmer, 2019). Outside the United States, researchers find a geopolitical diffusion of participatory budgeting in Estonia (Krenjova and Raudla 2018), climate policy in Germany (Abel 2019), policy transfer in regional development policy in Turkey (Ertugal 2018), and administrative reforms in China (Zhu and Zhang 2016).

In Russia, Gel'man and Lankina (2008) and Golosov, Gushchina, and Kononenko (2016) have led the study of policy transfer. Their results demonstrate that coercion became the main mechanism for policy diffusion during the presidency of Vladimir Putin. During this period, municipalities lost a significant part of their financial and political autonomy as compared to the 1990s. Similarly, the powers of regional capitals have also been significantly reduced because of the latest wave of federal reforms in 2014 (Turovsky 2015). Since the direct elections of municipal heads have been replaced by de facto appointments, the federal and regional authorities expect local heads to provide votes; therefore, signaling the mayor's loyalty to the federal center is of higher priority than providing public goods (Zavadskaya and Shilov 2021). Under this policy, any positive incentives for subordination, such as transfers or grants, are replaced by coercion.

Despite the evidence of growing coercion, organizations and platforms, such as the International Forum of Best Municipal Practices or the Association of Smart Cities, bring municipal heads and regional politicians together to exchange experience. These opportunities for different pathways of policy transfer do not act as incubators for policy change. The overwhelming majority of innovations in the field of urban government are tested and implemented in Russia's capital and largest city, Moscow. In this regard, creating a master plan for Perm deserves special research attention as it is a unique case of innovation developed outside of the capital city and transferred to a regional center. This case study allows us to understand better the possibility and limitations of policy transfers both to Russian municipalities and to cities and regional governments in states with similar political regimes.

The Perm Master Plan

In the years 2000–2009, urban planning in Russian cities was characterized by the preservation of traditional institutions and urban planning instruments (such as the chief architect in the city administration or the general plan), on the one hand, and by the rapid rejection of the Soviet model of urban development, on the other hand. The commodification of land through privatization processes brought developers with their interests and strategies to the forefront of urban development. Private construction firms acquired the opportunity to influence land-use and zoning regulations to initiate and expand projects and increase profits. One of the consequences of their involvement was an encroachment on public spaces such as parks and squares through the rapid growth of infill construction and the demolition of historic buildings. In general, these trends led to a reduction in the space in which citizens can live a comfortable life. As Golubchikov notes (2004, 233), "The planning system had ceased to be a real public good and started to serve the private interests of those who saw private benefits from the system of planning and development control." In other words, urban development became a tool to serve the economic interests of political and economic elites.

This problem was typical for urban planning in Perm and launched significant political contestation between developers and government officials. As in other Russian cities, in the first decade of the twenty-first century, urban planning in Perm was regulated by a general plan, which was developed in the late 1990s and approved by the Federal Agency for Construction (Rosstroy) in 2004. In 2005, in response to the initiative of Perm developers (represented by the general director of the Stroyindustriya company and the deputy of the regional legislature Sergei Levi), the head of the Perm administration, Arkady Kamenev, formed the City Planning Council to act in an advisory capacity. Officially, the council was aimed to formulate a unified urban planning and architectural policy for the city administration. It considered projects of urban planning complexes, engineering, and transport development for Perm. The council included developers, representatives of the financial sector, and representatives of the real estate business.

The representation of developers in government bodies is typical of many cities and regions of Russia (Szakonyi 2020). Perm is no exception; it has a diversified economy with a developed and competitive mass housing construction sector. In 2006, three representatives of the Perm Factory for Silicate Panels, two officials from the road-construction company Dorstroytrans and one representative each from Perm House Building Plant and Kamskaya Dolina won seats in the elections to the fourth convocation of the Perm City Council. In addition, candidates from three other construction agencies, Universal Stroy, KamaStroyInvest, and Zhilstroy, participated in the election but did not win seats. Having received parliamentary mandates, the developers formed a parliamentary Committee on Urban Planning and Development of the City's Territory.

During this period, the opinion of citizens and activists were not considered in the development of the general plan or the advisory council's discussion of urban planning issues. When civil activists Roman Yushkov and Denis Galitsky conducted an independent assessment of the general plan's project and revealed several significant drawbacks, the results were ignored by the Perm City Council (Borisova 2009). This lack of communication between the authorities and activists contrasted with the backdrop of overall assessments of governance in the Perm region and regional capital as open and competitive. Experts consistently evaluate both the region and the city as more competitive and democratic than most Russian cities (Petrov and Titkov 2013). These evaluations are based on comparisons of civil society activity, the low progovernment electoral support, particularly for the United Russia party, and low levels of electoral fraud (Shpilkin 2018; Rogov 2018).

My close study of the urban planning system demonstrates the gap between these governance measures and social inputs in critical policy processes. While parts of Perm civil society pretended to be significant players in urban politics, they were excluded from the decision-making process regarding urban development. As a result, the new project of the general plan did not satisfy the interests of the grassroots activists.

A good example of this gap between comparative assessments and local outcomes is that the document allowed for unpopular large-scale deforestation to support development mandates. In 2007, the initiative group For Saving the Akulovskaya Linden Grove found that the city administration had transferred 1.2 hectares of forest area to a developer even though, according to the law, forests were intended exclusively for recreational purposes. Residents of the Akulovsky district, together with activists and the public association the Union for the Protection of Perm Residents, challenged this decision in court. The court ruled against deforestation. As a result, the general plan that had been in place for three years was canceled in April 2007. This decision created the need for a new strategy to guide the city's spatial development and opened the policy to new actors.

Simultaneously, significant but contradictory changes occurred in the political sphere. In 2004, Oleg Chirkunov became the governor of the Perm region. The degree of involvement of the regional authorities in city-level policymaking and urban planning issues dramatically increased. Under direct orders from Chirkunov, the regional legislature adopted a new charter for the city of Perm. The new system abandoned direct mayoral elections and defined a dual governance system that increased the governor's influence on planning processes. Under the new charter, a city manager would be appointed by a special commission under gubernatorial influence. The Speaker of the City Council, a body under the influence of United Russia, would serve as nominal municipal head.

Under the new system, Chirkunov prompted the resignation of the sitting mayor, Arkadiy Kamenev, and promoted his ally, Igor Shubin, to the chairperson's post. These personnel shifts significantly strengthened the governor's influence in urban politics and extended the influence he built under the new charter. Subsequently, planning policy was developed under his direct patronage and control. The construction of highways, roads, and interchanges in the region and the regional capital increased, as did the construction of new inner-city districts (Borisova 2009, 44). Against the backdrop of the city authorities' inability to manage the city planning, the regional authorities intervened in urban governance processes.

Not surprisingly, the idea for the master plan as a key planning instrument first emerged among the members of the governor's team. In July 2007, the Legislative Assembly of Perm Krai elected Senator Sergey Gordeev, an entrepreneur and the main shareholder of the PIK development company, as Perm's senator to the Council of the Federation. As a billionaire, Sergei Gordeev became widely known in Russia and abroad for being a cultural philanthropist seeking to preserve Soviet architecture (Ouroussoff 2007). He became the primary advocate and ideologist of the master plan's development. The senator acted like a political entrepreneur. As one informant noted, "At some point Gordeev could have thought about making money," but his key goal was clearly "to do something to stay in the centuries, to enter history."[2]

According to the governor himself, he did not immediately agree with the idea of creating a master plan, but over the five years of work on the project, his views on urban planning "completely changed" (Chirkunov 2011). The transformation of the governor's outlook was facilitated by travel abroad in search of the best practices in urban planning. Another informant describes the process that led to this profound change in thinking: "First of all, the customer's team was formed so that the first person [Governor Chirkunov] understood what kind of document it was, what he was talking about; trips were made to Hamburg, Curitiba, and so on."[3] This process underscores the role of officials in educating the governor and exposing him to alternative viewpoints.

Other members of the Perm regional and city elite supported Chirkunov's new outlook. One respondent pointed to the key actors: "Shubin [the City Council's chairperson] very sincerely shared his position. For Katz [the head of Perm City Administration], this was also important; he was not just from Chirkunov's team but also a like-minded ally. As a result, [the master plan] was a joint project of the city and regional administration."[4] Importantly, the shift in perspective at the regional level increased the influence of city-level officials, creating the opportunity for collaboration.

Three international companies—KCAP Architects and Planners, Bureau Alle Hosper, and the Finnish company Pöyry—were also involved in the development of the document. In the next period, the Italian Systematica and employees of the Institute of Technology in Zurich also worked on the master plan. These companies had been commissioned to develop a master plan based on the principles of the "compact European city" with a comfortable environment by "European standards" (Zupan 2015). According to one of the respondents, the task was to make Perm a city that would be "medium-rise, compact, consisting of multifunctional street blocks with landscaped streets, embankments, and parks."[5]

An autonomous municipal organization, the Bureau for Urban Projects, was established to provide financial and organizational support for the project. The bureau was headed by Perm's former vice mayor for construction Andrei Golovin. Before joining the bureau, he worked as a top manager of the construction company Prospekt, which journalists associate with Governor Chirkunov (Zyryanova 2018). The bureau acted as the official customer of the master plan for foreign architects and was also responsible for the development of the city's general plan. In addition, the bureau was the link between the city administration and the master plan developers.

Throughout 2009, the work of developing a master plan was carried out in both open and closed formats. Planning officials organized public lectures, roundtables, and seminars devoted to discussing Perm's existing problems and the strategies of its development. These events took place in open formats at the university and public sites of the city. As my informant notes, "During the year, from ninety to one hundred open events were held in the city."[6] Citizens, scientists, private business owners, and representatives of NGOs were invited to participate in these discussions and present their views.

Key decisions, however, were made at closed meetings among the authorities. The main arena for these interactions was the Commission to Prepare the Drafts of General and Master Plans, created in February 2009 and chaired by Igor Shubin. The commission included a reduced form of the main advisory body on urban planning issues, the City Planning Council of Perm: two representatives of the city administration, four architects, two deputies of the Perm City Duma, and a developer. At the meetings of the commission, foreign experts presented their views and often met strong opposition from both representatives of the city administration and local architects.

Although the master plan developers envisioned the document to be "a political agreement adopted by the City Council and other most important interest groups in the city,"[7] in practice, they faced opposition from the professional community, developers, and law enforcement agencies. Even in the design stage, the document was criticized by the Perm Union of Architects since local architects were not substantively involved in the direct development of the new document. Despite this opposition, the development of the master plan was completed in February 2010; in December 2010, on its basis, the Perm City Council approved a new general plan.

After the adoption of the master plan, several Perm architects, including the former chief architect of the city and creator of the previous general plan, Sergei Shamarin, published an open letter in the newspaper *Zvezda* explaining the position of local experts. The authors of the letter emphasized the Dutch origin of the creators of the master plan and the inapplicability of their ideas to Perm. The architects called the master plan "a collection of lectures on urban planning for educational institutions in the Netherlands" (*Zvezda* 2010). Master plan opponents argued that their criticism was based on professional expertise and not on political goals or economic rent seeking.

One of the opponents believed that the master plan has a different purpose: "The master plan is planning and architectural ideas that are made in problematic areas to fix some issues. In fact, the master plan should be developed only for problem areas—here is a wasteland, let's make a master plan for three quarters. And it makes no sense to present the master plan of the city. . . . A compact city is absurd, we do not have a compact city along the river."[8] Despite this strong criticism, the respondent emphasized that there are many areas in Perm for which a master plan would be relevant. He argued, "Let's develop a master plan for the Motovilikha Factory [a Soviet-era industrial and military giant] because half of the territory there is empty."[9] These nuanced statements demonstrate the complexity of opinion and opposition around the master plan's proposals and goals.

Another informant saw these critiques as rooted in the threats the new process posed to the professional self-interest of local architects and interests. One of the developers of the master plan noted that "the local architectural community immediately rejected new approaches because of the competition. They wrote letters and protested. They still lived in the paradigm that someone distributes projects, that you are not working in a competitive market, but that projects are distributed from top to bottom."[10] This community feared that the new competitive process to win projects had the potential to disrupt the existing hierarchy and salaries.

The master plan also became a wedge in the relationship between the public authorities and businesses. In accordance with the provisions of the plan, Perm's mayor instructed the chief architect not to issue permits for high-rise construction on the city's periphery, a move that faced fierce opposition from some developers. They filed lawsuits against the city administration because they already owned the land but did not receive the city permits necessary to start construction. However, legal regulations were changed anyway. In particular, the height of buildings in the city center was limited. At the same time, as some observers noted, "by 2017, dozens of new buildings were built, but not a single project was brought in line with . . . the [height] norm" (Zayakina and Sedurina 2017).

The key problem for the creators of the master plan, however, came from repeated audits by law enforcement agencies and the resulting administrative and criminal cases against the head of the Bureau of Urban Projects, Andrei Golovin. As a result of the inspections, Golovin was charged with several infractions, including negligence and corruption. Following these charges, the prosecutor's office opened a criminal case based on suspected embezzlement from the city budget. In October 2010, the Federal Security Service started investigating the divulging of state secrets, but within a year, criminal proceedings were suspended.

It is unclear whether there were any political reasons apart from bureaucratic shortfalls on behalf of Golovin, but in parallel with investigations of the bureau, the Prosecutor General's Office opened an investigation of members of the governor's team in connection with abuse of power and corruption. The Perm master plan became a convenient excuse for federal TV channels to harshly criticize Chirkunov (Polina and Emelyanova 2011). As a result, Chirkunov prematurely resigned, officially voluntarily. After the resignation, the press stressed the Perm governor's disloyalty to the federal center (Gordienko 2007). They mentioned the governor's support of opposition parties and the poor results of the United Russia Party in federal and regional races, and they compared the attack on Chirkunov with the persecution of Yuri Luzhkov, the former mayor of Moscow (*Lenta.ru* 2012).

Chirkunov's successor, Viktor Basargin, emphasized developers' interests. As a result of this shift in personnel, almost none of the principles underlying the master plan were implemented. As one respondent observed, "When it came to implementation, the authorities changed, and the value was gone. The edge has already overflowed but has not spilled into the implementation system. Nothing happened. . . . Within the framework of the idea of a compact city, we removed 3–4 thousand hectares from potential construction, the new authorities came in and gave it back for development."[11]

Another respondent amplified this sentiment, focusing on the failure of new planning institutions to constrain the new leaders: "Under Chirkunov, some rules of the game were set, no matter how we liked them. In the City Council, a committee for spatial development was created, which considered issues related to the master plan, general plan, the relations between developers and the authorities. With the change of governor, the paradigm shifted."[12]

According to experts, the city planning documents became hostage to the change of governors and the lack of support for the draft master plan by other interest groups, including local experts, businesspeople, and civic activists.

This disconnect between plan and interests emerged because the business with the greatest influence on the decision-making process was not included in developing the master plan, which negatively affected its fate. The response was to undermine the plan. The respondents emphasize that under the new governor the "rules of the game" changed significantly: "Over the years of Viktor Basargin's governorship, the authorities have moved away from the norms of the master plan in a diametrically opposite direction, including acting in the interests of key developers and to the detriment of social facilities. The recent deviations from the master plan's principles undermine its future feasibility. In several places, large objects that did not fit into the master plan have been constructed. It is very difficult to rebuild the city in the future so that the transport system is organically used, the load on the networks is evenly distributed, and so on."[13]

In short, the plan did not constrain elite interests from bypassing regulations and creating development patterns that will necessarily shape future actions.

The Result of Transfer

Conflicting parties differ on the reasons for the failure of policy transfer. Supporters point out that the master plan was not "blindly copied by foreign experience" (*Lenta.ru* 2013), but the project team failed to convince the local community of its importance. One of the project's developers, Markus Appenzeller, commented, "We were tasked with creating a master plan. When we finished it, other people would implement it. If they cannot understand what this Plan is about, if they do not have the necessary knowledge, it will be difficult for them to discern its most essential aspects" (*Archsovet* 2015).

Other critics emphasize the absence of mechanisms for coordinating interests in the process of developing a political course: "The authorities, residents, specialists, and businesses cannot make a decision separately. Of course, all interests must be considered. It should be a real working town planning council, in which experts, developers, and citizens are represented. Moreover, this should not just be a chamber, or closed meeting of a narrow circle of people."[14]

This understanding echoes claims that a successful plan can only emerge from consensus born of coordination. Such consensus can only be achieved through an open policy process. As another respondent argued, "The master plan must be revived. It is necessary to determine the priorities for the next five years and the distant future; to outline how the projects laid down in the master plan can be implemented; and what we want from the builders, from the townspeople, from the authorities, and officials. It is necessary to create platforms for discussion, inform where residents can participate. There should be responsible companies and officials. In addition, control is important and at all stages. Finally, there should be interested people everywhere, like Chirkunov and Shubin."[15]

In short, successful urban planning demands both consistent rules and strong supporters in key political and economic positions. Representatives of legislature point to the ineffectiveness of public hearings as an institution of public participation, which creates problems with public support for projects: "Public hearings are not yet working for support or involvement."[16]

Largely because of informal processes and changes in political interests, the transfer of the new urban planning policy was premature and short-lived. Under the new governor, all projects were curtailed. Yet, from a political diffusion perspective, the creation of the master plan seems relatively successful. First, the resonance of the case gave a new impetus to the discussion around the need to revise approaches to urban planning, including at the federal level. In June 2014, the federal government adopted a new law, titled "On Strategic Planning in the Russian Federation." Although this law shifted the transfer paradigm from training to coercion with elements of competition, the new framework pushed many regional and local politicians to initiate the development of their strategic documents.

The Yekaterinburg Spatial Development Strategy and the project initiated by the city administration—100 Thoughts about Yekaterinburg—provide a striking example of this process. Officials launched both projects in response to two impulses. The first impulse was the influence of the new federal law. The second was grounded in local politicians' desires to create an alternative to compete with the Perm master plan to attract capital, investment, and human resources. The Perm example laid the idea of building a compact city as the basis for Ekaterinburg's document. Similarly, the experience and ideas of Andrei Golovin and architects from KCAP and Systematica allowed Yekaterinburg policymakers to avoid many of the problems that derailed the Perm process, including criminal charges. Eventually, strategic documents like Perm's master plan began to appear in cities such as Vladivostok, Omsk, Samara, and Ufa.

Under the new governor, Maxim Reshetnikov, whose political career began under Chirkunov, the regional administration raised the issue of transforming the urban space following the ideas and projects laid down in the master plan. At the Moscow Urban Forum in 2017, Reshetnikov declared his commitment to the master plan (Belkina 2017). The governor called developmental sprawl in the suburbs one of Perm's key problems and proposed to create "comfortable, compact cities for the creative class" (Bykova 2017). Reshetnikov also suggested concentrating construction in the central part of the city and entrusted building social infrastructure—such as public spaces, hospitals, schools, and clinics—to the builders. In addition, the tool of the master plan began to be applied to specific areas of the city. For example, an embankment project was implemented, and the master plans for the public lighting (*Vesti Perm* 2021) and opera house (*ProPerm* 2017) were developed.

Finally, even though platforms for public participation in the decision-making process have not been institutionalized, the master plan revitalized Perm's urban community. In this regard, the master plan became a document that defenders of small rivers of Perm refer to when interacting with government officials. One of the activists emphasizes that "the Dutch in the master plan clearly stated that there is a valley where a small river flows, and there it is necessary to create something like greenbelts without cars for pedestrians or cyclists. Thus, we will get an alternative transport system where people can walk or cycle quickly and conveniently."[17] The idea of the uniqueness of small rivers as part of the Perm cityscape was reflected in the repertoire of urban activism. In 2016, a group of activists launched a citywide public festival called Bridges with intent to draw the community's attention to the growing pollution of small rivers and other waterways. In 2020, the new governor, Dmitry Makhonin, met with activists, supporting the proposal "to make public spaces comfortable for jogging, walking, and cycling" (*Kommersant* 2020).

To halt the destruction of green areas around small rivers, he introduced a new law, "On the Protection of Urban Green Spaces," to the regional legislature. These developments demonstrate the cyclical nature of change influenced by policy diffusion, political interests, and activism. Despite ups and downs, Perm's experience with the master plan continues to influence urban planning and the development decisions in other Russian cities.

Conclusion

The borrowing of urban planning tools represents one of the countless repertoires within the global urban policy transfers. Bringing best practices can serve different purposes: from the improvement of public spaces, enhancing civic participation, or fostering investments (including more business-friendly strategic planning techniques), to policy legitimation of other agendas and strengthening the power positions of incumbents (González 2011). The mechanisms that allow policy diffusion are also on a continuum between voluntary and coercive adoption, varying from learning to mimicry of a policy model taken from another political setting. As scholars note, the success and failure of policy transfer may depend on importing mechanisms, but transfer is likely to be more effective when it involves not only formal bureaucrats and politicians but also businesspeople, researchers, and activists (Stone 2004).

By focusing on the example of Perm's master plan, the chapter demonstrates how the subnational political elite initiated and implemented policy transfer in urban governance. I argue that this transfer became both a focal point for the convergence of certain interests regarding the long-term prospects of urban development in Perm and also a target for opposition from multiple interest groups. The policy transfer process in Perm started in a top-down manner with the initiative of a particular businessman, philanthropist, and politician, Sergei Gordeev. The master plan was conceived as a new arena setting novel institutional conditions for urban planning. At the same time, the master plan did not become a long-term policy document. Investigations, litigation, and press coverage negatively shaped reference groups' dissatisfaction with policy. After Governor Chirkunov's departure, the plan lost political support, and grassroots activists enthusiastically resisted its implementation.

The contradictory combination of the diffusion mechanisms—the learning process, imitation, and coercion—and the introduction of new political practices explains this result. The learning consisted of the trips abroad taken by the governor and his associates, the selection of foreign specialists, and the commission's work for the preparation of the general and master plans. The learning process prompted the decision-makers to change their beliefs about the "fair" and "right" urban planning policy to meet modern urban-development standards. As a result of this shift, they are more willing to consider alternatives that have proved effective in other countries. At the same time, unlike mimicry based on imitating other politicians and copying their decisions without considering the consequences, learning requires focusing on the policy itself—how it was adopted, what caused its effectiveness, and what political effects it had. Moreover, the sustainability of policy needs the creation of institutions, primarily in harmonizing interests and protecting those who carry out a policy transfer. In Perm, the large-scale financial and organizational investments were made without considering these issues. Instead, we observe officials forcing the master plan on the urban community and local experts. The lack of institutional platforms for various actors to voice opinions, as well as the desire of politicians to improve their own authority and receive political dividends from the implementation of the project, indicate a high degree of imitation as the mechanism of policy transfer.

Does this mean that any transfer of urban planning policy in Russia is doomed? Under authoritarian rule, it probably is, because low electoral accountability leaves politicians with few incentives to involve civil society in the decision-making process: they seek to co-opt the expert community and convince that community that they are competent and progressive even if that is not true. Although the adoption of the master plan laid the foundation for the discussion of alternative models of urban development (even outside Perm), the federal center seized the agenda. Russia has been increasingly centralized during the last decade, which implies an intrusive policy style, whereby the federal center is in the driver's seat and subordinates are expected to implement its policy, leaving little space for either top-down or bottom-up local activism.

Notes

1. See Gorodperm 2016.
2. Interview 1, public figure, Perm, March 25, 2019.
3. Interview 2, architect, Perm, September 13, 2018.
4. Interview 2.
5. Interview 2.
6. Interview 2.
7. See Gorodperm 2016.
8. Interview 3, architect, Perm, December 18, 2017.
9. Interview 3.
10. Interview 2.
11. Interview 2.
12. Interview 4, Perm City Duma deputy, Perm, August 1, 2018.
13. Interview 5, Perm City Duma deputy, Perm, January 26, 2018.
14. Interview 6, architect and businessman, Perm, December 4, 2017.
15. Interview 7, journalist, head of the PR company, Perm, March 15, 2018.
16. Interview 8, assistant to the deputy of the Perm City Duma, Perm, December 15, 2017.
17. Interview 9, civic activist, Perm, May 23, 2017.

Bibliography

Abel, Dennis. 2019. "The Diffusion of Climate Policies among German Municipalities." *Journal of Public Policy* 41, no. 1 (March): 111–136.

Archsovet. 2015. "Markus Appenzeller: How to Decentralize a City." January 13, 2015. https://archsovet.msk.ru/article/ot-pervogo-lica/markus-appenceller-kak-decentralizovat-gorod.

Belkina, Anna. 2017. "Reshetnikov Announced the Rules of the Game for Perm Builders" [Reshetnikov ob"yavil pravila igry dlya permskikh stroiteley]. URA.ru, July 10, 2017. https://ura.news/articles/1036271472.

Borisova, Nadezhda. 2009. "Institutional Environment and Participants in Intersectoral Interaction in the Perm Region" [Institutsional'naya sreda i uchastniki mezhsektornogo vzaimodeystviya v Permskom kraye]. *Bulletin of Perm University, Political Science* 8 (4): 40–47.

Braun, Dietmar, and Fabrizio Gilardi. 2006. "Taking 'Galton's Problem' Seriously: Towards a Theory of Policy Diffusion." *Journal of Theoretical Politics* 18 (3): 298–322.

Bykova, Svetlana. 2017. "The Top View Is Better: Urban Planning Results of 2017 in the *Kommersant* Guide 'Perm Territory: Results of the Year'" [Vid sverkhu luchshe. Gradostroitel'nyye itogi 2017-go v Guide «Permskiy kray. Itogi goda»]. *Kommersant*, December 27, 2017. https://www.kommersant.ru/doc/3508931.

Campbell, Heather. 2002. "'Evidence-Based Policy': The Continuing Search for Effective Policy Processes." *Planning Theory & Practice* 3 (1): 89–90.

Chirkunov, Oleg. 2011. "Urban Planning Arithmetic" [Arifmetika gradoplanirovaniya]. *Expert*, March 14, 2011. http://expert.ru/expert/2011/10/arifmetika-gradoplanirovaniya/.

Crain, Robert. 1966. "Fluoridation—Diffusion of an Innovation among Cities." *Social Forces* 44 (4): 467–476.

Dolowitz, David, and David Marsh. 2000. "Learning from Abroad: The Role of Policy Transfer in Contemporary Policy Making." *Governance* 13 (1): 5–23.

Einstein, Katherine Levine, David Glick, and Maxwell Palmer. 2019. "City Learning: Evidence of Policy Information Diffusion from a Survey of US Mayors." *Political Research Quarterly* 72 (1): 243–258.

Ertugal, E. 2018. "Learning and Policy Transfer in Regional Development Policy in Turkey." *Regional Studies* 52 (9): 1181–1190.

Evans, Mark. 2009. "Policy Transfer in Critical Perspective." *Policy Studies* 30 (3): 243–268.

Gel'man, Vladmir and Tomila Lankina. 2008. "Authoritarian versus Democratic Diffusions: Explaining Institutional Choices in Russia's Local Government." *Post-Soviet Affairs* 24 (1): 40–62.

Gerrits, Lasse, Ward Rauws, and Gert de Roo. 2012. "Policy & Planning Brief." *Planning Theory & Practice*, 13 (2): 336–341. https://doi.org/10.1080/14649357.2012.669992.

Golosov, Grigorii, Kristina Gushchina, and Pavel Kononenko. 2016. "Russia's Local Government in the Process of Authoritarian Regime Transformation: Incentives for the Survival of Local Democracy." *Local Government Studies* 42 (4): 507–526.
Golubchikov, Oleg. 2004. "Urban Planning in Russia: Towards the Market." *European Planning Studies* 12 (4): 229–247.
González, Sara. 2011. "Bilbao and Barcelona 'in Motion': How Urban Regeneration 'Models' Travel and Mutate in the Global Flows of Policy Tourism." *Urban Studies* 47 (7): 1397–1418.
Gordienko, Irina. 2007. "Ex-Governor Has Nothing to Fear?" [«EKS» gubernatoru nechego boyat'sya?]. *Novaya Gazeta*, August 22, 2007. https://novayagazeta.ru/articles/2007/08/22/32240-eks-gubernatoru-nechego-boyatsya.
Gorodperm.ru. 2016. "The Master Plan." Accessed August 22, 2022. https://www.gorodperm.ru/actions/building-up/genplan/master_plan/.
Harvey, David. 1989. "From Managerialism to Entrepreneurialism: The Transformation in Urban Governance in Late Capitalism." *Geografiska Annaler. Series B, Human Geography* 70 (1): 3–17.
Knoke, David. 1982. "The Spread of Municipal Reform: Temporal, Spatial, and Social Dynamics." *American Journal of Sociology* 87 (6): 1314–1339.
Kommersant. 2020. "The Master Plan of Small Rivers of Perm May Be Financed by Sberbank." August 30, 2020. https://www.kommersant.ru/doc/4474178.
Krenjova, Jelizaveta, and Ringa Raudla. 2018. "Policy Diffusion at the Local Level: Participatory Budgeting in Estonia." *Urban Affairs Review* 54 (2): 419–447.
Lenta.ru. 2012. "Self-Rejection: Oleg Chirkunov Left the Post of Perm Governor ahead of Schedule" [Samootvod. Oleg Chirkunov dosrochno pokinul post permskogo gubernatora]. April 30, 2012. https://lenta.ru/articles/2012/04/30/perm/.
———. 2013. "All the Same, the Prison Turns Out: The Development of the Master Plan for Perm Ended in Four Criminal Cases" [Vse ravno tyur'ma poluchayetsya. Razrabotka master-plana Permi zavershilas' chetyr'mya ugolovnymi delami]. June 27, 2013. https://lenta.ru/articles/2013/06/27/plan/.
Marsh, David, and Jason Sharman. 2009. "Policy Diffusion and Policy Transfer." *Policy Studies* 30 (3): 269–288.
Mintrom, Michael, and Philippa Norman. 2009. "Policy Entrepreneurship and Policy Change." *Policy Studies Journal* 37 (4): 649–667.
Ouroussoff, Nicolai. 2007. "For Soviet-Era Architecture, a White Russian Knight Emerges." *New York Times*, October 10, 2007. https://www.nytimes.com/2007/10/10/arts/design/10olig.html.

Petrov, Nikolai, and Aleksei Titkov. 2013. *Democracy Rating of the Regions of the Carnegie Moscow Center: 10 Years in the Ranks* [Reyting demokratichnosti regionov Moskovskogo Tsentra Karnegi: 10 let v stroyu]. Moscow: Carnegie Endowment for International Peace.

Polina, Dina, and Nadezhda Emelyanova. 2011. "Oleg Chirkunov Is Punished on TV" [Olega Chirkunova nakazyvayut po televizoru]. *Kommersant*, July 11, 2011. https://www.kommersant.ru/doc/1676622.

ProPerm. 2017. "Reshetnikov: There Will Be a Master Plan for the Opera House, the Gallery Needs to Look for a Building, There Are No Problems with the Zoo" [Reshetnikov: budet master-plan dlya opernogo teatra, galereye nuzhno iskat' zdaniye, s zooparkom problem net]. March 22, 2017. https://properm.ru/realty/news/136662/.

Rogov, Kirill. 2018. "One and a Half Russia: Dominance Technologies and Social Orders" [Poltory Rossii. Tekhnologii dominirovaniya i sotsial'nyye poryadki]. *Inliberty*, April 27, 2018. https://www.inliberty.ru/article/regime-rogov/.

Scott, Mark, Arthur Parkinson, Declan Redmond, and Richard Waldron. 2018. "Placing Heritage in Entrepreneurial Urbanism: Planning, Conservation and Crisis in Ireland." *Planning Practice & Research*, February 15, 2018. https://doi.org/10.1080/02697459.2018.1430292.

Shipan, Charles, and Craig Volden. 2008. "The Mechanisms of Policy Diffusion." *American Journal of Political Science* 52 (4): 840–857.

Shpilkin, Sergei. 2018. "Tails and Pikes: History of Abnormal Voting in Russia" [Khvosty i piki. Istoriya anomal'nogo golosovaniya v Rossii]. *Inliberty*, April 27, 2018. https://www.inliberty.ru/article/regime-shpilkin/.

Simmons, Beth A., and Zachary Elkins. 2004. "The Globalization of Liberalization: Policy Diffusion in the International Political Economy." *American Political Science Review* 98 (1): 171–189.

Stone, Diane. 2004. "Transfer Agents and Global Networks in the 'Transnationalization' of Policy." *Journal of European Public Policy* 11 (3): 545–566.

Szakonyi, David. 2020. *Politics for Profit: Business, Elections, and Policymaking in Russia*. Cambridge: Cambridge University Press.

Turovsky, Rostislav. 2015. "Russian Local Self-Government: An Agent of State Power in the Trap of Underfunding and Civil Passivity" [Rossiyskoye mestnoye samoupravleniye: agent gosudarstvennoy vlasti v lovushke nedofinansirovaniya i grazhdanskoy passivnosti]. *Polis*, no. 2, 33–51.

Vesti Perm. 2021. "At a Meeting of the City Planning Council, the Possibility of Adopting a Master Plan for Lighting Perm Was Discussed" [Na soveshchanii Gradostroitel'nogo soveta obsudili vozmozhnost' prinyatiya master-plana osveshcheniya Permi]. July 2, 2021. https://vesti-perm.ru/pages/562250ea97fe49fa97cc379922de4de6.

Zavadskaya, Margarita, and L. Shilov. 2021. "Providing Goods and Votes? Federal Elections and the Quality of Local Governance in Russia." *Europe-Asia Studies* 73 (6):1037–1059.

Zayakina, Katerina, and Olga Sedurina. 2017. "Research by RBC Perm: Will the Master Plan Help the Development of Perm?" [Issledovaniye RBK Perm': pomozhet li Master-plan razvitiyu Permi?]. *RB*, August 15, 2017. https://perm.plus.rbc.ru/news/5992bbae7a8aa94259babb6e.

Zhu, Xu-Feng 2017. "Inter-regional Diffusion of Policy Innovation in China: A Comparative Case Study." *Asian Journal of Political Science* 25 (3): 266–286.

Zhu, Xu-Feng, and Zhang Youlang. 2016. "Political Mobility and Dynamic Diffusion of Innovation: The Spread of Municipal Pro-business Administrative Reform in China." *Journal of Public Administration Research and Theory* 26 (3): 535–551.

Zupan, Daniela. 2015. "Local Debates on 'Global' Planning Concepts: The 'Compact European City' Model in Postsocialist Russia—the Case of Perm." *Europa Regional* 22 (1–2): 39–52.

Zvezda. 2010. "Poor Dutch" [Bednoye gollandskoye]. LiveJournal, February 9, 2010. https://gazetazwezda.livejournal.com/11094.html#cutid1.

Zyryanova, Tatiana. 2018. "Who Is Andrey Golovin? And What Will He Do on His Third Return to Perm Politics?" [Who is Andrey Golovin? I chem on zaymetsya v svoye tret'ye vozvrashcheniye v politiku Permi?]. *ProPerm*, April 17, 2018. https://properm.ru/news/society/152749.

Eleonora Minaeva is a PhD student in Political Science at European University Institute in Florence. Her research focuses on machine politics at the municipal level in Russia and urban conflicts under authoritarianism.

10

Urban Planning and Civic Activism

CAROLA NEUGEBAUER, ANDREI SEMENOV, IRINA SHEVTSOVA, AND DANIELA ZUPAN

Urban activism relates to the contestation of forms of urban space production; it unfolds in multiple arenas, such as arts, media, or street politics. Urban planning, the process that governs land allocation and the development of the built environment, constitutes a distinct arena in which public authorities, experts, businesses, and citizens interact and produce the decisions that set the course for urban developments. In this chapter, we explore how urban planning as a mode of governance affects urban activism by comparing conflicts in the cities of Perm, Russia, and Bonn, Germany.

The study contributes to research on activism and urban planning. The literature on urban activism rarely engages systematically with urban planning institutions and instruments because of its tendency to understand planning as a pure technical and technocratic process. In contrast, we conceptualize urban planning as a mode of governance and argue that it matters for activism in at least three ways. First, the planning process serves as an arena in which active urbanites interact with public officials and forge alliances to advance or contest urban development projects. Second, urban planning institutions provide access points to decision-making processes for various stakeholders. Finally, urban planning codifies normative frameworks, such as public interest, property rights, and collaborative principles, that can turn into reference points for activists to strengthen their position. In other words, we demonstrate that the planning institutions form part of the political opportunity structure that might foster or hinder participation in urban development. We also demonstrate, however, that operations of the planning institutions are constrained by power arrangements regardless of the national political context.

We advance this argument by examining public conflicts over urban renewal projects in Perm and Bonn.[1] These two cities have distinct trajectories of urban development, allowing for a systematic comparison of urban activism in contrasting environments: the permissive and comprehensive planning system in Bonn versus a restricted and often contradictory one in Perm. Accordingly, we expected to find profound differences in the scope and outcomes of the conflicts in the two cities. Contrary to our expectations, we found that urban activists across contexts and conflict episodes faced the similar challenges of elite alliances, incoherent and opaque decision-making processes, and a lack of institutionalized power. In both cases, they employed a similar repertoire, forged coalitions with elected politicians, and relied on the normative premises enshrined in planning documents to justify their claims.

In the following section, we discuss urban planning as a mode of governance and relate it to the political opportunity structure. Then we consider the historic trajectories and characteristics of the local planning and political institutions in Perm and Bonn before we analyze the four conflicts. Finally, we discuss the implications of the comparison and reflect on the core arguments of this study.

Urban Planning as a Mode of Governance

Why is urban planning important for activism? For decades, planning has been regarded as a field of state power and technical expertise, where architects and planners have a primary voice and bureaucrats steer the process. The public, in turn, was relegated to watch urban development from the back seat. Since the late 1970s, the field of urban planning has undergone profound transformations. In many European cities, citizens started to contest the rigid, technocratic, and top-down form of urban planning, pushing the public authorities toward more collaborative forms of planning (Healey 1997). These changes are often referred to as the shift from the modernist planning paradigm (expert based, state governed, and sectoral) to communicative-collaborative planning. Advanced democracies such as West Germany underwent this shift in an incremental manner, while countries such as Russia started to adopt this approach more recently and with abrupt changes in legislation and governance models (Golubchikov 2004).

Regardless of the national context, urban planning deals with the allocation of land and the subsequent transformation of territories. Many European and post-Soviet countries share certain commonalities of urban planning systems. These include the different levels of governance and the core set of instruments, which define the land use and coordinate the actions across different sectors relevant to urban development (such as the environment, economy, mobility, and culture). At the city level, planning professionals elaborate the general land-use plan that defines functional zones for development, such as residential, service, or recreational areas. The plan incorporates national and regional specifications like designated areas of heritage or environmental protection. The general plan is meant to integrate different sectors of urban development, including traffic, health care, social affairs, and many more, thus seeking to balance the multiple needs of urban communities. On the local level, detailed land-use planning governs the development of land plots. Tools such as strategic master plans can complement this set of statutory instruments at different levels.

Planning processes are not limited to planning professionals within the city administration; rather, they are embedded in a political system where a variety of actors—such as active citizens, private businesses, elected officials, bureaucrats, and experts—interact with one another. On the city level, the City Council, city administration, and Mayor's Office play the leading role in urban development. Citizens and interest groups have multiple legal instruments at their disposal to affect the outcomes of the planning process: from elections and petitions to contracts and collaborative forms of governance such as citizens' workshops or participatory design. Figure 10.1 outlines these legal opportunities for interactions.

The figure highlights the political nature of planning processes by displaying its embeddedness in power structures. In a competitive political environment, the interconnectedness of institutions governing the planning process with the local political regime can create incentives for activists to contest seats in the City Council and public offices in the city administration. At the same time, it also provides stimuli for candidates and incumbents to engage with the activists' agendas. In a less competitive political environment, however, regulatory capture of political and administrative bodies by interest groups such as developers is widespread; it magnifies power asymmetries and further impedes the successful mobilization of activists. This process is illustrated in Minaeva's chapter in this volume.

While the planning institutions provide opportunities for activists and interest groups, access to them is often uneven for different stakeholders. For instance, citizens might lack political representation or capital to enter the planning process. Developers, in turn, may be incentivized to engage with the local community before they receive a construction permit if public hearings are compulsory to a planning process. However, developers might also consider

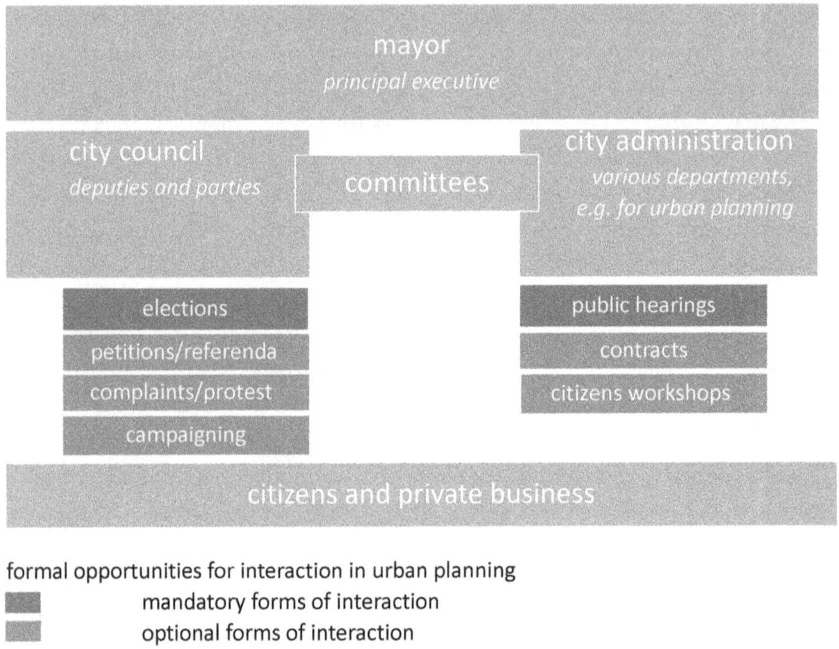

Figure 10.1. Formal opportunities for interactions in urban planning.

circumventing the formal procedures or opting for alternative arrangements with the public authorities, such as through public-private partnerships (PPP), to evade public scrutiny and citizens' supervision.

Finally, the planning institutions and instruments also encompass norms, convictions, and values, which are often manifested in locally specific visions of the city. These values and norms can become a point of reference for activists: confronted with violations of the declared standards and norms, citizens can appeal to these visions to enhance mobilization.

Urban Planning Institutions and Instruments in Bonn and Perm

Urban planning institutions reflect a rich history of development embedded in national systems. In this light, Perm and Bonn share many common planning institutions, but their political contexts differ. In this section, we outline the formal institutions and instruments of urban planning and embed them within the political environments of the two cities.

After the collapse of the Soviet Union, urban planning in Russia underwent a dramatic transition from a centralized-socialist to a centralized-neoliberal governance model. Initial deregulation led to chaotic urban developments in the 1990s. The federal government tried to address these challenges in the new millennium by tightening regulation, inter alia by adopting the Kodeks Zemplepl'zovaniya (Land Use Code) in 2001 and the Gradostroitel'nyi Kodeks (Urban Planning Code) in 2004. The former established the general principles of land allocation and identified major actors, their rights, and their responsibilities in this process. It also introduced mandatory public hearings for construction projects, thereby formally institutionalizing a collaborative planning model. The latter stipulated that by 2010 every municipality had to develop a new general plan, the main instrument of urban planning that defines functional zones; the existing ones had been set up during the Soviet Union and were considered outdated. Other federal laws regulate the status of protected areas such as rivers and lakes, natural parks, and historical sites, where particular rules of development apply. The rapid pace of regulatory change led to multiple inconsistencies and contradictions within the legal framework, which invited abuse by developers and public officials.

At the local level, Perm city administration held major responsibility for planning and urban development until 2020.[2] The Department of Urban Development designed and implemented the principal planning documents, like the general plan; issued construction permits; and negotiated contracts with developers. The City Council adopted the general plan and approved changes in land allocation. Besides the mandatory public hearings within the formal planning process, further access points for citizens included the Public Council and the Council for Urban Development within the City Council. The former is an arena for interactions with nonprofit organizations on "the needs and interests of the local community regarding the city's social-economic development" (Perm City Public Council 2020). At the moment of this study, however, it only comprised developers, public officials, and experts, hardly allowing for participation of citizens in practice.

The Council for Urban Development was established in 2014 "to form and pursue coordinated and coherent urban policies aimed at improving the quality of life and comfort of the urban environment" (Perm City Urban Development Council Statute 2018). In particular, the council "considers the spatial aspects of social and economic development; defines priority projects for the development of public spaces and the urban environment." Formally, it comprises the representatives of the city administration, council members, developers, planners, architects, and civil society organizations. In practice, the council suffers from lobbyists and inconsistencies in decision-making. One of our informants reported that its influence is limited to discussing aesthetic aspects of urban developments, arguing that "it is useless to evaluate images of a project when its construction has already been approved."[3]

Public hearings constitute another access point to the planning process. These hearings are a mandatory procedure. Their results, however, are nonbinding, and in practice they often suffer from misuse on behalf of the authorities and developers. For example, cases have been reported in which the city administration has hidden the information about certain hearings or has not publicized it in a transparent way. Several informants mentioned that the whole procedure can be faked with developers hiring people to attend and vote for a project. While formally Russian urban planning follows the collaborative model, actual practices and routines in Perm showed that it is still very much expert based and lacks sufficient transparency and access for citizens.

In (former West) Germany, both legislation and practice underwent a stepwise transition from an expert-based, state-centered, and sectoral planning model to a communicative and collaborative one since the late 1970s. This shift went hand in hand with economic liberalization and the rise of neoliberal ideas of "market-oriented, market-disciplinary regulatory restructuring" (Peck, Theodore, and Brenner 2009, 51). Thus, new instruments such as enhanced citizen participation, strategic planning, or PPP emerged slowly in the context of stable legislation.

The major German legislation for urban planning consists of the Baugesetzbuch and the Baunutzungsverordnung, which correspond with the Russian Urban Planning Code and the Land Use Code, next to the legislation on environmental protection and monument conservation. At the city level, the Flächennutzungsplan takes the role of the statutory general land-use plan. At the local level, the detailed land-use planning (Bebauungsplan), which is set up either by the city administration or by a private developer through a PPP, is meant to guarantee a balance of interests of different stakeholders. The land-use planning process formally regulates public participation within the formal planning procedure, by assuring the provision of information at early stages and by opening planning documents to public inspection.

The city administration, in particular the Department for Planning, Environment, and Traffic, elaborates and coordinates the urban planning process. In contrast to Perm, in Bonn the City Council is the decision-making institution in the planning process. Several committees of the City Council advise and in some cases guide its executive's decisions. The Committee for Planning, Traffic, and Monument Conservation, for example, decides whether land-use planning processes should start. The Committee for Citizens' Affairs collects, forwards, and moderates the so-called Bürgeranträge (questions and complaints that individuals send to the City Council).

Each committee consists of representatives of the council, whose seats are distributed among the political parties, representatives of the city administration, and citizens appointed by the political parties. What is more, the members of the Bezirksvertretungen (District Council) also represent the citizens' interests: directly elected, they decide on issues of relevance for the urban district in coordination with the City Council and the mayor. While in the case of Bonn we can assert that urban planning follows a collaborative mode not only in form but also in practices and routines, citizens and activists do bemoan shortcomings and infringements. Most often these concern the unequal access to decision-making processes among the different stakeholder groups.

Besides the differences in urban planning institutions and instruments, there are also marked differences in the local political environment. Against the backdrop of Russia becoming a consolidated autocracy, the local political regime in Perm for a long time was praised among the most competitive and liberal in Russia (Borisova 2011; Titkov 2018). Independent political actors, competing business groups, and a dense network of civic organizations served as a check on growing centralization during the first decade of the twenty-first century. However, the authoritarian turn and adoption of the new legislation on urban governance in 2004 led to a gradual decline in the openness of the local regime: direct elections of the mayor were abolished in 2010, and executive powers were transferred to the office of an appointed city manager. In November 2020, the key planning responsibilities were transferred to the regional level, a trend that has been observed across Russian regions.

From 2010 to 2016, the City Council's chair formally served as a mayor and a legal representative of the city. Since 2016, the City Council appoints half of the members of the commission (the governor appoints the other half) that conducts the mayoral selection, which effectively consolidates the power of the governor, making him or her the most powerful player in urban politics.[4] The council approves key planning documents like the general plan and land use and development rules; however, it mostly serves as an arena for lobbying the interests of developers. For example, the chair of the council's Committee for Planning and Land Use for the last three convocations was Aleksei Demkin, ex-CEO of Perm Factory for Silicate Panels, the largest mass-housing construction company in Perm. In April 2021, he became the mayor of Perm.

Germany, in contrast, is a democratic federal parliamentary republic. The citizens of Bonn directly elect the mayor and the City Council every five years. The mayor heads the city administration and the City Council. The city is

Table 10.1. Variation in urban governance structure and political context in Perm and Bonn

	Perm	Bonn
State of institutions in planning and policy	Inconsistent & changing	Coherent & stable
Urban planning paradigm by law	Collaborative	Collaborative
Planning practices	Expert based	Collaborative
National political regime	Autocracy	Democracy

politically and financially independent, although it has to follow the general rules of regional planning as well as the laws of the German federal state of North-Rhine Westphalia, to which it belongs. In sum, the cases of Perm and Bonn share many similarities in terms of key institutional arrangements and instruments of urban planning as well as in terms of formal access points for citizens to urban planning, but they drastically differ in political regime. Besides, planning institutions and policymaking keep changing in Perm, while in Bonn they have been relatively stable. As a result, planning practices (the realization of legal opportunities to engage with urban development by multiple stakeholders) remain restricted and expert based in Perm. Table 10.1 summarizes the differences in local context.

The similarity in institutional structures against the contrasting backdrop of political contexts and planning practices allows one to better understand how the activists use planning institutions and instruments and, ultimately, the latter's role in the urban development process. We expected a sustained and effective urban activism in Bonn and intermittent and fragmented attempts to challenge planning projects in Perm. While these expectations are partially confirmed, the four conflicts below demonstrate a far more complicated picture.

Urban Renewal Conflicts in Perm and Bonn

The case studies analyzed in this section illustrate how the differences in governance structures and context shaped mobilizations in the cities under scrutiny. The selected urban conflicts in Perm and Bonn germinated from the attempts to remake parts of the existing urban fabric. In Perm, we explore the cases of a local park in decay that was turned into a shopping mall in the Krasnova district and a recreational area that is maintained by locals and that faces the threat of residential apartment development. In Bonn, we study the attempted

Table 10.2. Overview of the conflict cases in Perm and Bonn

Case, location, and duration	Planning specifics	Repertoire of objection	Outcome
Perm: Krasnova Shopping Mall, Krasnova district, 2014–2015	General plan & construction permit: no prior public hearings. The mall replaced an abandoned park in a residential neighborhood.	Meetings, court trials, petitions, direct actions	Construction of the mall with minimal concession from the developer
Perm: Nightingales' Garden, Sadovyi district, 2010–2018	General plan, national regulations & aspired construction permit. New housing might replace a protected park.	Meetings, petitions, roundtables	Stalemate between the activists and developer/ landowner
Bonn: Viktoriakarree, downtown, 2012–2018	PPP-driven detailed land-use planning & aspired construction permit. The shopping mall might replace a mixed-use, inner-city quarter.	Meetings, petitions, protests, workshops	Stalemate between the activists and developer/ landowner
Bonn: Railway station's square, downtown, 2002–2016	PPP-driven detailed land-use planning, statutory detailed planning & construction permit. New constructions replaced the modernist ensemble in the city.	Meetings, petitions, workshops	Construction of the project with amendments

transformation of a lively inner-city historical quarter called Viktoriakarree into more profitable real estate by an international developer, as well as sustained citizen opposition to the city's plans to redevelop the railway station's square and its adjacent buildings. Table 10.2 summarizes these conflict cases.

The selected conflicts reflect the specific challenges that the case study cities face with regard to urban renewal projects: The city of Perm dates back to Peter the Great's modernization ambitions; it has a modernist regular grid layout that stretches along the Kama River. It is a large metropolitan area with over one million residents (2012) and holds a strong industrial profile. Residential areas encircle a number of military, aviation and space, and oil refinery enterprises. The heyday of industrialization and urban growth—the second half of the twentieth century—was associated with the development of densely populated housing districts. Krasnova and Sadovyi districts, the sites of our case studies, are typical examples of residential areas facing the perils of privatization and marketization of the land and housing stock in the post-Soviet period.

Unlike Perm, the city of Bonn has a long uninterrupted history of urban development, germinating from the times of the Roman Empire. Over centuries, the city developed continuously on the banks of the Rhine River. After World War II, Bonn became the capital of Western Germany, home for the federal government. Following the reunification in 1990, the government moved to Berlin, but some federal and international institutions remained in Bonn. Bonn has a growing population of 330,000 inhabitants (2018) and will keep growing, according to forecasts. One of the main challenges that urban development in Bonn faces today is the question of how to accommodate this growth within the city boundaries, where land is scarce. Accordingly, the topic of densification of the existing urban fabric and urban renewal projects dominate local planning debates and often become trigger points for conflicts, as in the two cases selected.

Perm: Replacing a Park with a Shopping Mall in Krasnova District

Perm's Krasnova district is a typical residential area adjacent to a large Soviet-era industrial complex. Over time, trees populated a wasteland territory between buildings, and residents used it as a recreational area, which had a land-use category of C-2 (service and business activity), not P-1 (parks and squares). The Department for Land Use (DLU) leased the area in 2013 to a businessperson who proposed to build a shopping mall on the plot. The initial project faced opposition from the DLU, but its rejection was overruled by the court.

Construction started suddenly on October 25, 2014, without mandatory public hearings. Convinced by local activist and popular local blogger Anton Tolmachev, who later became an informal leader of the mobilization, that the construction is illegal, the residents sued the developer and the DLU for the misappropriation of land and demanded the cancellation of the land-lease contract. They also petitioned the governor, the president, Perm Krai Ministry of Construction, and a number of other public officials. Much as in the chapter by Smyth, McCann, and Hitchcock in this volume, the attachment to place played an important role in interviews: the locals clearly expressed the grievances of unwanted developer intrusion into neighborhood life.

Despite these actions, on November 4, the workers secured access to the site and started to cut the trees. Their actions provoked a spontaneous gathering of about one hundred residents. The power inequalities and the perceived illegality were the major reference points; as one activist put it, "I've noticed that where money is involved, illegal construction starts, the trees are cut, so there is no law."[5] Later in November, the residents met with the developer's representative. Having received no concessions or answers, they organized a rally against the construction. In a reference to the developer's surname, Kozlov, which has the same root as *kozel* (or "goat," often used as a moniker in Russian), the locals put slogans like "Save the square from the goats" and "No to the goathouse" on display.

In March 2015, the initiative group attended the Commission for Land Use session and proposed to change the status of the area from commercial development to recreational area. While the commission approved the change of status, the case was eventually lost in the court, and the mall was built by summer 2015. The steam of mobilization had faded away by that time; the developer, however, agreed to allocate some funds to compensate the residents with a much smaller park nearby.

Perm: A Recreational Area under Threat (Nightingale's Garden)

The Nightingales' Garden is at the center of a protracted conflict complicated by the incongruence of regulations and regulatory bodies. It started as an environmental initiative from residents living near the small Uinka River—a wild ravine and a habitat for many bird species. The river constitutes the border between two densely populated Perm districts in need of green spaces—Sadovyi and Gorodskie Gorky. For years, the valley served as a landfill. In 2007, volunteers began to organize regular cleanups and named the area the Nightingales' Garden. At the same time, the regional government issued an ordinance "on demarcation of cultural heritage protection zones in Perm intra-city districts" that aimed at protecting the small river valleys. Uinka River received an L-3 status, which prohibited the construction of buildings not designated for recreational use. The initiative group of locals also advocated for a special status of urban park (P-1), which was granted for a part of the area in February 2009 by the City Council. Finally, the activists raised the funding for area beautification and established relationships with the city administration.

The City Council's sudden decision in January 2010 to change the status of the area to R-3, which permits residential and commercial construction, instigated the conflict. The decision was made without public hearings. As was revealed later, the group of landowners of the cooperative adjacent to the garden privatized their parcels and attempted to consolidate land plots to sell to developers. Recognizing the threat and using the momentum of the debates around the adoption of a new general plan, the initiative group launched a campaign advocating an incorporation of the Uinka valley into the plan as a recreational area. The group received a response from the Department of Architecture and Planning confirming the L-3 status.

In April 2014, public hearings were carried out to build residential apartments near the garden. Local citizens opposed these plans, but the landowner, in alliance with the *Permskii Kvartal* development company, continued to lobby for a construction permit in the area. In July 2015, the city administration by its ordinance stated that the garden was a part of Specially Protected Environmental Territory *Ivinskya*. Meanwhile, in October 2016 the landowners constructed a fence around the garden, thereby completely cutting off access to the area. To resolve the confrontation, on February 13, 2017, new public hearings put competing proposals on the agenda. The developer proposed a change in the zoning type from P-1[6] to C-2 (service and business areas), which would permit the construction of a multistory apartment building, while the initiative group insisted on maintaining the recreational status of the area. At the hearing, the developer said that the sufficient argument in favor of the project is the commercial interest based on property rights. As its representative put it, "We bought this land. That is why we will decide for ourselves what to build on it without consulting with you [the opponents of the project]." The activists contended that the project violates the public interests and the general plan regulations. No compromise was reached.

By that time, the coalition behind the garden included residents, environmental and urban activists, and Perm council members. To protect the garden, the coalition advocated for systemic changes in the regulation of the development in the small river valleys through petitions, roundtables, and other public events. In parallel, the developer sued the city administration for the refusal to change the zoning category. The last public hearing in April 2019 again led to a standoff between the developer and the activists, with both sides blaming each other for the unwillingness to compromise.

Bonn: An Inner-City Neighborhood under Threat (Viktoriakarree)

In contrast to Perm, the conflicts in Bonn unfolded in the inner city. The case of the Viktoriakarree concerns a vibrant quarter close to the city's university that comprised housing, small shops, cultural amenities, and a public swimming hall. Discussions about the redevelopment of the area germinated from the City Council's decision in 2007 to close the swimming hall. Consequently, several planning concepts were developed to strengthen the retail function in this area,[7] while the "Masterplan Inner City Bonn" (drafted since

2010 and approved by the City Council in 2013) foresaw mixed functionality for the area.

In 2010, developers began to buy plots in the Viktoriakarree, expecting the area's commercialization. In 2012, two investors presented their proposals for the development of the area to the City Council's Committee on Economic Affairs: the Austrian-based firm Signa envisioned a demolition of the whole structure and the construction of a shopping mall, and the investor PDP suggested a culture-focused concept. The city administration favored Signa's idea, and the governing Social Democratic Party (SPD) together with the Liberal Party (FDP) pushed the decision process forward. The council's Committee for Planning, however, postponed their decision because of opposition from two other political parties, the Christian Democratic Union (CDU) and the Green Party. The District Council of Bonn Inner City (Bezirksvertretung Innenstadt) was also against a shopping mall.

Because of this conflict, in March 2014 the City Council decided to carry out a European-wide tender to sell and develop the municipal plots within the Viktoriakarree. The tender included provisions to hold the area open to the public and to preserve the university's library. At the same time, the council decided to initiate a land-use planning process in which the investor would work out the plan, thus seeking to stimulate investors to develop the area. In May 2014, the City Council elections took place, leading to a change in the ruling coalition: the CDU, Green Party, and FDP took power. While before the elections the CDU had agreed with its coalition partner, the Green Party, on supporting the project, after the elections the latter distanced itself from the project.

The Greens called to preserve the existing milieu of Viktoriakarree and tried to mobilize support from citizens "before another part of the historic city center becomes a victim to the profit interest of foreign investors" (Beu and Lohmeyer 2014, cited in Akalin 2014). By using this specific vocabulary (for example, *Kahlschlagsanierung*, "urban clearance"; *Profitinteresse*, "profit interests"), the Greens referred to the controversies that characterized West German planning debates in the 1960s and 1970s. The outcome of these debates was a shift in perception, namely toward the recognition of the need to preserve existing urban structures and their socio-spatial milieus. By explicitly linking the Viktoriakarree project to these debates, the authors referred to values that are enshrined in contemporary German planning approach concerning the sensitive urban renewal, thereby seeking to strengthen their position.

Political support for the project was already shaky at this moment. But the conflict really arose in 2015 when the City Council presented its decision to sell the municipal plots to Signa, which despite the provisions in the tender offered again a bulky shopping center. Consequently, a citizen initiative, Viva Viktoria, was launched in August 2015 to protect the area from the project. Several other initiatives joined them in staging public protests every Wednesday. They launched a petition for a public referendum that the City Council members of the SPD, the Green Party, and the Left Party (against CDU and FDP) joined in December 2015. In consequence, the decision to sell the municipal land was canceled and the tender procedure stopped.

The project restarted in 2016, this time with a costly citizen workshop of eight months (February–September 2017), whose mission the City Council, in cooperation with the planning department, had agreed on in advance, namely "to make a clear recommendation on further development planning for the Viktoriakarree, underpinned by planning concepts."[8] The workshop itself was led and documented by an external agency that specialized in citizen participation and conflict mediation. However, Signa left this process before a consensus among all stakeholder groups could be reached. In parallel, Signa acquired other plots in the Viktoriakarree, thus becoming the dominant property owner. From 2016 onward, the company halted rental-contract extension for local businesses, stoking people's fears that Signa intended to ruin the lively atmosphere of the Viktoriakarree to increase pressure on officials. On the basis of the citizens' workshop results, the city of Bonn launched a detailed land-use planning process for the Viktoriakarree. In 2019, the majority of the City Council approved the land-use plan, yet some of the local activist groups, like Viva Victoria, stand against any physical change in the quarter. Much as in the Nightingales' Garden case in Perm, the city administration elicited compromise but stumbled over conflicting regulations and interests.

Bonn: A New Commercial Entrance to the City

The second case in Bonn concerns the development of the railway station's square, which has been a site of contention since the 1970s. Because of civic protests at that time, the city stopped the already-begun construction. In the first decade of the twenty-first century, the public authorities decided to give it another try and made a call for expression of interest for European investors. From the eight competitors, the City Council selected the project from the developer Brune, which consisted of a glass-construction complex with retail spaces. This decision spurred a conflict. By the end of 2002, citizens' initiatives and other lobby groups criticized the project, but above all the planning and decision-making process. Opponents argued that key decisions had been made before the project was even presented to the public, and they requested more participation in the planning process.

Despite the resistance, the City Council gave the formal mandate to the city administration to continue working with Brune. Between 2003 and 2004, the investor, in coordination with the city administration, further developed and amended their proposal. Although amendments were made and additional forms of participation, such as meetings, were carried out, the conflict intensified. The public interest groups demanded significant changes, and a group of citizens initiated a public petition against the renewal of the square. Even though the CDU had been a strong supporter of the Brune concept, the party joined the public petition during the campaign for mayoral elections in autumn 2004. Consequently, the City Council canceled the project in December 2004.

After this failure, supporters of the petition (CDU, Bürger Bund Bonn, and Green Party) pushed for a quick restart and proposed to proceed differently. The city organized a public workshop with citizens, lobby groups, politicians, and city officials between October 2005 and January 2006 to find consensus on key planning objectives. The resulting agreements included the provision of a sufficient distance between the new buildings and the railway station; the reduction or demolition of the Südüberbauung (the unloved modernist architecture by Friedrich Spengelin); the creation of a public square; and the commitment that planning competence must remain with the city and would not be given to a private investor.

Despite these agreements, in 2007 the City Council decided to develop the plots of the whole territory separately, and an interested investor, German Development Group (GDG), started to work on a project to replace the Südüberbauung at its own cost. During the development, GDG demanded concessions from the city—namely, that it be granted the land-use concession for the plot as investment protection. The city, however, rejected this request and launched a solely state-run detailed land-use planning process in 2008. At that point various citizen initiatives started to heavily oppose the city. They called for the city to actively support the private investor in their attempt to demolish the unloved Südüberbauung, opposing the former workshop agreement that the city would not merely serve the interests of private investors.

Yet the alliance between the activists and the investor broke after the investor presented his design by the end of 2009. Opponents now came back to the agreements of the workshop and systematically criticized the project on the basis of these principles. An observer from the Green Party rightly announced that every decision would be followed by discussions because it would be impossible to fulfill all agreements from the citizen workshop. And, indeed, the agreements of this workshop became a reference point during the whole process, from which all stakeholder groups made selective and shifting use conforming with their also shifting interests and positions. Though GDG made several amendments to its project, it could not build consensus and finally dropped the project because of financial problems in 2014. Another investor, Ten Brinke, jumped in with a new proposal for the Südüberbauung and received building permission in 2016 in line with the detailed land-use plan that had entered into force in 2013. The project construction was completed in summer 2019, and several activists now lament the lost heritage of the once-unloved modernist Südüberbauung.

Urban Activism, Planning, and Local Political Regimes

What do these conflicts reveal about the linkages between urban planning and activism? First, as the planning process regulates the access to information and decision-making, it establishes opportunities and constraints for activists to contest development projects. In both cities, the citizens used the established formal planning procedures to voice their concerns and enter the decision-making process. But we also observed differences between our cases. In Perm, the lack of public information about developers' proposals and the failure to establish arenas for communication and interaction between conflicting parties through conventional instruments like public hearings sparked collective action. In Bonn, planning processes are generally more transparent and participatory. Citizen workshops, public hearings, and committee meetings are the primary arenas to elicit information and voice concerns about the development projects.

As in Perm, Bonn public authorities found a way to limit public participation. For example, the instrument of PPPs, as the railway station case demonstrates, enhanced the opportunities for closed-door deals between the investors and authorities. Consequently, activists often fought for disclosing the project details as early as possible and before any key decisions were made. Perm activists also pointed to the necessity of entering the process at the early stages.

The conflicts also revealed the multiple channels through which civic actors can intervene in planning. Official meetings, public hearings, committee gatherings, workshops, and petitions provide formalized and legitimated spaces where activists can communicate their demands and negotiate project proposals. At the same time, our study indicates that access to these formal institutional arrangements is not equally distributed among the different stakeholder groups and that they create opportunities for informal ties and interactions, both in Perm and in Bonn.

These interactions are mostly invisible to the public and often escape public oversight, establishing conditions for shadow brokerage and deals. The members of a powerful lobby group in Bonn, for example, praised the "short distances" to official channels, especially the mayor, who is always open to meet them informally on Saturday mornings for discussion.[9] While powerful actors have access to several informal channels such as lobbying, urban activists often do not enjoy the same privileges. Even in Bonn, activists frequently complained that they were not heard: "[The current situation in planning] is not a representation of citizens. [Investors who rule the process] don't know at all what citizens want. They just know what the administration and politics have in mind."[10]

The study also shows the activists' use of and dependence on the normative frameworks enshrined in planning documents and practices. The planning regulations serve as a reference point when the activists appeal to the public and the authorities to substantiate their claims. In Nightingales' Garden, they invoked the legislation on environmental protection to convince the other parties that building in the area was not allowed. In the Krasnova case, the locals contested the construction in the court, believing that it was illegal with regard to official planning documents. In the case of the railway station's square in Bonn, activists selectively referred to the planning agreements of the citizen workshop when it fitted their interests and position. And in the case of the Viktoriakarree, references to West German planning history were used to fuel fears of demolition and spur mobilization against the project. In other words, the planning documents, practice, and history allowed the interested parties to maintain or contest the legal and moral basis for the projects.

Some contradictions and impediments emerge with regard to normative frameworks, concerning, for example, participation and property rights. Regarding the latter, in the Nightingales' Garden case, the landowner consistently emphasized his property rights as a way to deflect the activists' demands. The absence of the delineation between the private rights and public interests breeds a stalemate between the parties. In Bonn, the social obligation of property is a formal institution anchored in the constitution, which renders the contradiction between private rights and public interests less acute.

Regarding the idea of participation, the Bonn activists often fight for direct access to decision-making power instead of access to information only. Their aspirations, however, contradict German regulations, which strictly limit direct decision-making power to specific cases to protect the general working of parliamentary, representative democracy. Nevertheless, the participation in urban planning is institutionalized and provides multiple access points and a comprehensive framework for citizens' engagement with urban affairs. Activists in Perm, in contrast, struggle to find their place in the urban planning process. As access to formal arenas is restricted and informal practices undermine the binding effects of instruments such as the general plan, they have to make extra efforts to find relevant information, identify channels to raise their concerns, and mobilize.

Finally, we have highlighted that the planning processes are embedded in the larger political environment. In Bonn, politicians frequently seek alliances with citizens to secure their reelection. They readily take positions on salient projects that might easily spark public conflicts; they also change sides depending on their party's position in the government. Consequently, political parties play an important role and frequently side with one stakeholder or another. Elected officials in Perm also react to urban mobilizations: some support activists by attending the public events and advocating the regulatory changes; others either directly represent business interests or try to mediate between the conflicting parties. However, they engage with activists mostly on an individual basis rather than according to party affiliation.

Despite the differences in political environment, the activists use a strikingly similar repertoire: they hold public rallies, mobilize public opinion, contact and petition officials, bring their cases to court, and forge alliances with political groups. Although the repertoire in Bonn appears to be more robust and routinized because of the long-standing experience in a stable institutional setting, in Perm too, as the Nightingales' Garden case indicates, the mobilization can last for a long time and overcome the high costs of collective action in an unfavorable environment. However, there are constraints to activism and limits to the activists' reach: in Krasnova, depleted and having lost their case in the court, the locals gave up. The compensation the developer provided—a small renovated park area—is incommensurate to the territory lost to the construction. But even in environments generally conducive to urban activism, such as Bonn, activists in most cases do not fully achieve their goals.

Conclusion

The planning process constitutes an important part of urban activism and mobilization: the quality, stability, and coherence of formal and informal institutions of planning matter in structuring the relations between the different stakeholders and in coordinating and balancing their interests in urban development. We have shown how the local differences in urban planning and specific historical trajectories and political environments shaped the specific cases and outcomes of mobilization. Surprisingly, our study revealed more similarities than expected. The complexity and contradictions in legislation, weak law enforcement, and overt fraud on behalf of the powerful players in Perm often trigger citizens' engagement in urban affairs. Similarly, in Bonn, a city with a longer tradition of empowered citizens and business in collaborative planning, forms of publicly invisible and parliamentary uncontrolled power alliances trigger collective action. In both cities, activists at times feel powerless and irrelevant.

Both cases revealed that the political context shapes how planning institutions and instruments are practiced. While power inequalities are common, in Perm, the weak political competition deprives the City Council of its representative function. In contrast, in Bonn, politicians are generally more responsive to citizens' interests, and the withdrawal of support for a developer's project facing resistance is a commonly observed feature. Finally, the normative frameworks, which serve as a reference point during mobilization, also shape the trajectory of the activism. The juxtaposition between the private and public interests is more pronounced in Perm and often leads to irreconcilable situations. In Bonn, the social obligations of property rights are an established tradition; nevertheless, there exist other norms and values that become contentious during the conflict.

In the four cases we presented, one failed to achieve its purpose (Krasnova), two ended up in stalemates (Nightingales' Garden and Viktoriakarree), and only the reconstruction of the railway station's square can be considered as a (partial) success. Does this imply that the urban activism presented here made any difference? While such questions demand more study, we believe that the answer is positive. In the Krasnova case, the indirect consequence of the mobilization was the creation of the territorial self-government unit that took responsibility for the beautification and maintenance of the district and led the fight against the monopoly in service provision. The Nightingales' Garden activists successfully lobbied for amendments to the legislation on the small rivers' protection and pushed forward the agenda of a comfortable urban environment. Although the garden itself is still under threat, the sustained mobilization and resistance helped to raise awareness, preserve the site, and even make it a successful showcase for similar cases in the city.

In Bonn we can observe the emergence of a network of urban activist groups, who mutually support and actively learn from one another in different conflict cases throughout the city. What is more, as a result of several public conflicts over major projects in Bonn, the city has recently set up a new binding framework for participation that goes beyond the legally defined standards, the Guidelines for Citizen Participation Bonn. The results still have to be evaluated, but in general the guidelines seek to enhance opportunities for citizen participation and to systematically improve the accessibility of information on planning projects. In sum, the mobilization across the national contexts generated the social capital necessary for collective action.

The cases presented here also tell the complex story of the normative frameworks enshrined in the public institutions and rules that govern urban development. Designed to reconcile multiple and contradictory interests, the formal institutions of urban planning often fail to deliver on that promise. Although only a handful of development projects are contested at any point in time as compared to the entire volume of construction work in any city, the activists' actions are important in giving voice to the least powerful group in the planning process—the citizens.

Notes

This chapter was prepared within the TRIPAR research project funded by the Volkswagen Stiftung, grant number Az. 90 345–0.

1. We analyzed planning and policy documents, regulations, and media reports alongside interviews with participants of the conflicts. Through media screening we first identified urban conflicts in both cities between 2000 and 2016, before we selected matching cases for comparison. Overall, we conducted forty-eight semi-structured in-depth interviews (twenty-three in Perm and twenty-five in Bonn) in 2017–2018, complemented by fieldwork in both cities.
2. In November 2020, the City Council voted to transfer these responsibilities to the regional level.
3. Interview 1, activist, former member of City Council for Urban Development, Perm (November 17, 2017).
4. The governors played the central role in urban development even before these institutional changes: it was Governor Oleg Chirkunov in 2008 and not the mayor who proposed the development of the master plan and the transition to the compact city model (Zupan 2015). When Viktor Basargin replaced Chirkunov in 2012, the planning paradigm took a U-turn back to

the territorial expansion promoted by the developers affiliated with the new governor.

5. Interview 2, Krasnova district resident, activist, Perm (October 5, 2017).
6. Legally, the territory of the proposed development is a zone for parks (P-1), on which it is possible to place only fountains, sculptures, sports grounds, and greenhouses.
7. The "Integrated development concept for Bonn—inner-city" (2008) and a detailed retail report and potential analysis about the Viktoriakarree (2013).
8. For more details, see "Bürgerbeteiligung Viktoriakarree," Bonn Macht Mit, accessed June 23, 2021, https://www.bonn-macht-mit.de/dialog/b%C3%BCrgerbeteiligung-viktoriakarree).
9. Interview 3, lobby group member, Bonn (June 29, 2017).
10. Interview 4, activist, Bonn (December 13, 2017).

Bibliography

Akalin, C. 2014. "Grüne distanzieren sich. Pläne zum Viktoriakarree." *Generalanzeiger,* May 21, 2014. https://ga.de/bonn/stadt-bonn/gruene-distanzieren-sich_aid-41880035.

Borisova, N. 2011. "Perm: A Local Regime in a Large Russian City." *Russian Politics & Law* 49 (4): 85–96.

Fainstein, S. S., and J. Defilippis. 2016. "Introduction: The Structure and Debates of Planning Theory." In *Readings in Planning Theory,* 4th ed., 1–18. New York: Wiley and Sons.

Fröhlich, C. 2020. "Urban Citizenship under Post-Soviet Conditions: Grassroots Struggles of Residents in Contemporary Moscow." *Journal of Urban Affairs* 42 (2): 188–202.

Golubchikov, O. 2004. "Urban Planning in Russia: Towards the Market." *European Planning Studies* 12 (2): 229–247.

Healey, P. 1997. *Collaborative Planning: Shaping Places in Fragmented Societies,* London: Macmillan.

Peck, J., N. Theodore, and N. Brenner. 2009. "Neoliberal Urbanism: Models, Moments, Mutations." *SAIS Review of International Affairs* 29 (1): 49–66.

Perm City Public Council. 2020. PCPB official website. Last accessed August 21, 2022. https://web.archive.org/web/20210227042943/http://duma.perm.ru/sovets/sovet/.

Perm City Urban Development Council Statute. 2018. Postanovlenije (OMSU) ot 04.04.2017 289 "O Gradostroitelnom sovete pri Glave goroda Permi." Accessed August 21, 2022. https://docs.cntd.ru/document/446194453?marker.

Titkov, A. 2018. "Democracy Index in Russian Regions: Dynamics from 1990s to 2010s." *Bulletin of Perm University, Political Science,* no. 2, 83–106.

Zupan, D. 2015. "Local Debates on Global Planning Concepts: The Compact European City Model in Postsocialist Russia: The Case of Perm." *Europa Regional* 22 (1–2): 39–52.

Carola Neugebauer is Associate Professor of Cultural Heritage and Planning at RWTH Aachen University. She is editor (with Tsypylma Darieva) of *Urban Activism in Eastern Europe and Eurasia: Strategies and Practices*; (with Tauri Tuvikene and Wladimir Sgibnev) of *Post-Socialist Urban Infrastructures*; and (with Isolde Brade) of *Urban Eurasia: Cities in Transformation.*

Andrei Semenov is Associate Professor in the Department of Political Science and International Affairs at the Higher School of Economics, St. Petersburg. His work appears in *Russian Politics, Social Movements Studies,* and *Post-Soviet Affairs.*

Irina Shevtsova is Senior Researcher at the Sociological Institute, Russian Academy of Sciences. Her research focuses on Russian local politics and urban conflicts.

Daniela Zupan is Assistant Professor of European Cities and Urban Heritage at Bauhaus-Universität Weimar. Her research on urban studies and planning appears in *Antipode* and *Housing Studies.*

11

Manipulating Public Discontent in Russia

The Role of Trade Unions in the Protests against Pension Reform

IRINA MEYER-OLIMPIEVA

This chapter examines the role of trade unions in popular protests that erupted across Russia in response to the 2018 pension reform designed to increase the national retirement age. The research demonstrates that despite high popular dissatisfaction with the pension reform, the likely leaders of these protests, trade unions, failed to mobilize the general population and the rank-and-file union members, further undermining the ability of their capacity to influence policymaking.

On June 14, 2018, the Russian government approved a new bill raising the retirement age from sixty to sixty-five for men and from fifty-five to sixty-three for women. Pension reform had long been on the agenda of Russia's liberal economists (Maltseva 2018). The question of raising the retirement age arose every time the government faced a budget deficit and could not fulfill its social obligations. Since 2000, the regime has made several attempts to restructure the pension system (Cook, Asland, and Prisyazhnyuk 2019). Until 2018, these efforts failed, and the retirement age was unchanged. Pension reform remained highly unpopular and politically risky since President Putin made a promise in the beginning of the first decade of the twenty-first century that the pension age would remain the same while he was president.[1] Any increase in retirement age could damage his reputation.

The analysis focuses on the comparison of protest strategies of the two main trade union camps—the so-called official and alternative trade unions—to show how the struggle over pension reform revealed significant changes in the labor movement. By analyzing the repertoire of protest actions, I show that despite the remaining split into official and alternative camps, the actual distinctions among trade unions have been blurred. Both trade union leaderships refused to engage in direct protest such as strikes or work stoppages, confining the repertoire of contention to symbolic organized meetings and pickets. Similarly, both unions rejected organizational support of illegal protests to avoid violations of the laws about public actions.

While the opposition of official and alternative trade unions persists at the company level, they pursue the same institutional strategies. Both leaderships increasingly integrate into the political system through formal and informal ties with political parties and powerful political actors. In both camps, these alliances have undermined unions' capacity during the anti-reform campaign, although for different reasons. As a result, in both camps the anti-reform campaign has aggravated the discrepancy between leadership and grassroots activists as well as between active and passive trade unions.

Finally, this study highlights the manipulative character of the union-led anti-reform campaign as an example of a broader type of symbolic organized protests in authoritarian political regimes like Russia's. The symbolic depoliticized anti-reform protest could not stop regime plans to increase the pension age, since it was addressed to Kremlin-controlled, pseudo-democratic institutions. As an authoritarian body, the Kremlin can be forced to change its decision only under the threat of spontaneous protests demanding regime change. Both union camps worked to prevent politicization by keeping protests within the frame of symbolic depoliticized actions. On the background of pseudo-democratic policymaking institutions and weak civil society, organized depoliticized protests inevitably become manipulated as they are used by the authoritarian regime to channel public discontent and to avoid politicization of protesters' demands.

The chapter begins with a discussion of the closed opportunity structure in which the pension reform was enacted. It then outlines the configuration of the post-Soviet labor movement, with a focus on the role that protest plays in the strategies of different Russian trade unions. I then examine the features of the 2018 anti-reform campaign, such as repertoires of protest actions and political allies of different trade unions, as well as interactions between the leadership and grassroots levels of trade unions during this campaign. This discussion highlights the manipulative character of anti-reform protests and the reasons for trade unions' dependence on the regime. The final part of the chapter summarizes the outcomes of the anti-reform protests and their consequences for the Russian labor movement.

Suddenly Imposed Grievance: The Formation of Unpopular Policy

The bill about raising the retirement age appeared to come as a complete surprise to ordinary people. It was approved by the government just one month after the so-called May Presidential Decrees, Russia's six-year plan for top priorities of national development, in which the newly reelected president Vladimir Putin promised to ensure a steady growth in real incomes of citizens while reducing the poverty levels by half. The population's reaction was unanimously negative. According to Levada Center polls, about 90 percent of the population opposed raising the retirement age. Political leadership promoted the reform as a long-awaited improvement to the well-being of pensioners. The presentation prepared by the pro-Kremlin United Russia Party claimed that after the reform, all pensioners would receive an annual pension increase of 1,000 rubles, while before the reform increases were between 380 and 450 rubles. Despite these promises, ordinary people immediately labeled the pension reform as an "accounting maneuver" designed to make up for the shortfall in the ever-shrinking state budget by extracting the funds from people's pockets.

The new bill was also criticized on several technical points. It did not address a wide set of complex issues related to the reform, such as the inevitable growth of unemployment and age discrimination in the workplace, the restructuring of the vocational training and health-care systems, and many other issues that are usually taken into consideration. Some experts even refused to consider the proposed bill a reform, adopting alternative labels such as the "so-called reform." Another major criticism referred to the selective character of the changes. The bill did not change the early retirement age of forty to forty-five enjoyed by some state employees working in the military and law enforcement. The difference between these privileged groups and the rest of the population is even more striking with the new bill. This gap in the levels of pension benefits suggests that the pension reform was deliberately designed to buy the loyalty of the groups supporting the regime (Meyer-Olimpieva 2018).

While in democracies the introduction of a new pension system usually takes a long time because of wide public discussions, in Russia the whole process lasted a little longer than four months—from June 14, 2018, when the project was approved by the government, until September 27, 2018, when the law was adopted by the State Duma in the final reading. The government did everything possible to restrict open expressions of public discontent with the proposed increase of the retirement age. The time of reform coincided with the holding of the World Cup in Russia, which, because of a ban on holding mass rallies during the championship, severely limited the possibility of protest in major cities.

The process of adopting the new retirement age unfolded very rapidly and with little opportunity for opponents to influence the policy, demonstrating a closed opportunity structure within the legislative process. On June 19, 2018, the Russian State Duma adopted the bill on its first reading. While three opposition parties—the Communist Party of the Russian Federation (KPRF), Liberal Democratic Party of Russia (LDPR), and A Just Russia (JR)—voted against the bill, they could not prevail against United Russia's parliamentary majority. Rare opposition to the bill did extend the deadline for amendments to the bill until September 24.

On August 21, the State Duma held open parliamentary public hearings entitled Improving Pension Legislation. Representatives of political parties, advocacy groups, and civil society organizations were invited to express their opinions and criticism of the pension reform. The hearings included six hundred participants and lasted for more than four hours. Notably, the major targets of criticism of the pension reform—Prime Minister Dmitrii Medvedev, Finance Minister Andrey Siluanov, and Deputy Prime Minister for Social Policy, Labor, Health, and Pension Provision Tatiana Golikova—did not show up at the hearings, a clear sign of the event's low importance to the policymaking process. The hearings explicitly demonstrated that in the eyes of the government raising the pension age was a done deal and that there was only space to bargain over details.

After two months of silence, on August 29, President Vladimir Putin appealed directly to the Russian people, asking them to support reform. He suggested nine amendments aimed at softening the bill, chief among which was limiting the increase in the retirement age for women to five years. As he put it, "In our country, there is a special, gentle attitude to women" (*Vedomosti* 2018).

A month later, on September 24, the Duma Committee on Labor and Social Policy considered the 286 amendments to the bill. The amendments were made by the president and parliamentary parties, as well as by the Federation of Independent Trade Unions of Russia, the All-Russian NGO of Small and Medium Enterprises "Support of Russia," and the Russian Union of Industrialists and Entrepreneurs. Of 286 amendments, the committee adopted only 16—9 of which had been suggested by the president. Apart from the decrease in the raise in the pension age for women, he introduced the concept of preretirement age, of five years during which a person would be guaranteed protection against dismissal. The president also advocated the introduction of administrative and criminal liability for the dismissal or denial of employment of such employees. State Duma adopted the bill on the third and final reading on September 27.

Protest and the Role of Trade Union Organizations

The bill sparked a wave of popular protests across the country. According to the Center for Economic and Political Reform (CEPR), by the end of September, there had been 1,174 protest actions across forty-three Russian regions—a figure that accounted for almost half of all protest actions since the beginning of the year. Because of the scale, duration, and geographical coverage, scholars and analysts consider the anti-reform campaign a milestone of the post-Soviet protest movement similar to the "rail wars" of miners in the 1990s, the pensioner revolt against the monetization of social benefits in 2005, or truck drivers' protests against the Platon system in 2015–2016 (Bizyukov 2019).

Despite this scale, pension-reform protests are starkly different from the previous cases on the repertoire of collective action. While past actions were aimed at disruption and contentions action, the 2018 campaign relied exclusively on symbolic actions like meetings, rallies, and pickets as well as on appeals and petitions to the authorities. There were no direct protests such as strikes or the road blockades widely used by miners or truck drivers in previous protests. There were also no spontaneous uprisings to mark the pensioner revolt of 2005. The protests against the pension reform were well organized and held in strict accordance with the law on public gathering.[2] In ninety-seven Russian cities, organizers canceled demonstrations because they were not approved by city authorities.[3]

The anti-reform campaign turned out to be a complete failure for Russian trade unions. Not only could trade unions not stop or suspend the raising of the pension age; they could not change the bill—none of the nineteen amendments suggested by trade unions were accepted by the State Duma except for those that coincided with the amendments suggested by President Putin. The final softening of the bill seemed to be attributable not to public pressure but to the president's mercy. However, the protest campaign organized by Russian trade unions provides important insights into the state of the labor movement and its position vis-à-vis the state.

The protests against the pension reform constituted the first institutional nationwide protest campaign organized by Russian trade unions since the end of the 1990s. The campaign provides a good chance to test actual mobilizing capacity, which eventually defines trade unions' bargaining power in negotiations with employers and the state. Comparison of the repertoires and mobilizing efforts of different trade unions during the campaign allows better understanding of the configuration, vertical integration, and structure of the Russian labor movement. Finally, the union-led anti-reform campaign is an excellent case study to understand how public discontent can be manipulated by the authorities and why "symbolic" protests cannot be effective in authoritarian political regimes like Russia's.

In the next section, I compare the actions of different branches of the labor movement. The analysis is primarily based on the data collected from analytical reports on social and labor protests, such as the Monitoring of Labor Protests,[4] and the data on social protests and public opinion from the CEPR[5] and the Levada Center. To compare the repertoire of protest actions, I examined the groups created by the Federation of Independent Unions of Russa (FNPR) and the Russian Confederation of Labor (KTR) on Facebook and VKontakte to coordinate and monitor protest actions across Russian regions. Finally, I conducted interviews with trade unionists and labor activists in 2019, as well as participant observation during the Trade Union Master School in Saint Petersburg in the fall of 2019.

Two Camps of Russian Trade Unions and Protest Repertoire

Since the 1990s, the Russian labor movement has been divided into the so-called official (or traditional) and alternative (or free) trade unions. Official trade unions are affiliated with the FNPR, the successor of the Soviet-era unions, and bring together about twenty million members. Official unions have inherited Soviet-era traditions and have continued those roles, mostly serving as social departments of human resource management at the large state enterprises (Ashwin and Kozina 2020).

The official trade unions have a sophisticated structure built on territorial and industrial principles inherited from the Soviet era. Currently, the FNPR unites 122 all-Russia interregional industrial trade union organizations and 82 territorial organizations. In recent years, the FNPR federal leadership has been strengthening power vertically within the association to get more control over local member organizations.

The FNPR is known for its political loyalty to the regime. The history of FNPR's dependence on the Kremlin goes back to the early 1990s, when official trade unions found themselves under the threat of liquidation after losing in political confrontation with Boris Yeltsin.[6] After 2000, the loyalty to the regime grew even stronger. The FNPR started establishing the alliance with the ruling party and building informal ties with President Putin. FNPR bet on Putin during his first election campaign in 2000 and has backed him throughout the most difficult periods of his ruling, including the period of Dmitrii Medvedev's presidency and the protests of 2011–2012 (Olimpieva and Orttung 2013). However, neither political loyalty nor direct ties to the president can guarantee official trade unions institutional security. According to experts, "trade unions, both alternative and traditional, can be destroyed at any time."[7]

The "alternative" or "free" trade unions emerged against the background of the economic crisis of the 1990s as grassroots organizations, often replacing official unions that were unable to defend workers in conflicts with their employers.[8] Today, the alternative unions are mainly represented by the Confederation of Labor of Russia (KTR), which has about two million members. Unlike the FNPR, "the territorial representation of the KTR trade unions is very uneven, and there is no coverage throughout Russia."[9] Many alternative unions are built on a professional basis and therefore are not as massive as industrially based official unions, even if they unite 90 percent of workers of specific professions, such as the Trade Union of Air Traffic Controllers. The small membership of the alternative unions is amplified by the lasting contradictions related to the unification of trade unions into an association. According to the interviewed member of the KTR Council, while the nominal membership of KTR is two million, the actual number of paying members is only three hundred thousand.

To a large extent, the alternative trade unions have always had an image of political independence due to their ability to use protests. However, the situation has changed dramatically after 2000. The adoption of the new labor code that essentially restricted the possibility of legal protests—as well as the constantly increasing pressure on independent civil society—made alternative unions concerned for their own survival. After years of struggle with the employers at company level, the alternative trade unions realized they could not improve workers' rights without fundamental changes in state labor policy, which would require involvement in policymaking.

Since the 1990s, traditional and free unions have been engaged in a constant state of ideological war. The FNPR follows the ideology of social partnership and peaceful dialogue between labor and capital. Although some company unions use industrial actions to resolve conflicts with employers, the FNPR unions generally avoid open conflicts of any kind and are often accused of conciliation and taking the side of employers in labor disputes. In contrast, the alternative unions willingly resort to labor protests as an alternative to the conciliatory strategies of traditional unions. Despite their small size, the alternative trade unions are responsible for most protest actions in the labor sphere. In 2019, trade unions affiliated with KTR participated in 42 percent of all organized protest actions, while the FNPR-affiliated unions took part in only 33 percent of actions (Bizyukov 2020).[10]

Ideological differences extend into the repertoire of protest as well. Given that alternative trade unions are much more likely to turn to disruptive activities such as protests and strikes, one could expect that they would lead the trade union protest campaign against pension reform and that their strategies would stand in stark contrast to the strategies of the FNPR. In the following sections, I demonstrate that despite differences in how the official and alternative trade unions address labor conflicts, the repertoire of protest actions and the strategies used by these two types of trade unions in the campaign against the pension reform were not as different as might be expected.

Mobilizing Capacity of Trade Unions during the Anti-Reform Campaign

Official and alternative trade unions were the first to voice criticism and to campaign against the pension reform. According to the Russian neo-corporatist system of social partnership, bills on social policy should be discussed by the trilateral commission that includes the representatives of labor, employers, and the government before they are submitted to the State Duma. At the meeting of the Russian Tripartite Commission, which is the supreme body of the social partnership system in Russia, both trade unions unanimously voted against the government bill. After the bill was submitted to the State Duma, FNPR leader Mikhail Shmakov announced a nationwide protest campaign against the pension reform. He called for regional and local trade unions "to organize meetings, pickets, rallies and other protest actions against the raising of the pension age."[11] To coordinate trade unions' protest activities in the regions, the Committee for Solidarity Actions was established in Moscow FNPR headquarters.

The alternative trade unions organized a petition against the raising of the pension age, which was launched on the same day the government approved the bill. The petition relied on the internet platform Change.org and the Russian Public Initiative platform (ROI)[12] and collected over 1.7 million signatures in a week. Inspired by this success, the KTR leaders expressed hope that people would be just as enthusiastic in joining the street protests that KTR leaders promised to organize in the near future.[13]

While the beginning of the union-led protest campaign against the pension reform seemed promising, neither traditional nor alternative unions successfully brought people out into the streets. Despite the overwhelming level of popular dissatisfaction, both unions appeared unable to mobilize even their own members to protest. Faced with the inability to organize their own mass protest actions, trade unions, and especially alternative unions, joined the rallies and meetings held by political parties.

FNPR, Official Trade Unions

The scale of street actions led by official trade unions turned out to be far smaller than the union leaders expected. On October 31, 2018, FNPR leader Mikhail Shmakov regretfully announced the outcomes of the internal monitoring of the protest campaign. FNPR-affiliated trade unions managed to organize only 262 actions, including 73 meetings, 1 rally, and 188 pickets, of which 77 were single pickets. The overall number of participants was only 68,500 people, or about 0.29 percent of FNPR's total membership.[14]

The composition of protest actions was also disappointing. FNPR actions were mostly attended by the representatives of so-called *profsoyuznyi aktiv*, or a small group of union leaders (Bizyukov 2019). This group includes the chairs and governing bodies of grassroots trade union organizations, such as workshop committees and bureaus; members of elected trade union bodies at various levels of the FNPR; and employees of regional trade union bodies. This group represents a small percentage of the overall trade union membership. Most trade union members remained passive.

While most official trade unions turned out to be incapable of mobilizing their members, in a few locales where strong territorial or branch organizations of FNPR consistently fought against employers and where the trade union leaders were trusted and respected by the workers, mass protest actions were very successful. The territorial trade union organization of the Pskov region, known for its defense of workers' rights through protest actions, conducted four large meetings, twenty-two pickets, and four flash mobs against the raising of the pension age.[15]

In this case, the trade union initiated and organized the meetings and then invited political parties to join the protest: "We collaborated with all parties and invited everyone to participate in our events."[16] While trying to attract not only union members but also the general population, Pskov activists sought new forms of protest.

The picket was held in an open-mic format, from 8:00 a.m. to 8:00 p.m., and everyone who wanted to could speak out about the pension reform. Different people showed up—from children to senior citizens.[17] In addition to the events in the Pskov region, the FNPR trade unions organized mass protest actions in several Siberian and Far Eastern regions.[18]

KTR, Alternative Trade Unions

The leaders of the alternative trade unions (KTR) seemed to be similarly disappointed in the low protest activity of their members.[19] While summing up the results of the protest campaign against pension reform at the Tenth KTR Congress on May 5, 2019, Chairman Boris Kravchenko confessed that the KTR Council "clearly overestimated the level of interaction of our own affiliates in the regions, their ability to coordinate actions, to organize collective action on the ground as part of nationwide actions."[20] In an interview, a member of the KTR Council found it difficult to name any mass actions organized by the KTR, arguing, "I'm probably not even going to name what was really carried out."[21] The respondent went on, citing the rally on Suvorovskaya Square in Moscow on September 2 as the most successful action staged during the campaign. According to various estimates, the event gathered anywhere from 1,500 (as estimated by the Ministry of Internal Affairs) to 5,000 (estimated by KTR) people.[22] However, even if this meeting looks successful in comparison with other KTR actions, it was dwarfed by the KPRF's mass rally organized on the same day, which brought together 8,000–10,000 people.

Like official trade unions, the KTR was represented in the protests mainly by union leaders and activists (Bizyukov 2019). KTR leaders spoke at rallies, held press conferences, and published statements in the media, while ordinary union members remained invisible. None of the experts interviewed for the project could recall a single protest action organized by KTR trade union organizations. The largest alternative trade union, MPRA (Interregional Trade Union Workers' Association), known for its militancy and successful use of strikes in conflicts with employers, did not hold any independent protest action that would attract the attention of the press or the public.

Organization of Protests and Repertoire of Protest Actions

Both official and alternative trade union headquarters in Moscow had shifted responsibility for the organization of protest actions to regional-level and local-level organizations. Coordinating efforts on the part of the union leadership was ultimately absent and amounted simply to monitoring regional actions. It is remarkable that both trade union leaderships refused to engage in direct action, including strikes or work stoppages; rather, they confined the repertoire of contention to symbolic organized meetings and pickets. In fact, the FNPR banned such actions outright. This limit on protest repertoire highlights union concerns about compliance with the Kremlin's rules of the game and desire to avoid violations of the laws governing public actions. While the KTR leaders did not ban individual participation in unauthorized rallies, they did reject organizational support of illegal protest actions. One respondent confirmed: "Of course, no one prevented union members from taking unauthorized actions, but officially KTR, in general, abstained from this."[23]

In lieu of direction challenges, both FNPR and KTR leaders expressed opposition through dialogue with the authorities. This approach was manifested in the discourse of trade union leaders' speeches and statements. The FNPR traditionally resorted to social partnership mechanisms to deliver its message to the authorities through trilateral commissions at different levels; the KTR leaders relied on direct appeals to the authorities by filing petitions to the government, the State Duma, and President Putin.

Both unions sought to prevent politicization of the protests—that is, assigning political blame for the reform to the political regime or to Vladimir Putin personally. Instead, they relegated reforms to the nonpolitical realm that marks most grassroots protest actions. Union leaders directed their rhetoric at economic, demographic, or social arguments against the pension reform rather than calling for leadership change or even increased representation in the political system.

My respondents highlighted the FNPR's intention to limit contention, arguing that "from the very beginning the FNPR leadership took a dual position towards organization of protest actions"[24] and "removed itself from leading the protests."[25] The Committee for Solidarity Actions, established to coordinate trade union activities in the regions in relation to pension reform, never started working. Coordination of protests came down to displaying information about the protests organized by official trade unions across Russia on a monitoring web page created by the major FNPR media platform *Solidarnost'*.[26]

According to the FNPR Charter, organization of collective action should be coordinated by the trade union headquarters. However, appeals from the grassroots trade union organizations to organize interregional protests were ignored by the Moscow headquarters: "[We] wrote a letter to the FNPR with a proposal to organize a unified all-Russian campaign against pension reform, so that it could be coordinated from Moscow. We received an answer that they would not organize anything. The Committee for Solidarity Actions, about which they talked since the start of the campaign, had not met even once."[27]

The leaders of branch and regional organizations of trade unions, in their turn, were caught between two fires. FNPR chief Mikhail Shmakov had ordered them to mobilize union members to join street actions while also demanding that they keep expressions of public discontent under control and within the legal framework. As a result, the upper levels of the trade union organization often banned protest initiatives coming from the grassroots union activists.

According to the representative of the GMPR (Mining and Metallurgical Union of Russia), many workers of big metallurgical enterprises in Kachkanar, Novokuznetsk, and Chelyabinsk expressed indignation at raising the retirement age and were ready to join any form of protest. However, the GMPR leadership "drew a red line"[28] clearly defining acceptable protest formats and prohibiting direct industrial actions and any form of work stoppage. The only permissible form of protest was demonstrations and pickets organized in strict accordance with the law and with the agreement of local authorities. These actions were largely symbolic, as they communicated discontent but did not disrupt or impede economic production or daily life.

The union leadership not only banned direct action but also barred any grassroots initiatives that went beyond the formats outlined by the FNPR center. For example, some trade union activists at Novolipetsk Metallurgical Plant demanded to hold an extraordinary Congress of GMPR to develop a coordinated and effective protest strategy.[29] The Congress would also mandate that the deputies from FNPR in the State Duma must vote against the pension reform—linking activism to formal politics. A similar proposal to convene an emergency trade union conference was made by the activists of the Neftegazstroy trade union.[30] Trade union leadership did not support either of these initiatives.

The FNPR leadership encouraged regional and territorial unions to use mechanisms of social partnership to deliver the position of trade unions to regional and local authorities: "In almost all regions, meetings were held with governors. In a significant part of the regions, meetings of local tripartite commissions were held, where our leaders of affiliates reported on the trade union position to local deputies."[31] These actions did not have any effect on the results of voting at the level of regional parliaments.

The protests organized by the FNPR unions did not call for any change in political regime but were aimed exclusively against the change in the pension age. The protest organizers strictly banned political slogans during the rallies. As one respondent reported, "We always carefully watch what slogans are revealed during [rallies]. And if they refuse to turn off [political slogans], then we are already acting together with the police."[32]

This mandate stood in sharp contrast to protests organized by systemic opposition political parties, which displayed anti-Putin and other political slogans. In contrast, unions restricted their political demands to the dismissal of Prime Minister Dmitrii Medvedev (a safe demand in this context) and the ministers responsible for labor and social policy.

The KTR leadership took the same position as FNPR, leaving the initiative to member trade union organizations in the regions. Coordination was limited to creating an interactive map displaying all anti-reform protests across Russia.[33] The KTR failed to hold a single interregional protest, asking local unions in the regions "to coordinate dates of the meetings on their own."[34] This decision limited KTR involvement in unauthorized rallies if local authorities did not approve the appointed date and time.

Although there were no open statements by KTR leaders warning trade unions against strikes, they did not welcome direct actions that would violate the law. Russian Labor Code does not allow political or solidarity strikes. In addition, because of complicated formal procedures, it is almost impossible to organize a legal strike. At the beginning of the campaign, the leaders of some alternative trade unions such as Uchitel' (Teacher), Deistvie (Action, emergency doctors), and the Profsoyuz Aviadispetcherov (Air Traffic Controllers Union) announced plans to hold strikes. Air Traffic Controllers suggested staging hunger strikes, a strategy they had used effectively in the past. However, as the anti-reform campaign unfolded, the threat of strikes disappeared from KTR statements, surprising many trade union activists. Commenting on Facebook on KTR leaders' video clips calling for participation in the rallies, many wondered why there was no call for strikes: "Well said, but not a word about the strike. It's time to understand that rallies and demonstrations in themselves are just an opportunity to meet and organize. If you require something, you need to declare what will happen if you do not get it."[35] This surprise was rooted in the history of the alternative unions, famous for their reliance on illegal strikes—actions that posed a direct economic threat to employers—to resolve grievances. The KTR leadership's refusal to use direct protest deprived the alternative unions of their most effective tool.

Rhetorical and writing activities used by KTR leaders seem to outweigh street actions. Various authoritarian bodies, including President Putin,[36] were sent multiple petitions and letters, in which the KTR leaders stressed the negative consequences of the pension reform for Russian economy and society and asked for a public dialogue about pension reform. This idea to establish better connection between the government and the people was central to the KTR anti-reform campaign, and the notion of dialogue was prioritized in the discourse of KTR leaders (Kulaev 2020). Political issues were avoided both in protest actions and in the petitions. The only trade union leader who openly spoke about the need for politicization and called for a political strike was former MPRA chairman Alexei Etmanov.[37]

A Shift in Opportunity Structure: Trade Unions' Allies against the Pension Reform and Collaboration with Political Parties

Union action is constrained by Russian law. The Russian Constitution of 1993 banned the participation of trade unions in political activities. As a result, because of limitations on political action, both trade unions developed ties to existing political parties that served as their voice in government. The main political ally of the FNPR is the ruling party, United Russia (UR). The FNPR started building relations with UR on its creation near the beginning of the twenty-first century. Today, the FNPR is well integrated into the Russian political system and has its representatives in the State Duma and in the regional parliaments. In the 2016 convocation of the State Duma, all eleven deputies from the FNPR were elected on the UR party list. The deputy of the chairman of the FNPR, Andrey Isaev, has represented FNPR in the State Duma since the beginning of the twenty-first century, serving in two important leadership positions: first deputy head of the UR faction and member of the State Duma Council.

The main political ally of the alternative trade unions is the much weaker JR Party, which signed a cooperation agreement with the KTR over ten years ago. In addition to the agreement with the JR, the KTR has a cooperation agreement with the ruling party. The key representative of the alternative unions in the Russian parliament is the KTR vice president Oleg Shein, Duma deputy from JR and a secretary of the party's Central Council for interactions with public organizations.

Growing politicization of trade unions in recent years (Olimpieva and Orttung 2013) has resulted in the merger between union leadership and political parties, which irritates grassroots activists who support the Communists (KPRF).[38] Among the alternative unions, the influence of Marxist ideas at the grassroots level is strong. Union activists often collaborate with the far-left political parties and groups, such as the Russian United Labor Front (ROT Front), the Russian Socialist Movement, and others who support trade unions in the organization of protest actions.

Alliances with political parties undermined union capacity during the antireform campaign. The FNPR and UR found themselves on the opposite sides of the barricades, which put the trade union in a difficult position. On the one hand, maintaining political partnership with the ruling party was vital for the FNPR to retain influence on the lawmaking process. On the other hand, the FNPR leaders could not support increasing the pension age, which would completely discredit them in the eyes of their members.

The quintessence of the dual status of the FNPR during the anti-reform campaign was the vote for the bill in the State Duma. While trade unions in the regions were busy mobilizing members for mass protests, the FNPR representatives in the State Duma unanimously supported the bill raising the pension age, not daring to violate party discipline. Respondent 4 summarized the membership's response: "People's activity faded after the vote on the first reading in the State Duma. In general, people became so disappointed after this moment . . . gravely [disappointed]."

The FNPR found itself in the anti-reform campaign without political allies. Cooperation with the Communists was impossible because of the historical confrontation between FNPR and KPRF, which goes back to the 1990s.[39] Although official trade unions in the regions often joined protest actions organized by the Communists, the interaction between KPRF and FNPR headquarters was competitive, and official unions clearly lost. As regional elections approached, the KPRF tried to use social discontent to strengthen electoral positions. According to CEPR figures, before the elections, the KPRF organized 36 percent of all protest actions, while FNPR initiated only 8.8 percent.

Unlike the FNPR, KTR followed the strategy of unification of political and social forces. Together with the Just Russia political party, the KTR created the anti-reform coalition People against Raising the Retirement Age (PA), which aimed to unite "trade unions, social and political associations to fight against the pension reform."[40] Apart from the leaders of KTR and JR, the PA headquarters included representatives from different political parties and civic groups, including Yabloko, ROT Front, the Civil Solidarity movement, the Russian Socialist Movement (RSD), and some unaligned deputies. The KPRF also joined the campaign but "were represented by the low-level officials."[41] Established in Moscow and Saint Petersburg, the PA created campaign web pages on Facebook and VKontakte detailing protest activities.

If the FNPR found itself without political allies during the protest campaign, the KTR had the opposite problem. It fell in the shadow of the Just Russia and practically failed to appear in the protest landscape as an independent actor. The most prominent figure in the PA campaign was KTR deputy chairman Oleg Shein. He criticized the bill on the floor of the Duma, participated in rallies, and expressed his negative position in the media, but in doing this, he did not represent the trade union but acted on behalf of the JR.

Like other parties of systemic opposition, the JR fought for electoral positions in the upcoming regional elections, so it "tried to pursue its own interest."[42] PA actions were often attributed to the JR, not KTR. Even the rally at Suvorov Square in Moscow, the most successful KTR action, was referred to in many media as a JR event.[43] Media outlets also reported a KTR petition against pension reform, including 2.5 million signatures, as a JR action.

It is remarkable that the KTR did not consider cooperation with Aleksei Navalny's party, "Russia of the Future," or invite its representatives to join the PA Coalition. The main reason was the fear that Navalny would use unauthorized protests, which KTR refrained from because it worried about retaining the image of a law-abiding organization.

Official and alternative trade unions did not consider each other as allies during the anti-reform campaign. Cooperation between FNPR and KTR was limited to a unanimous vote against the bill at the meeting of the Russian Tripartite Commission. Representatives of the FNPR were not invited to join the headquarters of the PA Coalition; there was no cooperation among trade unions at the grassroots level in organizing meetings or rallies, which further undermined the capacity of trade unions to oppose the pension reform.

Trade Unions and Manipulation of Public Discontent

While the call for protests by KTR was not unexpected given the militant image of free trade unions, FNPR's call for all-Russia protests against the pension reform looked quite unusual and fostered suspicions that the campaign was informally permitted by the Kremlin. According to the Russian business daily *Vedomosti*, the protests were included in plans for implementing the reform from the start.[44] The article argued that the Kremlin permitted trade unions to lead protest actions to reduce the risk of uncontrolled public unrest.

To survive and obtain the opportunity to influence the policymaking process, both types of Russian trade unions must play by the rules established by the regime. In this respect, they are similar to other civil society organizations in Russia. The principal of limited pluralism (Linz 2000; Owen and Bindman 2019) in Russian social policy means that the state allows selected NGOs to participate in policymaking in exchange for political loyalty (Gilbert 2016). In this context, there was no need for a special agreement between trade unions and the Kremlin to encourage union self-censorship, prevent direct protests, or avoid political demands. Union leadership acted to preserve their organizations and individual careers.

The symbolic, depoliticized anti-reform protest could not stop the reform, since it was addressed to pseudo-democratic institutions controlled by the Kremlin. Despite the union partnerships with parliamentary parties, they faced a closed opportunity structure. The State Duma, the recipient of the KTR petition, has a supermajority of UR and follows the Kremlin's orders when passing important laws. The government is likewise controlled by the president, who can appoint and dismiss the members of the cabinet, including the prime minister. Social policy reforms succeed in Russia only if they are approved by President Putin, who is the final arbiter in the policymaking process. Only the threat of spontaneous protests demanding regime change can cause the Kremlin, an authoritarian body, to change its decisions. This type of protest is precisely what the trade unions helped to prevent by keeping protests within the frame of symbolic depoliticized actions.

Even if popular expressions of discontent had been massive, the Kremlin would have scaled back the reform to the more moderate scenarios prepared by the government rather than scrapping the reform altogether. According to the main trade union newspaper, *Solidarnost'*, the government originally considered three different approaches to increasing the retirement age, which were never discussed with the broader public.[45] The toughest version was suggested by the Ministry of Finance, which wanted to raise the retirement age to sixty-five for men and sixty-three for women. The Ministry of Labor suggested a more moderate version, to increase the pension age to sixty-five or sixty-two for men and to sixty-two or sixty for women. The protests weren't even able to accomplish the moderation of the reform, let alone its fundamental reconsideration. The final softening in the increase of the retirement age was presented not as a response to public pressure but as result of President Putin's mercy.

Conclusion

The campaign against pension reform revealed that the Russian labor movement had changed significantly over the last decades. Despite the split into official and alternative camps, the actual distinctions between different trade unions have largely blurred when it comes to organized protest campaigns designed to influence the policymaking process. The KTR and FNPR leadership applied the same protest strategies, using exclusively symbolic protest actions to avoid politicization. The growing integration of the KTR leadership into the political system has led to the traditionalization of protest repertoire as it becomes more concerned with the Kremlin-defined rules of the game. The militant rhetoric of the KTR program documents and statements has given way to the discourse of social partnership. Trade union camps that were once ideologically opposed have been transformed into "trade union denominations" that have no fundamental differences. Although official and alternative trade unions remain in opposition at the company level, there are no contradictions among trade union leaderships regarding institutional strategies.

Yet, in both official and alternative unions, the anti-reform campaign broadened the gap between union leaderships and grassroots activists. Leaders in the upper echelons failed to support grassroots protest initiatives in both organizations. After the vote in the State Duma, official union activists were gravely disappointed in the FNPR leaders. Internal differentiation between active and passive trade unions was also pronounced within the FNPR camp. In the alternative camp, the anti-reform campaign also led to the decline in confidence toward KTR leadership, as grassroots leaders felt betrayed by their bosses.

The few active union organizations that still fight for workers' rights managed to organize large-scale street protests, while passive or traditional post-Soviet unions limited themselves to holding union meetings and appealing to the authorities. More generally, the anti-reform campaign proved the inefficiency of an institutionally organized protest as an instrument of trade unions' pressure on public policy. Limited by pseudo-democratic policymaking institutions and weak civil society, organized depoliticized protests are inevitably manipulated by the Kremlin to channel public discontent and to avoid the politicization of protesters' demands. While direct industrial actions and work stoppages remain effective tools of trade union struggle at the company level, organized institutional protest remains an instrument unlikely to change social policy under Russia's increasingly authoritarian state.

The failure of trade unions to organize a genuinely powerful public protest to stop the pension reform further undermined their ability to influence the policy process through the mechanisms of social partnership. Unable to support their bargaining power by effective protest campaigns, trade unions doomed themselves to be further marginalized by their social partners in negotiations on contentious policy issues. To compensate for the inefficient social partnership system, both trade unions will likely fortify instruments of direct political involvement by strengthening alliances with parties and other powerful political actors. This means further trade union integration into the political system and further weakening in their capacity as independent actors. Contestation over pension reform proves that as more trade unions get involved in systemic politics, they will inevitably become more dependent on the Kremlin and less able to represent or channel the demands of members.

Notes

1. *Current Time*, "'While I'm the President, This Decision Will Not Be Made': How Putin's Words about the Retirement Age Changed over Time" ["Poka ja president, eto resheniye ne budet prinyato." Kak menyalis' slova Putina o puvyshenii pensionnogo vozrasta], August 29, 2018, https://www.currenttime.tv/a/29459254.html.
2. Before illegal protests organized by the Aleksei Navalny Foundation on September 9, 2018, when about eight hundred participants were arrested, the police intervention in protests was minimal.
3. Yandex Maps, "Actions against Raising the Retirement Age" [Akcii protein pobysheniya pensionnogo vozrasta], last modified August 29, 2018, https://yandex.ru/maps/?ll=131.884132%2C43.112093&mode=usermaps&source=constructorLink&um=constructor%3A6bba315064dce6c325fc915ec3b5bb2dfd7f0438a9adef7158c4b0a917732d8b&z=16.
4. Trudprotest, Monitoring of Labor Protests [Monitoring Trudovyh Protestov], last modified May 7, 2022, http://www.trudprotest.org.
5. The Centre for Economic and Political Reforms (CEPR), accessed June 21, 2020, http://cepr.su/about-eng/ (site discontinued).
6. During the constitutional crisis of 1993, the FNPR took the side of the Congress of People's Deputies in its confrontation with then president Boris Yeltsin. It was the first (and last) time that the FNPR called for all-Russian protest against the regime. It cost FNPR its control over the social insurance system and put trade unions under threat of liquidation (Cook 2007; Ashwin and Clarke 2003). The new Russian constitution prohibited trade unions from engaging in any political activity and deprived them of the right to legislative initiative. FNPR leader Igor Klochkov was replaced with the more conciliatory Mikhail Shmakov, and the FNPR switched from a strategy of open pressure on power structures to one of negotiation and social partnership.
7. Interview 2, labor movement activist and trade union trainer, founder of the Trade Union Master School, Saint Petersburg, September 21, 2019.
8. For more about alternative trade unions, see Ashwin and Clarke (2003); Bizyukov (2009); Bizyukov and Olimpieva (2014).
9. Interview 3, member of the KTR Council, cochair of the trade union Universitetskaya Solidarnost, online, April 22, 2019.
10. The remaining quarter of protest actions include participants from the Doctors' Alliance, one of the trade unions organized with the support of opposition politician Aleksei Navalny, which organized 14 percent of protests, and from grassroots workers' organizations not affiliated with any trade union, which organized 11 percent of actions.

11. Elena Melik-Shakhnazarova, "FNPR Proposes the Collective Action Plan against Raising the Retirement Age" [FNPD predlagaet plan kollektivnyh deist vii protein povycheniya pensionnogo vozrasta], *Solidarnost*, June 19, 2018, https://www.solidarnost.org/news/FNPR_predlagaet_plan_kollektivnyh_deystviy_protiv_povysheniya_pensionnogo_vozrasta.html.
12. Russian Public Initiative (ROI) platform is a state resource for petitions created by presidential decree in 2013. The federal government is obliged to consider a petition if it gains more than one hundred thousand votes.
13. Taisia Bekbulatova, "To Stop the Bill Is an Achievable Goal" [Ostanovit' zakonoproekt—dostijimaja tsel] *Meduza*, June 19, 2018, https://meduza.io/feature/2018/06/19/ostanovit-zakonoproekt-dostizhimaya-tsel. This is an interview with Pavel Kudyukin from the Confederation of Labor, which has collected one and a half million signatures against raising the retirement age.
14. The full text of Mikhail Shmakov's speech at the General Council of FNPR is available at via Rosprofprom's website, October 31, 2018, at https://rosprofprom.ru/wp-content/uploads/2018/11/Doklad_Gensovetu_31_10_2018.pdf.
15. Interview 4, member of Pskov territorial organization of trade unions, Saint Petersburg, September 21, 2019; interview 5, leader of the Pskov territorial organization of trade unions, Saint Petersburg, September 21, 2019.
16. Interview 4, Saint Petersburg, September 21, 2019.
17. Interview 4, Saint Petersburg, September 21, 2019.
18. Interview 1, labor movement activist and founder of the "Monitoring of Labor Protests," Saint Petersburg, September 22, 2019.
19. Interview 3, online, April 22, 2019.
20. Confederation of Labor of Russia, "Report of the Executive Committee of the Confederation of Labor of Russia to the delegates of the X Congress of the Confederation of Labor of Russia" [Otchetnyy doklad Ispolnitel'nogo komiteta Konfederatsii truda Rossii delegatam X S'yezda Konfederatsii truda Rossii], May 15, 2019, http://ktr.su/x-congress/detail.php?ID=6333&sphrase_id=10460.
21. Interview 3, online, April 22, 2019.
22. Interfax, "In Moscow, 1,500 Took Part in Public Protest against Raising the Retirement Age Led by Just Russia" [V Moskve na aktsiyu "eserov" protiv povusheniya pensionnogo vozrasta vyshlo 1.5 tys. chelovek], September 2, 2018, https://www.interfax.ru/moscow/627584; Confederation of Labor of Russia, "On Suvorov Square in Moscow, the Rally against the Pension Reform Took Place" [Na Suvorovskoi ploschadi v Moskve proshel miting portiv pensionnoi reformy], September 2, 2018, http://www.ktr.su/content/news/detail.php?ID=6073.

23. Interview 3, online, April 22, 2019.
24. Interview 4, Saint Petersburg, September 21, 2019.
25. Interview 1, Saint Petersburg, September 22, 2019.
26. Yulia Ryzhenkova, "Trade Union Campaign's against Raising the Retirement Age" [Profsoyznya kampaniya protiv povysheniya pensionnogo vozrasta!], *Solidarnost*, June 20, 2018, https://www.solidarnost.org/topics/Profsoyuznaya_kampaniya_protiv_povysheniya_pensionnogo_vozrasta_.html.
27. Interview 2, Saint Petersburg, September 21, 2019.
28. Interview 6, member of the Chelyabinsk regional organization of GMPR, September 23, 2019.
29. Interview 1, Saint Petersburg, September 22, 2019.
30. Interview 1, Saint Petersburg, September 22, 2019.
31. Mikhail Shmakov's speech at the General Council of FNPR, October 31, 2018, https://rosprofprom.ru/wp-content/uploads/2018/11/Doklad_Gensovetu_31_10_2018.pdf.
32. Interview 4, Saint Petersburg, September 21, 2019.
33. Yandex Maps, "Actions against Raising the Retirement Age" [Akcii protein pobysheniya pensionnogo vozrasta], last modified August 29, 2018, https://yandex.ru/maps/?ll=59.451542%2C57.303804&mode=usermaps&source=constructorLink&um=constructor%3A6bba315064dce6c325fc915ec3b5bb2dfd7f0438a9adef7158c4b0a917732d8b&z=3.
34. Elena Mukhamethsina, "Unions Apply for Rallies against Pension Reform in 50 Regions" [Profsoyuzy podali zayavki na mitingi protiv pensionnoy reformy v 50 regionakh], *Vedomosti*, June 21, 2018, https://www.vedomosti.ru/economics/articles/2018/06/21/773426-profsoyuzi-mitingi-protiv-pensionnoi.
35. "Trade Union of Ground Services of Pulkovo Airport" [Profsoyuz nazemnykh sluzhb aeroporta Pulkovo], Marx Byl Prav, video, 1:34, September 9, 2018, https://www.youtube.com/watch?v=x3psdqPaDaU.
36. Confederation of Labor of Russia, "Russian Labor Confederation Addresses Vladimir Putin" [Konfederatsiya truda Rossii obraschaetsya k Vladimiru Putinu], July 23, 2018. http://ktr.su/content/news/detail.php?ID=6025.
37. Seafarers Union of Russia, "Your Pension Was Stolen by the United Russia MP" [Vashy pensiyu unes deputat-edinoross], September 3, 2018, http://sur.ru/ru/news/lent/2018-09-03/_vashu_pensiju_unes_deputat-edinoross_/?fbclid=IwAR1d98Zg4baoEJKowEauvnrwocFwWbJ1HdZvDxgga9eP2bAx2MxYivSKiw8.
38. The chairman of the Federation of Trade Unions of the Novosibirsk Region is a KPRF deputy of the Regional Legislative Assembly.
39. Ivan Zuev, "Trade Unions vs Communists. 'We Have Disagreements on the Land Issue—Who Will Lie in the Ground'" [Profsoyuzy VS kommunisty.

"U nas raznoglasiya po zemel'nomu voprosu—kto budet lezhat' v zemle"], Nakanune, August 13, 2018, https://www.nakanune.ru/articles/114186/.

40. "People against Raising the Retirement Age: All-Russian Public Campaign" [NAROD PROTIV problem pensionnogo vozrasta Obshcherossiyskaya obshchestvennaya kampaniya], VKontakte, June 9, 2022, https://vk.com/pensioncampaign; "People against Raising the Retirement Age" [Narod protiv povysheniya pensionnogo vozrasta], Facebook, accessed August 22, 2022, https://www.facebook.com/pensioncampaign/.
41. Interview 3, online, April 22, 2019.
42. Interview 3, online, April 22, 2019.
43. Interfax, "In Moscow, 1,500 Took Part in Public Protest against Raising the Retirement Age Led by Just Russia" [V Moskve na aktsiyu "eserov" protiv povusheniya pensionnogo vozrasta vyshlo 1.5 tys. chelovek], September 2, 2018, https://www.interfax.ru/moscow/627584.
44. Elena Mukhametshina, Svetlana Bocharova, and Olga Churakova, "Trade Union Protests against Pension Reform Benefit the Kremlin" [Protesty profsoyuzov protiv pensionnoi reformy vygodny dlya Kremlya], *Vedomosti*, June 22, 2018, https://www.vedomosti.ru/politics/articles/2018/06/22/773488-protesti-profsoyuzov.
45. Yulia Ryzhenkova, "Who and How Wants to Raise the Retirement Age" [Kto i kak hochet povysit' pensionnyi vozrast], *Solidarnost*, June 13, 2018, https://www.solidarnost.org/special/spetshran/spetshran_36.html#36_6.

Bibliography

Ashwin, Sarah, and Simon Clarke. 2003. *Russian Trade Unions and Industrial Relations in Transition*. New York: Palgrave Macmillan.

Ashwin, Sarah, and Irina Kozina. 2020. "Employment Regulation in National Contexts: Russia." In *Comparative Employment Relations in the Global Economy*, edited by Carola Frege and John Kelly, 427–449. Abingdon, UK: Routledge.

Bizyukov, Piotr. 2009. "Alternative Unions in Russia: The Reasons for the Continuation of the Split." [In Russian.] In *Trade Unions at the Enterprises of Modern Russia: Rebranding Opportunities*, edited by Irina Kozina, 116–138. N.p.: Lema.

———. 2021. "Protest against the Increase in Pension Age in 2018 as a Special Type of Protest." [In Russian]. Trudprotest, August 12, 2021. http://www.trudprotest.org/2019/07/08/протесты-против-повышения-пенсионно/.

———. 2020. "Worker Protest in Russia in 2019, Part 5." [In Russian.] Trudprotest. April 5, 2020. http://www.trudprotest.org/2020/04/05/трудовые-протесты-в-россии-в-2019-г-часть-5/.

Bizyukov, Piotr, and Irina Olimpieva. 2014. "Collective Labor Protest in Contemporary Russia." In *Syndicalist and Radical Workers Movements in the 21st Century: New Responses to Capital's Offensive*, edited by Dario Azzellini and Immanuel Ness, 62–83. Oakland, CA: PM Press.

Churakova, Olga, Svetlana Bocharova, and Elena Mukhametshina. 2018. "The Government Has Delegated Pension Reforms to the Deputies: But the State Duma Will Not Be Allowed to Change Its Key Provisions." [In Russian.] *Vedomosti*, August 28, 2018. https://www.vedomosti.ru/politics/articles/2018/08/22/778697-pensionnuyu-reformu-deputatam.

Cook, Linda J. 2007. "Negotiating Welfare in Postcommunist States." *Comparative Politics* 40 (1): 41–62.

Cook, Linda, Aadne Aasland, and Daria Prisyazhnyuk. 2019. "Russian Pension Reform under Quadruple Influence." *Problems of Post-Communism* 66 (2): 96–108.

Gel'man, Vladimir, and Andrey Starodubtsev. 2016. "Opportunities and Constraints of Authoritarian Modernisation: Russian Policy Reforms in the 2000s." *Europe-Asia Studies* 68 (1): 97–117.

Gilbert, Leah. 2016. "Crowding Out Civil Society: State Management of Social Organisations in Putin's Russia." *Europe-Asia Studies* 68 (9): 1553–1578.

Kulaev, Maxim. 2020. "Trade Unions, Transformism, and the Survival of Russian Authoritarianism." PhD diss., University of Tartu.

Linz, Juan José. 2000. *Totalitarian and Authoritarian Regimes*. Boulder, CO: Lynne Rienner.

Maltseva, Elena. 2018. "From Stagnation to Recalibration: The Three Stages in the Transformation of the Russian Pension System." *Russian Analytical Digest* 225:9–13.

Meyer-Olimpieva, Irina. 2018. "Russian Pension Reform: The Rise and Failure of Organized Protests." *Russian Analytical Digest* 225:14–16.

Olimpieva, Irina, and Robert W Orttung. 2013. "Russian Unions as Political Actors." *Problems of Post-Communism* 60 (5): 3–16.

Owen, Catherine, and Eleanor Bindman. 2019. "Civic Participation in a Hybrid Regime: Limited Pluralism in Policymaking and Delivery in Contemporary Russia." *Government and Opposition* 54 (1): 98–120.

Remington, Thomas F. 2014. *Presidential Decrees in Russia: A Comparative Perspective*. New York: Cambridge University Press.

Irina Meyer-Olimpieva is Director of the Center for Independent Social Research and Research Professor at the Institute for European, Russian, and Eurasian Studies at the George Washington University. She is author of *Russian Trade Unions in the System of Socio-Labor Relations Regulation: Particularities, Problems, and Research Perspectives* (in Russian).

12

Active Urbanites in an Authoritarian Regime

Aleksei Navalny's Presidential Campaign

JAN MATTI DOLLBAUM, ANDREI SEMENOV, AND ELENA SIROTKINA

The previous chapters have examined activism without explicit political aims. Here we shift the focus: As demonstrated by Aleksei Navalny's 2017–2018 presidential campaign, some urban dwellers were ready to take part in the organized effort to challenge the incumbent president, Vladimir Putin. The campaign unfolded against the backdrop of a consolidating authoritarian state that took a number of steps to protect the incumbent regime. Political opposition was divided, co-opted, and marginalized. The remaining independent media were frequently intimidated or threatened. Civil society was deprived of crucial resources to build organizations and promote collective goals. And despite the tactical innovations and local victories before Navalny's campaign, the regime remained solid (Smyth and Soboleva 2016; Semenov 2017).

Nevertheless, the campaign that began as an effort to collect signatures essential to gain ballot access attracted tens of thousands of participants and thousands of volunteers across the country, emerging as a focal point to unite different (but certainly not all) strands of the opposition. The campaign's mass anti-corruption rallies in March 2017 took the regime by surprise, exposing its vulnerabilities and forcing it to increase overt coercion against activists. Although the authorities eventually denied Navalny ballot registration, they were unable to completely disrupt the development of the organizational infrastructure, which became a backbone for future action.

In this chapter, we study the campaign's organization, activists, and supporters and demonstrate that although Navalny framed his efforts as a normal political campaign in abnormal circumstances, it was these abnormal conditions of electoral authoritarianism, the closed opportunity structure, that molded it into a very specific hybrid of a social movement and an electoral machine. In addition to illuminating one of the most important political developments in Russia's recent history, this work informs the debate on opposition in authoritarianism by demonstrating how the constrained opportunity structure shapes individuals' choices and the organizations that they build.

Campaigning under Authoritarianism

Aleksei Navalny's political career (perhaps not coincidentally) dates back to the beginnings of the Putin regime. From 2000 to 2007, Navalny was a member of *Yabloko*—the oldest democratic party in Russia. In 2004, he founded the Committee for the Defense of Muscovites, a Yabloko-affiliated activist group that fought against infill development in the capital, and in 2007 he was expelled from the party[1] and cofounded the national-democratic movement, the People. He became one of the leading figures in the 2011–2012 For Fair Elections! campaign that targeted the ruling United Russia Party and Vladimir Putin. In 2013, he ran for a mayoral office in Moscow and, to the surprise of most observers, won 27 percent, coming in second after the incumbent Sergei Sobyanin.

Navalny's signature political platform is the quality and transparency of governance. In 2011, he founded the Anti-Corruption Foundation (FBK),[2] which consolidated a number of related projects. FBK became an organizational backbone for his political career. Staffed by journalists, media managers, and lawyers, the foundation produced several investigations against high-profile officials and politicians, including Prosecutor General Yurii Chaika, Russian Railways ex-CEO Vladimir Yakunin, presidential spokesperson Dmitrii Peskov, and former president and prime minister Dmitrii Medvedev.

Through these projects, Navalny and his collaborators developed tools to deal with many of the regime's strategies to limit political competition. These tactics became the foundation of the 2017–2018 campaign. The key components of the model comprised gaining financial and organizational autonomy with the help of volunteers and crowdfunding, mobilizing the public via a combination of offline and online communication, and sustaining engagement through organizational development. These components helped to mitigate major obstacles for political opposition in authoritarian regimes: the lack of material and organizational resources, restricted access to media, and high costs of coordination. At the same time, the campaign sought to capitalize on every bit of limited freedom that the hybrid political system of electoral authoritarianism allowed to exist.

Navalny's presidential campaign organization faced the barriers that electoral authoritarian regimes erect to control political competition. Schedler's "menu of manipulation" lays out the most pertinent political infringements in today's Russia, focusing attention on free supply, free demand, and integrity (2002, 40). Concerning free supply, opposition candidates are frequently excluded from the electoral competition because of violations of obscure rules, manipulation, complex regulations, or a combination of these factors. In Navalny's case, the state manufactured legal charges and engineered convictions that prevented him from running.

The second, free demand concerns the flow of information to voters about political alternatives. While independent sources of information exist in Putin's Russia, the government's control over major news agencies and twenty out of twenty-two national TV stations means that Navalny does not appear on the traditional media. As a result, potential supporters can only access unbiased coverage when they actively seek it out (Greene and Robertson 2019). Moreover, authorities frequently obstruct public meetings and other means of political communication, limiting citizens' exposure to alternative messages. Finally, the regime violation of integrity refers to various kinds of fraud, such as ballot stuffing or manipulation of protocols, that substantially decrease the chances of winning for the opposition candidates.

To show how the campaign was able to partially overcome the regime-imposed constraints, we analyze it from three different angles: its organization, its activist core, and its supporters. We draw on participant observation, media reports, interviews, and an original survey.[3] Each of the chapter's sections summarizes a set of important regime features: the impediments to political competition, the nature of repression, and the structure of political discourse. The sections then detail how the campaign's organization, supporters, and activists reacted to the constraints and how the subsequent countermoves of the regime agents shaped its further development. Overall, the analysis reveals the complex and dynamic character of interactions between the regime and the challengers in urban settings.

The Campaign's Organization

Shortly after Navalny announced his bid for the presidency in December 2016, campaign chief strategist Leonid Volkov published the first steps of the campaign. For independent candidates, the law requires the collection of 300,000 signatures from no less than forty regions, with no more than 7,500 signatures from one region—an arduous task for any candidate without a national political organization. Because the authorities frequently eliminate opposition candidates from the ballot by declaring signatures invalid (for example, saying that the spelling is slightly different in the official documents or that the address or passport number is incorrect), Volkov set the goal of four or five hundred thousand registered voters to be enlisted to screen and select complete and valid signatures.

To achieve this aim, he launched an online preregistration platform for voters, scheduled the development of a network of regional offices, and set a fundraising goal of 150–200 million rubles ($2.5–3.3 million at the time).[4] Anticipating that elections would not be conducted fairly, Volkov also proposed to train one hundred thousand electoral observers. He declared the regional offices (*shtaby*) in seventy-seven cities (mostly regional capitals) "the main battle unit of the forthcoming campaign."[5] In February and March 2017, the campaign established offices in cities with over one million inhabitants. From April to June, they extended this effort to regional capitals with a population over five hundred thousand and some other key towns across the country.

To sustain the expanding organizational network, Navalny's team developed a model of financial autonomy that germinated from FBK's subprojects and Navalny's 2013 electoral campaign for Moscow mayor. As Leonid Volkov succinctly put it: "In the end, what is necessary for any electoral campaign? Honestly speaking: people and money, money and people."[6] Constant targeting of the supporters on social media coupled with YouTube video production and offline events attracted substantial individual donations. In 2017, FBK received 80 million rubles (approximately $1.33 million at the time) in donations from almost thirty thousand individuals, half the amount expected, but nearly double the 45 million rubles donated in 2016. By February 2018, it had reached another $3 million in recurrent monthly payments. This funding sustained the campaign headquarters and the regional network.[7]

Financial autonomy allowed the campaign to hire professional staff, including lawyers, media professionals, and coordinators. It also funded campaign materials such as leaflets, cubes (compact mobile structures used for street campaigning), and advertising. Finally, the funding allowed the campaign to build and maintain a significant network of volunteers. Thanks to Leonid Volkov's background in information technology, the campaign also developed a number of digital tools to facilitate recruitment and coordination. Intentionally copying Barack Obama's presidential campaigns, the Navalny team adopted web platforms for volunteers' registration, work assignment, and supervision. Likewise, social media (VKontakte, Facebook, Instagram, Twitter, YouTube) helped to spread information about the campaign. Activists relied on Telegram, a secured messaging platform, for internal coordination and communication.

This entire organizational infrastructure helped to mitigate the opposition's inability to access the mainstream media, especially television, which for decades has been the major source of political information for Russians. The key campaign media event was the release of a forty-five-minute investigation in March 2017 that accused then prime minister Dmitrii Medvedev of corruption. It was titled *On vam ne Dimon!* (Do not call him Dimon [pet name for Dmitrii]), mocking Medvedev's innocent and slightly clumsy appearance. The well-produced film reached a broad audience, gathering over twenty-five million hits on YouTube over the next months. In a national poll, 30 percent of survey respondents indicated that they had heard of the video (Levada Center 2017).

Astutely combining street action with Navalny's political ambitions, the campaign organized large protests after the release of the film. Thousands of people went to the streets on March 26, 2017. Framed as anti-corruption rallies, the events also allowed Navalny to appear as the movement's leader and the only alternative to Putin. The protests took place in ninety-five cities across the country. Officials only issued permits for eighteen of these events; the rest were unauthorized.[8] Consequently, the first wave of action elicited a harsh reaction. Over 1,600 participants, many of them young people under eighteen, were detained in forty-seven cities. The coercive measures, however, didn't stop the mobilization. The next rally, on June 12, attracted between fifty thousand and one hundred thousand participants in 159 localities.[9] Navalny and approximately seven hundred protesters were detained during unauthorized protests in the center of Moscow.

The regional network continued to spread during the summer of 2017—and so did the pressure from the regime. The police raided offices, seized materials, and detained activists in several cities in July.[10] Despite the pressure, by September 2017 the team had opened seventy-nine offices covering almost the entire country. Regional offices consisted of a coordinator, a few staff members, and several to dozens of volunteers. In addition to collecting signatures of potential voters, the *shtaby* organized door-to-door canvassing and street campaigns, as well as get-together events like movie screenings and discussions. In alliance with *Golos*, a national electoral watchdog association, regional offices also organized training for electoral observers in the September 2017 regional elections.

On September 7, a training session for regional coordinators (*Shtabikon*) took place in Moscow. Standing on a stage decorated in the campaign's highly recognizable design, Navalny gave a speech to the coordinators with all key campaign managers standing on the stage behind him, much like candidates do in democratic countries. Shortly after the Shtabikon, the federal headquarters launched Navalny's second tour across the regions, starting with Murmansk, Ekaterinburg, and Omsk. Continuing to frame public events as a presidential campaign, the tour aimed at delivering his political platform to the wider public. The authorities did not obstruct the first wave of meetings except in one location where they denied the application for the public rally. By the next round, the majority of the rallies were not authorized or were moved to periphery locations or different dates.[11] Following the eighth rally, in Arkhangelsk on October 2, Navalny and Volkov were arrested. Both called to the activists and supporters to take to the streets.

By the end of October, only four out of 1,276 applications for protest permits were authorized. Volkov called an additional 57 permits negotiable.[12] In response, some activists suggested holding the rallies on private property that did not require authorization. In Tambov, a local businessperson granted access to his privately owned land. In Perm, Navalny supporters gathered in the yard of a housing cooperative.[13] This practice was replicated on several other occasions. The activists won some lawsuits against the authorities or found sufficient legal grounds to hold rallies in the so-called Hyde parks—areas authorized as designated meeting spots. Overall, the regional network managed to organize twenty-seven meetings during the fall.

The symbolic pinnacle of the campaign, Navalny's public nomination as a candidate by initiative groups, took place on December 24 in twenty cities (fig. 12.1). Volkov called the participation of nearly fifteen voters in the nomination procedure unprecedented and noted that "never in Russian history was a nomination so popular."[14] By that time, the European Court of Human Rights had ruled that Navalny and his brother Oleg had been unfairly convicted in the so-called Yves Rocher case that served as the pretext for barring him from the ballot. On these grounds, Navalny claimed that he should be registered.[15]

The Central Electoral Commission barred Navalny from running anyway. In response, he called to his supporters to boycott the elections, arguing that without his name on the ballot they would merely reappoint Putin and thus there would be no reason to vote. Navalny also mobilized more than thirty-three thousand electoral observers. To nobody's surprise, Vladimir Putin won reelection with 77 percent of the vote and 67.5 percent turnout. Navalny accused the authorities of an immense administrative pressure to increase the turnout and declared his boycott a success. He stressed that the main result of the fifteen-month campaign was "the movement, which we created, with live

Figure 12.1. Nomination rally on December 24 in Perm. Image credit: Valerii Avramenko.

offices in every big city across the country and supporters in every town."[16] The campaign ended, but the work of the regional network continued, as forty of the regional campaign offices remained open, investigating local corruption, environmental problems, and other issues until they were shut down in April 2021.

Overall, to maximize its effectiveness in the given circumstances, the campaign combined elements of a social movement and of a highly professional political campaign. It built on years of interaction with the regime and took this experience to a new level, forging a large and nationwide oppositional structure that was the first of its kind in Putin's Russia. The campaign exploited every small opportunity within the closed political structure to reach out to the population and to coordinate the next moves. The campaign's organization, therefore, managed to adapt to the specific conditions of Russia's electoral authoritarianism.

The Campaign's Core: The Activists' Experiences

Apart from the campaign's organization, the regime-imposed constraints also shaped the composition of the activist core. The material and informational restrictions of public politics have made it hard for people to find opportunities to engage, so for individuals with an active oppositional urge, the opening of Navalny's offices was a rare chance to address their accumulated grievances.

Our twenty-three structured interviews with campaign staff in seven regional offices reveal that two distinct groups composed the backbone of the campaign. The first group consisted of the seasoned activists who were previously engaged in political or civic actions—environmental and human rights activists, political journalists, and political parties' affiliates. Some volunteers were directly engaged in urban activism: protecting parks and recreational areas, critically monitoring urban infrastructure development, and protesting corruption in local administration. This way the campaign served as a platform to link various strands of nonpolitical activism to institutional politics (see Dollbaum 2020). The activists often framed their participation in Navalny's campaign as a logical next step: "I got involved in ecological activism, because we didn't have any other option here. During Tkachev's governorship in Krasnodar Krai, civil society was totally eradicated. Environmental activism was the only activism possible. [When Navalny announced he would run for president] my friends advised me to join the campaign; I submitted my CV to the campaign headquarters and was hired as regional coordinator on a competitive basis" (male, 35).

The second group of people no had prior experience and usually indicated that they had no prior interest in politics. However, both groups shared a general hopelessness and disillusionment with Russian politics. They mentioned cumulative grievances and frustration among major triggers to engage in political activism in general and the Navalny campaign in particular. As one respondent put it, "I did not take a large interest in politics. During the 2016 Duma's elections, I felt that the running candidates are puppet-oppositionists without any individual programs they truly wish to implement once they get elected. I got very frustrated about that and finally felt that politics is a completely useless thing" (male, 27). In this case, the campaign's image as the only real alternative to the familiar faces of the tolerated semi-opposition was a decisive feature that attracted this respondent to the campaign. As we show below, the perception of a genuine alternative—and the only one available—was an important point of attraction for a sizable fraction of Navalny's online supporters.

The campaign's objectives and rhetoric resonated well with the volunteers' predispositions. They blamed the regime for being corrupt, abusive, and inefficient. A volunteer summed up this opinion: "Corruption is the fundamental cancerous tumor, the kind that produces a terrible metastasis" (female, 26). Another activist mentioned corruption as the main impediment to state development: "I see how the government rapaciously interferes in the economy, suppresses entrepreneurship, and breeds corruption. I advocate for the idea that the state should be regulated through legal procedures, through taxation. The state should care a lot about economic inequality and take efforts to bridge the inequality gap . . . but Putin is more than 20 years in power, and having him as the president is not a solution to these problems" (male, 21). These assessments contrast with the regime-driven narrative of the Russian state as a modernizing force that delivers on the promises of rising living standards and efficient governance.

Indeed, the campaign supporters faced the reality of a repressive rather than a modernizing force. Generally, unlike closed autocracies, electoral authoritarian regimes do not repress every instance of resistance but apply only a limited amount of pressure and coercion, mostly to signal the limits of dissent they are willing to tolerate. Furthermore, coercion is exercised by a variety of actors, which further increases unpredictability. Throughout interviews, three distinct groups of the regime agents can be distinguished: local authorities, the official coercive apparatus, and formally independent but often government-affiliated groups.

Interactions with the local authorities mostly encompassed the organization of the campaign and its events. Bureaucrats routinely refused to authorize the campaign's public events. Moreover, in many cases they obstructed the process of opening an office. As one respondent put it: "We regularly got kicked out, they did not permit us to lease an office space for the *shtab*, and they did not authorize our rallies . . . we probably got 180 refusals on different matters from the local authorities" (male, 35). Brought to the courts, activists' complaints faced further resistance and were rarely decided in their favor.

Encounters with law enforcement agents were more severe, and in some cases the activists were well aware of the coercive agents' tendency to cross the legal limits of their actions. One volunteer recalled, "My first attempt at political activism was at the age of fifteen when I came across a resonant murder case that happened in my city and which the police refused to investigate. . . . I was so shocked by that open defiance of the police. I called all people to gather for a peaceful demonstration in protest against this" (male, 20). Shortly after the announcement of the meeting on social networks, the police visited the activist and pressured him to remove the post and the negative comments about their actions.

Another activist encountered a similar state reaction while serving as an electoral observer during the 2011 State Duma elections: "I knew that the election committee members were going to falsify the protocols and they wanted me out on any basis. I called the police and reported that a crime is being committed here. They came . . . and pulled me out of the building" (female, 33).

Apart from the police and its special units (like the Center for Combating Extremism, commonly known as the E-Center), the National Guards (*Rosgvardia*) and the Federal Security Bureau (FSB) were engaged in surveillance and repression of the regional offices' activities. While the police and Rosgvardia were responsible for policing the public events, the E-Center and the FSB were involved in the monitoring of social networks, information gathering (including of compromising materials) on activists, and criminal charges against them. One activist recalled, "The local government with the help from the E-Center tracks us down, they wiretap private calls, watch us closely to find a way to organize pressure on us, they keep track of all people who support us, take photos of these people" (male, 54).

Another activist told us that when he met people from the E-Center, "they were saying that they were constantly spying on me" (male, 21). In concordance with the local authorities, the coercive agents disrupted the campaign's infrastructure through occasional office raids, confiscation of materials, detainments, and arrests. Apart from coercion, these agents also employed deceit: for instance, when they could not seize the whole package of the information materials, they collected the next load of materials at the post office under false names.

Finally, numerous government-friendly groups interacted with the campaigners, the most famous being self-styled Cossacks[17] and different progovernment organizations like Antimaidan, the National Liberation Front (NOD), "Putin's Troops," or bikers. A campaign volunteer from the southern city of Krasnodar claimed, "We have encountered the Cossacks multiple times. One of these episodes was when they came to our conference and started to throw eggs, water, flour, and dough at us. They instigated a fight by throwing tables and chairs" (male, 35). He alleged that the Cossacks were paid by the authorities to intimidate the activists and rally participants. They often threaten and sometimes use physical violence against the protesters, though the vast majority of their public actions consist of verbal bullying. An activist from Rostov recalled an instance of exceptionally aggressive behavior: "They blocked us in a hotel . . . then started throwing people out of windows from the second floor. Some of us they beat with whips; they put some activists on their knees, we did not understand what it was for, but they kept trying to put people on their knees" (female, 19).

Street gangs, athletes, bikers, and even pensioners occasionally intimidated and harassed the activists. The prominent case of Putin's Troops in Krasnodar exemplifies these agents. As explained by a campaign activist, this is a group of agitated pensioners sponsored by a local entrepreneur. The "Troops" frequently raided the regional office and demanded that the activists leave the city. In August 2017, when they were denied access to the building, they broke through the door and ravaged the *shtab*. In the end, it did not frighten the activists, but rather it gave them additional publicity (male, 27).

Given the mostly negative nature of their interactions with regime agents, the interviewed activists were well aware of the personal consequences of their participation in the campaign. Almost all of them mentioned the surveillance by the security services. Some felt that they had sacrificed their careers for the political cause; others were worried that they would not be able to return to their business or ever be employed by the state. However, many interviewees emphasized that the decision to join the campaign already incorporated the perceived risks and that the regime could not pose any threat that the activists would not be able to circumvent or counter. For example, some activists mentioned specific defense mechanisms against such threats: "I am a freelancer most of the time. They cannot force people to get me fired. Okay, they can initiate my expulsion from the university. I will appeal against that but that is it. They do not have other leverage to pressure me" (male, 21).

To respond to the well-known constraints on political action and the repressive character of the regime, the campaign strategists devised a tight top-down structure, a hierarchically organized electoral machine. Core activists and volunteers were allowed to innovate and communicate their ideas to the top, where these ideas would sometimes be diffused to the other branches.

Yet in terms of political message, style, and tactics, activists had no input. The federal headquarters selected regional coordinators on a merit-based procedure that resembled the standard practices of a large company more than a social movement. One of our respondents describes the process as follows: "There was an open competition, a democratic competition (*demokraticheskiy konkurs*), where everyone could apply for the position, and I sent my CV. About a month later I was interviewed and then invited to Moscow. Then my candidacy was approved" (male, 34). Coordinators and three to four staff members per office, whom they could hire themselves, received a salary throughout the entire campaign.

The hierarchical structure sometimes caused discontent among the regional activists, especially those who had much grassroots experience and were used to making their own strategic decisions. One activist complained about the campaign's top-down structure: "I don't like the process of organizing the campaign, everything depends on the leader, everything is very personalized,

I would say authoritarian. . . . The coordinator has no direct connection with Navalny, only with intermediaries, through Volkov and all the others." Concerning posts on social media, he alleged that everything had to be approved on a higher level: "One of the campaign's main demands is, 'Trust the regions, don't decide everything in Moscow.' We have a poster [with this slogan], but I don't see it [being implemented here]" (male, 21).

Some former volunteers also publicly criticized the campaign for an overall lack of transparency.[18] However, most core activists agreed that vertical coordination was necessary to ensure the achievement of the campaign goals. Except for this trade-off, activists were generally very positive about their engagement, frequently stressing the valuable experience and the sense of belonging to a community of like-minded people that came with their participation in the campaign.

These accounts gave insights into the everyday life of activists, which was filled with increasing pressure from various regime agents, on the one side, and community building and tactical innovations to counter these impediments, on the other. Core activists spent a significant amount of time working in the campaign offices, registering the supporters, organizing events, and fostering internal cohesion. Recognizing the importance of the campaign's urban infrastructure, the regime agents in some locations attempted to disrupt the daily routine by raids, vandalism, and other means. It is therefore not surprising that the solidarity forged in the campaign among its volunteers extended far beyond its time limits.

The Campaign's Supporters

Apart from attracting devoted volunteers, the Navalny campaign was also successful in gaining traction with a wider public. Despite its absence from the mainstream media, Team Navalny leveraged its presence on social media platforms such as Facebook, VKontakte, or YouTube. The digital infrastructure—regional public groups and YouTube channels—helped to spread the campaign's messages. More importantly, it allowed the campaign to present Navalny's platform as an alternative to the regime's agenda.

State-controlled media dominate the communicative environment in Putin's Russia. They spread official propaganda, ridicule the opposition, and combine outright falsehoods with well-crafted infotainment. As a result, the public discussion on policy-related issues lacks quality. In addition, in the 2010s, the Kremlin deliberately amplified or fabricated socially conservative tendencies in the population (Sharafutdinova 2014). These ideas support the master frame of the sovereignty and uniqueness of the Russian nation and state but do not prescribe any particular policy program (Greene and Robertson 2019, chap. 5). Somewhat simplifying, the Kremlin's media strategy has been to equate President Putin with Russia and his decisions with the "will of the people," hence rendering any criticism toward his rule as unpatriotic. This has made forging an effective political alternative extremely difficult.

In this environment, Navalny attempted to attract followers by clearly positioning himself against the regime as a whole and against Putin in particular, presenting himself as the only viable alternative. Taking into account that Russia had undergone a period of stagnating growth and declining real disposable incomes since 2014, the leading undercurrent of his program was economic, although cautiously voiced with attention to very different population groups. As a result, opposition-minded people of different political orientations could find a demand they supported. Navalny's signature emphasis on anti-corruption tied these issues together. Not surprisingly, given the constraints, Team Navalny found its audience on social media.

To explore the reception of the campaign's messages by its supporters, we conducted an original two-wave online survey in February and early March 2018.[19] We used a simple random sample stratified by age and gender to contact group members.[20] It is important to highlight that this sample is not representative of Navalny's follower base as a whole, because the selection procedure biases it toward online-savvy, younger, urban social media users.

However, this is exactly the category of people that Navalny's campaign appealed to in style and rhetoric (Dollbaum, Semenov, and Sirotkina 2018). The sociodemographics of the followers indicate the prevalence of young, educated, and relatively better-off citizens, although they are economically more diverse than urban dwellers overall. Figure 12.2 depicts the age distribution of our sample. Depending on whether one chooses the mean or the median, the average campaign supporter in our data was born between 1993 and 1995. Slightly over 16 percent are younger than eighteen, which is a substantial number but certainly not a majority. The bulk of online supporters (60%) are between eighteen and twenty-nine years old, while middle-aged people between thirty and forty-five make up 18 percent, similar to the share of those under eighteen.

In addition, there were substantially more males than females in the VK groups. Taking information on gender directly from the VK profiles yields a distribution of 68 percent males and 32 percent females.

How are Navalny's social media supporters positioned in terms of their socioeconomic status? We compare our sample to a representative opinion poll

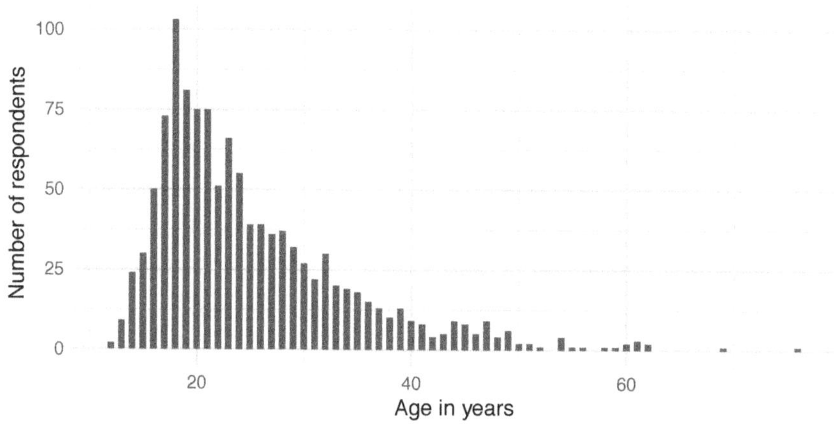

Figure 12.2. Age distribution of the sample. Source: Online survey, February–March 2018.

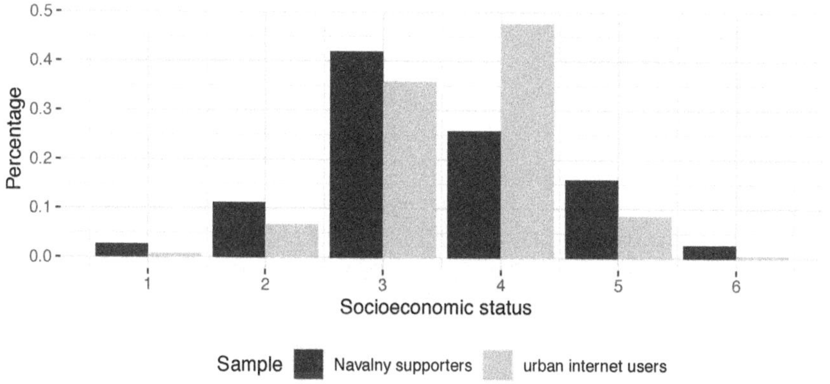

Figure 12.3. Socioeconomic status of sample compared to urban population. Source: Online survey, February–March 2018, Levada Center.

by the Levada Center from 2017. Since our survey was conducted only in large cities, we restrict the Levada sample accordingly to arrive at a more meaningful comparison.[21] Figure 12.3 plots the distribution of both groups on a six-point scale that measures a household's standard of living, ranging from "We do not even have enough money for food" (1) to "We do not have to deny ourselves anything" (6).

The distributions suggest two things. First, our sample of Navalny supporters is somewhat worse off than the population of urban dwellers as a whole. Second, our sample seems to be slightly more economically diverse. The categories at the ends of the spectrum (categories 1, 2, 5, and 6) are more populated than they are in the reference group.[22] Overall, the differences are not enormous, suggesting that in terms of socioeconomic characteristics the campaign attracted a fairly representative group of urban citizens.

Navalny's supporters have a substantially higher level of education. In our data, 67 percent report that they have received incomplete or complete university education, as compared to 43 percent in the reference group. A high share of well-educated participants is also a common characteristic of broadly prodemocratic political movements in the post-Soviet space (Smyth 2020; Volkov 2012). Concentrating mobilization efforts on well-resourced participants—for example, highly educated urbanites—as the campaign clearly did, also makes sense from the broader perspective of the "urban advantage of revolution" (Beissinger 2022). This follower base is well equipped to carry out the strategy that Navalny pursues in the restricted political environment—namely, using street protest as an important part of his political campaigns.

To explore the foundation of political support, we examine the degree of respondents' agreement with seven major demands of Navalny's campaign, including demands (1) to downsize the bureaucratic apparatus, (2) to increase the minimum wage from around 10,000 to 25,000 rubles, (3) to reduce the powers of the president, (4) to scrap income tax for small business owners with low income, (5) to sue state servants whose expenses do not match their official salary, (6) to increase the regions' discretion over tax revenue, and (7) to introduce a visa regime for citizens of Central Asian countries. These demands address liberal, left-wing, anti-corruption, and, with regard to the last item, moderately nationalist concerns (a remnant of Navalny's nationalist past; see Moen-Larsen 2014). They also reflect the wide net that the campaign cast to attract a maximum of aggrieved citizens (Dollbaum, Semenov, and Sirotkina 2018).

The campaign supporters tend to agree with all of these statements. Even for the least supported demand, the visa regime, the mean score does not drop below 4 on a scale from 1 to 5. This hardly comes as a surprise, but it evokes the question of whether respondents' agreement is driven by support for these political demands or by their support for Navalny. So what did really drive the support? In Andrei Loshak's documentary *The Age of Dissent*,[23] Yegor, an eighteen-year-old high school student and the coordinator of Navalny's local office in Kaliningrad, argues, "We are not Navalny's hamsters, we are hamsters of progress." He ironically refers to the term *net hamsters*, frequently used by government-affiliated media since 2011 to ridicule digitally mobilized protesters (Sharafutdinova 2014). Other episodes of the film series depict active supporters of the campaign as intelligent youngsters who are tired of the regime's ineffectiveness and pervasive corruption. Clearly, the campaign themes of accountability and transparency in the current government resonated with the campaign's supporters and activists, but this support does not preclude personalist attachment to Navalny.

To get at this in greater depth, we make use of an open question on respondents' reasons for supporting the campaign. An astonishing 94 percent of respondents articulated a clear focus of support. We divided each person's response into three substantive parts, each of which was assigned to one of twenty-one categories, like regime change (e.g., "we need to replace the authorities"), pluralism ("we need political competition"), or social issues ("he fights poverty and injustice").[24] Each of these categories was then assigned to one of five macro-categories: democracy and governance (including anti-corruption demands), material (comprising economic and social demands), anti-regime (comprising unspecific demands for change and other statements critical of the regime), personal (containing statements about Navalny's personal characteristics), and other demands (containing all categories that do not fit in any of the above).

Table 12.1 shows the distribution of demands across these five categories. It reflects the programmatic breadth of the campaign. About 16 percent of respondents explicitly make democracy and governance claims, such as the need for more pluralism and accountability and less corruption. Material claims yield a similar share. By contrast, anti-regime claims and unspecific demands for change feature much more strongly in the data, being voiced by 40 percent of respondents. Although the campaign did formulate different policy proposals, this agenda is clearly the most important self-reported reason to support the campaign, much more so than, for instance, anti-corruption or prodemocratic demands.

This finding is consistent with the two defining features of the regime outlined above: the tight restrictions on political competition, allowing no or only handpicked sparring partners and excluding all potential threats, and the political discourse that de-emphasizes policy differences in favor of an us-versus-them narrative. This structural feature of Russian politics was amplified by the campaign's rhetoric that positioned Navalny as the only challenger capable of seriously confronting the Putin regime, which is also reflected in the fact that more than one in ten respondents (12%) referred to Navalny as "the only one" (*edinstvennyi*). As one respondent put it, "[He] is the only one from the opposition who actually tried doing something."[25]

The answers also demonstrate how many respondents joined the campaign primarily because of their support for Navalny as a person. About a quarter of

Table 12.1. Supporters' demands in open text entries

Demands	**Share of respondents**[1]
Democracy and governance	16.3%
Material	15.6%
Political change	40.1%
Personal	24.3% (12.5%)[2]
Other	17.5%

Notes

1. The sum exceeds 100 percent because a number of respondents voiced more than one demand.
2. 12.5 percent refer exclusively to Navalny's personal features, without making other claims.

respondents made references to Navalny's personal appeal (for example, "I like him as a personality"). However, personal and political support may well go together. To identify the hard core of predominantly personal supporters, we additionally calculated the share of those who exclusively cite personal features in their answer to the open question. This share stands at 12.5 percent, suggesting that "Navalny's hamsters" constitute a minority of the overall sample.

The sociodemographics and political positioning of the respondents in our sample suggest that the campaign successfully targeted its core constituencies: young, educated, relatively well-off urbanites who embrace the agenda of contemporary social liberalism, some of whom advocate democratization, but who above all dislike the regime. They are likely to represent the most active and politicized part of the urban middle class that emerged in the country after almost three decades since the breakup of the Soviet Union. Moreover, a significant number of Navalny's core supporters also find value in him as a person, but, contrary to pundits' claims, substantive reasons by far outweigh personalistic ones.

Conclusions

In this chapter, we have examined central elements of Aleksei Navalny's presidential campaign of 2017–2018 through the lens of several important regime features: the impediments to political action, the nature of repression, and the political discourse. If the presented evidence is taken together, these structural features are mirrored in the campaign to a remarkable extent.

First, the restrictions to the political sphere meant that the campaign spent much of its energy on battling with the bureaucracy, getting its message out in the absence of mainstream media coverage, coordinating electoral observers, and avoiding or softening the effects of repression and obstruction. Second, the core activists' experiences on the ground reflected the limited potential to become politically active and the grievances accumulated in the process; these experiences also gave a clear picture of the complex nature of repression that is characterized by the parallel—and often uncoordinated—operation of different repressive agents. Third, the constraints in media environment and the lack of a clearly structured cleavage system in the public sphere meant that Navalny's best bet was his self-presentation as the only viable alternative to the regime, which was reflected in his followers' self-reported motivations. Although Navalny complemented his anti-regime agenda with a program that promised liberal political reforms and socioeconomic improvements through various measures like tax cuts for small and medium enterprises, investment in social infrastructure, and an increase in the minimum wage, material and democratic demands featured in respondents' self-reports to a much smaller degree than anti-regime claims and general demands for change.

Benefiting from the iterative refinement of strategies and the development of digital tools in Navalny's previous projects, the campaign fitted the environment better than any oppositional effort before. Given the various constraints, its mobilization and capacity building—particularly in the regions—were truly remarkable. However, despite Navalny's insistence that his campaign was conducted like a "normal" political campaign in Western liberal democracies (for example, with a regional network of offices and volunteers and with public appearances across the country), it was in fact a very specific hybrid between a social movement and a tightly controlled electoral machine whose characteristics were in many cases shaped by the nature of its antagonist.

The campaign's most important result was the regional network: instead of appropriating existing organizations, it created its infrastructure almost from scratch. Representatives of political parties, NGOs, and activist groups were visible, and their local connections and experience were harnessed, but they did not dominate. Moreover, the campaign managed to attract civic activists who had not taken any directly political action before, while at the same time tying in members of explicitly political local groups. Even though the campaign abstained from formal cooperation with other organizations, on the ground it had a profound integrating effect. As a result, the regional network of campaign offices represents a significant benefit to the regional activist spheres, an effect that extends beyond the campaign's end in March 2018: half of the eighty regional *shtaby* were transformed into local-level opposition hubs and continued coordinating corruption investigations, protest rallies, and other opposition activities.

The regional network played a significant role in Navalny's new initiatives: The first was a new trade union organization for state employees, whose aim is to pressure the state to deliver on its promises of rising salaries. The second is called Smart Voting; this strategy's idea is to concentrate the oppositional vote on the most promising contenders in each electoral district to jointly outweigh the votes cast for the candidate of the governing party (see Turchenko and Golosov 2021). Shortly after the regional elections of September 2019, during which the governing party lost its absolute majority in six of thirty-one regional and municipal parliaments, in part because of Smart Voting, the regime cracked down on Navalny's regional network with hundreds of searches and detainments across the country. In April 2021, after the mass rallies against Aleksei Navalny's arrest and imprisonment, the Moscow Prosecutor's Office demanded that Navalny's regional network offices and the associated organizations be labeled extremist. In early June 2021, the court imposed this designation, threatening anyone who supports the organization with criminal charges. As a result, the network's leadership decided to disband the organizations to avoid further danger to members and supporters.

Navalny's campaign and subsequent developments demonstrate the cycles of learning on both sides—the opposition and the regime. Navalny's network effectively exploited the limited opportunities (for example, the remnants of freedom of assembly, the relatively unrestricted social media environment, and the technological advancements) to build a solid organizational network for mobilization. At the same time, its actions helped the regime to identify the weak spots in its institutional facade, leading to increased repressions and eventually to the dissolution of the network. Moreover, the regime involved multiple agents—from local authorities to gangs and paramilitary groups—to counter the opposition movement. This brings a decade-long spiral of action and reaction to a repressive and depressing conclusion. Despite the increased pressure, however, the experiences of collective action and solidarity that supporters gained through their participation have already been valuable resources for them personally as well as for their local civil societies.

Notes

1. According to Yabloko's version of the story, Navalny was expelled because of his nationalist rhetoric (which he has now largely toned down). Navalny himself claimed that he was expelled because he criticized the leadership, calling for the resignation of then leader Grigori Yavlinsky. See Dollbaum, Lallouet, and Noble (2021) for the details.

2. The government enlisted the FBK (alongside its legal entity, Foundation for Citizens' Rights Defense, and the Navalny *Shtabs* movement) as an organization performing the functions of a foreign agent in 2019. In April 2021, Moscow's prosecutor opened a case against the FBK and Navalny's regional network to add them to the list of extremist organizations. On April 29, 2021, the organizations were disbanded.
3. We conducted an online survey of Navalny's social media followers (N = 1182) and twenty-three semi-structured interviews with campaign staff, gathered at the height of the campaign between September 2017 and February 2018.
4. Leonid Volkov, "Navalny's Presidential Campaign: The First Steps," *Leonid Volkov* (blog), December 15, 2016, https://www.leonidvolkov.ru/p/183/.
5. Leonid Volkov, "Campaign's Plan: Regional Networks and Tasks for Volunteers," *Leonid Volkov* (blog), January 19, 2016, https://www.leonidvolkov.ru/p/186/.
6. Leonid Volkov, "Let's Go! We Need Money and Volunteers," *Leonid Volkov* (blog), June 23, 2015, https://www.leonidvolkov.ru/p/24/.
7. Anti-corruption Foundation Annual Report 2018, accessed: August 21, 2022, https://report2018.fbk.info/fundraising/.
8. For meetings—large gatherings of people with sound amplification—the initiators are required to obtain an authorization from the municipality where the event takes place. The application should be filed within a ten-to-fifteen-day time frame before the event. The absence of a response from the local authorities has no clear legal consequences for the event organizers.
9. "Protest Map by Meduza and OVD-Info," *Meduza*, June 13, 2017, https://meduza.io/feature/2017/06/13/skolko-lyudey-protestovali-12-iyunya-i-skolko-zaderzhali.
10. "On 'Canvassing Saturday,' 130 Were Detained," *OVD-Info*, July 8, 2017, https://ovdinfo.org/express-news/2017/07/08/na-agitacionnyh-subbotnikah-zaderzhano-bolee-130-chelovek.
11. Leonid Volkov, "Two Tables," *Leonid Volkov* (blog), September 25, 2017, https://www.leonidvolkov.ru/p/233/.
12. Leonid Volkov, "Invite Navalny," *Leonid Volkov* (blog), October 30, 2017, https://www.leonidvolkov.ru/p/244/.
13. Aleksei Navalny, "Experimental Meeting in Tambov," *Navalny* (blog), October 29, 2017, https://navalny.com/p/5598/.
14. Leonid Volkov, "Invent Something Better," *Leonid Volkov* (blog), December 25, 2017, https://www.leonidvolkov.ru/p/261/.
15. Aleksei Navalny, "Elections Are Scheduled. Here Is Our Action Plan," *Navalny* (blog), December 18. 2016, https://navalny.com/p/5668/.
16. Aleksei Navalny, "On Electoral Boycotts and 'Elections' Results," *Navalny* (blog), March 20, 2018, https://navalny.com/p/5820/.

17. Historically, the Cossacks were members of paramilitary communities in southern regions of Russia and in Ukraine, while today they are often regime-sponsored paramilitary organizations.
18. Ilya Azar, "Disillusionment or Betrayal?," *Novaya Gazeta*, March 1, 2018, https://www.novayagazeta.ru/articles/2018/03/01/75659-razocharovanie-ili-predatelstvo.
19. Our sample is based on eight regional groups that the campaign had opened in the social medium VKontakte (VK) groups. We targeted VK groups rather than Facebook because the former is still much more widespread in the regions, as was also reflected in the campaign's organization. We selected the regions with regard to the performance of the regional economy and the degree of regional political openness. We used a standard regional democracy index (Petrov and Titkov 2013) and the log of GRP to design a two-dimensional space and randomly selected the regions from each quadrant. Selected regions are Altai Krai, the Republic of Tatarstan, Primorsky Krai, Ivanovo Oblast, Rostov Oblast, Tomsk Oblast, Moscow, and Saint Petersburg.
20. A team of interviewers made about five thousand personalized requests (the response rate was about 28%) holding the age-gender ratio constant, so that the sample (N = 1182) is representative for age and gender in each VK group.
21. From the Levada poll, we selected only those respondents who claimed to use the internet at least five times a week and who live in cities with over five hundred thousand inhabitants.
22. Navalny sample: mean = 3.49, sd = 1.05, urban internet users: mean = 3.60, sd = 0.78. The mean difference increases somewhat (3.36 versus 3.61) when both samples are restricted to respondents eighteen to twenty-nine years old. For comparison, the mean of those groups who do not live in large cities or do not frequently use the internet lies between 2.73 and 2.94.
23. Andrei Loshak, "The Age of Dissent," documentary, video, 35:00, 2018, https://artdoc.media/ru/movie/vozrast_nesoglasiya_2018_35/.
24. To sort the text entries into categories, we developed an inductive coding scheme based on 10 percent of the material. The resulting codes we applied to the whole material. Two raters coded in parallel, coding up to three separate demands per respondent. In the first round of 20 percent of the material, the inter-rater reliability (measured as Cohen's Kappa) for the first of three codes was acceptable (0.75). Then, we reconciled the differences and refined the coding rules. Next, the remaining 70 percent were coded, with Cohen's Kappa reaching 0.79. Again, we decided to resolve the remaining disagreements between the raters so we could use the full material.

25. It needs to be stressed that these are responses to an open question: the fact that anti-regime demands are the strongest category does not yet allow us to speak of a "negative coalition" (Goldstone 2011; Beissinger 2013), where rejection of the authorities is the only relevant attitudinal factor that unites participants.

Bibliography

Beissinger, Mark R. 2013. "The Semblance of Democratic Revolution: Coalitions in Ukraine's Orange Revolution." *American Political Science Review* 107 (3): 574–592.

———. 2022. *The Revolutionary City: Urbanization and the Global Transformation of Rebellion.* Princeton, NJ: Princeton University Press.

Dollbaum, Jan Matti. 2020. "Protest Trajectories in Electoral Authoritarianism: From Russia's 'For Fair Elections' Movement to Alexei Navalny's Presidential Campaign." *Post-Soviet Affairs* 36 (3): 192–210.

Dollbaum, Jan Matti, Morvan Lallouet, and Ben Noble. 2021. *Navalny: Putin's Nemesis, Russia's Future?* Oxford: Oxford University Press.

Dollbaum, Jan Matti, Andrey Semenov, and Elena Sirotkina. 2018. "A Top-down Movement with Grass-Roots Effects? Alexei Navalny's Electoral Campaign." *Social Movement Studies* 17 (5): 618–625.

Goldstone, Jack A. 2011. "Cross-Class Coalitions and the Making of the Arab Revolts of 2011." *Swiss Political Science Review* 17 (4): 457–462.

Greene, Samuel A., and Graeme B. Robertson. 2019. *Putin V. the People: The Perilous Politics of a Divided Russia.* New Haven, CT: Yale University Press.

Levada Center. "Do Not Call Him Dimon!" 2017. Levada Center public opinion poll, April 6, 2017. https://www.levada.ru/2017/04/06/film-on-vam-ne-dimon/.

Moen-Larsen, Natalia. 2014. "Normal Nationalism: Alexei Navalny, LiveJournal and 'the Other.'" *East European Politics* 30 (4): 548–567.

Petrov, Nikolay, and Aleksei Titkov. 2013. *Rejting Demokratichnosti Regionov Moskovskogo Centra Karnegi: 10 Let v Stroju.* Moscow: Carnegie Endowment for International Peace.

Semenov, Andrei. 2017. "Against the Stream: Political Opposition in the Russian Regions during the 2012–2016 Electoral Cycle." *Demokratizatsiya: The Journal of Post-Soviet Democratization* 25 (4): 481–502.

Sharafutdinova, Gulnaz. 2014. "The Pussy Riot Affair and Putin's Démarche from Sovereign Democracy to Sovereign Morality." *Nationalities Papers* 42 (4): 615–621. https://doi.org/10.1080/00905992.2014.917075.

Smyth, Regina. 2020. *Elections, Protest, and Authoritarian Regime Stability: Russia 2008–2020.* Cambridge: Cambridge University Press.

Smyth, Regina, and Irina V. Soboleva. 2016. "Navalny's Gamesters: Protest, Opposition Innovation, and Authoritarian Stability in Russia." *Russian Politics* 1 (4): 347–371.

Turchenko, Mikhail, and Grigorii V. Golosov. 2021. "Smart Enough to Make a Difference? An Empirical Test of the Efficacy of Strategic Voting in Russia's Authoritarian Elections." *Post-Soviet Affairs* 37 (1): 65–79. https://doi.org/10.1080/1060586X.2020.1796386.

Volkov, Denis. 2012. "The Protesters and the Public." *Journal of Democracy* 23 (3): 55–62.

Jan Matti Dollbaum is Postdoctoral Research Fellow at the University of Bremen. His work appears in *Perspectives on Politics, Post-Soviet Affairs,* and *Social Movement Studies.*

Andrei Semenov is Associate Professor in the Department of Political Science and International Affairs at the Higher School of Economics, St. Petersburg. His work appears in *Russian Politics, Social Movements Studies,* and *Democratizatsiya.*

Elena Sirotkina is a PhD student in Political Science at the University of North Carolina at Chapel Hill. She studies political behavior in autocracies, contentious politics, and protest movements.

13

Why Grassroots Activism Matters

JEREMY MORRIS, ANDREI SEMENOV, AND REGINA SMYTH

In an era in which national social movements have rocked governments everywhere from the Middle East and North Africa to Hong Kong, Ukraine, and the United States, it is easy to neglect the small-scale local mobilization as insignificant. As the chapters in this volume show, they are often short-lived collective action organized around demands for new government policies or services. Local mobilizations do not represent grand forces of modernity or the emphasis on transformative societal or political changes. These movements are short-term events designed to redress specific demands that emerge from the disruptions of the everyday, not to end political regimes or topple leaders.

From the vantage point of our chapters, Russian society appears vibrant, although disengaged from futile performances of formal politics. A quick look at the online magazine *Horizontal Russia (7 X 7)* highlights issue-based collective initiatives across Russia.[1] Rooted in shared efforts to improve everyday life, these examples of nonpolitical activism address challenges from environmentalism to the creation of open spaces for art and music and indicate steps to enrich and rebuild the shared spaces of the city. Our chapters amplify this view. Across the federation, citizens have organized in response to state actions, economic development, and the abrogation of rights. They collaborate to influence policies that shape daily life and address significant problems and shared demands that are not met by the regime.

Grassroots actions take many forms, from single pickets to flash mobs, from political campaigns to petitions, the provision of collective goods, and protest. The rich repertoire of contestation also occurs across a wide range of venues: on the graffiti on building walls, theaters, and art houses, as well as online through connective action. Our closely observed cases show that theories of grassroots activism in Russia can be explored using concepts developed in other contexts. Collective responses are rooted in new social infrastructures—identities or meanings developed through daily interactions, new understandings of shared ideas about governance and state responsiveness, practices of daily life, and local networks that enable communities to surmount disinformation campaigns and state intervention. Opportunity structures define the goals of mobilization as well as the economic, political, and social allies and ties that facilitate or stifle action.

This activism is recognizable to regional studies scholars, but we argue that it deserves wider attention as a mechanism of social development in transitional societies. Scholars are divided about the importance of bottom-up, grassroots movements to political development, particularly in an environment of increasing state repression and autocratic consolidation. The view from local politics highlights that national politics obscure much of the change that occurred in Russian social structures since the shared trauma of the 1990s.

By probing the variation in mobilization across issue areas and regions, and over time, the essays in this volume also provide new insights into how state-society interactions work in Russia. These chapters reveal the state-imposed boundaries across issues and instances of social mobilization, demonstrating state efforts to channel and control activism as well as state accommodation of grassroots demands. Even as the regime tightens its grip on social organization and narrows the scope of grassroots activism, it reveals an incoherent varied official response to mobilization across locations, issue areas, and repertoire. The state also seeks to capture the positive benefits of mobilization: new information about social demands, an impression of responsiveness, and increased social support. All these dynamics—around society, the state, and the interaction between the two—demand closer attention.

Our conclusions begin with the challenges of studying these localized efforts in the context of authoritarianism. We then examine the theoretic and empirical implications of our findings for societal development and change. We collect our insights into state actions, outlining a more variegated view of the state that resembles Migdal's concept of state-in-society. We conclude with a different view of state-society relations that focuses on the dynamic nature of Russian political and social development.

Studying Activism in Authoritarian States

Our collective work casts a wide net in terms of disciplines, theories, and research methods. This multifaceted inquiry is essential to tackle the complex issues of grassroots mobilization in nondemocratic systems. Authoritarian politics are notoriously (and deliberately) opaque. The lack of reliable, publicly available information helps autocrats to keep challenging forces at bay and forestalls the accumulation of shared knowledge (Ahram and Goode 2016). It also obscures the research focus, particularly when movements are localized or rely on infrapolitics or symbolic and clandestine repertoire.

Consequently, studying collective action in authoritarian settings is problematic and requires research sensitivity (Eliasoph and Clément 2020). These dilemmas are clear in Jeremy Morris's chapter, where he describes the necessity of trust between the researcher and his respondents. It is also clear in Anna Zhelnina's self-conscious recognition of her role as interviewer in shaping the trajectories of the interviews she reports. Regina Smyth, Madeline McCann, and Katherine Hitchcock use focus group data, or structured interactions among Muscovites affected by the housing policy, to explore how activism originates in small acts such as conversations among neighbors that generate common knowledge or understanding at the root of collective action. Studying the grassroots activism requires deep research and respect of subjects, which are common in the ethnographic work evident in these chapters based on participant observation, focus groups, and open-ended interviews.

Our volume also reveals new media platforms as an important tool in research on grassroots actions. Guzel Yusupova complements traditional interview data with digital footprints created by activists to demonstrate the logic of connective action. Similarly, Jeremy Morris relies on new media platforms to develop a deep case study of the couriers' strike and the activists of the left coalition. Jan Matti Dollbaum, Andrei Semenov, and Elena Sirotkina's chapter draws heavily on blogs, videos, and online discussions to understand the development of Aleksei Navalny's 2017–2018 presidential campaign.

These methods complement other research strategies involving event counts and survey data, some of which are collected through online tools and survey instruments (see, for example, Dollbaum, Semenov, and Sirotkina's chapter in this volume). While national protest actions like the 2011–2012 For Fair Elections protest cycles generate a lot of valuable data, they are rare and unpredictable. And while our first chapter demonstrates the value of event count data that illustrate the spread of the movement across regions and republics, their scale also makes them hard to observe in their entirety (see also Lankina and Tertychnaya 2020).

The premise of this project is that by comparing events over time, regions, and issue areas, we could bring the phenomenon of grassroots mobilization into focus. Studying local activism combines the advantages of direct observability with the accumulation of unique data. This comparison across issue areas requires deep knowledge of the subject, as is evident in Anna Dekalchuk and Ivan Grigoriev's exploration of the origins of activism launched by high school friends in Sosnovyi Bor. Local episodes of contention are more easily approached and described analytically because the effective researcher can identify the local contexts and relevant actors, claims, repertoire, and opportunities. The importance of contextual knowledge is clear in all these chapters, but the point is made very strongly in John Burgess's understanding of the complex nature of the Russian Orthodox Church. Burgess stresses activist priests and local parishes—a view obscured by studies of church leadership or its relations with the state.

Infrastructure, Framing, and Changing Opportunities

Our studies rely on three approaches common in the social sciences to explain grassroots mobilization: identities, framing, and political opportunity structures. These approaches are woven into our studies and provide new insight into how they operate in authoritarian contexts to encourage collective action in the form of individual participation and organization building.

The first section of the volume explores the building blocks of collective action—the infrastructure of seemingly spontaneous mobilization. For Stewart and Yusupova, these ties are rooted in ethnic and linguistic identities shared through cultural experiences or common causes. For Smyth, McCann, and Hitchcock and Zhelnina, the raw materials of mobilization around housing are neighborly ties or networks that constitute reciprocal relations, trust, and prosocial norms. In the second section, Jeremy Morris extends this work by developing a concept of entanglement, or the ways in which activists interact over time and in different ways to shape shared understandings of everyday life.

This first section also highlights and expands upon studies of the invisible sources of resistance that are described by James Scott (1990) as *infrapolitics*. Katie Stewart's distinction between acceptable and unacceptable efforts to preserve local culture and language highlights that citizens use a wide-ranging repertoire of hidden actions embedded in cultural events to protect their heritage against a hegemonic national culture. The strategies that she studies are not overtly political; they constitute hidden politics, conducted within regime-sanctioned institutions. Her work also underscores the regime's strategy to treat different actions differently to siphon off societal frustration and generate divisions among groups. These actions reinforce ethnic and linguistic identities through symbolic and cultural action. This theme reemerges in subsequent chapters, including John Burgess's study of grassroots actions within or in conjunction with local parishes of the Russian Orthodox Church. Dekalchuk and Grigoriev's study of the skate park begins in a stealth beautification project—graffiti—and grows from there.

In the second section of our book, the authors rely on close observation, interviews, and process tracing to identify the trajectory of grassroots actions in the context of existing organizations and networks. Reflecting arguments developed by Yusupova and Stewart, Jeremy Morris, and John Burgess underscore the role of historical trajectories in shaping current developments. Writing about different institutions, they invoke the legacy of the Soviet experience on church- and union-based activism to explain current patterns of engagement. Legacy-based union activism is also described by Irina Meye Olimpieva in the third part of the book. Without supposing a rigid sense of path dependency for subsequent developments, the repertoire moves from Scott's infrapolitics to more visible repertoire: petitions, protests, rallies, strikes, and the provision of public goods. These actions transform the institutional structure of new or existing civic organizations.

These studies also show the emergence of activist identities that occur through engagement in local activism. The longitudinal biographic trajectory from political consciousness to more substantive and connective activism—and its uneven outcomes—is a topic Morris's chapter explores. Stewart and Yusupova focus on how shared ethnic or linguistic identity can transform cultural identities into activist identities. Similarly, many of our chapters underscore that attachment to place, or shared experiences of growing up, can also inform activist identities. The exposure to urban activism does not necessarily pave the way into politics—many activists prefer to remain apolitical and withdraw from mobilization as soon as the problem is solved or further engagement is impractical. However, as conventional pathways into formal politics close, grassroots activism remains an important part of the biographies of politicians across the political spectrum.

Political Opportunities: Allies and Obstacles

Our strategy of pairing comparisons of similar types of activism around housing, ethnic identity, planning, and unions provides deeper insight into the role of opportunities in shaping mobilization. Writing about unions from a different perspective from Morris, Meyer-Olimpieva demonstrates that the Kremlin's influence over national unions, exercised through the co-optation of union leaders, limited protest in response to a very unpopular pension reform. Her chapter highlights that these strategies blurred the lines between official and alternative unions, undermining organizational influence. This finding contrasts to Morris's work, which demonstrates the existing capacity for bottom-up labor organization in response to COVID-19. The crucial difference is the level of integration with state officials.

The relative openness of the political system, the availability of powerful allies, and regional capacity to deal with activists are relevant for mobilization. These factors mattered for the Navalny campaign. If local activists were able to find extra resources or faced a relatively mild response from the regime agents, their organizations were stronger and more developed. It mattered for the advocates of skate-park construction in Sosnovyi Bor to find allies among the city officials who helped them to circumvent specific problems associated with the provision of club goods. And it mattered for the proponents of a new planning instrument to guide urban development in Perm to gain support from the governor. When he left office, the master plan lost its relevance. Moreover, it also mattered for activist priests who partnered with urban-based advocates to establish centers to treat drug addiction or educate and care for disabled children in rural communities where the opportunity structure was more open.

Anna Zhelnina's study of housing activism extends the concept of opportunity to consider multiple arenas in which contestation occurs. The multiple-arenas approach demonstrates how activism links across locations, constituencies, and issue areas to amplify action. In the case of the Renovation Program, interactions within apartment buildings are linked to neighborhoods, NGOs, and, finally, elections.

These movements can also create countermovements, sometimes fostered by state action and sometimes by new independent grassroots actions. Dekalchuk and Grigoriev show how activism in support of a public skate park produced a NIMBY-style backlash that was overcome only with a new partnership between local officials, and in particular corporate managers, and the activists. Their chapter links local networks to new NGOs designed to support subsequent organizational efforts without direct involvement in formal politics. In contrast, the pro–Renovation Program mobilization appears to be clearly directed by the state to shape opinion.

Our volume also highlights an understudied aspect of post-Soviet politics: the role of economic actors in policy and governance. Economic actors play an important role in opportunity structures. As we note in the introduction, market forces created new dynamics within the opportunity structure facing activists. While political-economic coalitions were critical to studies of regional politics in the 1990s, they largely dropped out of our inquiries as Putin centralized power (Stoner-Weiss 2002).

Our work shows that this shift in research focus was shortsighted. Neugebauer and her coauthors underscore that market-based authoritarian politics can experience some of the same dynamics and constraints as democratic politics, raising the question of the role of economic transformation in the emergence of activism. Eleonora Minaeva highlights economic-political partnerships in planning that limit societal voices as economic and political elites work together to secure their development goals. Similar interventions are apparent in Jeremy Morris's analysis of labor activism and in the concerns raised over the priorities in the Renovation Program.

The case studies of urban planning highlight how grassroots oppositions can use formal political processes to push forward social mobilization and create openings for activists to make demands on government. Neugebauer and her coauthors as well as Minaeva demonstrate the importance of formal planning structures and of elite networks in shaping urban development. Dollbaum, Semenov, and Sirotkina show how regularly scheduled elections allowed opposition leader Aleksei Navalny to harness regional grassroots energy to build a national organization. The work on Moscow housing shows how policies that demand consultation among residents and neighbors, and that link state and social actors, can lead to collective action.

Conversely, Meyer-Olimpieva clearly demonstrates that engagement with formal institutions can also close the opportunity structure by introducing new levers of state pressure to constrain leaders and organizations. Increasing integration of union and state actors through parties and legislative cohorts has severely constrained independent union action. This change over time reflects the state's attempts to replace grassroots actions with symbolic protests led by politically conformist union organizations. The critical goal was that protests would not become politicized or spill over into demands for political change. As is clear in many of our papers, the slow but steady erosion of space for activism has increased the gap between formal and informal action and between state and social actors. Yet, despite these changes, localized activism continues.

This collection makes a case for the relevance of local politics in autocracies, especially given the inconsistent degree of vertical institutional coordination, well illustrated by the weakness of the federal center during the COVID-19 pandemic in 2020. Earlier studies framed the question of the political regimes almost exclusively in terms of nation-level process. Scholars of Russian politics noted the importance of the local mobilization early on: Karine Clément and her collaborators (Clément 2008; Clément and Zhelnina 2019) documented the patterns of urban protests in the first decade of the twenty-first century; Robertson (2010), Lankina and Tertytchnaya (2020), and Semenov (2018) provided a more systematic analysis of these patterns. More recently, Gorokhovskaia (2018), Zhelnina (2020), Smyth (2020), and Dollbaum (2020) all argued that nationwide waves of mobilization had local forms of activism as antecedents.

The importance of geographic and institutional context in shaping activism is not new to the scholars of contentious politics. What is important, though, is the emphasis on the local characteristics of the context. Despite the claim that political opportunity structure theories are best applied to the national level (Kriesi et al. 1992), these studies show the importance of studying how national structures vary from one place to another and shape the patterns of activism. As our essays clearly demonstrate, in authoritarian regimes local politics matter in providing opportunities and constraints for civic actors to find support among political and economic elites. John Burgess reminds us that even institutions such as the Russian Orthodox Church are home to diverse and sometimes conflicting interests and are not monoliths working in slavish support of the regime, as is often depicted in the conventional wisdom. Jeremy Morris, and to a lesser degree Irina Meyer-Olimpieva, show similar divisions within unions. We return to this point below.

Information Politics and Frame Contestation

As the information-autocracy approach to nondemocratic politics stresses, governmental dominance of television and other traditional media outlets constitutes significant challenges for societal mobilization. To combat this state-directed deterrent, many of the chapters in this volume focus on framing processes, and the information battle between state and society to describe political reality, attribute responsibility, and define solutions is a key element of activism in authoritarian contexts. These chapters also demonstrate that frame contestation, or information politics, also occurs among local officials and between societal stakeholders engaged in policy battles.

The chapters reveal that activists are creative in their use of traditional media and face-to-face communication to frame their projects. Stewart highlights the role that cultural events play in communicating shared identities and societal preferences. Dekalchuk and Grigoriev's activists engage local television to redefine the identities of skaters. Smyth and her coauthors show how neighborly teas challenged the regime's narrative presented on web portals and news stories. Zhelnina underscores the value of Yuliia Galiamina's neighborhood newspaper in forging shared understandings across neighborhoods and city organizations. In several chapters, new media platforms provide important alternative information to challenge state narratives. Russians have been creative in working around state media control.

Many of our studies also support Scott's (2012) claim that new media platforms constitute an infrapolitics battleground. The chapter by Yusupova eloquently demonstrates how innovative citizens can amplify and redress their grievances with the help of online tools that communicate shared interests. Zhelnina demonstrates how Facebook and other internet platforms assist mobilization efforts around the Renovation Program, by providing critical tools for newcomers to political action. Morris's study of the food couriers and Dollbaum, Semenov, and Sirotkina's exploration of the Navalny campaign go a step further and make a case that it is possible to partially substitute digital infrastructure for formal organization. Morris shows very clearly the couriers' response to disinformation around the spread of COVID-19 as they mobilize on the basis of experiential density, identity, and shared commitment to safety. These studies outline the limits of state narratives and disinformation strategies in the face of rich information available in everyday life.

As the debate over the role of new media in grassroots mobilization rages on, these studies underscore that this role is not dichotomous as depicted in the slacktivist-versus-activist debates. More importantly, as Morris argues, online and offline activism often interact to create new entanglements that propel subsequent common action. Despite increasing limits on new media platforms, online communication can overcome state efforts to dominate the discussion, as in the case of housing renovation. These insights confirm the findings of a research collective focused on the 2020 postelection protests in Belarus that remind us that both new media and age-old strategies, such as flyers posted near mailboxes in apartment buildings, are critical to attempts to overcome the information control of contemporary autocrats (Gabowitsch 2021).

State-in-Society: Insights from the Bottom-Up Perspective

Our volume also provides a unique bottom-up perspective on Russia's consolidated autocratic state. While contestation over social and political reality constitutes one battleground between state and society, another plays out within formal institutions such as policy, elections, and urban planning. It is undeniable that informal acts, employed by state actors to undermine the open nature of formal political processes, are key drivers of political outcomes. Yet despite this fact, formal structures remain important to an understanding of grassroots activism.

In a groundbreaking essay in 2010, social movement theorists Doug McAdam and Sidney Tarrow (2010) defined the linkages between protest movements and elections as a new frontier of research. Increasingly, studies cited throughout our chapters show how elections and protest actions are linked, particularly at the local and regional levels (Gorokhovskaia 2018; Smyth 2020; Zhuravlev, Yerpyleva, and Savelyeva 2017). Apart from being a source of volunteers for opposition election campaigns, grassroots contention outlines the responsiveness gap—the failures of the regime to address the needs and grievances of the population. It also provides resources and models embedded in the organizations, fundraising strategies, and frames that provide a structure for mobilization.

Grassroots activism is also a training ground for new leaders. Anna Zhelnina describes the candidate schools that grew out of Moscow housing activism and led to greater representation in city councils across the city. A year later, the Central Election Commission barred some of these candidates from competing for office, prompting large street protests and a Smart Vote tactic that undermined United Russia's control of the capital's legislature, the *MosGorDuma*.

Local collective action is fertile ground for breeding new leaders such as those that Leonid Volkov identifies as central to Navalny's campaign. Similarly, the fight for property protections in Moscow gave rise to newcomers such as Kari Guggenberger as well as to new ties to elected opposition deputies such as Yabloko's Sergei Mitrokhin and Yuliia Galiamina. The critical role that Ukraintsev plays in left-leaning labor organizations highlights the ways in which individuals bring new ideas and tools to mobilization.

This link between formal and informal political participation extends to the creation of shared information challenging state narratives. For citizens, the struggle over urban space, local identities, service provision, and workplaces evokes neglected concepts of justice, accountability, and representativeness. Resources such as time, trust, and community capital previously oriented toward private life were increasingly spent in the public domain contesting shared grievances. In an authoritarian setting where the key resources are concentrated within relatively closed circles, the influx of autonomous resource flows (as with Navalny's 2017–2018 campaign) remains highly consequential.

Yet it is also extremely important for scholars to recognize some of the limits of the autocratic state. As our observers descend the ladder of governance into local politics and even household-level actions, it becomes harder to isolate agents of the regime as a coherent category of analysis: at times, the local bureaucrats and politicians have more in common with the local citizens than with their principals on the higher levels. As Bob Jessop (2016, 50) points out, "state systems never achieve complete separation from society" even in bureaucracies dominated by clientelistic interpersonal networks. Municipal officials emerge as both obstacles and partners in securing better social outcomes.

While these fluid coalitions are clear in the studies of urban planning and land use, Irina Meyer-Olimpieva demonstrates the regime's capacity to limit union action over the profoundly unpopular pension reform, although it could not eliminate all regional activism.

Some of our studies also show how the regime deploys informal institutions and actions to create an uneven playing field in contests between state and society. The two chapters focused on urban planning rely on detailed analysis of policy and interviews with key stakeholders to illuminate how the injection of informal practices into politics-as-usual crowds out societal voices, securing outcomes that are supported by political and economic elites. These chapters also demonstrate how case study comparisons can be used to tease out causal arguments (see also Aidukaite and Fröhlich 2015).

The bottom-up focus on activism highlights important variation in state responses and tactics across localities. In many instances, the grassroots emerge in a response to national-level stressors—a new language or cultural policy, a federal electoral cycle, or a changing economic fortune. In the near absence of national organizations that can address the grievances of underrepresented groups, such as ethnic minorities or working-class families, the local responses are inevitable even when they are costly for local or regional officials.

Our essays suggest that these local responses provide alternative policies and models that can inform national politics. Some contention starts as local and then gyrates to the national level or other localities—the examples of Mayor Sobyanin's renovation in Moscow, which has now taken the form of a national policy initiative, or the attempt to export Perm's master plan speaks to this point. More importantly, the variation across regions, cities, and neighborhoods defines a mosaic of state responses and the state as a "social relation" to society—where strategies, not all of them from the Kremlin, are tested and elaborated (Jessop 2018). Because of the multiple rivalries between and within state bodies, even the seemingly clearly defined area of competency of institutions does not necessarily lead to substantive coherence. As multiple chapters in this volume demonstrate, even within the same domain, for example opposition activism or cultural politics, there is a considerable variation in the trajectories and outcomes of the mobilization.

Despite the common authoritarian environment, which inhibits the general level of contention, urban activists face different opportunity structures across regions, cities, and neighborhoods. No simple function like the size of the population can fully explain the variation in the degree of activism across the country: successful collective efforts take place in small cities like Sosnovyi Bor or megacities like Moscow. Residents' struggles to defend their vision of the city, cultural identities, and rights to political participation unfold in poor and affluent environments, in closed and open local regimes.

Consolidated Authoritarianism and Grassroots Mobilization

As the previous discussions show, the Russian regime has changed over the course of our work, becoming more autocratic and reliant on intervention to stifle mobilization. Some studies of activism in authoritarian states posit that localized protest, often called rightful resistance, serves as a safety valve that lessens pressure on the government by facilitating co-optation or limiting the nature of social claims against the government (Chau 2019; O'Brien and Li 2006; Frye and Borisova 2019). This approach is clear in Meyer-Olimpieva's study of trade union activism. In its application to Russia, Catherine Owen (2017) focuses on the concept of *obshchestvennyi kontrol'*, or public oversight, as a tool to collect information about social pressures and increase government efficiency. The Russian state has increasingly moved to generate formal and informal mechanisms of public oversight. In this view, grassroots efforts create short-term support even as officials move to repress or channel societal demands to win support.

Yet our chapters show that while the Russian government has used permitted protest to collect information on social needs and manage societal claims, grassroots activism can have developmental effects of mobilization on social structures and prosocial norms. We are mindful of the regime's power to shape activism. In our chapters, this is evident in the attempt to discourage participation by refusing to offer housing opponents protest permits. Russians fearing arrest and violence are much less likely to attend an unpermitted action. Similarly, attacks on Navalny's regional *shtaby* and individual leaders over the past year illustrate the state's strategy of dividing grassroots civic leaders from political activists. More recently, the regime has limited freedom of expression by closing or harassing independent media outlets and limiting the voice of individual journalists who regularly document grassroots actions.

Authoritarian constraints on grassroots actions still come in the form of carrots and sticks. Russia's regime continues to adapt to increased societal capacity, implementing new strategies such as grant programs that create state dependencies (Laruelle and Howells 2020). Presidential Grants subtly channel activism in support of regime goals, providing funds to address social issues such as drug treatment or care for disabled people outside of the formal political process. The Sosnovyi Bor skaters also received this funding and built an NGO to help others secure grants to improve the local quality of life. Yet the chapters in this book testify that the regime relies on accommodation as well as coercion to maintain social peace, especially if the mobilization turns political. Yet, as exemplified by the Moscow Renovation Program, these state-directed efforts at policy consultation or funding incentives can also build societal resources such as networks, skills, and ties to local officials that transfer across issue areas.

State strategies to limit communication also extend to new media to challenge movement frames and disrupt communication with disinformation campaigns. While internet platforms can harness activism, as they did in Yusupova's case of language learning, autocrats can use these tools to channel or discourage collective action. In the case of Moscow Renovation, Smyth, McCann, and Hitchcock show that government-run information portals not only provided information for affected citizens but also created a new mechanism to track and counter popular attitudes to quell discontent with the program.

Grassroots actions continue to occur even as the state perpetuates narratives of inaction and passivity (Kukshinov 2021) or targets individuals to limit participation. Yet this clear increase in repression may logically lead to a rise in infrapolitics as opposed to direct action, which is increasingly dangerous. Governments across the globe, democratic and autocratic alike, increasingly rely on information and communication technologies to monitor, prevent, and disrupt mobilization. Closed-circuit television with face-recognition technologies, mobile data tracking, and excessive access to personal data provide other examples of how the governments can use digitalization to their own benefits. Many Russians expressed concerns that monitoring systems developed during the pandemic could eventually be used to track every movement. And the heavy-handed use of biosecurity measures, such as the development of an app tracing infected citizens, provoked a significant backlash in Moscow (Orlova and Morris 2021).

While we recognize the authoritarian nature of the Russian state and acknowledge the constant adjustment of state strategies to maintain centralized power, the focus on grassroots activism suggests a more complex picture of state control. The essays in this volume highlight both the extent of state control and the limits that structural factors such as urban space, the economic base of a city, the choices of local officials, opposition innovation, and creativity in repertoire and activist toolkits present to a federal state. While a top-down view of politics suggests a centralized state, firmly in control, the bottom-up view suggests a more incoherent state in which responses vary widely.

Explaining Activism, Understanding Change

Our overarching goal in this book is to provide a complement to the predominant focus on elite politics, centralization and the power vertical, and the central role of President Putin. These developments led Russian regional studies to focus largely on top-down processes that overlooked societal change. This research focus, while important, also overshadowed critical dynamics that are not apparent when one looks only at national politics or Kremlinology. We focused on two of those dynamics: the causes of grassroots mobilization and the consequences of mobilization for societal development.

Despite increased state repression, our studies illustrate the evolution of Russian society since 1991. Deeply rooted in the work of Karine Clément, the studies in this volume confirm that activism emerges from the disruption in everyday life and that it is closely connected to new understandings, languages, and institutions that affect citizens' shared experiences. Social movement theories suggest that mobilization is a two-step process in which people become "mobilizable" and then join an action, largely because they are asked to do so by members of their close circle or network. Subsequently, as Morris shows, the very process of becoming active and engaging in activism transforms individuals and their beliefs. This process of change is clear across the regional and institutional contexts and issue areas described in individual chapters.

The chapters in this volume suggest a developmental model of societal capacity. The book's organization highlights an overlapping progression of strategies that range from infrapolitics, or the invisible tactics that enable the weak to challenge entrenched political and economic elites, to street actions. We also show how organizations emerge from these efforts. The tactics employed by grassroots activists span cultural or symbolic acts, art and graffiti, and coded language. Such tactics are generally anonymous and indirect, but as the second section of our volume underscores, they can overlap with or lead to more legible political strategies of dissent, such as protests and strikes, or generate or transform organizational forms, although that is not an inevitable outcome of activism.

Dekalchuk and Grigoriev provide evidence of this development: activism among high school classmates creates the ties that enable the emergence of NGOs that in turn support a wider range of activism. Yet, in this case, the activists remain steadfastly outside of formal politics despite collaborating with some political officials. Zhelnina and Smyth and colleagues demonstrate that disruption in housing leads some citizens, but not all, to reengage with formal electoral politics as voters and candidates. Burgess shows that common belief is at the root of the provision of new social goods that come to be supported by state funds. This link is clearest in the analysis of Navalny's presidential election mobilization, which straddled social movement organization and campaign organizations.

This increased capacity for grassroots action is clear in the COVID-19 period. As Andrei Semenov and Vsevolod Bederson (2020) convincingly show, Russia's civic sphere has been resilient in the face of the pandemic. In his chapter, Jeremy Morris demonstrates that the COVID-19 pandemic did not dampen this type of action among couriers on the front line of virus exposure. Throughout the pandemic, persistent activism around Moscow Renovation continued through online and face-to-face protest, meetings with officials, and court cases. Similarly, COVID-19 sparked the online coordination of makers who produced masks and ventilators, and the activism by the Alliance of Doctors and the Memory List project, which stepped in to publicize and redress the lack of protection for frontline workers. These actions suggest that urban activism is a core element of politics, even in times of crisis (Asmolov 2015).

As the previous section suggests, we also gain some insight into how mobilization is changing state responses as well as the true nature of the state. The diverse research projects presented here converge on several issues that are critical for authoritarian governance in the twenty-first century, including aging infrastructure, social rights and the accommodation of mentally or physically disabled citizens, and the effect of globalization and technology. Our analyses highlight the political implications of the continued urbanization and rapid transformation of everyday life and beliefs. We underscore that transforming urban landscapes provokes sharp debates regardless of the size or centrality of the city in which it occurs. These studies also show the linkages that are often unrecognized between urban and rural spaces. Although rural areas are largely regarded as more conservative than urban regions, both Burgess and Yusupova remind us of the permeable boundaries between urban and rural localities.

Grassroots actions alter opportunity structures, frames, and policy processes available for future actions and formal politics. For many opposition leaders, their first experience with politics starts on the very local level. Aleksei Navalny's biography is exemplary in this regard: as a secretary of the Committee for the Defense of Muscovites (Komitet zashity moskvichei), he dealt with issues familiar to the readers of this book, including infill construction, illegal evictions, and other developmental projects in Moscow under Yurii Luzhkov. Others, like Vyacheslav Lyskov of the Automobile Movement, were co-opted into the dominant party and turned from activism to institutionalized authoritarian politics (Greene 2014).

As we note in the introduction, regime flexibility may reflect that few of these local movements directly challenge the authoritarian regime. As many activists continuously stress, their aims are not revolutionary; they just want to protect their localities and identities. Nevertheless, the grassroots mobilization draws the line where society is ready to fight back and defend their (limited) achievements vis-à-vis the autocratic state and provides an alternative route to the accumulation of societal capacity to make demands on the state. This mobilization may be transformed by increased repression, but it is unlikely to disappear.

* * *

The Russian invasion of Ukraine on February 24, 2022, dramatically changed the landscape of activism inside Russia. Anti-war mobilization erupted in the ensuing week bringing thousands of participants to unauthorized rallies across the country. Several professional communities—from designers and architects to political scientists and schoolteachers—issued public letters demanding a stop to the war. Renowned human rights defender Lev Ponomarev launched an online petition that collected over one million signatures in less than a week. The immediate crackdown on activists (sometimes using brutal force), however, halted the momentum, and in a matter of two weeks, the State Duma passed draconian laws prohibiting any type of public statements against the war.

The political discontent did not disappear: Russian activists continued to stage single pickets, artists staged numerous performances, and anti-war graffiti filled the streets. The Party of Dead held a photo session at a graveyard; journalist Evgeniya Isaeva painted herself with crimson red in front of a Saint Petersburg municipal council. Green ribbons, a symbol of peace promoted by the Vesna movement, colored public places, while No War signs were visible on the streets of almost every Russian city. A creative repertoire, for instance, using price tags in shopping malls to remind ordinary Russians about war crimes committed in their names in places like Bucha and Mariupol, has been developing as well. In short, an anti-war activism unfolds in multiple forms and on different arenas capitalizing on the years of capacity and network building.

The state response to the anti-war resistance has been harsh. Even the tiniest forms of dissent have been punished: Sasha Skochilenko, an artist who replaced store price tags with the names of Ukrainian towns, was put in a pretrial detention center (SIZO) despite having a health condition. The new legislation criminalizing "fake information" about, and "discrediting" of, the Russian military and public official actions has been effectively used to open administrative and criminal cases against hundreds of Russians who dare to criticize or even simply spread basic information about the war. Aleksei Gorinov, a municipal council member, received a seven-year jail sentence for speaking about the death of Ukrainian children during a council meeting. Prominent opposition figures who remained in the country, such as Il'ya Yashin and Evgenii Roizman, were also detained under this law. Dozens were labeled foreign agents or pushed into exile. As of September 2022, Putin's regime decimated the ranks of political activists and effectively left no opportunity to raise critical voices.

Yet other forms of activism survived. Russians continued to fight for urban commons and a better environment; they fought against social and economic injustice and targeted damaging policies such us the ongoing waste management reform. For example, in Chelaybinsk, a center of heavy industry, local residents organized a protest camp against an ice rink construction in a city park and did not face any repercussions. They also recorded a video appeal to Putin and offered to name the park after him. Against the backdrop of deteriorating socioeconomic conditions, "nonpolitical activism" gained momentum. And with the regime willing to tolerate contention that does not challenge the status quo directly, such activism will likely endure and even gain a permanent foothold in public discourse, presenting a dilemma to the authorities, given the weak spots in governance of the state.

As our edited volume demonstrates, activism in Russia is multifaceted, and it is unlikely to disappear in the course of the war. The strains caused by war and sanctions on Russia will inevitably aggravate governmental failures, which will require new formations of solidarity and collective action on behalf of the citizenry. The question remains whether this response will be civic in nature (which requires the continuing efforts of political activists now scattered across the world) or more parochial and even violent. Let us hope for the best.

Note

1. The platform includes an entire section called "Discovery: Successful Civil Society Practices from the Regions" [«Открытия»: успешные практики гражданского общества из регионов], and the articles are collected at https://7x7-journal.ru/tags/otkrityia.

Bibliography

Ahram, Ariel I., and J. Paul Goode. 2016. "Researching Authoritarianism in the Discipline of Democracy." *Social Science Quarterly* 97 (4): 834–849.

Aidukaite, Jolanta, and Christian Fröhlich. 2015. "Struggle over Public Space: Grassroots Movements in Moscow and Vilnius." *International Journal of Sociology and Social Policy* 35 (7/8): 565–580.

Asmolov, Gregory. 2015. "Vertical Crowdsourcing in Russia: Balancing Governance of Crowds and State–Citizen Partnership in Emergency Situations." *Policy & Internet* 7 (3): 292–318.

Chau, L. M. 2019. "'Extremely Rightful' Resistance: Land Appropriation and Rural Agitation in Contemporary Vietnam." *Journal of Contemporary Asia* 49 (3): 343–364.
Clément, Karine. 2008. "New Social Movements in Russia: A Challenge to the Dominant Model of Power Relationships?" *Journal of Communist Studies and Transition Politics* 24 (1): 68–89.
Clément, Karine, and Anna Zhelnina. 2019. "Beyond Loyalty and Dissent: Pragmatic Everyday Politics in Contemporary Russia." *International Journal of Politics, Culture, and Society* 33 (2): 9–20.
Dollbaum, Jan Matti. 2020. "Protest Trajectories in Electoral Authoritarianism: From Russia's 'For Fair Elections' Movement to Alexei Navalny's Presidential Campaign." *Post-Soviet Affairs* 36 (3): 192–210.
Eliasoph, Nina, and Karine Clément. 2020. "Doing Comparative Ethnography in Vastly Different National Conditions: The Case of Local Grassroot Activism in Russia and the United States." *International Journal of Politics, Culture, and Society* 33 (2): 251–282.
Frye, T., and Ekaterina Borisova. 2019. "Elections, Protest, and Trust in Government: A Natural Experiment from Russia." *Journal of Politics* 81 (3): 820–832.
Gabowitsch, Mischa. 2021. "Belarusian Protest: Regimes of Engagement and Coordination." *Slavic Review* 80 (1): 27–37.
Gorokhovskaia, Yana. 2018. "From Local Activism to Local Politics: The Case of Moscow." *Russian Politics* 3 (4): 577–604.
Greene, Samuel A. 2014. *Moscow in Movement: Power and Opposition in Putin's Russia*. Stanford, CA: Stanford University Press.
Jessop, Bob. 2016. *The State: Past, Present, Future*. Cambridge: Polity.
———. 2018. "The State as a Social Relation." In *State Formations: Global Histories and Cultures of Statehood*, edited by John L. Brooke, Julia C. Strauss, and Greg Anderson, 45–57. Cambridge: Cambridge University Press.
Kolessnikov, Andrei, and Denis Volkov. 2020. "Russians' Growing Appetite for Change." Carnegie Moscow Center, January 30, 2020. https://carnegie.ru/2020/01/30/russians-growing-appetite-for-change-pub-80926.
Kriesi, Hanspeter, Ruud Koopmans, Jan Willem Duyvendak, and Marco G. Giugni. 1992. "New Social Movements and Political Opportunities in Western Europe." *European Journal of Political Research* 22 (2): 219–244.
Kukshinov, E. 2021. "Discourse of Non-participation in Russian Political Culture: Analyzing Multiple Sites of Hegemony Production." *Discourse & Communication* 15 (2): 163–183.
Lankina, Tomila, and Katerina Tertytchnaya. 2020. "Protest in Electoral Autocracies: A New Dataset." *Post-Soviet Affairs* 36 (1): 20–36.
Laruelle, Marlene, and Laura Howells. 2020. "Ideological or Pragmatic? A Data-Driven Analysis of the Russian Presidential Grant Fund." *Russian Politics* 5 (1): 29–51.

McAdam, Doug, and Sydney Tarrow. 2010. "Ballots and Barricades: On the Reciprocal Relationship between Elections and Social Movements." *Perspectives on Politics* 8 (2): 529–542.

Migdal, Joel. 2001. *State in Society: Studying How States and Societies Transform and Constitute One Another.* New York: Cambridge University Press.

O'Brien, Kevin J., and Yuan Deng. 2017. "Preventing Protest One Person at a Time: Psychological Coercion and Relational Repression in China." *China Review* 17 (2): 179–201.

O'Brien, Kevin J., and Lianjiang Li. 2006. *Rightful Resistance in Rural China.* Cambridge: Cambridge University Press.

Orlova, Galina, and Jeremy Morris. 2021. "City Archipelago: Mapping (Post) lockdown Moscow through Its Heterogeneities." *City & Society* 33 (1): 1–18.

Owen, C. 2017. "The Struggle for Meaning of Obshchestvennyi Kontrol' in Contemporary Russia: Civic Participation between Resistance and Compliance after the 2011–2012 Elections." *Europe-Asia Studies* 69 (3): 379–400.

Robertson, Graeme B. 2010. *The Politics of Protest in Hybrid Regimes: Managing Dissent in Post-Communist Russia.* Cambridge: Cambridge University Press.

Scott, James C. 1990. *Domination and the Arts of Resistance: Hidden Transcripts.* New Haven, CT: Yale University Press.

———. 2012. "Infrapolitics and Mobilizations: A Response by James C. Scott." *Revue Francaise Detudes Americaines* 1 (131): 112–117.

Semenov, Andrei V. 2018. "Protest Activity of Russians in 2012–2013." *Sociological Studies* 11 (11): 53–63.

Semenov, Andrei, and Vsevelod Bederson. 2020. "Organizational Resilience: Russian Civil Society in the Times of COVID-19." PONARS Eurasia Policy Memo 663, July 2020. http://www.ponarseurasia.org/node/10873.

Smyth, Regina. 2016. "Studying Russia's Authoritarian Turn: New Directions in Political Research on Russia." *Russian Politics* 1 (4): 337–346.

———. 2020. *Elections, Protest, and Authoritarian Regime Stability: Russia 2008–2020.* Cambridge: Cambridge University Press.

Stoner-Weiss, Kathryn. 2002. *Local Heroes: The Political Economy of Russian Regional Governance.* Princeton, NJ: Princeton University Press.

Wedeen, Lisa. 1998. "'Acting as If': Symbolic Politics and Social Control in Syria." *Comparative Studies in Society and History* 40 (3): 503–523.

Zhelnina, Anna. 2020. "Engaging Neighbors: Housing Strategies and Political Mobilization in Moscow's Renovation." PhD diss., City University of New York.

Zhuravlev, Oleg, Svetlana Yerpyleva, and Natalya Savelyeva. 2017. "Nationwide Protest and Local Action: How Anti-Putin Rallies Politicized Russian Urban Activism." *Russian Analytical Digest* 210:15–18.

Jeremy Morris is Professor of Global Studies at Aarhus University. He is author most recently of *Everyday Post-Socialism: Working-Class Communities in the Russian Margins.*

Andrei Semenov is Associate Professor in the Department of Political Science and International Affairs at the Higher School of Economics, St. Petersburg. His work appears in *Russian Politics, Social Movements Studies,* and *Post-Soviet Affairs.*

Regina Smyth is Professor of Political Science at Indiana University. She is author most recently of *Elections, Protest, and Authoritarian Regime Stability: Russia 2008–2020.*

INDEX

www.ingramcontent.com/pod-product-compliance
Lightning Source LLC
Chambersburg PA
CBHW032344280326
41935CB00008B/445
* 9 7 8 0 2 5 3 0 6 5 4 6 9 *